A Practical Guide
to Studying History

A Practical Guide to Studying History

Skills and Approaches

Edited by Tracey Loughran

BLOOMSBURY ACADEMIC
LONDON • NEW YORK • OXFORD • NEW DELHI • SYDNEY

BLOOMSBURY ACADEMIC
Bloomsbury Publishing Plc
50 Bedford Square, London, WC1B 3DP, UK
1385 Broadway, New York, NY 10018, USA

BLOOMSBURY, BLOOMSBURY ACADEMIC and the Diana logo are trademarks
of Bloomsbury Publishing Plc

First published in Great Britain 2017
Reprinted 2017 (three times), 2018, 2019 (twice), 2020

For legal purposes the Acknowledgements on p. xii constitute an extension
of this copyright page.

Cover design: Liron Gilenberg

A catalogue record for this book is available from the British Library.

ISBN: HB: 978-1-4725-3226-8
PB: 978-1-4725-2998-5
ePDF: 978-1-4725-2342-6
ePub: 978-1-4725-3009-7

Library of Congress Cataloging-in-Publication Data
Names: Loughran, Tracey, editor.
Title: A practical guide to studying history: skills and approaches/
edited by Tracey Loughran.
Description: London; New York: Bloomsbury Academic, 2017. |
Includes bibliographical references and index.
Identifiers: LCCN 2016012260 (print) | LCCN 2016014811 (ebook) |
ISBN 9781472529985 (paperback) | ISBN 9781472532268 (hardback) |
ISBN 9781472523426 (epdf) | ISBN 9781472530097 (epub)
Subjects: LCSH: History–Study and teaching. | History–Methodology. |
History–Research. | Historiography. | Public history. |
BISAC: HISTORY/ Study & Teaching. | HISTORY/General.
Classification: LCC D16.P685 2017 (print) | LCC D16 (ebook) |
DDC 907.2–dc23 LC record available at http://lccn.loc.gov/2016012260

Typeset by Integra Software Services Pvt. Ltd.
Printed and bound in Great Britain

To find out more about our authors and books visit www.bloomsbury.com
and sign up for our newsletters.

CONTENTS

PART III: HISTORY IN PUBLIC

LIST OF FIGURES

NOTES ON CONTRIBUTORS

Chiara Beccalossi is Senior Lecturer in Modern European History at the University of Lincoln. Her publications include *Female Sexual Inversion: Same-Sex Desires in Italian and British Sexology, c. 1870–1920* (Palgrave Macmillan, 2012). She is currently working on a Wellcome Trust–funded project on sexology in transnational contexts.

Lloyd Bowen is Reader in Early Modern and Welsh History at Cardiff University. His publications include *The Politics of Principality: Wales, c. 1603–1642* (University of Wales Press, 2007). He is currently researching the political culture of popular royalism, c. 1637–62.

Federica Ferlanti is Lecturer in Modern Chinese History at Cardiff University. She has particular research interests in China's state-building and political history in the 1930s and 1940s. She has published extensively on China's New Life movement.

Matthew Grant is Reader in History at the University of Essex. He is a historian of modern Britain, specializing in the domestic impact of the Cold War. His publications include *After the Bomb: Civil Defence and Nuclear War in Britain, 1945–68* (Palgrave Macmillan, 2010).

Jane Hamlett is Reader in History at Royal Holloway, University of London. She researches the history of women, gender and the family in modern Britain, with special interests in material and visual culture. Her most recent publication is *At Home in the Institution: Material Life in Asylums, Lodging Houses and Schools in Victorian and Edwardian England* (Palgrave Macmillan, 2014).

Tracey Loughran is Senior Lecturer in Modern British History at Cardiff University. She is a historian of psychology, gender and the self in twentieth-century Britain. Her publications include *Shell-Shock and Medical Culture in First World War Britain* (Cambridge University Press, 2016).

Siobhan McGurk is a doctoral candidate in Modern European History at the University of Wisconsin, Madison. She is interested in how nineteenth-century gendered and raced identities were concurrently constructed at local, national and transnational levels. She has published on the French surrealist artist Claude Cahun.

Helen J. Nicholson is Professor of Medieval History at Cardiff University. She is a specialist in the history of the Knights Templar and Hospitaller and has edited and translated a major two-volume edition of *The Proceedings against the Templars in the British Isles* (Ashgate, 2011).

Kevin Passmore is Professor of History at Cardiff University. He is a specialist in historical methods, modern French history and European fascism. His publications include *Writing History: Theory and Practice* (Bloomsbury, 2nd revised edn, 2010; 3rd revised edn, forthcoming 2017).

Toby Thacker is Senior Lecturer in Modern European History at Cardiff University. His research interests centre on music, art and culture in modern Europe. His most recent publication is *British Culture and the First World War: Experience, Representation and Memory* (Bloomsbury Academic, 2014).

Shaun Tougher is Reader in Ancient History at Cardiff University. He specializes in late Roman and Byzantine history. His publications include *Julian the Apostate* (Edinburgh University Press, 2007) and *The Eunuch in Byzantine History and Society* (Routledge, 2008). He is currently completing a book on Roman eunuchs.

Keir Waddington is Professor of History at Cardiff University. He has published widely on the social history of medicine, hospitals and public health in nineteenth-century Britain. His most recent publication is *An Introduction to the Social History of Medicine: Europe since 1800* (Palgrave Macmillan, 2011).

Garthine Walker is Professor of History at Cardiff University, with research interests in early modern crime and gender. Her publications include *Crime, Gender and Social Order in Early Modern England* (Cambridge University Press, 2003). She currently holds a Leverhulme Trust Major Research Fellowship to research rape in early modern England and Wales, c. 1500–1800.

Stephanie Ward is Senior Lecturer in Modern Welsh History at Cardiff University. She is the author of *Unemployment and the State in Britain: The Means Test and Protest in 1930s South Wales and North-East England* (Manchester University Press, 2013). She is currently researching industrial masculinity in interwar Britain.

Mark Williams is Lecturer in Early Modern History at Cardiff University. His specialisms include British, Irish and North Atlantic history. He is the author of *The King's Irishmen: The Irish in the Exiled Court of Charles II, 1649–1660* (Boydell & Brewer, 2014).

Martin Wright is Lecturer in History (Welsh Medium) at Cardiff University. His research interests centre on the history of socialism and radicalism in modern Britain and Wales. His publications include *Wales and Socialism: Political Culture and National Identity before the Great War* (University of Wales Press, 2016).

David Wyatt is Senior Lecturer in Early Medieval History, Community and Engagement at Cardiff University. His most recent publication is *Slaves and Warriors in Medieval Britain and Ireland, 800–1200* (Brill, 2009). He is involved with numerous community and engagement projects, including the AHRC-funded Caerau and Ely Rediscovering (CAER) Heritage Project.

ACKNOWLEDGEMENTS

I vividly remember the first item I read as part of my undergraduate degree in history. Reading E.H. Carr's *What Is History?* in the autumn of 1998, nearly forty years after it was first published, I was thrilled. It opened up an entirely new perspective on history for me, and I realized that from now on, I could not rely on anything I previously thought that I knew about the subject. In that first year at university, I was immensely fortunate to find myself in a seminar group run by Professor William Lamont, an early modern historian and veteran of Sussex since the mid-1960s, especially as he was due to retire that year. William Lamont played a crucial part in setting up 'Historians and Historical Controversies', the undergraduate module which not only introduced me to Carr, R.G. Collingwood and R.H. Tawney, but made me read these historical masters alongside Milton's *Areopagitica* (1644) and Anthony Burgess's novel *A Clockwork Orange* (1962). It was a strange and wonderful module, and I cannot count all the ways I have benefitted from it. I do know that I owe a great debt to William Lamont, a patient, inspiring tutor with the accumulated wisdom of thirty years' experience of teaching and research, and none of the cynicism which others might have gathered along the way.

Without that year at Sussex University, and the early encouragement of William Lamont, I might not be a professional historian today. It was perhaps inevitable that some years later, when I took part in setting up an undergraduate module similarly designed to introduce undergraduates to historical debate, I insisted on a chapter from E.H. Carr as the required reading for the first seminar. I still see this as an act of generosity towards these new students, though it is possible that not all those I have taught over the years would agree with this interpretation. This book arises out of the Cardiff University undergraduate module 'History in Practice', but its roots spread further and deeper than this: they extend back to my own undergraduate years, and those of all my contributors and, even further, to the inspirational teachers who encouraged us to read History at university (a nod to Sally Sellers, my own A-Level history teacher, seems in order here).

Any book, and especially an edited collection, emerges out of several stories, not all of which are apparent to readers, and encompasses too many debts to be remembered, never mind repaid. I say this by way of an advance apology to anyone neglected in these acknowledgements. Thanks are due to colleagues, past and present, in the History Department at Cardiff

University. Many have contributed directly to this book, but in supporting the Year 1 module 'History in Practice', many more demonstrated their commitment to educating and enthusing new generations of undergraduates. Special mention should be made of Lloyd Bowen and Stephanie Ward, who were instrumental in getting 'History in Practice' off the ground, and have continued to go beyond the call of duty in providing encouragement, advice and proofreading skills whenever the project of this edited collection seemed daunting. Likewise, teaching on historiographical modules designed by Kevin Passmore has indelibly marked my own approach to history. I am fortunate to work in such a rewarding environment, and this book reflects the collegiality and dedication to research-led teaching which characterizes the Department.

The School of History, Archaeology and Religion at Cardiff University generously provided monies towards image permissions and indexing. Several individuals and institutions helped to source images, or provided useful advice, including Olly Davis, Paul Evans, Kirsty Harding, Rachel Roberts, Adam Stanford, Gareth Taylor, Vivian Paul Thomas, Nicolle Watkins and several staff at The Geffrye, Museum of the Home, Jersey Heritage Collections, The National Archives, the Parker Library, Tyne and Wear Archives, the V&A and the Wellcome Library. As ever, Matthew Grant has juggled the roles of intellectual stimulus, sounding board and Teasmade with aplomb; his versatility is appreciated as much as his patience.

Above all, thanks are due to all the undergraduates taught by the contributors to this book over our many combined years as university tutors. We've learnt a lot from you.

Tracey Loughran
Cardiff University

Introduction

Tracey Loughran

The Museo del Noreste is like no other museum I have ever visited. As with most museums, its name indicates what visitors will find inside. Located in Monterrey, this 'Museum of the Northeast' is dedicated to the history of Mexico's northeast region (the states of Coahuila, Nuevo León and Tamaulipas): its name refers to a geographical region within a specific nation. On entering the museum, I was therefore surprised to find that it defines this regional history as encompassing the bordering US state of Texas. From a historical point of view, this makes sense. Between 1821 and 1836, Texas was part of Mexico, and between 1836 and 1846, it was an independent nation bordered by Mexico on one side and the United States of America on the other. The modern borders of the state were not established until 1854, and so it is impossible to tell the history of the region without reference to Texas. The museum's first exhibit, a floor map of northeast Mexico and Texas big enough for visitors to walk around on, is a startling visual reminder that national borders are permeable and changeable. The perspective of the present can distort the past.

This lesson is emphasized by another unusual curatorial choice: the exhibition starts in the present and works its way back to archaeological evidence from the region dated c. 12,000 BCE. For this visitor at least, walking round the exhibits was a disorienting experience. The narration of any event involves implicit or explicit reference to what happened before. The logical sequence seems to be beginning, middle, end, with each step following on from the previous one taken. Walking backwards, we can't see where we're going: the path from a known end to an unknown beginning places the traveller on uncertain ground. The advantage of this mode of storytelling is precisely that it undermines existing assumptions about what happened when, and why. It forces us to look at the past from a different angle – but the degree to which the perspective is altered depends on the outlook of the visitor. Mexicans with family living in Texas, or Texans used to sprinkling jalapeño sauce on their breakfast burritos, are well aware of the extensive cultural exchange across the region. Students on both sides of the border are taught the interlaced history of Mexico and the United States, and learn Spanish and English in school. The Museo del Noreste subverts the standard curatorial practice of museums, but its overall effect is far more destabilizing for a visitor such as myself, a monoglot English speaker from another continent, with little knowledge of Mexican or US history. The traditional way of telling stories about the past provides an anchor which we do not always realize is there.

The potential reactions of visitors to the Museo del Noreste demonstrate that our understandings of history depend on many different variables: how the subject of the history is framed, how it is integrated into a particular narrative and what prior knowledge audiences bring to these constructions of the past. The three parts of this book deal with each of these variables in turn. Part One examines how and why historians assume particular perspectives on the past. Whether deliberately chosen or unintentionally espoused, historians cannot avoid adopting specific geographical, chronological or methodological frameworks to view the past, and to organize its chaos into some kind of coherence. These organizational strategies inevitably embody particular assumptions, often unspoken, about the purpose of history. Part Two looks in more detail at the skills and methods used to transform provisional questions and raw materials into 'History', including using archives, different kinds of printed texts and digital sources; the relationship between evidence and interpretation; and the formulation and execution of research projects. Finally, Part Three examines different forms and uses of history outside universities, including in schools, government policy, novels and museums, and invites undergraduates to get involved in 'taking history into the world'. This section reflects on the differences between popular and academic history, and further demonstrates how history is shaped by the needs and perspectives of different audiences.

To study history at degree level, it is essential to understand different perspectives, skills and audiences for history. Thinking about history in this way might challenge some of your preconceptions about the subject. New undergraduates are often surprised to find that they are required to take modules in historical theory or historiography (the study of how historians have researched and written about history in particular ways). Resentful students sometimes complain that they came to university to find out more about what actually happened in the past, not to speculate about the nature of history. This volume shows that there is nothing abstract about the ability to identify how and why historians approach their subject(s) in certain ways: this skill is absolutely necessary to research and write history, whether this skill is applied to first-year essays based on secondary sources, final-year dissertations grounded in primary research or research articles published in peer-reviewed journals. From the outset of a history degree, in essays on topics such as the causes of the First World War or the Russian Revolution, students must adjudicate between different interpretations, and explain why X's account is more convincing than Y's. At the culmination of the degree, students are expected to intervene more directly in historical debates – to locate primary sources which enable investigation of specific historical questions, to marshal these sources into a convincing argument and to show the relevance of this research to a broader field. This is not possible without an understanding of how history 'works', no more than it is possible to be fluent in a language without some grasp of grammar, or to drive a car without comprehending the rules of the road. You might get some way without this knowledge, but a metaphorical or literal crash is always on the cards.

Let's think in a different way about why it is important for undergraduates to learn about how history 'works'. At some time, almost all history graduates are confronted by friends or family members who have never studied history with a question on some topic the student never tackled on their degree course. On honestly admitting ignorance, the shocked exclamation invariably follows: 'But I thought you did a history degree!' If you are reading this book, it is likely that you have already spent several years studying history before starting higher education. You know that it is impossible to learn about the sweep of history in its entirety, from the dawn of human consciousness to the present day, across the expanse of the whole globe, in a further three or four years. Indeed, history is recognized as an unusual case by the Quality Assurance Agency for Higher Education (QAA), an independent body which monitors and advises on standards in UK universities. The QAA statement on history begins by acknowledging that this discipline 'differs from many subjects in that historians do not recognise a specific body of required knowledge or a core with surrounding options'. Instead, history degrees employ 'an approach which concentrates on using knowledge in order to develop certain skills and qualities of mind'. These include 'understanding of the problems inherent in the historical record itself', such as limitations of evidence, and 'understanding of the nature of the subject, including what questions are asked by historians, and why'.[1] While non-historians often think we do nothing but learn dates, the study of history can never be reduced to a list of what happened.[2] It always involves thinking about *how* we come to know about this past – through specific forms of evidence, which are interpreted in specific ways. In turn, this means understanding how historians are oriented towards the past.

History is a discipline in which knowledge of what happened in the past is inseparable from how that knowledge is acquired, interpreted and represented to different audiences. The logical conclusion of this outlook on history is that approaches to the study of the past cannot be isolated from the skills necessary for this study. This volume provides a *practical* guide to studying history at university because it combines discussion of frameworks, perspectives and audiences with guidance on reading, interpreting and using evidence. Because the skills of the historian embrace qualities of mind which cannot be reduced to a list of instructions on how to write essays, it aims to nurture these qualities of mind through detailed explanations of the processes of historical research, criticism and debate. These processes are best illustrated through concrete examples of historical research, and so chapters use case studies ranging from the later Roman Empire to contemporary Britain. The very diversity of these examples shows that the underlying principles of historical research and writing discussed in these chapters can be applied to the even greater diversity of periods, regions and societies the collective readership of this book will encounter.

This book is practical in another sense. It assumes that it is difficult to apprehend the purpose of specific schools of historical thought (such as Marxism, the Annales or poststructuralism) without some understanding of why historians ask certain questions and adopt certain perspectives on the past. It therefore does not provide detailed chapters on historical theory or historiography, but instead considers particular orientations to the past, such as adopting the nation as a unit of analysis, or choosing to study individuals rather than societies. This approach should help readers to feel more confident about tackling complex historical theory in the future. Although this volume was conceived with the specific needs of first-year undergraduates in mind, it tackles many important historical questions and topics, and so should provide a valuable resource throughout your years of undergraduate study. Different readers will use this book in different ways, according to their interests and the requirements of their degree course. While each chapter can stand alone, the text clearly indicates when and where other chapters discuss related topics. These cross-references allow readers to build their own reading patterns; likewise, the Study Questions and Further Reading lists at the end of each chapter will help interested readers to reflect more deeply on specific topics in a structured and productive way.

All the contributors to this book believe that understanding of the past enables people and societies to locate themselves within the present, and that transmitting the qualities of mind of the historian to future generations of students is crucial. History matters because it fosters an analytical, critical, curious mentality. Good historians do not simply accept the word of others. They investigate. When they make a claim, they support it with evidence. And they are always asking questions of the world around them: Why is this happening? What different factors have contributed to this event? Have similar things happened before? If so, what happened last time, and what should be done differently in the future? Curiosity and a critical attitude do not prevent laziness, cruelty or selfishness, but they do stop people being lazy, cruel or selfish because they are ignorant, or complacent, or they cannot think through the consequences of their actions. The world would be a better place if everyone asked questions instead of accepting assumptions. If everyone knew how ordinary people had contributed to changing the world in the past, they would refuse to believe that it is not possible to change the world now. They would look at their own responsibilities and possibilities for action as citizens differently. An undergraduate degree in history develops a mental outlook you will carry with you always, wherever you go and whatever you do next. I hope this book helps you to become a historian. I hope you change the world.

Notes

1   QAA Subject Benchmark Statement for History: http://www.qaa.ac.uk/en /Publications/Documents/SBS-history-14.pdf. Accessed 16 January 2016.

2   See P. J. Corfield, 'All People Are Living Histories – Which Is Why History Matters', Institute of Historical Research, Making History: The Changing Face of the Profession in Britain: http://www.history.ac.uk/makinghistory/resources /articles/why_history_matters.html. Accessed 16 January 2016.

PART ONE

Framing Histories

Introduction: Frameworks and Perspectives

Tracey Loughran

History is not simply the story of what happened in the past. It is an active process of enquiry, and what we are able to discover depends on the questions we ask. The German poet and playwright Bertolt Brecht (1898–1956) imagined history as a series of questions lacking answers:

Who built Thebes of the seven gates?
In the books you will find the name of kings.
Did the kings haul up the lumps of rock?
And Babylon, many times demolished.
Who raised it up so many times? In what houses
Of gold-glittering Lima did the builders live?
Where, the evening that the Wall of China was finished
Did the masons go? Great Rome
Is full of triumphal arches. Who erected them?[1]

Each question condemns the assumptions and priorities of conventional history books. We know about kings and generals, Brecht tells us, but not about the labourers who built their worlds. We do not know about them because we have not asked the right questions.

Regarding history as a set of questions helps us to think about the discipline in a new way. This conception of history emphasizes the role of the historian in making history. A question cannot exist without someone to ask it. History does not exist without historians. What happened in the past has already happened and cannot be changed, but our *knowledge* of that past is dependent on someone asking questions and seeking out answers. Although it is sometimes difficult to detect her presence, the historian is at the centre of each history we read, busily making decisions about the relative importance of kings and builders, and which group deserves most space in her pages. This way of thinking about the relationship between history and historians is not new. In *What Is History?* (1961), E.H. Carr argued that because it is impossible to comprehend the past in its entirety, the historian has to select specific aspects of the past to investigate. This inescapable act of selection is simultaneously an act of interpretation. Each decision about what to research involves judgements about what is or is not relevant. Each question asked of the past involves assumptions about what is or is not important. Each stage of the research process involves decisions made by a living, breathing human, whose perspective on the past is shaped by his position in time and space. This is why Carr argued that the 'element of interpretation enters into every fact of history', and that no historical fact exists independently of the historian.[2] The perspective of the historian inevitably shapes the history produced.

We might put this another way, and say that historians must always decide how to frame their histories. We can demonstrate what this means through a visual illustration. Figure I.1 shows the neurologist Jean-Martin Charcot (1825–93) delivering a clinical demonstration of the symptoms of hysteria to medical students and colleagues at the Salpêtrière Hospital in Paris. Charcot was widely recognized as the premier theorist of hysteria in late nineteenth-century Europe. It is easy to see why historians of nineteenth-century medicine and psychiatry would be interested in the scene depicted here. However, historians could write about this episode from several different perspectives, and frame their histories in several different ways. One historian might zoom in on the figure of Charcot as the central pivot on which all the action turns

FIGURE I.1 *Jean-Martin Charcot demonstrating hysteria in a patient at the Salpêtrière Hospital in Paris. Lithograph after P.A.A. Brouillet,* Une leçon clinique à la Salpêtrière *(1887). Courtesy of Wellcome Library, London.*

(Figure I.2a). Another might turn her gaze to the right of Charcot, and consider the experiences of female patients in institutions such as the Salpêtrière (Figure I.2b). Hysteria was a highly gendered diagnosis, applied to many more women than men. How might the stories of female hysterics such as Blanche Wittman, pictured here, open up new understandings of prevalent ideas about femininity in this period? A third historian might decide the real locus of interest is the group of men to the left of the picture, watching the demonstration (Figure I.2c). In the late nineteenth century, physicians debated whether hysteria was a physical or psychological disorder. The illness came to be seen as crucial to interpretations of mind–body relations. Doctors from across the continent, including Sigmund Freud (1856–1939), the founder of psychoanalysis, flocked to the Salpêtrière to witness demonstrations by the *grand maître*. How did other doctors who attended Charcot's lectures influence medical culture? In turn, what might their experiences tell us about medical education in this period? Indeed, can we find out anything at all about ordinary practitioners, who never reached Charcot's level of prestige and fame?

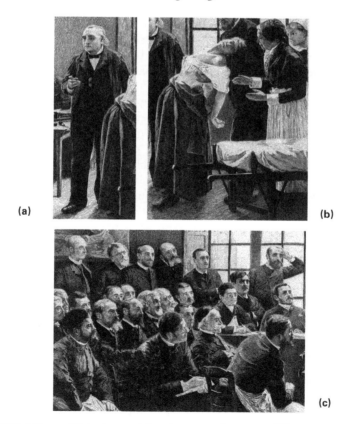

(a)

(b)

(c)

FIGURES I.2a–c *Historians might choose to focus on different aspects of this picture. The choice of perspective and frame affects the history which is produced.*

Crucially, difference in perspective does not mean that one historian is right and others wrong. These are all legitimate perspectives: each historian is simply looking at the picture from a different angle, and asking different questions about its historical significance. However, if these historians focus on different parts of the picture, they will write different histories. As literary historian Alison Light reminds us, 'The place from which one writes, but also from which one understands the past, is a matter of perspective and will alter the focus of what can be grasped near to hand, what can only be glimpsed on the horizon'.[3] A historian who decides to write about Charcot will consult different sources to one who tries to understand the experiences of female psychiatric patients in the 1880s. In reading their histories, it is important to consciously examine how the historian frames the history, the decisions (both deliberate and unwitting) which lie behind this choice, and the consequences of this choice for the overall interpretation and argument. All students of history must acquire this skill of critical reading. Without some awareness that the historian has made certain choices about what to include and exclude, it is impossible to assess whether any history is valid: that is to say, whether the historian started out with appropriate questions, consulted the best possible range of evidence, interpreted this material convincingly and marshalled the evidence into a coherent argument. No findings can be challenged or confirmed without understanding how the history has been framed.

This is not easy. Certain frames are so ubiquitous as to be almost invisible. Consider the titles of history textbooks such as *The Stuart Age: England 1603–1714*, or *Lenin and the Russian Revolution*. We tend to take it for granted that histories are organized around particular events, geographical entities, political leaders or time periods. However, the decision to write about nations, rulers or specific periods always involves further judgements about who, what and where is important enough to merit historical attention. Such categories are highly constructed, but we are so used to organizing historical material in this way that these strategies appear 'natural' rather than the result of conscious choice. If we cannot see that a frame exists, we cannot think outside it. We cannot know what is neglected, and we cannot think of new questions. It is all too easy to accept the terms of a debate as they are presented to us: to understand that argument X is opposed to argument Y, and that we must come down on one side or another. But this risks missing the argument which has not been stated, or the angle which has been ignored, simply because no one has thought about it. One of the dangers of assuming that history can be neutral is not realizing that blind spots exist.

Awareness of common framing devices opens up the possibility of subversion, and the production of new histories. This is illustrated by a thought-experiment recommended by the walker-writer Robert Macfarlane in his discussion of the mapping of prehistoric sea roads (optimal routes for sailing across open sea) by early twentieth-century archaeologists. Research on sea roads, Macfarlane states, 'necessitated a radical re-imagining of the history of Europe':

> Try it yourself, now. Invert the mental map you hold of Britain, Ireland and western Europe. Turn it inside out. Blank out the land interiors of these countries – consider them featureless, as you might previously have considered the sea. Instead, populate the western and northern waters with paths and tracks: a travel system that joins port to port, island to island, headland to headland, river mouth to river mouth. The sea has become the land, in that it is now the usual medium of transit: not barrier but corridor.

The consequences of this 'photo-negative flip' are manifold: coastal settlements must now be seen as 'thriving crossroads'; the Orkney Islands are no longer remote, but the focal point of a trade and pilgrimage network; and 'today's national boundaries shiver and collapse':

> Instead of belonging to particular nations that happen to possess coastlines, these outward-facing coastal settlements – from the Shetlands and the Orkneys all the way round and down to Galicia in Spain – become a continuous territory of their own: Atlanticist in nature, sharing culture, technologies, crafts and languages.[4]

The act of looking reveals a new history, lying dormant under the old, and forces us to interrogate the most basic assumptions about our subjects.

This section encourages you to look afresh at familiar histories. It deals with some common frameworks adopted in historical research, the implications of implicit or explicit adoption of particular frameworks, and challenges posed to particular perspectives from the 1960s to the present day. Just as all historians must make choices about how to frame their histories, editors and authors of works on historiography must select which frameworks and approaches to include. Here, the focus is on precisely those concepts and frameworks so often taken for granted that students rarely recognize them as involving theoretical choices and stances. Mark Williams shows how the prioritization of national frameworks has privileged particular narratives to the neglect of others, and considers alternative modes of analysis, including transnational and 'connected' histories. This examination of challenges to the 'nation' as a focus of historical inquiry is continued in Chiara Beccalossi's chapter, which explores the uses of comparative history through a case study of the history of sexuality. In his chapter on periodization, Shaun Tougher reveals how the periodization 'Late Antiquity' contests a host of assumptions about the later Roman Empire, and has resulted in innovative historical research. The remaining chapters explore different historical perspectives on identity. Toby Thacker shows how biography can illuminate multiple aspects of a society and culture; Martin Wright argues that histories of 'the people' defy top-down narratives and hold urgent political purpose; and Siobhan McGurk examines current modes of conceptualizing identity within history, with particular focus on gender and sexuality. These different ways of looking at history each involve certain assumptions which not only guide writing and research, but also contain the potential to generate exciting new perspectives and reveal hidden histories.

A word of encouragement: It can be disorienting to focus on differences between historians, the constructed nature of history, and the fluid and shifting boundaries of historical knowledge. Yet this instability is an inevitable aspect of tackling the human past, for humans are messy and complex creatures. As historian Stefan Collini puts it, there is 'no one agreed account of what it is to live a life', and therefore it should not surprise us that 'all attempts to understand aspects of human life, past or present, no matter how disciplined they may be in their analysis of concepts and their handling of evidence, will reproduce some of this fundamental lack of agreement'. We should welcome this disagreement as a sign that we are working with topics of real, living importance. A frame still exists, even when it is not recognized; and what remains invisible often operates with most power, because it cannot be challenged. Making discourse visible is a means of confronting power and determining whether it should hold this dominant position. Critique does not undermine history: most often, it is 'a way of registering the pressure of wider social and cultural changes on the always restless, never settled, attempt to expand understanding'.[5] Embrace new ways of looking at history, and the rewards are potentially limitless.

Notes

1   Bertolt Brecht (1987) 'Questions from a Worker Who Reads' ['Fragen eines lesenden Arbeiters'], trans. M. Hamburger, in R. Manheim and J. Willett (eds), *Bertolt Brecht: Poems, 1913–1956*, rev. edn (London and New York: Methuen), pp. 253–4.

2   E. H. Carr (1987) *What Is History?* 2nd edn (London: Penguin), p. 13. See also Kevin Passmore's chapter in this volume on 'Evidence and Interpretation'.

3   A. Light (1991) *Forever England: Femininity, Literature and Conservatism between the Wars* (London and New York: Routledge), p. 1.

4   R. Macfarlane (2012) *The Old Ways: A Journey on Foot* (London: Hamish Hamilton), pp. 92–4.

5   S. Collini (2012) *What Are Universities For?* (London: Penguin), pp. 68–70.

1

Nations

Mark Williams

What is a 'nation'? It may seem a deceptively simple question to the modern eye, familiar as it is to consulting a map and tracing the usual borders of recognized nation-states. Looking at atlases, it is easy to assume not only that these borders have always existed, but that the creation of international boundaries through the drawing of lines represents the most sound and historically rational means of comprehending 'the nation'. Borders, in such instances, represent beginnings and endings: the points at which systems of government, common cultures, shared languages and a unified sense of the 'character' of a nation converge upon one another and acknowledge their mutual limits.

As historians, it is essential to acknowledge that the apparently 'natural' existence of nations as we know them is an assumption inextricably grounded in the past, and subject to an ever-changing future. The borders which help us to define nations in the present day are products of long and contested histories: they have rarely been fixed for long periods of time, and are unlikely to remain so as political and cultural agendas change. Moreover, the place of these boundaries as clear-cut indicators of 'us' and 'them' in historical terms is a relatively new one, with many would-be 'nations' defining themselves in terms which might have included, but were not exclusive to, geographical borders. There is no singular definition of what, precisely, constitutes a 'nation'. The *Oxford English Dictionary* (*OED*) provides no quick and easy answers, only further ambiguity: is a nation 'a people or group of peoples; a political state', as the first definition suggests? If so, how do we understand terms like 'people', 'peoples' or 'political state'? By this definition, we might consider a 'people' as one united by any number of common characteristics (for instance, ethnic background or language) or as a comparatively diverse community which shares a common state (for example, Canada). Further *OED* qualification only begs further questions: an 'aggregate of communities and individuals united by factors such as common descent, language, culture, history, or occupation of the same territory, so as to form a distinct people' may be helpful in suggesting a common grounding in identity, place and a sense of mutual interest – but these are hardly fixed categories! Can we, as historians, trace wholly 'distinct' histories, languages or cultures without risking oversimplification? Such definitions easily slip into the realm of dangerous politics, inviting exclusion and notions of ethnic, religious or cultural 'purity' in a way which the history of the twentieth-century grimly underscores.

Definition, however, misses the point of the whole historical exercise. Even in these first couple of paragraphs, employing 'the nation' as a unit of analysis has raised further questions about how we as historians think about our craft. As this book will reinforce, a central part of historical analysis is maintaining awareness of not only *what* we study, but also *how* and *why* we study it. There is no such thing as a neutral approach to historical analysis: every method we adopt fundamentally alters how we gather evidence, what we 'see' when we finally put our findings to paper and, at the other end of the process, how we read what others have written. For these reasons, historians very often disagree with one another, whether amicably or otherwise. The study of the past is always open to the questions and re-evaluations of shifting cultural priorities.

The status of 'the nation' as a unit of historical analysis has been among the most influential and contentious ways of writing history for precisely these reasons. In many respects, the nation appears a sensible and recognizable way of framing historical analysis. For many historians, it has provided a way of connecting the unfamiliar past with the recognizable present, affording an opportunity to tell audiences 'this is how we arrived at what you now see before you'. To this day any casual scan over the titles available on bookstore shelves produces a majority of books grouped according to the nation concerned, whether a conventional *History of England*, a conceptual study focused on ethnicity or gender in modern France or (more controversially) *The Making of the British Isles*. It is essential, however, that we do not mistake this ubiquity – the fact that 'the nation' surrounds us in the history we read, hear and see – as a sign that it is an unproblematic category of analysis. As this chapter will explore, the writing of 'the nation' has a long and complicated history which shapes how we construct our past, bringing with it agendas and attitudes towards evidence which have given way to as much forgetting as remembrance.

This is not to suggest that we are all 'wrong' in looking at the nation as a unit for these studies: there are many advantages to adopting this approach, both for the questions it asks and the answers it can raise. However, it is vitally important that, as historians, we maintain a critical understanding of what sort of history we create when we set out to write the history of a 'nation'. Each selection brings its own set of assumptions and perspectives, rooted (consciously or otherwise) in the present day. We need not sever these roots to be good historians; we do, however, need to be sensitive to them if we are to begin to understand the past and our place within it. This chapter therefore outlines the history of writing about 'the nation', looking in particular at the influence of this approach while also noting its pitfalls and challenges posed to it. By way of conclusion, I reflect on some alternatives to national history which historians have developed and continue to debate today.

The origins of national histories

National histories occupy a unique category in terms of their origins: depending on the definition used, they are both the oldest and among the newest 'varieties' of history. If one adheres to the looser definitions of 'nation', in which communities are bound by common languages, ethnicity, region and so forth, then 'national histories' are very old indeed. Even in the foundations of historical writing, one finds definitions of 'nations' by their perceived characteristics and, moreover, what marked them out as 'different' (more often than not, better!). The roots of this sort of 'nation' in the writing of history extend back to the very origins of the discipline. The supposed 'father' of history writing – the Greek historian Thucydides (c. 460–400 BCE) – devoted much of his *History of the Peloponnesian War* to defining the 'national' characteristics of the warring Athenians and Spartans. These became part of the explanatory framework of his account of the war. One might include key religious texts such as the Jewish Torah among 'national' histories. In the Torah – as with the Old Testament (as it is known in the Christian Bible) and Tawrat (in Islam) – historians can see a very particular distinction made between God's 'chosen people' and the other peoples of 'God's creation'. Here, history serves as a means of demarcating the characteristics of 'the chosen', set apart by their covenant with God, and those not belonging or separate from that 'nation'. As we will see, this was by no means the last appeal to the divine in circumscribing the limits of a nation.

In the early modern period, humanist scholars frequently enlisted the past in order to articulate, if not a coherent idea of 'a nation' in the current sense of the word, then at least a clear distinction between 'us' and 'them'. An enduringly relevant example can be drawn here from the histories written soon after the accession of James VI and I to the throne of England, Scotland and Ireland in 1603, known as 'the Union of the Crowns'.[1] With the hope of ensuring that this unprecedented attempt to unite these kingdoms succeeded, James made proclamations of Britain's common foundations in 'a community of Language, the principal means of Civil society, and unity of Religion'. Even today, this claim would rankle some within Britain; still, with the aim of reinforcing the 'ancientness' of the union between Scotland and England, James VI and I made use of some of the best politicians and philosophers of his day to trace the historical roots of the political present.[2] Among James's Irish subjects, appeals were made to the connections between the ancient Stuarts (or Stewarts) and the great kings of Ireland, supported by Irish antiquarians eager to establish an unbroken line of legitimate sovereigns in Ireland.[3] As now, these claims did not always convince; however, history nevertheless played a central part in the framing of 'the nation'.

Histories such as these suggest that history was employed as a means of providing community cohesion long before the 'modern' era. However, it was not until the late eighteenth and early nineteenth centuries that the process of employing history to build the 'nation-state' in the modern sense began to take form. Here we can distinguish more clearly between 'histories of nations' and 'nationalist' history. This change coincided with, and was the product of, a number of late eighteenth-century events. In the wake of the American (1776–83) and French (1789–99) revolutions, and especially the turbulence of the Napoleonic Wars (1799–1815), history became a means of both justifying radical innovation and reinforcing the shaken foundations of ruling powers.[4] Aiding this effort was a boom in the print trade: not only thick tomes of history, but cheap pamphlets and ballads illuminated the past for a wider public increasingly engaged with these national narratives.[5] What followed was the creation of a set of symbols and representations of 'the nation' which, though in many instances novel, reinforced these claims: national flags, anthems and rituals of state were born out of this period, each traced (often tenuously) to a distant past. School syllabi and instructional books reinforced a sense of national identity from an early age, while civic pageantry and festivities celebrating the 'birth' of, or pivotal events in, each nation reinforced these ideas across broad swathes of society. These provided a way of establishing both the enduring appeal of what came before and, as often, laid a safe historical foundation for otherwise novel and (potentially) subversive nation-building practices.

With this call for tracing the 'character of the nation' came a trend towards turning the study of history from a pursuit of gentlemen and philosophers into a profession in itself. Universities and their scholars were increasingly recruited to provide a more convincing veneer of legitimacy for their respective (often newly founded!) states. This was coupled with the *professionalization* of history as a field. Emphasizing 'objectivity' in the gathering and application of knowledge, historians increasingly upheld ideals of scholarly distance from their subject matter. History was to be grounded upon the rigorous gathering and analysis of historical documents and the subsequent assembly of a clear historical narrative.[6] Finally, as part of the rising importance of universities and the broader national role of historical study, there arose a greater concern for *modernization*. Especially in areas such as the German and Italian states (as shown by Figures 1.1 and 1.2, neither could be referred to as 'Germany' or 'Italy' at this stage beyond geographical distinctions), the Napoleonic Wars were thought to have exposed the 'backwardness' of their people and institutions. Foregrounding their universities as places of innovation and the creation of new disciplines – history foremost among them – became a venue through which these humiliations could be remedied and the dignity of the nation restored through the past.

FIGURE 1.1 *The German states, c. 1800. Courtesy of Kirsty Harding.*

ITALIAN PENINSULA, c. 1800

FIGURE 1.2 *The Italian Peninsula, c. 1800. Courtesy of Kirsty Harding.*

Naturally, these high ideals of empirical knowledge and academic disinterest mingled with the realities of political change and cultural contexts. A clear example of this can be seen in the person of Leopold von Ranke (1795–1886). Often credited in the past as the 'grandfather' of modern historical scholarship, Ranke authored epic histories of the Germanic peoples which mapped the German national character against the perceived corruptions and impositions of the Roman Catholic Church and the Latin peoples of Europe. For Ranke, history became the fulfilment of a people's potential through the benevolent marching of great men like Martin Luther and Otto von Bismarck.[7] With this interest in writing 'national histories' came a concern for compiling the evidential foundations upon which they were based: national archives were created to collect and preserve the records of these 'nation-builders' to aid in the conservation (or invention) of a national past. These repositories were meant to provide an 'empirical' foundation for research in the 'Rankean' mode, using 'evidence' of this kind to arrive at an unequivocal, professionally analysed 'truth'.

This 'empiricism' blended with interest in charting 'the nation'. As the methods associated with Ranke and German universities more generally caught on, they blended with and reacted to other academic cultures and notions of nationhood. For instance, the English historian Thomas Babington Macaulay (1800–59) wrote in celebration of his own nation's perceived characteristics, elevating those who had forwarded Victorian ideals of liberalism, religious freedom (at least for Protestants) and constitutional monarchy. In Macaulay's words, '[the English] never lost what others are wildly and blindly seeking to regain...It is because we had freedom in the midst of servitude that we have order in the midst of anarchy'.[8] Others, like the Scottish Thomas Carlyle (1795–1881), peered across the Channel to provide a mirror to contemporary morals. In Carlyle's *The French Revolution* (1837), he employed the lessons of the recent past, with particular remembrance of The Terror of 1793–94, in order to challenge the moral decay he saw in the Britain of his day. Like his contemporaries, Carlyle adhered to ideals of historical rigour: he later published a (flawed) collection of the letters of Oliver Cromwell, and even his *French Revolution* spoke with the authority of historical evidence drawn from burgeoning national archives.[9] Nevertheless, Carlyle read the histories of nations and men as a warning for his own time. It seems that Britons soaked up these lessons with enthusiasm: an editor of the 1907 edition estimated that nine out of ten English men or women who read anything about the French Revolution had read only Carlyle.[10]

For historians within this blossoming professional field of history, the nation became the central unit of analysis and the point at which much historical change pivoted. These developments mirrored what has been classically referred to as the 'rise of nationalism' in nineteenth-century Europe, providing grist for the mills of politicians and pundits alike to advance 'national' causes. The newly professionalized writing of history, for all its aims of empirical objectivity, nevertheless continued to be shaped by shifting attitudes towards evidence, audience and the purpose of history itself. Writing the history of nations created new ways of writing and thinking about history, as well as new institutions – libraries, archives and universities – through which it could be pursued.

Historians must be aware of the complexities that shaped how history was being written at this time. While nationalist histories were on the rise generally, others wrote histories which actively rejected the nation as the natural unit of analysis and model for historical study. Karl Marx, while now known for his philosophical/economic works *The Communist Manifesto* (1848) and *Das Kapital* (1867), was also a historian in the 'modern' vein, conducting extensive research for many of his publications. For Marx, the nation was the antagonist in a much wider, international struggle: that of class. In Marx's works, the construct of the nation hides the real driver of historical change: the division of mankind according to the production and consumption of material goods, and the role of broader historical changes – for instance, industrialization – in challenging or reinforcing these class divisions. Through this lens, Marx mapped the arc of history onto a wider awareness of social classes – what Marx called 'class consciousness' – and the conflicting interests between them. History itself was not the story of the triumph of national character, but rather the progress of human society towards a state of classlessness, with socialism finally rising out of the exhausted ruins of capitalism. This approach to the past brought about its own sense of periodization, determined less by the rise and fall of great men and institutions than by the pulse of economic change. While this view of history was perhaps flawed in its own right, within the context of nineteenth-century historiography Marx and other socialist historians offered an important counterblast to the dominance of the nation in these burgeoning historical analyses.[11]

Other approaches, of course, prevailed in this period as well, with subject matter and motive further altering the lens of analysis. Massive histories of – for instance – the Roman Catholic Church or the Renaissance necessarily worked across national boundaries in the search for empirical evidence while still promoting clear moral and cultural ideals. Nevertheless, it is essential that we understand the historical moment out of which interest in 'the nation' as a unit of analysis emerged. Though drawing upon a much older tradition of writing of 'nations' as exclusive, 'us and them' histories, the national history now familiar to us is a relatively recent invention born of nineteenth-century contexts and attitudes towards evidence. Such approaches were from the outset subject to particular ideological agendas of which all historians must be aware.

Dangers, challenges and new approaches to nations

In the previous section, we saw both the historical innovations established by the nineteenth-century turn towards national histories and, even from their onset, the challenges and dangers which they posed. As a unit of analysis, the 'nation', as it came to be known in the nineteenth century, offered a sort of organizing principle through which to evaluate the past and, in the views of many who practised national history, to aid in explaining, and in some cases aggrandizing, the origins of those national qualities which were most valued in their own time. With the professionalization of history came a determination to archive and catalogue the past in a way which still holds much value in the present day. From these origins in modern Germany and Britain, professionalization and recognizably 'modern' systems of historical enquiry internationalized, spreading globally over the following century (though not without controversy or transformation). Though imbalanced in terms of where, when and in what form this historical enquiry took root – often it was a consequence of imperial expansion – this was nevertheless a significant inheritance.

There were also clear agendas at work here which left the writing of national histories open to significant abuses and noticeable absences in their depictions of the past. The first of these dangers, the use of national histories to stigmatize particular groups within a polity, became most apparent at the outset of the twentieth century. The most familiar examples of this practice are those national pasts constructed by the fascist regimes of Italy, Germany and Japan in the 1920s and 1930s. At their most toxic, these national histories employed the past – with the appearance of academic rigour and empirical analysis – to support notions of racial purity and natural hierarchy. They fused notions of an intrinsic national character with cold scientific certainty in the course of justifying the ascent of one nation above all others. German Nazism, for instance, entrenched itself in constructions of ancient Germanic militarism and racial strength to manufacture 'Aryanism' (the 'ancient' master race from which 'pure' Germans were descended) and marginalize the genetically 'weak' (Slavs, Jews, Roma and Sinti, blacks and homosexuals).[12] East Asia also saw an increased push towards employing notions of a historically and racially 'pure' nation to substantiate aggression and empire building. While Japanese historians played an important role in casting the Chinese and Koreans as inferior and elevating themselves as the inheritors of an as-yet-unrealized greatness, Chinese historians meanwhile looked to the writing of history to construct ideas of the 'barbarians' who surrounded them.[13] Nor were these ideological aims unique to the non-democratic governments of the world in the early twentieth century: notions of intrinsic national character and historicized superiority underpinned first the slave trade and then deep racial division in the Americas; lent justification to the global practice of empire by Britain, France and other states; and spoke to the natural exclusion of broad swathes of society from the 'national story', pinning them instead to subservient roles.

The deficiencies in such approaches to national history brought about a variety of changes in attitude towards using the nation as a unit of historical analysis. In some instances, a more acutely developed and historically grounded sense of nationhood legitimated political and cultural opposition and subversion. In Ireland, for instance, the 'Gaelic Revival' of the late nineteenth and early twentieth centuries – as much a cultural phenomenon as a political one – helped to develop a sense of 'national' unity in opposition to the governing British state. This period saw a resurgence of the Irish language, a blossoming of Irish writers, an interest in Irish folklore and the institution of the Gaelic Athletic Association. When the Easter Rising erupted in Dublin in 1916 against the backdrop of the First World War, it was as part of a wider sense of opposition to a state which many no longer felt represented their nation.[14] This use of history in order to 'create' a nation or lend legitimacy to opposition through looking to a shared, timeless past was common globally: the emancipation of India from the British Empire in 1947, the creation of the state of Israel in 1948, even the dissolution of the Union of Soviet Socialist Republics (USSR) in 1991 all arose out of (and further necessitated) the articulation of historicized ideas of nationhood. While this did not shift the *writing* of history away from 'the nation' as a unit of analysis, it is important that we acknowledge that the recovery, articulation and in some cases creation of a national history could provide a powerful tool of political opposition and cultural change.

The defining of 'the nation', even in these seemingly emancipatory moments, often divided as much as it united. New nations rarely emerged with a sense of comprehending a variety of faiths, creeds, ethnicities and languages; rather, they tended to define themselves in exclusive terms. This is what the historian Linda Colley has referred to as the creation of 'the Other': the identification of characteristics – whether religious, political, cultural or otherwise – *against* which a nation comes to define itself.[15] Both India and Ireland, for instance, were torn in two by deep religious and ethnic divisions (Hindus and Muslims in the former, Catholics and Protestants in the latter), in no small part due to a failure on the part of each group to allow for difference in its imagining of the nation. The writing of national histories also played a significant part in the exclusion of these 'others'. In the nineteenth and early twentieth centuries, the usage of national history to aid in the formation of a nation-state relied heavily upon source material which, for many groups, simply did not exist or had been destroyed. The institutionalization and professionalization of history and the concurrent creation of national archives were meant to have put many of these rising nations 'on the map', but those entrusted with the creation of such archives also spurned the use of oral histories, material goods and other media through which many cultures – especially the marginalized and less powerful – recorded and understood their past.[16] Roma and Sinti ('gypsies') had no devoted 'national' archive through which to document their past; the songs and poetry of the Haida or Sioux were rarely seen as legitimate source material against the state records of Canada or the United States. Thus, while writing histories of 'the nation' had, in many respects, provided a useful unit of historical analysis, there remained fundamental issues about what that nation comprised, those it incorporated and excluded, and most of all the place of historians in facilitating narratives of the nation and belonging.

Some of the most innovative turns in historical thought in the last fifty years have arisen out of attempts to respond to the problems and challenges of using the 'nation' as a unit of historical analysis. Many historians have turned towards interdisciplinary approaches, blending techniques drawn from such fields as anthropology, sociology, literary studies and semiotics. Early pioneers in this field were the social historians of the 1970s, who drew from a broad Marxist influence to write the history of 'ordinary people'.

Many of these historians took as their most important point of historical enquiry the act of *creating* the nation and the subsequent discourses which that process provoked (or suppressed). The point here was to shift the focus of analysis away from 'great men' and essential institutions believed to be intrinsic to the nation (for instance, parliament or monarchy) and towards alternate venues where 'the nation' was created by 'ordinary people'. This, as Eric Hobsbawm suggested, means looking more to the role of football in the creation of urban working-class culture in Britain and its place within (or outside of) 'the nation' than to the affairs of Westminster or Washington. For Hobsbawm and others, the 'invention of tradition' in the establishing of historical continuity and, in particular, the use of history to 'inculcate certain values and norms' has proven essential to explaining the ways in which nations have been variously created or challenged in a much broader social sense. One example might be seen in the singing of folk songs or the relating of folklore (think of the Brothers Grimm), in which tunes or tales plucked from 'time immemorial' are employed to suggest the ancient roots of a people when, in fact, they are often much more recent inventions.[17] For historians, this begs questions not so much of how this now informs 'our nation' but rather of the ways in which power relations were enshrined in these traditions, how different communities understood 'the nation' and of the place of history in the framing of what is 'modern'.

An analogous movement, particularly evident in Indian historiography, has been the development of postcolonial perspectives on the history of the nation which also sought to look at history 'from below'. Informed by Marxist theory (in particular the Italian Antonio Gramsci), South Asian scholars looked to the history of the masses, rather than the elite, to challenge the narrative of nationalism and colonialism. History in this vein turned away from nationalism as the sole response to postcolonial questions by looking to the common experience of non-elites – for instance, the experiences of the Indian 'peasantry', of women and of religious minorities. This shift in focus has not gone without criticism, especially for its use of 'professional' ideas of history – largely Western and European – to 'liberate' the voice of the oppressed; nevertheless, it has done much to question the dominant models of historical study by further questioning who constitutes and defines 'the nation'.[18]

This notion of looking at how nations have been defined and imagined, and the power of history in legitimating particular visions of the nation, resonated in another highly influential work by political scientist and historian Benedict Anderson. In his *Imagined Communities* (1983), Anderson mapped out his own narrative of how modern nations have come into being, working forward from the feudal and religiously grounded medieval monarchies through to the advent of capitalism. Anderson was intrigued by the idea that non-European groups – most notably in the Americas – had attained a sense of nationhood different from those (such as linguistic, ethnic, religious and other 'nations') which had proven essential to European traditions. To explain this, Anderson put forward the idea of nations as 'imagined communities' which come into being through the spread and incorporation of images of 'the nation' into wider cultures. For instance, Anderson emphasizes the role of the media (reading newspapers, literature and, of course, now television), of memory (museums, galleries, memorial observances) and other factors in determining how a nation *imagines itself*. Think, for instance, about what the Smithsonian Museum or the British Museum say about how Americans or the British think about *who they are as a nation* – what they value, what they keep, what they remember and what they have discarded. Through this lens of analysis, what distinguishes one nation from another is 'the style in which they are imagined'.[19] Thus, as historians, we might challenge ourselves to move beyond the traditional halls of power in assessing how the 'nation-state' came into being and instead look to, say, how 'Britain' is debated in the comment section of broadsheet newspapers, how the ethnic composition of the French football team challenges notions of French nationhood or how architecture shaped identity in modern Singapore. All of these comprise acts of 'imagining' nationhood in differing registers.

What is most important here is that we acknowledge, once again, how a change in perspective and an alternate idea of how to assess 'the nation' can dramatically change the end result of the research which we, as historians, undertake. By comprehending 'the nation' in terms beyond those set out in the nineteenth-century origins of professional history, we can retain it as a useful and challenging unit of analysis while still asking important questions about its basic assumptions.

Alternate approaches: Beyond the nation

As this shows, we need not see the nation as the 'natural' and most logical unit of analysis for historical study. Earlier historians in many respects realized this when looking to chart wider historical movements like the Renaissance and Reformation, or in analysing the mass movement of people between and across regions and nations. For instance, Fernand Braudel's *The Mediterranean and the Mediterranean World in the Age of Philip II* (1949) adopted the Mediterranean itself as a unit of analysis, setting change in human societies within broader geographical and economic changes. Others have followed similar lines by looking at the Atlantic, the Indian Ocean and other geographical areas and the peoples whose lives were shaped by them. Another approach, discussed in Chiara Beccalossi's chapter in this volume, has been to compare regions or nations in order to isolate or illuminate the specific reasons for similarities or differences in historical experiences.

More recently, many historians have begun to adopt what is commonly referred to as 'transnational' history. Pierre-Yves Saunier has identified this as a perspective which 'is not written against or without nations but simultaneously pays attention to what lives against, between, and through them'.[20] For instance, many transnational histories adopt as their focus the movement of people (immigrants, students, scholars, athletes), institutions (corporations, aid organizations, the UN) and ideas across and between national boundaries. These perspectives may, at once, reinforce and challenge more traditional historical narratives of national character and belonging by looking at what precipitated such movements, how movement transformed those people/institutions/ideas and how these forces changed 'the nation'. We might, in a nice turn of historical irony, think here of the influence which transnational factors had upon the formation and dissemination of 'German' styles of history writing in the nineteenth century: scholars, bureaucrats and ideas moved across Europe and the Americas to entrench this model, but it was subsequently challenged and altered as it found roots (or was rejected) in a wider global history. Even the process of debating 'nationhood' and the identities it often entailed was influenced by transnational factors, shaped by encounters with the wider world, the departure and arrival of migrants and ideas of meeting a broader standard of what the new, 'modern' nation should look like. This has led some historians to beg the question whether one can write about 'the nation' without writing about the transnational.[21]

Like all other historical approaches, 'transnationalism' itself is a debated term. Medievalists and early modernists have challenged 'transnationalism' as a term in part because it assumes the presence of a coherent 'nation-state' in periods where these entities were ambiguous at best, bearing little resemblance to their modern counterparts in terms of centralized power, bureaucracy or institutional structures. This has led some to call for approaches which emphasize connection and inter-crossing without employing the nation as a default unit. For instance, influential works by Sanjay Subrahmanyam have explored the intersection and changeability of cultural and political boundaries across South Asia, particularly in the early modern period. Informed by historical anthropology and other disciplines, Subrahmanyam set out to challenge studies which focused on fixed areas by looking for 'the at times fragile threads that connected the globe'. In Subrahmanyam's case, this has meant a historical focus on merchants, travellers, cartographers, imperial bureaucrats and any number of those who moved (or were moved by) an expanding world.[22] Similarly, Michael Werner and Bénédicte Zimmerman have employed the term *histoire croisée* (or 'entangled history') to suggest the importance of historical *relations* in the generation of divergent and overlapping histories. They argue that historians should look at not just a single 'crossing' or 'transfer', but rather all the movements that facilitated it, the transformations it engendered and how those intercrossings were, and are, perceived. At first, this seems extraordinarily abstract, but consider, for instance, the 'intercrossings' which characterized engagements with the 'New World' in the fifteenth and sixteenth centuries. Western historiography has conventionally told a simple story of Europeans crossing the Atlantic. In contrast, an approach informed by *histoire croisée* would trace the ways in which that travel and encounter was facilitated through the exchange of geographical ideas within and across Europe and Asia, through later interactions with communities and other empires in the Americas and through the crossing of material goods gathered and managed locally across the Atlantic. It would also trace the broadening of mental horizons to comprehend an 'entangled' world, not only in the halls of power but in the shops and markets where the arrival of foreign goods expanded and challenged world views. As Werner and Zimmerman underscore, this approach requires that we, as historians, also become exemplars of *histoire croisée* ourselves, challenging the fixedness and fluidity of the boundaries within which our own reading and research operate.[23]

Conclusion

This question of *reflection* brings us back to the fundamental argument here about 'the nation' in the writing of history: namely, that there is no singular, 'natural' way of looking at the past which supersedes all others. As we have seen, the lens we adopt as historians must always be a critical one. We must be aware of the benefits of particular frameworks for addressing certain historical questions, but we must also be alert to the blind spots these frameworks may create. We have seen how particular historical contexts have shaped, reinforced and challenged ideas of 'the nation', and its uses as a unit of historical analysis, over time; but we must not fall victim to the notion that we are now, somehow, 'better than that'. While historians have now set different challenges for ourselves and looked to other shores to trace the dimensions of our historical worlds, we must ultimately maintain an acute and ever-questioning awareness of the choices we make and the ways in which those choices shape what we create.

STUDY QUESTIONS

- How have differing ideas of 'the nation' shaped the ways in which historians have studied the past?
- What is the relationship between historical 'evidence' and the ways in which 'the nation' has been understood?
- How successful are approaches 'beyond the nation' in shifting historical attention away from the nation as the 'natural' unit of study?

Notes

1   S. G. Ellis (2007) *The Making of the British Isles: The State of Britain and Ireland, 1450–1660* (Harlow: Pearson Longman), p. 291.

2   M. Smuts (2003) 'Political Thought in Early Stuart Britain', in Barry Coward (ed.), *A Companion to Stuart Britain* (Oxford: Blackwell), p. 273.

3   B. Cunningham (2010) 'Seventeenth-Century Constructions of the Historical Kingdom of Ireland', in M. Williams and S. Forrest (eds), *Constructing the Past: Writing Irish History, 1600–1800* (Woodbridge: Boydell & Brewer).

4   S. Berger with M. Donovan and K. Passmore (1999) 'Apologias for the Nation-State in Western Europe since 1800', in S. Berger, M. Donovan and K. Passmore (eds), *Writing National Histories: Western Europe since 1800* (London: Routledge), p. 6.

5   R. Chartier (1991) *The Cultural Origins of the French Revolution* (London: Duke University Press); R. Darnton (1997) *The Forbidden Best-Sellers of Pre-Revolutionary France* (London: Harper Collins).

6   P. Lambert (2010) 'The Professionalization and Institutionalization of History', in S. Berger, H. Feldner and K. Passmore (eds), *Writing History: Theory and Practice* (London: Bloomsbury); Berger with Donovan and Passmore, 'Apologias for the Nation-State'.

7   S. Berger (2007) 'The Power of National Pasts: Writing National History in Nineteenth- and Twentieth-Century Europe', in S. Berger (ed.), *Writing the Nation: A Global Perspective* (Basingstoke: Palgrave Macmillan).

8   T. B. Macaulay (1867) *The History of England, From the Accession of James II*, 5 vols (London: Spottiswoode & Co.), Volume II, p. 242.

9   T. Carlyle (1845) *Oliver Cromwell's Letters and Speeches, with Elucidations*, 2 vols (London: Chapman and Hall).

10 K. Robbins (2008) 'Ethnicity, Religion, Class and Gender and the "Island Story/ies": Great Britain and Ireland', in S. Berger and C. Lorenz (eds), *The Contested Nation: Ethnicity, Class, Religion and Gender in National Histories* (Basingstoke: Palgrave Macmillan), p. 234.

11 For wider discussions, see G. McLennan (1981) *Marxism and the Methodologies of History* (London: NLB); H. J. Kaye (1995) *The British Marxist Historians: An Introductory Analysis* (Basingstoke: Palgrave Macmillan).

12 H. Schleier (1999) 'German Historiography Under National Socialism', in Berger, Donovan and Passmore (eds), *Writing National Histories*.

13 See, for instance, R. A. Morse (1990) *Yanagita Kunio and the Folklore Movement: The Search for Japan's National Character and Distinctiveness* (New York and London: Garland).

14 R. F. Foster (1990) *Modern Ireland, 1600–1972* (London: Penguin), especially Chapters 18 and 19.

15 L. Colley (1992) *Britons: Forging the Nation, 1707–1837* (New Haven: Yale University Press).

16 Lambert, 'The Professionalization and Institutionalization of History', pp. 54–6.

17 E. Hobsbawm (1983) 'Introduction: Inventing Traditions', in E. Hobsbawm and T. Ranger (eds), *The Invention of Tradition* (Cambridge: Cambridge University Press).

18 For instance, R. Guha (1983) *Elementary Aspects of Peasant Insurgency in Colonial India* (Delhi: Oxford University Press).

19 B. Anderson (1983) *Imagined Communities* (London: Verso), p. 6.

20 P.-Y. Saunier (2013) *Transnational History: Theory and History* (Basingstoke: Palgrave Macmillan), p. 11.

21 S. Berger (2007) 'Introduction', in Berger (ed.), *Writing the Nation: A Global Perspective*.

22 S. Subrahmanyam (2004) *From the Tagus to the Ganges: Explorations in Connected History* (Oxford: Oxford University Press); S. Subrahmanyam (2011) *Three Ways to Be Alien: Travails and Encounters in the Early Modern World* (Waltham: Brandeis University Press). Other groups of interest to these historians include exiles, diplomats, and scholars. For instance, see M. Williams (2014) *The King's Irishmen: The Irish in the Exiled Court of Charles II, 1649–60* (Woodbridge: Boydell & Brewer); G. Janssen (2014) *The Dutch Revolt and Catholic Exile in Reformation Europe* (Oxford: Oxford University Press); J.-P. Ghobrial (2013) *The Whispers of Cities: Information Flows in Istanbul, London, and Paris in the Age of William Trumbull* (Oxford: Oxford University Press).

23 M. Werner and B. Zimmerman (2006) 'Beyond Comparison: *Histoire Croisée* and the Challenge of Reflexivity', *History and Theory*, 45:1.

Further Reading

B. Anderson (1983) *Imagined Communities* (London: Verso).

M. Bentley (2005) *Modernizing England's Past: English Historiography in the Age of Modernism* (Cambridge: Cambridge University Press).

S. Berger (ed.) (2007) *Writing the Nation: A Global Perspective* (Basingstoke: Palgrave Macmillan).

S. Berger, M. Donovan and K. Passmore (eds) (1999) *Writing National Histories: Western Europe since 1800* (London: Routledge).

L. Colley (1992) *Britons: Forging the Nation, 1707–1837* (New Haven: Yale University Press).

E. Hobsbawm and T. Ranger (eds) (1983) *The Invention of Tradition* (Cambridge: Cambridge University Press).

P.-Y. Saunier (2013) *Transnational History: Theory and History* (Basingstoke: Palgrave Macmillan).

S. Subrahmanyam (2011) *Three Ways to Be Alien: Travails and Encounters in the Early Modern World* (Waltham: Brandeis University Press).

2

Periodization

Shaun Tougher

Asked for his definition of history, Rudge (one of the pupils studying for exams for entrance to Cambridge or Oxford in Alan Bennett's play *The History Boys*) responds: 'How do I define history? It's just one fucking thing after another'.[1] This response echoes the famous quotation attributed to the British historian Arnold J. Toynbee (1889–1975), about those who view history as 'just one damned thing after another'. Periodization is used to bring definition and meaning to history, to prevent it from being 'just one damned thing after another'.[2] 'Periodization' refers to the dividing of history into discrete periods, shaped by diverse unifying features, such as culture or political organization. The broadest periods are of course Ancient History, Medieval History and Modern History, but within these there are multiple further divisions: for example Classical, Hellenistic, Tudor, Regency and Victorian, to name but a few.

We are so used to thinking about history as divided into discrete periods that it is easy to forget that there is nothing self-evident or 'natural' about these categorizations. Decisions about periodization involve problems of definition and meaning, and often invoke value judgements. They are not neutral. As William Green asserts, 'The organizing principles upon which we write history, the priorities we assign to various aspects of human endeavour, and the theories of change we adopt to explain the historical process: all are represented in periodization.'[3] The operation of such principles, priorities and theories can be seen in the emergence of the periodization 'Middle Ages'. This phrase, coined during the Renaissance, implied a value judgement of the culture that existed after the Classical period and before the Renaissance itself. It developed out of the ideas of the Italian scholar Petrarch (1304–74) about the 'Dark Ages', a more obviously pejorative label he first used in the 1330s to describe an apparent cultural deterioration between the sixth and thirteenth centuries. For these reasons, the term 'Middle Ages' is still controversial today. At the 50th International Congress on Medieval Studies in 2015, a roundtable on 'The Nature of the Middle Ages: A Problem for Historians?' addressed the issue of periodization. One discussant argued that perhaps the period should be relabelled 'early modern' as a way of addressing the negative (and inaccurate) connotations of the periodization 'medieval'. This solution, of course, might cause even more confusion: 'early modern' is already an established periodization which conventionally refers to the period c. 1500–1800.

This chapter discusses the topic of periodization through the prism of one specific case study, that of 'Late Antiquity'. Broadly speaking, this period covers the third to the eighth centuries CE, and overlaps with other periodizations used for East and West in the same time span: late Roman, early medieval, early Byzantine (discussed later in this chapter), Sassanid (a dynasty that ruled Persia from the early third century CE until 651) and early Islam. 'Late Antiquity' is my own period of specialization. It is also a relatively new periodization, which has generated much reflection and debate. This case study allows for close consideration of the self-conscious construction of a particular periodization. It illuminates many more general issues around periodization, including how particular labels and periodizations come into being; why particular periodizations are deemed appropriate, and what they signify; how periodizations are problematized and continually contested; and how each periodization affects other periodizations and terms, too (in this instance, the overlapping periodization of Byzantium and the Byzantine Empire). This close examination of the construction of 'Late Antiquity' as a discrete period serves as a model for thinking about and exploring periodization in general.

Forging 'Late Antiquity'

'Late Antiquity' has established itself very quickly as a familiar term and a popular field of study. Most universities which teach history in its broadest sense now include courses and modules covering late antiquity, and some universities even have recognized centres of late antique studies. The term is especially associated with the historian Peter Brown's ground-breaking and field-defining *The World of Late Antiquity: From Marcus Aurelius to Muhammad* (1971).[4] Since this date, several guides and handbooks to 'Late Antiquity' have been published.[5] An *Oxford Dictionary of Late Antiquity* is now in the process of being produced, distinct from the *Oxford Classical Dictionary*. In 2008, the Johns Hopkins University Press began to publish the *Journal of Late Antiquity*, the first English-language journal of late antique studies.[6] Tellingly, the first volume of this journal was dedicated to Peter Brown 'in appreciative recognition of the service he has done for the development, expansion, promotion, and even the creation of our period and our discipline'.[7] Thus, 'Late Antiquity' has been established as a distinct periodization rapidly and effectively.

But what is distinctive about the concept and period of 'Late Antiquity'? Here, comparison between Brown's seminal text and earlier works on the same period is instructive. A.H.M. Jones's iconic three-volume text *The Later Roman Empire 284–602: A Social, Economic, and Administrative Survey* (1964), published shortly before Brown's fundamental book on 'Late Antiquity', illustrates the more traditional focus of works on the late Roman Empire.[8] Jones divided his book into two parts. Part I, 'Narrative', takes us from the Principate of the Antonines (96–192) through the reigns of Diocletian (284–305) and Constantine I (305–337) to the fall of the western Roman Empire, the establishment of the barbarian kingdoms in the west and the reigns of the eastern Roman emperors Justinian I (527–565) and his successors in the sixth century. Part II, 'Descriptive' (more than two-thirds of the book), supplies analysis of various topics, including government, administration, the army, the cities, the land, the church, education and culture, and the decline of the empire. Jones's survey considers political, administrative and social features of the later Roman Empire and traces its ultimate decline in its final centuries. Until Brown's work, this was the standard mode of treating the history of the later Roman Empire; Jones's work followed in direct descent from other great monuments of historiography on the later Roman Empire, most obviously Edward Gibbon's six-volume *The History of the Decline and Fall of the Roman Empire* (1776–88),[9] and J.B. Bury's two-volume *History of the Later Roman Empire from the Death of Theodosius I to the Death of Justinian* (1923).[10]

Traditional histories of the later Roman Empire have shared certain concerns, and established as the defining characteristics of the period the Christianization of the Roman Empire, the influx of barbarians into the empire and the eventual establishment of barbarian kingdoms on former Roman territory. For instance, Gibbon famously referred to his history as describing 'the triumph of barbarism and religion'.[11] Another major concern of these histories was to establish key moments and turning points marking the end of the Roman Empire and the beginning of the medieval period. It was usually argued that the reigns of Diocletian and Constantine initiated a new phase of the Roman Empire, marked by significant administrative and religious change. The years 395, 410 and 476 were designated as iconic moments in the failing fortunes of the Roman Empire. 395 marked the division of the empire between east and west when the Christian Roman emperor Theodosius I divided his empire between his young sons Arcadius (in Constantinople) and Honorius (in Italy). 410 marked the sack of Rome by the Goth Alaric and his band of supporters. 476 marked the end of the Roman Empire in the west when the barbarian general Odoacer deposed the young emperor Romulus Augustulus and did not appoint another in his stead. Much attention was also paid to the long reign of the emperor Justinian I (527–565) ('The Age of Justinian') and his attempted re-conquest of the west. In these traditional histories, then, historians were largely concerned with the political fortunes of the period and specific religious changes.

Against this background, Peter Brown's work achieved a revolution. Brown described his book as 'a study of social and cultural change'. His aim was to show how and why 'the Late Antique world (in the period from about 200 to about 700 CE) came to differ from "classical" civilization', and how the 'changes of this period, in turn, determined the varying evolution of western Europe, of eastern Europe and of the Near East'.[12] Unlike most earlier historians, Brown did not position himself as just writing a history of the fate of the Roman Empire: his wider purview also takes in broader European and Near Eastern history. Crucially, he also moved away from 'a melancholy tale of "Decline and Fall"', instead creating an exciting portrait of a vital period of transformation and transition, in which the classical world moved towards the modern. This reappraisal of the significance of the period was, as we shall see, related to his strong emphasis on cultural history, rather than the more traditional concerns of religion and politics. Notably, his book is richly illuminated, with 130 illustrations and 17 in colour. From the outset, and throughout the book, Brown is concerned to show the 'modern' qualities of art and literature of the period. Thus Brown's history of 'Late Antiquity' offers a very different type of history, as well as a very different periodization, to the traditional histories of the later Roman Empire.

Brown's reconceptualization of this era was partly a response to previous negative presentations of the later Roman Empire, but he also placed new emphasis on evidence of the vibrancy of the later Roman Empire, which had emerged in the work of earlier scholars despite their own predominantly pessimistic assessments.[13] Brown remarks on how aspects of Jones's *Later Roman Empire* chimed with his own more positive view of the period, observing that 'By Jones' workaday criteria, at least, a large part of the ancient world proved to have been alive and well for three centuries after [the historian] Rostovzteff had signed its death-warrant'.[14] There is no doubt, however, that Brown's vision outstripped Jones's. His aim was to replace 'colourless and unreal' pictures of the age, which focused entirely either on 'emperors and barbarians, soldiers, landlords and tax-collectors' or on 'the monks, the mystics, and the awesome theologians' with a more inclusive and wide-ranging account of the culture of the period.[15] Moreover, Brown asserted that the scholarly context of the late 1960s and early 1970s was crucial in enabling him to reject 'the widespread notion of decay' and catastrophe, and instead chart ('with palpable enthusiasm') 'the religious and cultural revolution associated with the end of the ancient world'.[16]

Brown's vision has had immense influence on the acceptance and growth of 'Late Antiquity' as a term and as a field, as well as on the main concerns of historical scholarship on this period. One of the prime features of this scholarship is the emphasis on cultural history. The culture of the period is appreciated on its own terms, rather than viewed in the shadow of the classical past. The period also came to be seen as an age of transition and transformation rather than one of decline and fall: for example, one University of California Press series (which Brown edits) is entitled 'Transformation of the Classical Heritage'. The scope and flavour of scholarship on 'Late Antiquity' is also conveyed by the definitions of the aims and coverage of the recently founded *Journal of Late Antiquity*. The first volume asserted the 'multi- and interdisciplinary' scope of the journal's coverage of 'the late Roman, western European, North African, Byzantine, Sassanid, and Islamic worlds, ca. CE 200–800 (i.e. the late and post-classical world up to the beginnings of the Carolingian period)'. The editor described the unifying theme of the journal as the conceptualization of 'Late Antiquity as a discrete period with its own idiosyncratic characteristics', even if contributors might also acknowledge relevant 'elements of continuity with the past and harbingers of the future'.[17] The 'Late Antiquity' project thus recognized distinctive features of the understanding of late Roman history but presented them in fresh and broader terms.

This new form of periodization ('Late Antiquity') entailed and encouraged a significantly different focus from older histories (of 'the later Roman Empire'). Rather than concentrating on politics, specific religious changes and catastrophic decline, historians of 'Late Antiquity' highlighted the rich cultural life of the period and gradual transformations rather than dramatic shifts and breaks. They also broadened the focus from Rome specifically to take in both different external cultures (e.g., Persian, Arab) and internal local cultures (e.g., Syrian, Coptic). Significantly, Brown himself was particularly interested in religious history, and is known especially for his work on the emergence of the holy man in this period, so an increased emphasis on spiritual life was evident (in contrast to the previous focus on the process of Christianization alone).[18] To an extent then a more positive view of the period emerged, one that minimized the narrative of political disruption and decline, and sought to trace the history of social and cultural change, to the point where the classical world had completely transformed. Thus 'Late Antiquity' stood as its own discrete period, post-classical and pre-medieval but fundamental to both.

Why did this change in the perception of the period come about? Historians of 'Late Antiquity' have been notably preoccupied with the same question, and have written much about periodization; in its first volume, the *Journal of Late Antiquity* included no fewer than three contributions dealing directly with the periodization. From these writings, a broad consensus emerges that the shift in perceptions is attributable partly to borrowings from art history, partly to a new emphasis on certain strands of scholarship within the history of the later Roman Empire, and partly to the specific political context in which the concept of 'Late Antiquity' was developed.

It is commonly asserted that the term 'Late Antiquity' first emerged in the field of art history, and its first traceable use (the German *Spätantike*) is attributed to the German art historian Alois Riegl (1858–1905).[19] In his account of the genesis of his book, Brown says that the term 'Late Antiquity' was fairly new to him, and that it might have been his editor Geoffrey Barraclough, a historian of medieval Germany with knowledge of historiographical writings on *Spätantike*, who suggested the title.[20] The emergence of the term in German art history partially explains the emphasis on cultural history in late antique studies, especially changes in the style of art, away from classical preoccupations with 'realism' towards symbolism and abstraction.

It is also clear that notions of a longer antiquity, a more positive bill of health for the later Roman Empire, and of transformation rather than a sudden break, existed before Brown's book. For instance, Brown draws attention to works of French historiography which influenced his own outlook, including works by Henri-Irénée Marrou (1904–77) and André Piganiol (1883–1968).[21] Other scholarship which anticipated some of the central concerns of historians of 'Late Antiquity' includes the Belgian Henri Pirenne's *Mahomet et Charlemagne* (1937), which posited that it was only the birth of the Arab empire that ruptured the ancient Mediterranean world.[22] Thus the notion of 'Late Antiquity' was already developed before Brown's book put it firmly on the map.

Finally, modern commentators have noted how the changing political history of the twentieth century affected understandings of the late Roman period. In the wake of the First World War, there was a preoccupation with understanding the decline and fall of empires, whereas following the Second World War and the subsequent rehabilitation of Germany, different responses and agendas emerged. The move towards European union required a different understanding of the past, one that minimized the story of invasion by 'Germans'.[23] In this context, the transition model of the history of the period was very attractive. This is clearly seen, for instance, in the *Transformation of the Roman World AD 400–900* programme, a European Science Foundation Research Project supported by the European Union from 1993 to 1997.[24] Thus, the understanding of history, and the periodization of it, is very much informed by the present.

A problematized periodization

In recent years, however, there has been a distinct reaction against the notion and periodization of 'Late Antiquity'. This has largely focused on the emphasis on comfortable transformation as opposed to dramatic crisis: the notion of decline and fall has struck back. This is emphatically demonstrated by Bryan Ward-Perkins's *The Fall of Rome and the End of Civilization* (2005). Many of the concerns voiced by Ward-Perkins were pre-empted, and have since been echoed, by other scholars, but this is nevertheless a useful case study of the questioning of the 'Late Antiquity' brand.[25] Ward-Perkins takes Gibbon and the traditional notion of the decline and fall of the Roman Empire as his starting point, and argues against more positive notions of the period which emphasize relatively peaceful transitions. He asserts that 'the coming of the Germanic peoples was very unpleasant for the Roman population, and that the long-term effects of the dissolution of the empire were dramatic'.[26] Ward-Perkins argues that the quality of life in the empire did decline in this period, and that value judgements can be made about 'civilization'. This echoes Liebeschuetz's earlier work on *The Decline and Fall of the Roman City* (2001) (itself an echo of Gibbon's iconic history), which argued strongly for a decline in the quality of life in the later Roman Empire.[27]

Ward-Perkins reflects on why such polarized views of the period (the more positive transformation narrative versus the more traditional focus on crisis and collapse) exist. He argues that modern-day conditions and attitudes (including the identity of modern Germany, the project of the European Union, the rejection of empires, the decline of classics and the unwillingness to use civilization as a tool of assessment) have affected the vision of the period. However, much of his discussion deals with the different perspectives of historians. These can be ethnic and cultural: Italians tend to have a rather different (negative) view of the impact of barbarians than those living in northern Europe and North America (Ward-Perkins himself was born and raised in Rome).[28] Wolf Liebeschuetz has also drawn attention to the influence of different national perspectives on interpretations of the period, noting that the English-speaking world tends to favour the notion of 'Late Antiquity' more than France and Germany.[29]

It also matters which part of the world historians focus on: a focus on the East can produce a more positive narrative, as the East had better fortunes and remained more prosperous than the West, which experienced distinct crises (Ward-Perkins's own focus is very much on the West). He asserts that 'the imposition of a single and dynamic period, "Late Antiquity", to cover the years between 250 and 800' does not fit the experience of the West after 400 and the Aegean region after 600, because it ignores 'dramatic change and discontinuity in political, administrative, military, social, and economic life'.[30] Other scholars have also noted that historians of 'Late Antiquity' have tended to privilege the history of the East at the expense of that of the West. Edward James, whose own concerns, like those of Ward-Perkins, are more Western, is notably pessimistic about the idea of 'Late Antiquity'. He declares that the 'rejection of decline and the emphasis on continuity make no sense in Britain or northern Gaul; they probably make little sense anywhere in the former western empire'.[31] Against these criticisms, it must be acknowledged that Brown recognized his concentration on the East in

The World of Late Antiquity, and explicitly advised scholars to consult other works to discover more about western Europe.[32] In a more recent article, Brown has also confessed that his later book *The Rise of Western Christendom* (1996) was produced to redress the picture.[33]

In Ward-Perkins's view, only a focus on religion (Christianity and Islam) makes the periodization of 'Late Antiquity' work. In his view, historians of 'Late Antiquity' focus on 'spiritual and mental' worlds, and neglect institutional, military and economic history, the 'secular and material' worlds. Ward-Perkins illustrates this point through reference to Bowersock, Brown and Grabar's *Late Antiquity: A Guide to the Postclassical World* (1999), a volume of almost 800 pages which includes an Alphabetical Guide covering subjects from 'Abbasids' to 'Zurvan'. Ward-Perkins notes the focus of the Alphabetical Guide on religious topics and people, but the absence of information about peoples and secular officials. He memorably remarks, 'I looked in vain for one of the most powerful figures in late Roman politics and administration, the "Praetorian Prefect", but found nothing between the entries for "Pornography" and "Prayer".'[34] The tendency of late antique historians to focus on the subject of religion and spirituality at the expense of more traditional institutional and political history has also been noted by other scholars.[35]

Further problems that arise with 'Late Antiquity' relate to dating and terminology. The beginning and end dates of 'Late Antiquity' often vary from historian to historian.[36] Brown's *The World of Late Antiquity* first identifies Marcus Aurelius (reigned CE 161–180) and Muhammad (died CE 632) as beginning and end points, but the title of the 1989 reprint gave the specific dates CE 150–750, though even the first edition utilized Harun al-Rashid and Charlemagne as terminal poles (they both died in the early ninth century). The *Guide to the Postclassical World* takes as its span CE 250–800, and the *Journal of Late Antiquity* pushes that back to 200. A sourcebook on 'Late Antiquity' asserts that it is the period 'stretching roughly from Diocletian's reforms in the late third century to the rise of Islam in the seventh and covering a swath across Europe and the Middle East'.[37] The value of the term 'Late Antiquity' is also disputed. O'Donnell laments the fact that 'there is no term in use for the period 200–700 C.E. in the Mediterranean world that is not in some way derivative: late antiquity, sub-Roman, later Roman, early medieval, early Byzantine, post- or pre- something… What would this period be if it had its own name?'[38] Contrastingly, Ward-Perkins believes 'Late Antiquity' and 'late antique' are useful terms because they are 'relatively new coinages, which have not yet entered into popular usage, and have therefore been spared the rich accretion of misleading connotations that the "Middle Ages" and "medieval" (not to mention the "Dark Ages") carry with them'.

In all, the problematization of the concept of 'Late Antiquity' – whether on the grounds of national bias in uses of the term, the partial geographical coverage of many histories of the period, historians' focus on spirituality and mentalities at the expense of politics and administrative change, or more basic disagreements about what and even *when* the term signifies – constitutes a significant trend in recent scholarship. In part, this reflects the inevitable to-and-fro of historical debate. Ward-Perkins acknowledges that the new 'Late Antiquity' corrects a previous bias, 'which assumed that the entire Roman world declined in the fifth century, because this is what happened in the West', but believes that the pendulum has now swung too far. However, Ward-Perkins also summarizes the view of other opponents of 'Late Antiquity' when he concludes that 'The transition from Roman to post-Roman times was a dramatic move away from sophistication towards much greater simplicity'.[39]

Competing periodizations?
Byzantium and the Byzantine Empire

One further problem worth highlighting, as it illuminates the effect which any new form of periodization has on existing ways of understanding specific eras, is the question of how pre-existing periodizations fit within the 'Late Antiquity' framework. We have touched already on late Roman and early medieval, and one could also reflect on the Sassanian and early Islamic periods, for instance, but here I consider further the case of Byzantium and the Byzantine Empire. 'Byzantium' is a modern term given to the eastern Roman Empire which survived into the medieval period. Its origins are traditionally associated with Constantine I (306–337), the first Christian Roman emperor, who in 324 re-founded the ancient Greek city of Byzantium (modern-day Istanbul), as Constantinople (the 'city of Constantine'). Formally dedicated in 330, Constantinople became established as the capital of the eastern Roman Empire in the course of the fourth century CE. The end of this empire is traditionally defined as occurring with the fall of the city to the Ottoman Turks on 29 May 1453, during which the last emperor, Constantine XI (1404–53), perished.

'Byzantium' is a problematic concept, as the Byzantine Empire never existed. The Byzantines (as we call them), the inhabitants of this empire, did not call themselves Byzantines. They thought of themselves as Romans, and understood their history as part of the history of the Roman Empire. The term 'Byzantine' was created in 1557 by the German philologist Hieronymus Wolf (1516–80), who was the private secretary and librarian of the nephew of the proprietor of the commercial firm Fugger, which was involved in trade between the Ottoman and Habsburg empires. Wolf invented the term when he was ordered to edit Byzantine historiographical texts from manuscripts brought from Istanbul.[40] The chequered history of the term 'Byzantium' is another example of the way in which periodization usually involves the *retrospective* imposition of temporal (and often, by extension, geographical) unifying labels which would have been quite alien to the past peoples and societies they describe.

While the existence of the Byzantine Empire overlaps with the period covered by 'Late Antiquity', Byzantium can be studied in its own right, as apart from 'Late Antiquity', and has specific resonances which are not fully encompassed by the latter term. Byzantium has its own periodization, too. Some see the beginnings of the empire as intimately connected with Constantine (the adoption of Christianity and the founding of Constantinople). Consequently, the divisions of Early (fourth to seventh centuries), Middle (eighth to twelfth centuries) and Late (thirteenth to fifteenth centuries) Byzantium have become established. Once again, however, there are divisions of opinion, which can have national variations, too. As with 'Late Antiquity', concepts of continuity and change are important here. French historiography tends to argue that Byzantium begins with Constantine, but there is also the view that Byzantium proper only begins in the seventh century, with the rupture wrought by the birth of Islam and the concomitant early Arab conquests in which much of the eastern territories of the empire were lost.[41] This is also associated with a recasting of the Byzantine Empire along more obviously Greek lines, and with significant institutional change.[42] Others have argued that the critical age of transformation was the extended reign of Justinian I himself (527–565), and that over the course of the period of his rule ancient Rome gave way to medieval Byzantium.[43]

Against this emphasis on moments of change, there is intense debate on the degree to which Byzantium also had continuity with past cultures back into the fourth century, or even earlier. In recent work, Anthony Kaldellis has stressed the Romanness of the Byzantine Empire.[44] Likewise, Averil Cameron has recently observed that the expansion of 'Late Antiquity' 'threatens to sideline Byzantium once again', but also warns that the field of Byzantine Studies is in danger of cutting itself off from that of 'Late Antiquity'. She argues that we need to see Byzantium in connection with its Roman past, even the early Roman imperial period.[45]

This emphasis on continuity echoes the view of earlier historians of the later Roman Empire that Byzantium was inextricably connected with the history of Rome. Gibbon, despite his dim view of Byzantine history and culture, continued his story of Rome to 1453, thus embracing a much longer periodization than even Brown did. It is also notable that Bury established himself as a leading 'Byzantinist', even if he was not keen on the term 'Byzantine'. He wrote histories of the later Roman Empire from CE 395 to 802, and of the period from 802 to 867 (from the fall of Eirene to the rise of Basil the Macedonian).[46] In his *A History of the Later Roman Empire from Arcadius to Irene (395 A.D. to 800 A.D.)*, Bury expressed robust views on issues of periodization and terminology. He claimed that the history of the later Roman Empire has been 'constantly misunderstood', and its character 'misrepresented', because of the use of 'incorrect and misleading titles'. In Bury's view, the 'essential fact' that 'the old Roman Empire did not cease to exist until the year 1453' was obscured 'by applying the name "Byzantine" or the name "Greek" to the Empire in its later stages', especially as historians who used these terms were 'not very consistent or very precise as to the date at which the "Roman Empire" ends and the "Byzantine Empire" begins'. Indeed, because the Byzantine Empire as such never existed, it could even be claimed that '*Byzantine* is a dangerous word, when it is used in a political sense'.[47] As this demonstrates, the debate about the identity of Byzantium and how it relates to the Roman Empire has a long history. Clearly, debates and views of periodization ebb and flow, and repeat themselves. At the core of this fact lies the challenge of how to understand and define history.

Conclusion

Periodization is a necessary mechanism for dividing up history in order to make it manageable. How history is divided up into discrete periods is, however, not a straightforward or purely scientific matter. It often involves value judgements, as in definitions of the Dark Ages or the Middle Ages. The case of 'Late Antiquity' testifies to the attempts of historians to make sense of the central and challenging question of the fate of the Roman Empire, or indeed the wider European, Mediterranean and Near Eastern worlds. In attempts to understand this complex age, the issue of perspective is crucial. Where one stands to view the period (West or East, North or South) affects one's sense of it (different parts of the world experienced different fortunes). There is also the issue of where one is looking ahead to; historians can have different end points to reach. In addition to particular territorial or cultural concerns which affect perspective, contemporary concerns can also influence how periods are understood and constructed. As we have seen, the changing political and intellectual circumstances of twentieth-century Europe resulted in the institution of a positive and long concept of late antiquity. This is now being challenged by the revival of the model of decline and fall, a challenge which itself may be a response to current economic and cultural crises. It is also evident that different periodizations can co-exist, following different cultural or national perspectives for instance. Ultimately, periodization is a vital and fascinating aspect of the study of history itself. Historians need to know not just the details of the periods they study but also why their relevant periodization/s came to exist. The circumstances, perspectives and judgements which result in the creation and maintenance of specific periodizations tell us much about the frameworks, assumptions and beliefs which colour and shape the writing of history. Periodization is history, too.

STUDY QUESTIONS

- How and why do historians divide history into different periods?
- Why are some periods seen as more important than others, and is this judgement influenced by contemporary concerns?
- To what extent do competing periodizations exist? Why?
- How useful is periodization?

Notes

1   A. Bennett (2004) *The History Boys* (London: Faber and Faber), p. 85.

2   On periodization, see P. N. Stearns (1987) 'Periodization in World History Teaching: Identifying the Big Changes', *The History Teacher*, 20; W. A. Green (1995) 'Periodizing World History', *History and Theory*, 34.

3   Green 'Periodizing World History', p. 99.

4   P. Brown (1971) *The World of Late Antiquity: From Marcus Aurelius to Muhammad* (London: Thames and Hudson). The title was later simplified to *The World of Late Antiquity AD 150–750*. For a fascinating account of the genesis of the book, see P. Brown (1997) 'The World of Late Antiquity Revisited', *Symbolae Osloenses*, 72.

5   G. W. Bowersock, P. Brown and O. Grabar (eds) (1999) *Late Antiquity: A Guide to the Postclassical World* (Cambridge, MA and London: Harvard University Press); P. Rousseau (ed.) (2009) *A Companion to Late Antiquity* (Chichester and Malden, MA: Wiley-Blackwell); G. Clark (2011) *Late Antiquity: A Very Short Introduction* (Oxford and New York: Oxford University Press); S. Johnson (ed.) (2012) *The Oxford Handbook of Late Antiquity* (Oxford and New York: Oxford University Press).

6   Brepols has published the French language *Antiquité tardive* since 1993.

7   R. Mathisen (2008) 'Dedication', *Journal of Late Antiquity*, 1.

8   A. H. M. Jones (1964) *The Later Roman Empire 284–602: A Social, Economic, and Administrative Survey*, 3 vols (Oxford: Basil Blackwell). For Jones and his history, see D. M. Gwynn (ed.) (2008) *A. H. M. Jones and the Later Roman Empire* (Leiden and Boston, MA: Brill).

9   D. Womersley (ed.) (1994) *Edward Gibbon, The History of the Decline and Fall of the Roman Empire*, 3 vols (London: Allen Lane). Volume 1 appeared in 1776, volumes 2 and 3 in 1781, and volumes 4, 5 and 6 in 1788.

10 J. B. Bury (1923) *History of the Later Roman Empire from the Death of Theodosius I to the Death of Justinian* (London: Macmillan and Co. Ltd). This covers the years from 395 to 565 CE.

11 Womersley, *Edward Gibbon*, Vol. 3, p. 1068 (Gibbon, Volume 6, chapter 71.2).

12 Brown, *The World of Late Antiquity*, p. 7.

13 Brown, 'The World of Late Antiquity Revisited', pp. 5–6.

14 Brown, 'The World of Late Antiquity Revisited', p. 14. M. Rostovtzeff (1926) *The Social and Economic History of the Roman Empire* (Oxford: Clarendon Press).

15 Brown, *The World of Late Antiquity*, p. 9.

16 Brown, 'The World of Late Antiquity Revisited', p. 15.

17 R. Mathisen (2008) 'From the Editor', *Journal of Late Antiquity*, 1.

18 See for instance P. Brown (1971) 'The Rise and Function of the Holy Man in Late Antiquity', *Journal of Roman Studies*, 61.

19 See, for example, E. James (2008) 'The Rise and Function of the Concept "Late Antiquity"', *Journal of Late Antiquity*, 1, pp. 20–1. See however J. H. W. G. Liebeschuetz (2004) 'The Birth of Late Antiquity', *Antiquité tardive*, 12. Liebeschuetz says that Riegl did not use the term and notes that Henri-Irénée Marrou attributed the first use of the term to Riegl's contemporary Richard Reizenstein (1861–1931).

20 Brown, 'The World of Late Antiquity Revisited', p. 17.

21 H.-I. Marrou (1949) *Saint Augustin et la fin de la culture antique: Retractatio* (Paris: De Boccard); A. Piganiol (1947) *L'empire chrétien (325–395)* (Paris: Presses Universitaires de France).

22 H. Pirenne (1937) *Mahomet et Charlemagne* (Paris: Alcan).

23 'German' is a problematic term itself in a late Roman context: see, for instance, G. Halsall (2007) *Barbarian Migrations and the Roman West 376–568* (Cambridge: Cambridge University Press), especially pp. 22–5.

24 See, for example, L. Webster and M. Brown (eds) (1997) *The Transformation of the Roman World AD 400–900* (London: British Museum Press).

25 B. Ward-Perkins (2005) *The Fall of Rome and the End of Civilization* (Oxford: Oxford University Press).

26 Ward-Perkins, *The Fall of Rome and the End of Civilization*, p. 10.

27 J. H. W. G. Liebeschuetz (2001) *The Decline and Fall of the Roman City* (Oxford and New York: Oxford University Press); Liebeschuetz, 'The Birth of Late Antiquity', especially p. 17, on the 'rejection of judgementalism'.

28 On Italy, see also A. Giardina (1999) 'Esplosione di tardoantico', *Studi Storici*, 40; A. Marcone (2008) 'A Long Late Antiquity? Considerations on a Controversial Periodization', *Journal of Late Antiquity*, 1, p. 5 and especially p. 18.

29 On the Anglocentric aspect of 'Late Antiquity', see also A. Cameron (2002) 'The "Long" Late Antiquity: A Late Twentieth-Century Model', in T. P. Wiseman (ed.), *Classics in Progress: Essays on Ancient Greece and Rome* (Oxford and New York: Oxford University Press).

30 Ward-Perkins, *The Fall of Rome and the End of Civilization*, pp. 170–1.

31 James (2008) 'The Rise and Function of the Concept "Late Antiquity"', p. 29.

32 Brown, *The World of Late Antiquity*, p. 9.

33   Brown 'The World of Late Antiquity Revisited', pp. 13–14 and 23;
     P. Brown (1996) *The Rise of Western Christendom: Triumph and Diversity
     AD 200–1000* (Malden, MA and Oxford: Blackwell Publishers).

34   Ward-Perkins, *The Fall of Rome and the End of Civilization*, p. 174. See also
     James, 'The Rise and Function of the Concept "Late Antiquity"', p. 26.

35   Cameron, 'The "Long" Late Antiquity', p. 180.

36   James, 'The Rise and Function of the Concept "Late Antiquity"', p. 24.

37   M. Maas (2000) *Readings in Late Antiquity: A Sourcebook* (London and
     New York: Routledge), p. li.

38   J. J. O'Donnell (2004) 'Late Antiquity: Before and After', *Transactions of the
     American Philological Association*, 134, p. 210, n. 23.

39   Ward-Perkins, *The Fall of Rome and the End of Civilization*, pp. 170–1, 174;
     see also James, 'The Rise and Function of the Concept "Late Antiquity"',
     p. 25.

40   See, for instance, D. R. Reinsch (2010) 'The History of Editing Byzantine
     Historiographical Texts', in P. Stephenson (ed.), *The Byzantine World* (London
     and New York: Routledge), especially pp. 438–9.

41   See A. Cameron (2014) *Byzantine Matters* (Princeton, NJ and Oxford:
     Princeton University Press), p. 5.

42   See J. Haldon (1990) *Byzantium in the Seventh Century: The Transformation
     of a Culture* (Cambridge: Cambridge University Press).

43   See A. Cameron (1985) *Procopius and the Sixth Century* (London:
     Duckworth).

44   A. Kaldellis (2012) 'From Rome to New Rome, from Empire to Nation-
     State: Reopening the Question of Byzantium's Roman Identity', in L. Grig
     and G. Kelly (eds), *Two Romes: Rome and Constantinople in Late Antiquity*
     (Oxford and New York: Oxford University Press).

45   Cameron, *Byzantine Matters*, p. 5.

46   J. B. Bury (1889) *A History of the Later Roman Empire from Arcadius to
     Irene (395 A.D. to 800 A.D.)*, 2 vols (London and New York: Macmillan and
     Co. Ltd); J. B. Bury (1912) *A History of the Eastern Roman Empire from the
     Fall of Irene to the Accession of Basil I (A.D. 802–867)* (London: Macmillan
     and Co. Ltd).

47   Bury, *A History of the Later Roman Empire*, vol. 1, pp. v, ix.

Further Reading

C. Ando (2008) 'Decline, Fall, and Transformation', *Journal of Late Antiquity*, 1,
     pp. 31–60.
P. Brown (1971) *The World of Late Antiquity: From Marcus Aurelius to
     Muhammad* (London: Thames and Hudson).
P. Brown (1997) 'The World of Late Antiquity Revisited', *Symbolae Osloenses*, 72,
     pp. 5–30.

A. Cameron (2002) 'The "Long" Late Antiquity: A Late Twentieth-Century Model', in T. P. Wiseman (ed.), *Classics in Progress: Essays on Ancient Greece and Rome* (Oxford and New York: Oxford University Press), pp. 165–91.

A. Cameron (2014) *Byzantine Matters* (Princeton, NJ and Oxford: Princeton University Press).

W. A. Green (1995) 'Periodizing World History', *History and Theory*, 34, pp. 99–111.

J. Haldon (1990) *Byzantium in the Seventh Century: The Transformation of a Culture* (Cambridge: Cambridge University Press).

E. James (2008) 'The Rise and Function of the Concept "Late Antiquity"', *Journal of Late Antiquity*, 1, pp. 20–30.

A. H. M. Jones (1964) *The Later Roman Empire 284–602: A Social, Economic, and Administrative Survey*, 3 vols (Oxford: Basil Blackwell).

J. H. W. G. Liebeschuetz (2004) 'The Birth of Late Antiquity', *Antiquité tardive*, 12, pp. 253–61.

A. Marcone (2008) 'A Long Late Antiquity? Considerations on a Controversial Periodization', *Journal of Late Antiquity*, 1, pp. 4–19.

J. J. O'Donnell (2004) 'Late Antiquity: Before and After', *Transactions of the American Philological Association*, 134, pp. 203–13.

P. N. Stearns (1987) 'Periodization in World History Teaching: Identifying the Big Changes', *The History Teacher*, 20, pp. 561–80.

B. Ward-Perkins (2005) *The Fall of Rome and the End of Civilization* (Oxford: Oxford University Press).

D. Womersley (ed.) (1994) *Edward Gibbon, The History of the Decline and Fall of the Roman Empire*, 3 vols (London: Allen Lane).

3

Comparative Histories

Chiara Beccalossi

Comparative history is not new. As far back as 1928, the use of comparative techniques was advocated by Marc Bloch, one of the most eminent historians of his day.[1] Even before then, analysis of similar historical phenomena in different geographical settings was not rare. In the nineteenth century, for example, writers concerned with sexual matters researched how prostitution had been regulated in different countries across the centuries.[2] Yet, over the last twenty years, comparative, transnational, international, world and global histories have become far more common. As demonstrated in Mark Williams's chapter, 'Nations', these histories encompass a variety of approaches, and in some cases, even their practitioners do not agree on the scope and remit of each.[3] Nevertheless, approaches which look beyond the nation as the unit of analysis are now considered on the cutting edge of history.

Scholars have compared diverse aspects of historical change in different geographical settings, including the development of political and economic systems, the elaboration of artistic and scientific movements, religious sensibilities and moral codes. This chapter examines comparative history through case studies relating to the regulation of sexuality in England and Italy in the second half of the nineteenth century. In the early 1980s, George Mosse, a prominent cultural historian and a pioneer historian of sexuality, declared that scholars could no longer treat the histories of the nation and of sexuality as separate and autonomous. Instead, discourses of nationhood and sexuality should be considered as powerful and intertwined forces shaping contemporary notions of identity.[4] Following Mosse's insight, other historians of sexuality demonstrated that the history of sexuality is part of national history, and then began to overcome the constraints of national borders to consider how sexual attitudes have changed across countries and continents.

There are a number of questions we can ask when examining similarities and differences in sexual attitudes and behaviour in different countries. These questions relate to key analytical categories and aspects of identity, such as gender, class, ethnicity, age, religion and urban versus rural, as well as important elements of the social system, such as law, politics and science. So, for example, are the sexual attitudes of men and women different in two or more countries in a specific historical period? Have different classes developed different codes of moral and sexual behaviour in different countries? How do different religions affect gendered sexual conduct? Do people in rural areas manifest the same sexual behaviour as those in cities? How do different legal systems regulate sexuality? This chapter considers what elements may legitimately be compared within the history of sexuality, and how comparison challenges common assumptions. It uses the history of sexuality as a case study to illuminate the kinds of issues addressed in comparative history, and what comparison can reveal.

Comparative history, risks, challenges and rewards

Comparative history is the study of similar historical phenomena in different geographical and/or temporal settings. Comparative historians do not adopt a single nation-state as their main framework of analysis; they thus move away from national history. There is no single comparative historical approach or method, but broadly speaking, comparative historians choose at least two cases for detailed study, and then attempt to identify important similarities and differences between these cases. Historians have compared various phenomena such as the outbreak of revolutions, the advance of eugenics and the growth of nationalism, just to name a few, in different geographical contexts.[5] Any historical period or geographical area can be used as a unit of comparison, and the method may involve rejecting the standard chronological or geographical focus of established national histories. As Marc Bloch wrote, 'Those who wish finally to drop the burden of artificial separations must find the appropriate geographical context for every aspect of European social life and for different periods; one that is defined not from the outside, but from the inside.'[6] Bloch's comments can of course extend to other geographical areas.

Comparison invariably involves two fundamental aims: to discover *similar* causal conditions recurring in different geographical or temporal settings; and to reveal *different* historical contingencies that lead two or more cultural contexts to develop similar social, cultural or political conditions. Comparison can therefore help to identify regularities across time or in different geographical contexts. So Theda Skocpol, for example, sought correspondences between the French, Russian and Chinese revolutions.[7] It also, however, illuminates differences within recurring social mechanisms and structures. For example, Peters Stearns, who has studied the revolutions of 1848–49 in Europe, claims that 'each revolution must be assessed in its own context' and has highlighted how the revolutions across different countries 'interacted to a limited extent'.[8] Comparison can yield significant rewards, but it is as well to be aware of some of the potential pitfalls involved in practising comparative history.

The most important risk involved is the tendency towards overgeneralization. In order to practise comparative history, scholars need to attain both a certain degree of abstraction, and a plausible level of generality. These qualities are not always fostered by historical training, which encourages historians to look for details and for what is unique to specific historical developments. Consequently, some within the profession believe that comparative history often leads to unjustified and excessive generalizations. Yet this criticism is perhaps unwarranted. To a certain extent, all historians have to provide synthesis and abstraction. Moreover, in assessing the significance of any historical event, there is always an element of implicit or explicit comparison to other times or places. This is an inevitable aspect of historians' attempts to understand the influences between diverse countries and peoples, and the development of different cultures.

The main challenge in comparative history is to find appropriate terms of comparison. We cannot compare oranges with apples; for a comparison to be useful, there must be some similarities between two phenomena. The criteria which determine whether a unit of comparison is useful or not depend on the sources we analyse and on the questions we pose.[9] We can compare, for example, the process of urbanization in two very different geographical settings, such as Europe and Asia, and in two different historical epochs, but it does not make sense to compare the process of urbanization in one country and the development of prostitution in another, even though prostitution has tended to expand with urbanization. At the outset of any comparative project, the terms of comparison must be clearly defined.

If there are dangers in using comparative history, there are also many rewards. Historians can deploy all kinds of comparisons, including cross-cultural connections and transnational flows of individuals, ideas and movements, to challenge simplistic assumptions or received wisdom about causation and to understand the combinations of factors that determine changes in history. Each unique national and temporal case can also help to shed light on other national cases. Did industrialization, for example, follow the same patterns in all European countries? Was prostitution increasingly regulated in all Western countries in the modern period?

Comparative history can also be used to test hypotheses. Among other things, historians look for causes of historical phenomena. If a historian explains the appearance of phenomenon x in one society in terms of the existence of condition *y*, he or she can check this hypothesis by trying to find other societies where *x* occurs without *y* or vice versa.[10] Comparative history is also helpful in formulating problems for historical research. For example, in the 1980s many historians interested in the history of sexuality suggested that the formation of homosexual identity in the modern period was dependent on the medicalization of same-sex desires in the late nineteenth-century Western world. According to a number of historians, men who desired other men started asserting membership in a community of individuals sharing the same sexual orientation at the end of the nineteenth century when medical doctors started to classify sexual behaviours. Medical knowledge, therefore, offered men who loved other men a language with which to speak about their desires.[11] Ancient and early modern historians then researched whether men or women who loved individuals of the same sex before the modern period expressed a sense of homosexual identity.[12] In doing so, they forced modern historians to rethink certain categories they used to talk about sexuality and to provide more nuanced accounts.

History of sexuality

This example leads on to this chapter's two case studies, which illustrate some of the factors that must be taken into account in practising comparative history. In the last twenty years, historians of sexuality have been active in developing comparative, transnational and global approaches.[13] The history of sexuality, like comparative, transnational, international, world and global history, can bring together work on cultural representations and economic, social and political phenomena. Historians of sexuality studying the modern period, like their colleagues in comparative and transnational history, have been committed to deconstructing the nation-state. Moreover, as we saw in the previous section, some historians of sexuality have provided new insights by comparing the pre-modern period with the modern period.[14] The case studies scrutinized here consider how sexuality was regulated in England and Italy in the second half of the nineteenth century. To further limit the terms of comparison, the second part of this chapter will focus on how female prostitution and male homosexuality were regulated and controlled in these two countries.

First of all, it is worth asking whether we are comparing oranges with apples in this case. Is the proposed comparison meaningful? The answer is yes. England and Italy are two Western countries with a long history; we propose to study these two countries in the same historical period; and, by confining our analysis to two specific historical developments (the regulation of female prostitution and male homosexuality), we choose to analyse the same phenomena, and therefore avoid the risk of implausible comparison. There are also clearly identified points of difference between England and Italy: these European countries were traditionally dominated by different religious traditions, went through different political shifts in the late nineteenth century and had two different legal systems. From the many analytical categories and aspects of social organization which could be used in comparisons between the history of sexuality in two geographical areas, in these case studies I focus on gender, religion and the legal regulation of sexual behaviours. So identifying similarities and differences between these two countries will allow us to discern not only patterns of sexual regulation in modern Europe, but also which political and cultural factors shaped the attempts of two different governments to control sexual behaviour. We can also consider some questions which situate this comparison within wider debates on the history of sexuality in both nations. For example, which country was more tolerant towards non-reproductive sexual behaviour? Is it true, as is commonly believed, that Italy, traditionally associated with erotic freedom, was more liberal in regulating the sexual sphere than Victorian England, so often associated with sexual repression and control?

So, let us start by putting gender at the centre of our analysis. Throughout Western history, men have enjoyed more power and privileges than women. The sexual conduct of men and women has also been appraised and controlled in different ways. In the case studies examined here, we could ask a number of questions about gender differences in relation to sexuality. For example, how were women and men's sexual behaviours regulated? Did both English and Italian legislators subscribe to the view that sexual behaviour should be subject to different formal constraints depending on gender? The short answer to the above questions is yes. But it is also necessary to identify key similarities and differences to contextualize our case studies. During the nineteenth century, both England and Italy passed several laws that increasingly regulated conjugal life, the family, and the sexual conduct of men and women. For example, in 1837, England introduced the civil registration of marriage, and in 1857 the Matrimonial Causes Act made divorce more widely accessible. Under the latter, a husband could divorce his wife simply on the accusation of adultery, on the basis that an adulterous wife might bring a spurious child into the family. A woman, on the other hand, had to prove that her husband had been adulterous *and* that he had committed an additional 'matrimonial offence' such as cruelty, desertion, bigamy or incest. Despite this double standard, the Matrimonial Causes Act represented a blow to the ecclesiastical doctrine of the indissolubility of marriage in England, and it did grant women some rights in cases of intolerable unions. Moreover, under common law, married women's legal rights and obligations were subsumed by those of her husband, but this Act gave divorced and legally separated women the status of 'femme sole', which enabled them to own property and sign contracts.[15]

Similarly, marital life was increasingly regulated in nineteenth-century Italy, but here laws that attempted to control sexual behaviour were inextricably linked to the political situation. The unification of Italy in 1861 meant that new, homogenous regulation was necessary. Italy remained without legislation on the dissolution of marriage until 1970,[16] but marital life was regulated through the 1865 Italian Civil Code and the 1889 Zanardelli Penal Code. The 1865 Italian Civil Code, based on the Napoleonic Code, declared that the sexes were equal before the law. However, in practice, women had fewer rights than men, and the Code reinforced their dependence on men. Women were still not allowed to practise liberal professions such as law and medicine, and did not have unrestricted access to higher education. Under a provision termed 'marital authorization', married women could engage in trade; inherit, own and manage property; and make wills and bequests only with the express permission of their husbands.[17] A woman who owned property could not even give it to her own children without her husband's consent. This meant, for example, that a woman could not act independently of her husband to provide a dowry for her daughter, and so fathers had the legal power to determine whom their daughters married. The 1889 Zanardelli Penal Code established that an adulterous woman could be punished with three to thirty months in prison, while a man could be punished only if he brought his mistress to the house he shared with his wife.[18]

There are a number of similarities so far. In both England and Italy, the laws mentioned above partially reflected the increasingly secularized regulation of moral conduct. Likewise, women did not have access to the same rights as men in England or in Italy, and in both countries the family was the only legitimate sphere for sexual activities. Finally, the English and Italian legal systems shared ideas about the different sexual natures of men and women. Adultery by a woman was so horrendous that a single act justified her husband divorcing her. In a man, however, the offence was so trivial that it was not regarded as sufficient reason for a woman to terminate her marriage unless aggravated by some other offence. In different ways, then, both English and Italian nineteenth-century legislation asserted the inferiority of women within the family.

The laws regulating female prostitution and male homosexuality in these two countries show more plainly both similarities *and* differences. Female prostitution was widespread and visible in nineteenth-century English and Italian cities and both national governments passed a series of laws that aimed to control the conduct of women engaged in selling themselves.[19] The earliest modern laws against prostitution-related activities in England were passed in the second decade of the nineteenth century. The 1824 Vagrancy Act introduced clauses that allowed police and night watchmen to arrest 'common prostitutes behaving in a riotous or indecent manner'; the 1839 Metropolitan Police Act included a clause prohibiting any 'common prostitute' from soliciting to the annoyance of residents or visitors; and a section in the 1847 Town Police Clauses Act enacted similar provisions outside London.[20] These laws were complemented by a series of Disorderly Houses Acts, which allowed local authorities to prosecute brothels (and other establishments) if they were disturbing the peace, and by the 1871 Prevention of Crimes Act which allowed police to search and close down brothels if they were found to be a resort for criminals and thieves.[21] More controversial were the Contagious Diseases Acts, passed in 1864, 1866 and 1869. These acts, partially inspired by the French system of state regulation of prostitution,[22] ruled that any unaccompanied woman in garrison towns and sea-ports could be required to submit to gynaecological examination to ascertain whether she carried a transmissible disease. If found to be suffering from venereal disease, she would be incarcerated in a lock hospital until 'clean', and thereafter would remain on a register of 'common prostitutes' and have to submit to regular inspections.[23] Finally, the 1885 Criminal Law Amendment Act made brothel-keeping a summary offence (an offence tried without a jury), raised the age of consent and made procuration for the purposes of prostitution illegal.[24] In effect, brothels were outlawed.

English feminists and social reformers immediately reacted strongly against the Contagious Diseases Acts, arguing that they legitimized men's sexual urges and restricted women's civil liberties; they also protested at the injustice of examining the prostitute but not the male client. Feminists objected to the assumption that prostitution was necessary because of the particular nature of male sexuality, arguing that the male sexual urge was socially rather than biologically determined, and that a single moral standard should be applied to both sexes. Women attacked the Contagious Diseases Acts while claiming the right to promote wider moral and social reforms. Under the inspired leadership of Josephine Butler (1828–1906), the Ladies National Association for the Repeal of the Contagious Diseases Acts established a powerful national movement. Finally, thanks to public outcry, the Contagious Diseases Acts were repealed in 1886.[25]

Before Italian unification, prostitution was regulated in a number of different ways on the Italian Peninsula. In Rome, Pope Pius IX (r. 1846–78) did not accept prostitution at all; he considered it a sin and, consequently, a crime. Other parts of Italy were more tolerant. Several cities adopted the Napoleonic model.[26] For example, from 1823, the municipal government of Palermo allowed police to issue 'licences of toleration' (*patenti di tolleranza*) for brothels in the name of public order. In 1841, legislation emanating from Naples, the capital of the Kingdom of the Two Sicilies, strengthened regulation by requiring regular medical inspection of all prostitutes. In February 1860, the Cavour Regulation (*Decreto Cavour*), designed to halt an apparent increase in the number of cases of syphilis, was passed. It took effect first in Piedmont and those provinces already annexed: Lombardy, Tuscany, Modena, Parma and the Romagna. With the unification of Italy, this regulation was extended to the Kingdom of the Two Sicilies in 1861, Venice in 1866 and Rome in 1870.[27]

The Cavour Regulation aimed to concentrate prostitution in closed houses and to limit the freedom of movement of registered prostitutes. It established that women over the age of sixteen who sold their bodies had to be registered as 'public prostitutes'. A special passport stating their profession was used to record and track their movements from one city to another. Public prostitutes had to reside in brothels and could not move from one brothel to another without police permission. Owners of brothels had to declare to the state all women working for them, and pay taxes to the government. The fees for prostitutes' customers were fixed by law and prostitutes had to undergo medical examination twice a week (the lower ranks of soldiers also had to undergo periodic examination). If found to be infected with venereal disease, prostitutes were confined to so-called *sifilicomi*, venereal hospitals similar to English lock hospitals. Finally, from October to March, prostitutes were not allowed to walk the streets after 8 pm, or after 10 pm from March to October.[28] In 1888, the Crispi Law revised the Cavour Regulation. It prohibited the sale of food and drink, and parties, dancing and carousing, in brothels, and the opening of such premises near places of worship, schools and kindergartens. It also stipulated that the shutters of brothels must always remain closed, hence the name *case chiuse*, or 'closed houses'. In 1891, the Nicotera Law made a further amendment, which made prostitution fully legal in Italy if practised in private houses.[29]

In both England and Italy, regulation of female prostitution escalated between the 1860s and 1870s, with somewhat similar underlying causes: the influence of the French model in the regulation of prostitution, and fears of the effects of an apparent increase in venereal disease on military prowess and morale. In the Italian case, unification brought about uniform regulation of female prostitution, although parts of Italy had implemented measures like compulsory medical inspections for prostitutes and a legal system of brothels from at least the 1840s. This earlier development was in part caused by the Napoleonic influence in some parts of Italy. England was relatively late in adopting the French model and introducing medical inspections. Importantly, the Contagious Diseases Acts did not apply to the entire national territory, but only to areas in which there were barracks or sea-ports. Another difference was that whereas in both countries it was legal for women to sell sexual services, in England there was no system of licensing or approving brothels; most prostitutes acted individually rather than being organized into a profession. This made it more difficult, but not impossible, to regulate their activities. In a sense, then, the English regulation of prostitution was more liberal than the Italian. Moreover, in Italy there was no public outcry when the government introduced the Cavour Regulation. There were certainly feminists who campaigned against the Cavour Regulation, such as Anna Maria Mozzoni (1837–1920), but unlike the English campaign, the Italian feminist movement was not successful in obtaining abolition of the state regulation of prostitution.[30]

There is also another striking similarity. Both the English Contagious Diseases Acts and the Italian Cavour Regulation responded to military concerns. The Contagious Diseases Acts attempted to stem the steady increase in venereal infection among men, in particular soldiers, since the 1820s. By the mid-nineteenth century, the massive expansion of British military and naval activities, the rapid growth of towns and new understandings of contagion led many to see prostitution as primarily a medical rather than a moral problem, its chief evil being, they supposed, its connection with venereal disease.[31] Britain's imperial ambitions are also important for understanding the implementation of the Contagious Diseases Acts. Crucially, they were passed in the aftermath of the Crimean War (1853–56), which had shown how sanitation was important for the health of the soldiers and therefore for the efficacy of the army itself.[32] In Italy, the Cavour Regulation had its roots in the 1850s when Piedmont was preparing for war. Crucially, Camillo Benso di Cavour (1810–61), prime minister of Piedmont after 1852, needed a healthy army to unify Italy. Cavour's reforms, such as the extension of the railway network, the creation of an armaments industry and the establishment of banks, were designed to provide the transportation, weapons and capital necessary for unification.[33]

It is possible to go even further and draw other parallels between the two countries. The regulation of prostitution in the last fifty years of the nineteenth century shows that both in Italy and England the state combined legal sanction of sexual practices with medical control of the human body and sexual behaviours.[34] Because it was believed that venereal diseases were caused by vice and promiscuity, prostitutes were usually blamed for the increase in such diseases. In both countries, the adoption of medical measures to combat the spread of venereal diseases, such as the compulsory internment of infected women, furthered control over women's bodies. At the time, scientific understanding of venereal disease was limited: the relationship of syphilis to its late manifestations as debility, paralysis and insanity had not yet been established and treatments were largely ineffectual, often severely debilitating, and sometimes even punitive, including cauterization and the application of caustic substances.

A cursory comparison of how prostitution was regulated in England and Italy might lead readers to think that England showed a more liberal attitude to sexual matters than Italy. However, if we compare how male homosexuality was regulated in these two geographical areas, the picture is completely different. In England, ever since the 1533 Buggery Act, it had been possible to punish men involved in acts of sodomy with death. This act remained the basis for legal treatment of homosexuality in England until 1967.[35] In the nineteenth century, the death penalty was seldom enforced as punishment for sodomy, and in 1861 the law was modified so that sodomy was penalized with imprisonment for a period of ten years, and more lenient sentences for those conspiring to commit sodomy. However, during the eighteenth century, common law had made it possible to prosecute a number of relatively new offences under the label of 'unnatural crimes', including sodomy, bestiality and any same-sex act or invitation to such an act, usually described as indecent assault or 'assault with intent to commit sodomy'.[36] In 1885, Section 11 of the Criminal Law Amendment Act, commonly known as the Labouchère Amendment, redefined which kinds of same-sex acts could be punished.[37] It made acts of 'gross indecency' between males, such as mutual masturbation and fellatio, misdemeanours liable to imprisonment for up to two years. This change expanded the definition of a homosexual act and, because it introduced a new and very broad category of homosexual misdemeanour, made prosecution easier and conviction more likely. This measure inaugurated an era of persecution of homosexuals by blackmailers and moral purity brigades such as the National Vigilance Association. Moreover, the clause also enabled punishment of same-sex acts performed in private. English legal regulation therefore contrasted starkly with that of Continental countries under the influence of the Napoleonic Code, where homosexual acts carried out between consenting adults in private did not fall under the jurisdiction of the law.[38]

As in the case of female prostitution, before unification different Italian states operated different standards for the punishment of male same-sex practices (see Figure 3.1 below).[39] In the Papal States, male same-sex

FIGURE 3.1 *Punishment of male same-sex practices in the Italian Peninsula, c. 1853. Courtesy of Kirsty Harding.*

acts were punished with life imprisonment.[40] In the Lombardo-Veneto region (current Trentino-Alto Adige, Friuli-Venezia-Giulia, Istria and Fiume), which was under Austrian domination, sodomy was punished with custodial sentences from six months to one year. In the kingdom of Sardinia, under the Savoy monarchy, male same-sex acts could land men in prison for up to ten years.[41] The rest of Italy adopted the Napoleonic Code, which was silent on the issue of homosexuality. This meant there was no legal framework for the repression of same-sex acts, and in practice they were not criminalized. Formal repression increased from the mid-nineteenth century, but was not equally applied across the country. In 1861, the criminal code of the kingdom of Savoy was extended to the rest of the country. In southern Italy, however, the law against homosexual acts was not enforced. The government acknowledged that in Mediterranean culture, it was considered normal for young boys to engage in same-sex practices, and that punishing same-sex acts in southern Italy would entail a complete transformation of the indigenous culture.[42] Thus, government authorities conceded cultural differences between the country's northern and southern regions.

With the promulgation of the 1889 Zanardelli Penal Code, private homosexual behaviour between consenting adults ceased to be a punishable offence, except in cases that involved 'public scandal' or violence. The latter were subject to private prosecution under criminal law, for example, in cases of rape. Homosexuality was thus decriminalized throughout Italy and tolerated as long as it did not cause public disturbance. In the 1887 parliamentary debate that led to the decriminalization of male same-sex practices, the Minister of Justice, Giuseppe Zanardelli (1826–1903), explained that in dealing with 'acts against nature', ignorance of the 'vice' was more useful than its advertisement through the law. This line of argument was informed by the legal doctrines of prominent authority Giovanni Carmignani (1768–1847) which argued that the most prudent way to confront the 'vice' of same-sex practices was to deny their existence. Political caution led Italian legislators to believe that unveiling sexual practices usually shrouded in silence was against the public interest, the effectiveness of the legal system and especially against traditional customs.[43]

Despite this, the Italian ruling classes were not prudish in discussing sexuality and so-called sexual perversions. Following Italian unification, there was bitter conflict between the state and the Church, as the latter did not recognize the new Italian kingdom. The state sought to replace the Church's moral authority, and to take control of citizens' sexual morality. Doctors and criminal anthropologists played a critical role in this process and began to talk openly about sexuality, considering silence over sexual matters, the characteristic stance of the Catholic Church, to be a profoundly dangerous attitude towards a fundamental part of human life. They contributed to the creation of sexology, that is, the interdisciplinary study of human sexuality. Much of the sexological work of men like Cesare

Lombroso (1835–1909) and Paolo Mantegazza (1831–1910) was directed at religious sexual tenets.[44]

Why did English legislators feel the need to punish male same-sex practices for such a long time when their Italian counterparts did not? Why was the English government partially influenced by the Napoleonic Code when it came to regulating female prostitution, but not with regard to male same-sex practices? Comparative history can shed light on these kinds of questions. Historians have debated why different parts of Europe adopted different legal approaches to male homosexuality from the early nineteenth century. Religion is important here: sexual behaviours are not only regulated by laws, but also by religion and other beliefs. We should therefore always consider how religion affected sexual conduct in given geographical areas. Predominantly Roman Catholic countries such as France, Belgium, Italy and Spain tended not to criminalize male homosexuality between consenting adults, while predominantly Protestant countries and mixed-confessional but Protestant-dominated countries, like England and Germany, criminalized male homosexuality until well into the twentieth century. As a result, some scholars have argued that Catholic countries were more superficially tolerant because the Church exerted a powerful influence on private moral issues and succeeded in suppressing deviant sexualities. These studies highlight the fact that, because religion had less influence on private affairs in Protestant countries, the sanctioning of sexual behaviour became the state's prerogative. According to these studies, tolerant Mediterranean legislators sought to cloak deviant sexualities in silence; their intention was to prevent the disorder being named.[45]

Conclusion

When comparing the history of sexuality, or any other cultural phenomena, in different geographical contexts, a number of factors must be considered. Attitudes towards gender, political contexts, legal frameworks, the cultural role of religion and national traditions, and reactions to attempts to control sexual behaviour are of crucial importance. Class, age, ethnicity and differences between urban and rural settings, although not considered in this chapter, are also central to any sustained attempt to compare different countries. Comparison does not yield easy answers, but it does illuminate the role of specific factors and help us to avoid simplistic moral judgements.

Comparison deepens historical analysis and challenges common assumptions. The above overview of the regulation of female prostitution and male homosexuality in England and Italy shows that it is difficult to decide which country was more tolerant towards non-reproductive sexual behaviour. If we look at female prostitution, England certainly had a more liberal approach to prostitution than Italy. While in both countries prostitution was legal, the English authorities never managed to regulate prostitution to the same extent as their Italian counterparts. In England, prostitutes enjoyed more freedom, the Contagious Diseases Acts applied only to limited areas and they had a relatively short life. Conversely, attitudes towards male homosexuality were more liberal in Italy. It is not a coincidence that Oscar Wilde (1854–1900), convicted of acts of gross indecency with other men, went into exile in Italy following his release from prison in 1897. John Addington Symonds (1840–93), the eminent Victorian interpreter of classical thought and Renaissance history, and self-identified homosexual, considered the Zanardelli Code well in advance of the English legal system, which still punished male same-sex practices carried out in private. He hoped that his own country would in time follow Italy's legal example in dealing with male same-sex acts.[46]

As the Italian case has shown, specific political contexts are very important when comparing two countries. Laws such as the Cavour Regulation and the Zanardelli Penal Code responded to the perceived need for uniform regulation of sexual conduct on the Italian Peninsula. The implementation of these laws cannot be understood without considering the unification of Italy. Yet Italy was also influenced by the French model in regulating both female prostitution and male homosexuality, while England, if not completely immune to French influence, resisted the Continental model until the passing of the Contagious Diseases Acts in the 1860s, and eventually rejected it entirely. In both countries, laws such as the Contagious Diseases Acts and the Cavour Regulation were passed in response to military concerns. Despite the fact that different confessional allegiances might have played a central role in guiding individual sexual conduct in different ways in England and Italy, both countries went through a process of secularization in the regulation of sexual conduct, with the state increasingly taking on the role formerly played by the Church.

This chapter has dealt with two specific case studies on the regulation of sexuality in England and Italy, but in showing how comparative analysis can provide valid and rewarding insights into specific societies, it has aimed to illustrate the wider applicability of this approach to history. Comparative history helps to identify typologies of development, structures, differences, similarities and reciprocal influences. It is also crucial in helping to *explain* these differences. For example, systematic comparison of factors which shaped the legal regulation of sexual behaviour in England and Italy enables historians to isolate the most important reasons for differences in these systems, such as religion. Above all, comparative approaches help historians to rethink accepted historical explanations, as in the argument that in some times and places, the strong influence of the Catholic Church on private life might actually have resulted in more liberal legislation regarding some aspects of sexual behaviour. While comparative history moves beyond the nation to elucidate broader political, cultural and social patterns, it also fosters original insights into national histories which could not be gained through focusing exclusively on single national contexts. In the twenty-first century, comparative history still has much to offer historians.

STUDY QUESTIONS

- Why do historians compare?
- What are the potential problems of using a comparative methodology?
- In what ways do comparative histories differ from national and transnational histories?

Notes

1   M. Bloch (1928) 'Pour une histoire comparée des sociétés européennes', *Revue de synthèse historique*, 46; M. Bloch (1969) 'A Contribution Towards a Comparative History of European Societies', in M. Bloch, *Land and Work in Mediaeval Europe: Selected Papers by Marc Bloch*, trans. J. E. Anderson (New York: Harper Torchbooks).

2   M. Ryan (1839) *Prostitution in London, with a Comparative View of That of Paris and New York* (London: H. Bailliere); G. Tammeo (1890) *La prostituzione. Saggio di statistica morale* (Naples: Roux).

3   M. Werner and B. Zimmermann (eds) (2004), *De la comparaison à l'histoire croisée* (Paris: Seuil); P.-Y. Saunier (2008) 'Learning by Doing: Notes about the Making of the Palgrave Dictionary of Transnational History', *Journal of Modern European History*, 6:2, p. 177.

4   G. L. Mosse (1982), 'Nationalism and Respectability: Normal and Abnormal Sexuality in the Nineteenth Century', *Journal of Contemporary History*, 17.

5   T. Skocpol (1979) *States and Social Revolutions: A Comparative Analysis of France, Russia and China* (Cambridge: Cambridge University Press).

6   Cited in H. G. Haupt and J. Kocka (2004) 'Comparative History: Methods, Aims, Problems', in D. Cohen and M. O'Connor (eds), *Comparison and History: Europe in Cross-National Perspective* (New York and Abingdon, Oxon: Routledge), p. 31.

7   Skocpol, *States and Social Revolutions*.

8   P. N. Stearns (1974) *The Revolutions of 1848* (London: Weidenfeld and Nicolson), p. 5.

9   Haupt and Kocka, 'Comparative History', p. 27.

10   W. H. Sewell (1967) 'Marc Bloch and the Logic of Comparative History', *History and Theory*, 6:2.

11   J. Weeks (1979), 'Movements of Affirmation: Sexual Meanings and Homosexual Identities', *Radical History Review*, 20; J. Weeks (1981) *Sex, Politics and Society: The Regulation of Sexuality since 1800* (London: Longman).

12 D. M. Halperin (1990) *One Hundred Years of Homosexuality and Other Essays on Greek Love* (New York: Routledge); R. Norton (1992) *Mother Clap's Molly House: The Gay Subculture in England, 1700–1830* (London: Gay Men's Press); T. van der Meer (2007) 'Sodomy and Its Discontents: Discourse, Desire, and the Rise of a Same-Sex Proto-Something in the Early Modern Dutch Republic', *Historical Reflections/Reflexions Historiques*, 33:1.

13 M. Canaday (2009) 'Thinking Sex in the Transnational Turn: An Introduction', *American Historical Review*, 114:5.

14 D. M. Halperin (2002) *How to Do the History of Homosexuality* (Chicago, IL: University of Chicago Press).

15 L. Stone (1990) *Road to Divorce: England, 1530–1987* (Oxford: Oxford University Press), pp. 368–90.

16 M. Seymour (2006) *Debating Divorce in Italy: Marriage and the Making of Modern Italians, 1860–1974* (New York: Palgrave Macmillan).

17 J. J. Howard (1978) 'The Civil Code of 1865 and the Origins of the Feminist Movement in Italy', in B. Boyd Caroli, R. F. Harney and L. F. Tomasi (eds), *The Italian Immigrant Woman in North America* (Toronto, ON: Multicultural History Society of Ontario); P. Willson, (2004) 'Introduction: Gender and the Private Sphere in Liberal and Fascist Italy', in P. Willson (ed.), *Gender, Family and Sexuality: The Private Sphere in Italy, 1860–1945* (Basingstoke and New York: Palgrave Macmillan).

18 E. Sarogni (1995) *La donna italiana. Il lungo cammino verso i diritti, 1861–1994* (Parma: *Pratiche* Editrice), p. 97.

19 S. L. Gilman (1985) *Difference and Pathology: Stereotypes of Sexuality, Race, and Madness* (Ithaca, NY and London: Cornell University Press), pp. 76–108.

20 J. Laite (2012) *Common Prostitutes and Ordinary Citizens: Commercial Sex in London, 1885–1960* (Basingstoke and New York: Palgrave Macmillan), pp. 6 and 32–3.

21 Laite, *Common Prostitutes and Ordinary Citizens*, pp. 6–7.

22 J. Walkowitz (1980) *Prostitution and Victorian Society: Women, Class and the State* (Cambridge: Cambridge University Press), pp. 36–47. In 1804, Napoleon had passed a law rendering the registration and bi-weekly health inspection of all prostitutes compulsory. Many leading British regulationists were venereologists who had studied in Paris and influenced the political debate that led to the passing of the Contagious Diseases Acts.

23 The Act of 1864 stated that infected women could be interned in lock hospitals for up to three months. The period of incarceration was gradually extended until the 1869 Act increased the sentence to a year. Walkowitz, *Prostitution and Victorian Society*, pp. 67–148.

24 Laite, *Common Prostitutes and Ordinary Citizens*, pp. 54–69.

25 Walkowitz, *Prostitution and Victorian Society*, pp. 90–136.

26 M. Gibson (1986) *Prostitution and the State in Italy, 1860–1915* (New Brunswick: Rutgers University Press), p. 15.

27   R. Macrelli (1981) *L'indegna schiavitù: Anna Maria Mozzoni e la lotta contro la prostituzione di stato* (Rome: Editori Riuniti), p. 68.

28   Macrelli, *L'indegna schiavitù*, pp. 11–13; Gibson, *Prostitution and the State in Italy*, p. 24.

29   Macrelli, *L'indegna schiavitù*.

30   Howard, 'The Civil Code of 1865 and the Origins of the Feminist Movement in Italy', p. 16.

31   Walkowitz, *Prostitution and Victorian Society*, pp. 48–66.

32   F. Mort (1987) *Dangerous Sexualities: Medico-Moral Politics in England since 1830* (London: Routledge & Kegan Paul), pp. 58–9.

33   Gibson, *Prostitution and the State in Italy*, pp. 23–34.

34   L. A. Hall (2000) *Sex, Gender and Social Change in Britain since 1880* (Basingstoke and New York: Palgrave Macmillan), p. 22.

35   S. Brady (2005) *Masculinity and Male Homosexuality in Britain, 1861–1913* (Basingstoke and New York: Palgrave Macmillan), p. 27.

36   H. G. Cocks (2003) *Nameless Offences: Homosexual Desire in the Nineteenth Century* (London: I. B. Tauris Publishers), pp. 17–18.

37   F. B. Smith (1976) 'Labouchère's Amendment to the Criminal Law Amendment Act', *Historical Studies*, 17.

38   This was similar to the situation of German homosexuals, who were judged under the Prussian legal code after unification. J. Steakley (1975) *The Homosexual Emancipation Movement in Germany* (New York: Arno Press).

39   For further details, see Codici penali italiani preunitari e omosessualità: http://www.giovannidallorto.com/saggistoria/tollera/codici.html. Accessed 16 January 2016.

40   In 1832, Pope Gregory XVI ruled that sodomy should be punished with a life sentence: 'delitto consumato contro natura'. See Regolamento Gregoriano, art. 178. Quoted in Oliari, 2006, p. 17.

41   Art. 425 'Codice Penale per il Regno di Sardegna, 20/11/1859 – Libro II, Titolo VII, Dei Reati contro il Buon Costume'.

42   L. Benadusi (2005) *Il nemico dell'uomo nuovo. L'omosessualità nell'esperimento totalitario fascista* (Milan: Feltrinelli), pp. 98–9.

43   Benadusi, *Il nemico dell'uomo nuovo*, p. 103.

44   C. Beccalossi (2012) *Female Sexual Inversion: Same-Sex Desires in Italian and British Sexology, ca. 1870–1920* (Basingstoke and New York: Palgrave Macmillan), especially pp. 43–78, 117–71.

45   G. Dall'Orto (1988) 'La "tolleranza repressiva" dell'omosessualità. Quando un atteggiamento legale diviene tradizione', in Arci Gay Nazionale (ed.), *Omosessuali e stato* (Bologna: Cassero); Benadusi, *Il nemico dell'uomo nuovo*, p. 103.

46   C. Beccalossi (2015) 'The "Italian Vice": Male Homosexuality and British Tourism in Southern Italy', in V. Babini, C. Beccalossi and L. Riall (eds), *Italian Sexualities Uncovered: 1789–1914* (Basingstoke and New York: Palgrave Macmillan).

Further Reading

C. Beccalossi (2012) *Female Sexual Inversion: Same-Sex Desires in Italian and British Sexology, ca. 1870–1920* (Basingstoke and New York: Palgrave Macmillan).

C. Beccalossi (2015) 'The "Italian Vice": Male Homosexuality and British Tourism in Southern Italy', in V. Babini, C. Beccalossi and L. Riall (eds), *Italian Sexualities Uncovered: 1789–1914* (Basingstoke and New York: Palgrave Macmillan), pp. 185–206.

M. Bloch (1969) 'A Contribution Towards a Comparative History of European Societies', in M. Bloch, *Land and Work in Mediaeval Europe: Selected Papers by Marc Bloch*, trans. J. E. Anderson (New York: Harper Torchbooks), pp. 44–81.

S. Brady (2005) *Masculinity and Male Homosexuality in Britain, 1861–1913* (Basingstoke and New York: Palgrave Macmillan).

M. Canaday (2009) 'Thinking Sex in the Transnational Turn: An Introduction', *American Historical Review*, 114:5, pp. 1250–57.

M. Gibson (1986) *Prostitution and the State in Italy, 1860–1915* (New Brunswick: Rutgers University Press).

L. A. Hall (2000) *Sex, Gender and Social Change in Britain since 1880* (Basingstoke and New York: Palgrave Macmillan).

D. M. Halperin (2002) *How To Do the History of Homosexuality* (Chicago, IL: University of Chicago Press).

H. G. Haupt and J. Kocka (2004) 'Comparative History: Methods, Aims, Problems', in D. Cohen and M. O'Connor (eds), *Comparison and History: Europe in Cross-National Perspective* (New York and Abingdon, Oxon: Routledge), pp. 28–40.

J. Laite (2012) *Common Prostitutes and Ordinary Citizens: Commercial Sex in London, 1885–1960* (Basingstoke and New York: Palgrave Macmillan).

P.-Y. Saunier (2008) 'Learning by Doing: Notes about the Making of the Palgrave Dictionary of Transnational History', *Journal of Modern European History*, 6:2, pp. 159–79.

W. H. Sewell (1967) 'Marc Bloch and the Logic of Comparative History', *History and Theory*, 6:2, pp. 208–18.

J. Weeks (1981), *Sex, Politics and Society: The Regulation of Sexuality since 1800* (London: Longman).

4

Biography

Toby Thacker

How and why would a historian write a biography of a man considered, almost universally, to have been singularly evil, in the words of Victor Klemperer, 'the most poisonous and mendacious of all Nazis'?[1] Joseph Goebbels (1897–1945) is notorious as the Propaganda Minister of the 'Third Reich', a brilliant public speaker who used his talents to encourage hatred of the Jews, to build support for Hitler and to justify the most horrible excesses of the Nazi regime during the Second World War. In the public mind, he is typically imagined as the sinister manipulator of radio and cinema, who used these technologies to brainwash a whole population, and to turn them into fanatical supporters of the 'Hitler myth'. No television documentary on the Nazis is complete without archive film of Goebbels speaking to huge audiences, jeering about his opponents, excoriating foreigners and rousing his listeners into a hysterical frenzy. When all was lost for the Nazis at the end of the war, he was not content to kill himself, but, together with his wife Magda, murdered his six young children. He is one of the monsters of the twentieth century, identified with the worst abuses of dictatorship.

We have of course moved on from the nineteenth century, when biography was largely confined to the stories of 'great men', kings, diplomats, statesmen and artists. We are now equally used to seeing biographies of tyrants and despots, or of historical figures like Stalin or Cromwell, who are seen by some as heroes, and by others as villains. And biography, as a historical form, is making a comeback after decades in which it was seen as better suited for popular consumption than for serious academic readers. In this chapter, I draw on my own experience to ask what biography as a form can offer to history, above all in exploring the relationship between an individual and the times in which that person lived and died. I examine the kinds of evidence which biographers use, and how this can shape the kinds of biography which are produced. Drawing largely on examples from the history of Nazi Germany and the twentieth century, I explore recent developments which have brought new vitality to biography, and placed it again at the forefront of historical enquiry.

Goebbels as a biographical subject

As a historian of modern Germany, there appeared to me to be numerous legitimate reasons for writing a new biography of Joseph Goebbels when I embarked on this project in 2006. This was a man, however unpleasant, who had undoubtedly exercised a major influence in one of the most significant episodes in modern history. He was critically important in the late 1920s and early 1930s in building popular support for Hitler and the Nazis, and in helping them come to power. His skilful use of propaganda after 1933 was vital in building support for Hitler's foreign policy, and for the reconstruction of German society at home. During the Second World War, Goebbels was of vital importance in maintaining popular support for the regime, particularly after the disaster at Stalingrad in 1943, and as the British bombing of German cities intensified. And from 1925 onwards, Goebbels had played an influential role within the Nazi movement, constantly putting hatred of the Jews at the centre of the Party's programme, and demanding, after 1933, that they be relentlessly persecuted. In 1941, Goebbels, who had a uniquely close relationship with Hitler, urged him to take the opportunity provided by the war to move to what the Nazis called the 'Final Solution', the murder of all of the Jews under their control, and until the end of the war Goebbels sought to prosecute this end.[2] Goebbels also presents the historical biographer with a paradox: he was, unlike many of the leading Nazis, an intelligent, cultivated and well-educated man. He loved literature, music and theatre. He was a talented and energetic writer who had dreamed of being a playwright and a poet when he was younger, and he was a father who cared for his children. As an individual, Goebbels encapsulates and embodies one of the most difficult problems confronting historians of modern Germany: how could a people, a society which was in many ways so 'advanced', so 'developed', so 'modern', embrace the violence, the cruelty and the banality of Nazism?

This highlights a further dimension to biography. Although primarily concerned with one person, a biography which takes account of the wider circumstances in which an individual lived offers potential insights into a period of history, and particular aspects of that period. In the case of Goebbels, his path from a lower middle-class childhood in the Rhineland through to early adulthood in the troubled early years of the Weimar Republic offers a unique view, through the prism of one individual's experience, of Germany's transition from empire through defeat in war to a chaotic and unsettling new post-war world, one in which extreme views flourished. Goebbels was not an early member of the Nazi Party, so his personal history tells us nothing about the Party's beginnings in Munich, but from March 1924 onwards his fate was intimately bound up with that of the Party; his biography offers new light on the institutional and structural development of an organization which is often overlooked by students concentrating their attention on its charismatic leader. It need hardly be stressed how much a biography of Goebbels has to offer to the student of propaganda in the twentieth century.

The evidence for a biography of Goebbels

A further compelling reason for writing a biography of Goebbels was the availability of new evidence. All historians are dependent on evidence, and biographers are particularly interested in personal documents, what is called 'life writing', that is to say diaries, journals and letters. In the chaos at the end of the Second World War, Goebbels's own diary had almost completely disappeared. Fragments of his diary from 1942 to 1943, and from 1925 to 1926 were found, transcribed and published in German and in English; later the final few weeks of his diary, from January through to April 1945, were found and published in a widely selling edition.[3] Not until the final years of the Cold War did it become clear that the diaries which Goebbels had kept almost uninterruptedly from 1923 until the end of his life had survived almost intact, micro-photographed onto glass plates and kept hidden in the Soviet State Archives in Moscow. After complex negotiations, the diaries were returned to the Federal German Republic, where over the next decade, a team of historians worked painstakingly to transcribe the material, and to publish all of it in a huge edition of twenty-nine volumes containing some 15,000 printed pages. This project to publish what is undoubtedly one of the most significant historical documents of the twentieth century was only completed in 2006 with the publication then of the earliest section of the diary, starting from October 1923, and dealing with the critical period in Goebbels's life when he made the transition from being an unemployed loner to a new life as a Nazi Party activist.[4]

Diaries come in many forms. Some consist of nothing more than fragmentary notes giving times and dates of meetings and appointments. Some contain details of public events, and the perceptions of the writer about those events. Others are more intimate and personal, with reflection on the inner life of the writer. Many are intermittent, with much more written at some points in an individual's life than others, and with gaps of varying length. Joseph Goebbels took to writing almost daily from October 1923, using his diary as a private space to reflect on his own mental state and on what was happening around him. When he moved into political activism and then into public life, he used his diary to record larger events and to portray the people around him. By the early 1930s, when he had become a politician of national importance, he was becoming aware of the potential value of his diary as a historical document, and he began to write with future publication in mind, taking care to record his impressions of political developments. He continued this habit as a minister after March 1933, now recording summaries of international affairs. After July 1941, as the war intensified, Goebbels included every day a military communiqué from the headquarters of the *Wehrmacht*, and dictated his diary to a stenographer. He had by this time developed the habit of setting aside time every day to work on his diary, and the entries became correspondingly longer. This habit – one might call it a compulsion – ended only in April 1945, a few days before Goebbels moved with his wife and children into Hitler's bunker under the Reich Chancellery.

There were before 2006 several biographies of Goebbels, many of dubious reliability, but none were written with access to all of this extraordinary material. Several, lacking evidence from the early 1920s, took at face value and rehearsed Goebbels's own *later* suggestion that he had joined the Nazi Party in Munich in 1922 after seeing Hitler speak at a public meeting.[5] I found this to be only one of several completely inaccurate ideas about Goebbels which were frequently repeated, even in recent books about him and about Nazi Germany.[6] The newly available evidence does not only tell us about Goebbels. Ian Kershaw wrote in 1998 that one of the main reasons for his writing a new biography of Hitler, which was published to great critical acclaim, was because of the new insights available from Goebbels's diary.[7] How much greater then the potential for a new biography of Goebbels himself!

Inevitably, readers will ask whether Goebbels's diary is to be trusted. The man was, after all, one of the great liars of history. Clearly, this is a document to be approached with the greatest scepticism and care. Where possible, the 'facts' presented in it must be cross-referenced with other sources to test their accuracy. When this is done, Goebbels's diary is found to be extraordinarily accurate. Most aspects of the history of Nazi Germany are well documented, as this was a highly literate country with a particularly developed publishing and media sector. A mass of photographs, of film and of sound recordings have survived to complement a rich written record. Hundreds of memoirs have subsequently been produced, and there is now a flourishing oral history movement which has added to our knowledge of this period. Goebbels was a careful and detailed chronicler, and his record of events stands up to close scrutiny. Of course, the subjective impressions he recorded of people and events are just that, and should be taken as such. Goebbels even wrote with surprising candour about some of the most ghastly Nazi crimes, such as the gassing of the Jews and the implementation of a policy of 'extermination through labour' for slave workers in Nazi Germany. True, his comments on these topics were brief and oblique, offering little detail. Nonetheless, there is consensus among serious historians of Nazi Germany that as a factual record, Goebbels's diary is extremely accurate, and that it is one of the most important documents from the period. No historian of Nazi Germany can ignore it.

Use of these newly available diaries begs a question. Do we need extensive 'life writing' to underpin a biography? Is it possible to write a good biography of a historical figure who has not left a diary, or extensive personal correspondence? Here the comparison with Hitler is instructive, and suggests that the answer is yes. Hitler did not keep a diary, and as an adult wrote very few letters. We have very little surviving personal writing by him. There are of course literally thousands of official documents, protocols of meetings, memoranda, public pronunciations, transcriptions of speeches and broadcasts, to say nothing of his monologues which were recorded by people around him. This material lends itself to a very different kind of biography, one where an individual is seen much more from the outside, as a public persona. Isaac Deutscher, in the preface to his classic 'political biography' of Stalin, wrote, 'It is impossible to narrate the private life of Stalin, since only one private letter of his has come to light.'[8] Even the most recent biography of the Soviet leader by Stephen Kotkin, drawing on evidence from a wide range of people who knew Stalin, has presented him as a professional revolutionary, a man of extraordinary determination who exercised an immense influence on twentieth-century history, but says little about his inner life. Kotkin notes that he avoids 'speculative leaps or what is known as filling in the gaps in the record of Stalin's life'.[9]

Where there is an extensive and frank personal record, as with Goebbels, the potential exists for a biography which seeks to reveal the inner life of its subject. And, we should add, there is no shortage of surviving material revealing Goebbels as a public figure. As a practising journalist, he wrote between 1919 and 1933 no fewer than 791 articles in different newspapers![10] Transcriptions of his speeches run to hundreds of pages. As with any individual there are lacunae. Most frustratingly, we have no sound recordings of his early speeches, and we are left largely to imagine what extraordinary qualities he must have had to rise from nowhere in the 1920s to become the Nazi Party's favourite speaker, second only to Hitler himself (see Figure 4.1).

Biography and 'great men'

Is biography a historical form appropriate only for reconstructing the lives of significant figures? To this day biography – both academic and popular – is dominated by accounts of famous people, those who by dint of personality, talent and circumstance have stood out from their fellow men and women, and who typically have enjoyed remarkable lives, whether in

FIGURE 4.1 *Anger, energy and aggression: this picture of Goebbels speaking in the open air at Bad Freienwalde near Berlin in 1929 demonstrates some of the qualities that made him one of the most influential orators of the twentieth century.* Source: F. Maier-Hartmann (1938), Dokumente der Zeitgeschichte *(Munich: Franz Eher Verlag), p. 304.*

politics, sport, the media or in other fields. Well into the twentieth century, biography as a literary form was considered more or less exclusively fitted to record the lives of exceptional figures in history. This idea chimed well with the popular nineteenth-century idea that history was made by 'great men', a preoccupation which resulted in numerous biographies of leaders such as Napoleon and Frederick the Great, imagined as colossal figures who had taken history into their own hands and reshaped it through the force of will and personality. Even when Lytton Strachey pioneered the idea of 'critical biography' in the early twentieth century, challenging hero-worship with a satirical approach to his subjects, he concentrated his attention on what he called 'Eminent Victorians'.[11]

Several developments in the twentieth century have changed this. As discussed in Martin Wright's chapter in this volume, the emergence in the 1960s and after of 'history from below' turned historical attention towards ordinary people, and led in subsequent decades to new forms of social history which concentrate on the experience of everyday life. Women's history has sought to recover the lives of women, so long hidden from view, and opened up new fields for biography.[12] In the 1980s, historians further developed the idea of prosopography, or collective biography, hoping by studying similar groups of people to understand better the lives of others like them.[13] By turning to oral testimony, historians have sought to record the voices of people who did not leave copious written records. The whole field of micro-history, which sought to turn away from the great events around which earlier narratives had been structured, and to examine historical situations from a local and small-scale perspective, deliberately used as a major source of evidence the life-writing of hitherto obscure and unknown individuals.[14] In recent years, biographers have often consciously sought to reconstruct the lives of ordinary people, men and women, sometimes using them to challenge existing accounts which focus more on the rich and famous. In 2014, this was particularly apparent in the numerous commemorations of the First World War, many of which centred on reconstructing the biographies of ordinary people who were involved, and who were previously unknown to posterity.[15]

All of these newer forms have been applied to modern German history, and in particular to the history of Nazi Germany. A flourishing social history has developed, seeking to understand how ordinary people reacted to the rise of Nazism in the 1920s and then lived – and died – in the 'Third Reich'. Many historians have concentrated on the experience of women, long considered marginal to the history of Nazism because they were largely excluded from the public sphere. Oral history, often based on local community initiatives, has complemented these developments. Most recently, academic historians have turned to prosopography, seeking to isolate groups or types of people in Germany, and to explore their experience.[16] Writing the life of Joseph Goebbels, I was for the most part concerned with a figure who played a role in politics, in national and then in international affairs. When he was appointed by Hitler to the new post of Propaganda Minister in March 1933, Goebbels was proud to be the youngest man ever to serve as a minister in Germany, and he enjoyed being at the centre of events. He did not confine his role to shaping, or trying to shape public opinion, but liked to have a finger in every pie. Particularly through his close relationship with Hitler, Goebbels sought to influence policies towards the churches, on the treatment of the mentally and physically disabled, and of male homosexuals. He made himself the public face of Nazi anti-Semitism, fronting the public boycott of Jewish businesses in April 1933, and the organized pogrom of November 1938 which became known as *Kristallnacht*, or 'The Night of Broken Glass'. The story of his life between 1933 and 1939 is also the story of the Nazi effort to create inside Germany a *Volksgemeinschaft*, what Burleigh and Wippermann called the 'racial state', and to reshape the map of Europe.[17] Between 1939 and 1945, Goebbels's fate was intimately bound up with Germany's fortunes in the Second World War. Building on his earlier obsession with the persecution of Jews in Germany, Goebbels took it upon himself to try to influence policy towards the Jews of Germany and in Occupied Europe. His life in these years was not that of an ordinary person. He was wealthy, lived in considerable comfort and enjoyed mixing with politicians, businessmen, artists, generals and even film stars.

But in his early life, Goebbels's life history was much more closely linked to that of many more ordinary people in Germany, and a close study of his individual experience can illuminate much more than his own life. It seems clear, for instance, that the disability which resulted from failed operations on his foot in childhood resulted in bullying and humiliation at school, and helped to turn the young schoolboy into a loner and a bookworm. Goebbels, unlike many other Nazis, did not serve in the First World War, and was not one of the brutalized and traumatized ex-servicemen who gravitated towards paramilitary violence and male comradeship in the post-war years.[18] In common with most of the civilian population, he did experience great material hardship and family tragedy. One of his brothers was taken prisoner by the French, and in 1915 his sister Elisabeth died of tuberculosis at the age of twelve. For the young Goebbels, now an undergraduate student, the collapse of the German war effort, the abdication of the Kaiser and the defeat of the German army in November 1918 came as huge shock. For the next six years, he shared the common experience of many young German men, of struggling to find gainful employment in a chaotic economy, and of trying to make sense of an external world in which the proud German people appeared to be victims of a vengeful conspiracy. He was forced to live without money of his own, in his parents' house. Goebbels also tried, and failed, to build meaningful relationships with women of his own age. In these years, he was not involved with party politics, and was not in any sense a public figure, but his individual experience reflects that of many others. Goebbels was one of many who knew little or nothing about the activities of the Nazi Party in Munich, or of its leader Adolf Hitler, but who came in these years to see the Jews as the antithesis of everything German, and as somehow responsible for all the country's problems.

Biography and psychoanalysis

In seeking to understand this vital period of Goebbels's early adulthood, I drew in my biography on a psychoanalytical concept, Erik Erikson's idea of the 'second birth', a formative and frequently troubled period when the individual makes a transition from adolescence to adulthood. How can this, and other psychoanalytic ideas, inform a historical biography? Slowly, at different speeds in different cultural contexts, the ideas developed in the late nineteenth century by Freud and other psychoanalytic thinkers have seeped through academic disciplines, and into the public consciousness. Many of them are now part of the common cultural capital of the Western world. Before Freud, biographers had accepted that adult subjects had previously been children. James Boswell (1740–95), widely credited with having written the first modern biography in 1791, had famously proclaimed his intention to narrate Samuel Johnson's life 'from his cradle to the grave'.[19] But in practice, most biographers had only provided a few anecdotes from the childhood of their subjects, typically using them to show the early emergence of a particular talent or aptitude. The psychoanalytic emphasis on the determining influence of the earliest stages of childhood, and of a child's relationships with its parents, pointed towards an entirely different understanding of adult behaviour, and towards a new form of biography.

As Freudian ideas have been disseminated, historians have wrestled with the consequences they might have for their own discipline. While some have welcomed psychoanalysis as offering, even demanding, totally new ways of understanding human motivation and action, others have argued that psychoanalysis presents fundamental problems. These controversies have been particularly sharp when applied to biography. If, as psychoanalysts hold, human behaviour is best understood through an analysis of repressed childhood experience and the interpretation of dreams, where is the body of reliable empirical evidence which historians and biographers normally rely on to be found? Long dead historical figures cannot easily be placed on the psychoanalyst's couch and invited to explore their memories. If adult behaviour is completely or even largely determined by childhood experience, is there any point in a biographer examining anything other than the formative stages of a life? And, given the increasing complexity of psychoanalysis as a discipline, how can a biographer without specialized psychoanalytical training hope to understand any given individual?[20]

There have been several original and highly successful biographies of historical figures written which have tried to overcome these problems: Erik Erikson's *Young Man Luther*, published in 1959, is still pre-eminent in the field.[21] The Harvard psychoanalyst John Mack wrote a brilliant biography of T.E. Lawrence – Lawrence of Arabia – in 1974 which skilfully combined psychoanalytical interpretation of his subject with a historian's appreciation of the wider circumstances in which Lawrence carved out his famous career.[22] Most recently, the critical acclaim accorded to Jonathan Steinberg's new biography of Otto von Bismarck (1815–98), the statesman widely credited with having unified Germany in 1871, suggests that psychoanalysis still has an important role to play in biography. Steinberg though wears his psychoanalytic learning lightly. He avoids using too much opaque psychoanalytical jargon, and concentrates on a set of ideas about Bismarck which are easily understood, and not unduly speculative. Convincingly, he argues that Bismarck's personality was fundamentally shaped in childhood through his relationships with a weak, easy-going father and an intellectually powerful but emotionally cold mother. Steinberg suggests that throughout his adult life as a politician Bismarck found himself playing out repetitions of this Oedipal drama, for example, in his relationship with Kaiser Wilhelm I and his wife, the Empress Augusta. 'He had', writes Steinberg, 'to re-enact day after day, year after year, the agony of his childhood, the little boy at the point of an upside-down triangle and at the mercy of the struggle between the threatening woman and weak man.'[23]

Notably, and this is where the influence of psychoanalysis is strongest today, Steinberg constantly portrays Bismarck in a holistic manner, not just as a public figure, but as a human being who struggled with his health and with personal relationships. In his portrayal, we hear almost as much about Bismarck's hypochondria, his gluttony, his ill-will and his raging temper as about his consummate diplomacy and statecraft. This kind of biography, in which an individual is portrayed not merely as an adult in public life, but as a whole person, with a childhood, adolescence, early adulthood, with sexual desires, with dreams and with issues of physical and mental health, is a far cry from the hero-worship characteristic of so many nineteenth-century works.

When considering how to approach Joseph Goebbels, I faced a number of particular problems. The evidence for Goebbels's infanthood and childhood is derived almost entirely from his own anecdotes, first committed to paper when he was a young man, and subsequently ossified in frequent repetition to subordinates. By the time Goebbels produced these anecdotes, he had become active in politics, and already wanted to recast his early life, in particular to suggest that he had been attracted to Nazism early in its history. When, as an adult he wrote and spoke about his parents, he felt obliged to cast them as stereotypes displaying characteristics widely recognized and celebrated in German society. He described his father, therefore, as an archetypal Prussian, 'a man of duty', a 'fanatic for work', and his mother as an idealized German matron who, unbowed by poverty, sacrificed everything for the upbringing of her children.[24] By any token, this is unreliable material to work from. In fact, Goebbels had struggled to maintain good relations with both of his parents, particularly after leaving university. He was painfully aware that he had not fulfilled their fond earlier hopes that he might become a priest, and, for his part, he came to despise what he perceived as their philistine and petty bourgeois values. Goebbels did record his memories of a few dreams, but I felt it unwise to construct an edifice of speculation on these insubstantial foundations. Other biographers of Goebbels, drawing largely on the revelatory comments in his diary, have gone further, and have characterized him as having a 'severe narcissistic personality disorder', seeking in this diagnosis a key to unlock the understanding of his complex personality.[25]

The evidential record for Goebbels's early adulthood is much broader and more reliable than that for his childhood, and here I found ideas which Erikson had applied to Martin Luther (1483–1546) extremely helpful. Erikson, better known for his concept of the 'identity crisis', focused on Luther's adolescence and early adulthood, a 'second birth' where, he argued, the individual leaves childhood, and has to determine and to create an adult identity. Erikson argued that this period was, in certain individuals, extended over several years, and might result in a prolonged crisis before the individual found a new and settled path to follow. Strikingly, he moved beyond the consideration of the family and parental orbit to include the wider societal context in which this 'second birth' was played out, and argued that in times of 'pervasive ideological unrest', it might be exacerbated. Although Erikson was writing about the religious and ideological struggles of the early sixteenth century in which Martin Luther came to maturity, his ideas appeared to me to apply with equal strength to the turbulent period of the early twentieth century in which Goebbels reached adulthood. Arguing that for some individuals this crisis resulted in delinquency or mental illness, Erikson wrote:

> others, although suffering and deviating dangerously through what appears to be a prolonged adolescence, eventually come to contribute an original bit to an emerging style of life: the very danger which they have sensed has forced them to mobilize capacities to see and say, to dream and plan, to design and construct, in new ways.[26]

Critically, Erikson's model suggests a close relationship between the development of the individual personality, and the wider society in which that person develops. This is much more appealing to the biographer who wants to see individuals not as entirely free agents, or as prisoners of infantile experience, but as people living and maturing in specific historical contexts.[27] It is particularly applicable to the young Goebbels, who, even before he was actively involved in politics, was a close observer of events and trends in society around him.

Using the idea of the 'second birth', it became clear to me that the paradigmatic image of Goebbels, deeply entrenched in popular consciousness and still present in academic work, as the great opportunist, the cynic willing to take up any idea which he thought might serve his cause, was entirely mistaken. Working with the new evidence available, and integrating this with a wide range of other primary sources, I realized that there were red threads of conviction, developed in this critical period between 1917 and

1924, running through Goebbels's life until its grisly end in 1945. He was firstly a passionate German nationalist, a sense he identified closely with his understanding of German culture, and which was developed during the First World War. His later involvement with Nazism only strengthened this feeling. Secondly, Goebbels maintained an obsessive hatred of the Jews, whom he saw as enemies of Germany and German culture. This was clearly central to his world view in the immediate post-war years, well before he met Hitler, and was a key factor in the subsequent relationship between the two men. Thirdly, Goebbels had a genuine belief in 'socialism', or what he would have called 'German socialism'. Again this was developed in the chaotic early years of the Weimar republic, when Goebbels came to identify his own, and Germany's economic miseries with the failings of international capitalism. When he became a politician and propagandist with the Nazis, Goebbels identified strongly with those elements of the Party – notably the paramilitary *Sturmabteilung* (SA) – with a socialist agenda. Even during the Second World War, particularly as the Allied bombing of Germany intensified, Goebbels worked with characteristic energy to try to mitigate the suffering of ordinary German civilians. Finally, from 1924 until 1945, Goebbels developed and maintained a passionate veneration for Adolf Hitler. When he wrote in 1926, in a passage addressed to 'Dear, honoured Adolf Hitler', that if at some stage in the future everything collapsed, he and other loyalists would stand with Hitler, singing their defiance to the world, and ready to face death, this might have appeared to some readers as bombastic nonsense.[28] In April 1945, when other leading Nazis such as Himmler, Göring and Speer deserted Hitler and sought to make individual accommodations with the Allies, Goebbels alone joined Hitler in the bunker under the Reich Chancellery and followed him by committing suicide as the Red Army closed in around them.[29]

Goebbels's attraction to these ideas about German nationalism, community, leadership and race can be seen, with variations, in many other German men and women who lived through this period, and suggest that his is more than an individual story. The consolidation of these ideas and their convoluted genesis encourage us to revisit the complex questions of continuity in German and in European history, rather than to imagine the 'Third Reich' as some kind of bizarre aberration, a departure from history. Steinberg's work on Bismarck, concerned with nineteenth-century history, suggests something similar. Although focused on one remarkable individual, he has much to say about the development of larger attitudes and ideas in the newly unified Germany, and argues that Bismarck left a powerful legacy which can be traced into the twentieth century, notably in attitudes towards authority and decision making. He writes, looking chronologically forwards rather than backwards: 'Bismarck's legacy passed through Hindenburg to the last genius-statesman that Germany produced, Adolf Hitler, and the legacy was thus linear and direct between Bismarck and Hitler'.[30]

Conclusion

Does biography still have vitality as a historical form? Does it have anything to contribute? If we judge by the great number of recent biographies in all fields of history, including those of important politicians and statesmen, of artists and thinkers, of men and women, of people both obscure and famous, the answer must be yes. The value of biography is being acknowledged by historians working with other analytical frameworks, such as Adam Tooze, who states in the introduction to his acclaimed economic history of Nazi Germany: 'It is not for nothing that biography – both individual and collective – is one of the most illuminating ways to study the Third Reich'.[31] Brutally rejecting E.H. Carr's idea that 'circumstances make the man, not the man the circumstances', Stephen Kotkin now argues that 'Stalin made history, rearranging the entire socioeconomic landscape of one sixth of the earth'.[32] Human history is the record of what people have done, and while there will always be a place for studies of impersonal forces and structures, the analysis of the individual, and of that person's place in history, still has much to offer.

STUDY QUESTIONS

- Does biography distort history by overstating the importance of one individual?
- Does the tendency of biographers to identify or to sympathize with their subjects undermine the value of their work?
- How do different kinds of evidence affect different biographies? Does a good biography depend on the availability of intimate 'life-writing'?
- Can biographies offer a different way of looking at the periodization of an area of history?

Notes

1 V. Klemperer (1998) *I Shall Bear Witness: The Diaries of Victor Klemperer 1933–41*, trans. M. Chalmers (London: Book Club Associates), 30 July 1936, p. 172.

2 For fuller details, see T. Thacker (2009) *Joseph Goebbels: Life and Death* (London: Palgrave Macmillan).

3   See L. Lochner (ed.) (1948) *The Goebbels Diaries* (London: Hamish Hamilton); H. Heiber (ed.) (1962) *The Early Goebbels Diaries: The Journal of Joseph Goebbels from 1925–1926*, trans. O. Watson (London: Weidenfeld and Nicolson); and H. R. Trevor-Roper (ed.) (1978) *The Goebbels Diaries: The Last Days*, trans. R. Barry (London: Book Club Associates).

4   See E. Fröhlich (ed.) (1998–2006) *Die Tagebücher von Joseph Goebbels: Teil I, Aufzeichnungen 1923–1941*, 14 vols (Munich: Saur); and E. Fröhlich (ed.) (1993–1998) *Die Tagebücher von Joseph Goebbels: Teil II, Diktate 1941–1945*, 15 vols (Munich: Saur).

5   See, for example, C. Riess (1949) *Joseph Goebbels* (London: Hollis and Carter), pp. 22–5.

6   It is rehearsed, for example, in Anna Klabunde's 2003 biography of Goebbels's wife Magda. A. Klabunde (2003) *Magda Goebbels*, trans. S. Whiteside (London: Time Warner)

7   I. Kershaw (1998) *Hitler 1889–1936: Hubris* (London: Allen Lane), p. xii. Even Kershaw did not have access to the full diaries, but used the substantial 'fragments' which were published in four volumes (covering 1924–41) in 1987, and in five volumes (covering 1924–45) in 1992. E. Fröhlich (ed.) (1987) *Die Tagebücher von Joseph Goebbels. Sämtliche Fragmente, Teil I, Aufzechnungen 1924–1941* (Munich: Saur); and R. G. Reuth (ed.) (1992) *Joseph Goebbels. Tagebücher 1924–1945* (Munich and Zurich, Piper).

8   I. Deutscher (1979) *Stalin: A Political Biography*, rev. edn (London: Penguin), p. 18.

9   S. Kotkin (2014) *Stalin. Volume I, Paradoxes of Power, 1878–1928* (New York: Penguin Press), p. 9.

10 See S. Richter (2010) *Joseph Goebbels – der Journalist. Darstellung seines publizistischen Werdegangs 1923 bis 1933* (Stuttgart: Franz Steiner), Anhang Nr. 5, pp. 517ff.

11 L. Strachey (1986) *Eminent Victorians* (London: Penguin) [1918].

12 A good example is J. Hannam (1989) *Isabella Ford* (Oxford: Blackwell). Biographers have also presented female subjects from Nazi Germany. See J. Lomax (1988) *Hanna Reitsch: Flying for the Fatherland* (London: John Murray); and A. Salkeld (1996) *A Portrait of Leni Riefenstahl* (London: Jonathan Cape).

13 See, for example, B. Harvey (1993) *Living and Dying in England, 1100–1540: The Monastic Experience* (Oxford: Clarendon Press).

14 The classic microhistory of Nazi Germany, which focused on the experience of one small German town in the month before Hitler's accession to power is H. A. Turner (1997) *Hitler's Thirty Days to Power: January 1933* (London: Bloomsbury).

15 See, for example, R. David (2014) *Tell Mum Not to Worry: A Welsh Soldier's World War One in the Near East* (Cardiff: Deffro); one of many recent anthologies of life-writing from hitherto unknown figures is D. Young (2005) *Forgotten Scottish Voices from the Great War* (Stroud: Tempus).

16 Some prosopographies have concentrated on significant male groups in Nazi Germany. See, for example, R. Smelser and R. Zitelmann (eds) (1993) *The*

Nazi Elite (London: Macmillan), and B. Campbell (1998) *The SA Generals and the Rise of Nazism* (Lexington: University of Kentucky Press). On women, see, for example, E. Harvey (2003) *Women in the Nazi East: Agents and Witnesses of Germanization* (New Haven and London: Yale University Press); and W. Lower (2014) *Hitler's Furies: German Women in the Nazi Killing Fields* (London: Vintage Books). For an oral history which explores women's memories of everyday life in Nazi Germany, see A. Owings (1995) *Frauen: German Women Recall the Third Reich* (London: Penguin).

17 M. Burleigh and W. Wippermann (1991) *The Racial State: Germany 1933–1945* (Cambridge: Cambridge University Press).

18 Curiously, this does not prevent Klaus Theweleit from using Goebbels as one of the subjects in his influential study of 'Fascist' paramilitaries in Germany after the First World War. See K. Theweleit (1987) *Male Fantasies*, 2 vols (Minneapolis: University of Minnesota Press) [1977].

19 R. W. Chapman (ed.) (1970) *Boswell, Life of Johnson: A New Edition, Corrected by J. D. Fleeman* (London, Oxford and New York: Oxford University Press), p. 29.

20 See G. Walker (2010) 'Psychoanalysis and History', in S. Berger, H. Feldner and K. Passmore (eds), *Writing History: Theory and Practice*, 2nd edn (London: Bloomsbury).

21 E. Erikson (1959) *Young Man Luther: A Study in Psychoanalysis and History* (London: Faber and Faber).

22 J. Mack (1976) *A Prince of Our Disorder: The Life of T. E. Lawrence* (Boston, MA: Little, Brown).

23 J. Steinberg (2011) *Bismarck: A Life* (Oxford: Oxford University Press), pp. 469–71.

24 Thacker, *Joseph Goebbels*, pp. 107 and 327.

25 See in particular P. Longerich (2012) *Goebbels. Biographie* (Munich: Pantheon).

26 Erikson, *Young Man Luther*, p. 12.

27 It is of course the point famously made by Karl Marx, when he wrote: 'Men make their own history, but they do not make it as they please; they do not make it under self-selected circumstances, but under circumstances existing already, given and transmitted from the past.' Karl Marx (1979) 'Excerpts from 18th Brumaire of Louis Napoleon', in Lewis Feuer (ed.), *Karl Marx and Friedrich Engels: Basic Writings on Politics and Philosophy* (London: Fontana), p. 360.

28 J. Goebbels (1927) 'Dr Generalstab', *Wege ins Dritte Reich* (Munich: Eher Verlag), pp. 7–9. Goebbels had in 1926 published this article in the Nazi Party newspaper *Nationalsozialistische Briefe*.

29 For further development of these ideas, see Thacker, *Joseph Goebbels*, pp. 324–32.

30 Steinberg, *Bismarck*, p. 478.

31 Adam Tooze (2007) *Wages of Destruction: The Making and Breaking of the Nazi Economy* (London: Penguin), p. xx.

32   E. H. Carr (1958) *Socialism in One Country, 1924–1926* (New York: Macmillan), Volume I, p. 151; and Kotkin, *Stalin*, p. 739.

Further Reading

'Roundtable: Historians and Biography' (2009) *American Historical Review*, 114, pp. 573–8.

B. Caine (2010) *Biography and History* (London: Palgrave Macmillan).

E. Erikson (1959) *Young Man Luther: A Study in Psychoanalysis and History* (London: Faber and Faber).

I. Kershaw (1998) *Hitler 1889–1936: Hubris* (London: Allen Lane).

I. Kershaw (2000) *Hitler 1936–1945: Nemesis* (London: Allen Lane).

I. Kershaw (2004) 'Personality and Power: The Individual's Role in the History of Twentieth-Century Europe', *The Historian*, 83, pp. 8–19.

S. Kotkin (2014) *Stalin. Volume I, Paradoxes of Power, 1878–1928* (New York: Penguin Press).

W. Lower (2014) *Hitler's Furies: German Women in the Nazi Killing Fields* (London: Vintage Books).

J. Mack (1976) *A Prince of Our Disorder: The Life of T. E. Lawrence* (Boston, MA: Little, Brown).

J. Steinberg (2011) *Bismarck: A Life* (Oxford: Oxford University Press).

L. Stone (1971) 'Prosopography', *Daedalus*, 100:1, pp. 46–71.

L. Strachey (1986) *Eminent Victorians* (London: Penguin) [1918].

T. Thacker (2009) *Joseph Goebbels: Life and Death* (Basingstoke: Palgrave Macmillan).

K. Urbach (1998) 'Between Saviour and Villain: 100 Years of Bismarck Biographies', *Historical Journal*, 41:4, pp. 1141–60.

5

People's History

Martin Wright

What is 'people's history'? The term is difficult. Some would prefer 'labour history'; others favour 'history from below'. The less politically committed may simply opt for 'social history'. The words of James McLachlan (1869–1937) serve well, though, as a starting point from which to capture the spirit of this branch of the discipline:

> I believe in telling children the truth about the history of the world, that it does not consist in the history of Kings and Lords and Cabinets, but consists in the history of the mass of the workers, a thing that is not taught in the schools. I believe in telling children how to measure value, a thing that is not taught in any school.[1]

McLachlan, a Scots-born miner, was leader of the Cape Breton mineworkers in early twentieth-century Canada. His life was bound up with the rise of the international labour movement. A self-educated man and ardent socialist, his view of history grew directly out of his life experience: it was strongly partisan and asserted that the only history of value was the history of the common people. McLachlan contended, moreover, that the teaching of history had a revolutionary purpose. Its aim was not to celebrate the achievements of society's rulers, but to provide the workers with an account of their past from which they could build a consciousness that would enable them to make a better future.

To contemporary British readers this partisan, revolutionary, class-based view of history may appear extreme. It has nevertheless served to inspire and define an important impulse within the discipline of history – an impulse that has played a crucial role in challenging, widening and expanding the discipline as a whole. Focusing on British historiography, this chapter will explore people's history by first examining the growth of labour history in the nineteenth and twentieth centuries, and then discussing the ways in which labour history has been broadened into a wider people's history. Finally, it will examine some of the problems this has raised, and reflect on the current state of people's history.

Foundations: The making of labour history

People's history is the intellectual child of the nineteenth- and early twentieth-century labour movement. In Britain, its development may be traced to the period immediately after the French Revolution, when radicals such as Thomas Paine (1737–1809) constructed a view of the past that stressed the loss of the people's natural rights to usurpation by an elite 'banditti of ruffians'.[2] This view of history intellectually nourished the radical movement of the early 1800s. In their debating societies and newspapers, radicals discussed not just the contemporary condition of the common people, but also its historical roots. Works such as William Cobbett's *History of the Protestant Reformation in England and Ireland* (1824–26) elaborated narratives of dispossession and oppression, while in their autobiographies and memoirs, and in one or two exceptional historical works, such as R.G. Gammage's *History of the Chartist Movement* (1854), radicals also began to write the history of their own struggles. Thus in the febrile atmosphere of the industrial revolution were laid the foundations of working-class history.

An increasingly strident working-class presence in politics across Europe also encouraged academic interest in the study of the history of the common people.[3] In Britain, this was represented in the work of Liberal historians such as Goldwin Smith and J.R. Green. Green's *Short History of the English People* (1877) purported to present 'a history not of English kings or English conquests, but of the English People', which focused not on 'foreign wars and diplomacies' or the 'personal adventures of kings and nobles', but 'the incidents of that constitutional, intellectual, and social advance, in which we read the history of the nation itself'.[4] The common people also played a central role in the work of another radical Liberal, James Thorold Rogers (1823–90). In order to understand the past, he concluded in his influential *Six Centuries of Work and Wages* (1884), the student 'must take account not only of the process by which the machinery of our social condition has been made and constantly marred, but much more of the opinion and action which have developed and moulded the character of the English people'.[5]

Rogers's work was widely read by students of the growing adult education movement, which was a powerful agent in the popularization of social history. From the 1870s onwards, a variety of adult education colleges and associations promoted the study of such people's history.[6] These institutions were guided by liberal values; their aim, as expressed by the founders of Oxford's Ruskin College, was to turn students into 'sandbags for stability not windbags for revolution'.[7] In the historical texts used in such institutions, the villains were usually grasping landlords, and the heroes were industrious workers, allied with a virtuous middle class in pursuit of the great Whiggish project of (English) national evolution.[8] In its blandest form, this type of history could become, in the words of its last advocate G.M. Trevelyan (1876–1962), 'the history of a people with the politics left out'.[9]

A sharper political edge to the study of history was provided in the closing decades of the nineteenth century by the emergence of a more militant labour movement. The aftermath of Chartism (a political movement which sought rights for the working classes and which reached its height in the 1830s and 1840s) had witnessed the growth of moderate, conciliatory labour organizations. However, by the 1880s, more aggressive trade union expansion was accompanied by increasing demands for the creation of an independent Labour Party, fuelled by increasing acceptance among labour activists of the ideology of socialism. At one end of its ideological spectrum, socialism could virtually merge into Liberalism. At the other, though, the ideas of Karl Marx (1818–83) and Friedrich Engels (1820–95) were more influential. Marx and Engels placed a theory of economic exploitation at the centre of their social analysis, allied with a supposedly scientific view of history that identified class struggle as the driver of a dialectical process of social development. This supposition was to have huge ramifications for the writing of history.[10]

This said, the first modern labour historians were shaped less by Marxism than by a concern to document the rise of their own movement. One important agent in this process was the Fabian Society (founded 1884). This small but influential group of middle-class socialists rejected the Marxist analysis of class struggle, and instead asserted that careful, evolutionary social planning was the key to progress. The intellectually well-connected backgrounds of Fabians such as Sidney and Beatrice Webb allowed them to become prominent in both the world of politics and the writing of history. Works like their monumental *History of Trade Unionism* (1894) form the bedrock of British labour historiography. They initiated a classic age of British labour historiography, during which the history of the labour movement was first defined, narrated and celebrated. From the 1890s until the Second World War, labour historians developed a narrative in which the labour movement developed from riotous and unlawful beginnings into a model of reason, discipline and moderation, befitting it to play a central role in the governance of the nation. Its heroes were temperate, moderate, self-educating, male trade unionists, generally skilled craftsmen, who – along with a cast of supportive middle-class sympathizers very much like the authors of the works themselves – guided the labour movement towards power.[11]

From the 1880s, British socialists began writing Marxist history which contested the influential narratives of Fabian labour historians.[12] In the early twentieth century, their efforts were supplemented by organizations that represented a direct challenge to both the moderate labourism of the Fabians and mainstream liberal adult education. In 1909, the Plebs League, formed by a group of worker-students at Ruskin College, initiated the establishment of the Central Labour College (CLC) with the aim 'of equipping organized workers with the knowledge adequate for the accomplishment of their industrial and political tasks' (i.e., the overthrow of capitalism).[13] The time had come, according to Noah Ablett (1883–1935), one of the movement's leaders, 'when the working class should itself enter the educational world to work out its own problems for itself'.[14] This development coincided with a sharp upturn in labour militancy in the years immediately preceding the Great War, and was further encouraged by the Russian Revolution of 1917 – an event which led to the consolidation of those on the left of British politics into the Communist Party of Great Britain (CPGB) in 1920.

The nature of the early twentieth-century Marxist contribution to labour history may be illustrated with reference to one of the CLC's early textbooks, Mark Starr's *A Worker Looks at History* (1917). A coal miner in south Wales,[15] Starr based his book on CLC classes he taught in the south Wales coalfield in the years after 1915, and his work is people's history in two senses: it is a history *of* the people, written *by* one of them. Starr explained the genesis of the book:

> Written by a wage-worker for the use of other wage-workers, by one alternately using a mandrill and a pen, these Outlines were composed in week-ends, evenings, and other intervals snatched from the time occupied by classwork, and the getting of a living 'by helping to milk the black cow.' While the disadvantages of such conditions are obvious, yet they have had their compensations in keeping the writer close to the objective world of reality, often ignored by college professors, which will have to be faced and altered by the workers before they have the sufficiency of means, time and energy to demand for themselves books giving a more adequate treatment of the history of the Labour-process.[16]

Starr's explicit purpose was to equip the labour movement to undertake its revolutionary work of social transformation. Class struggle was central to his interpretation of English history. Starr therefore consciously applied the Marxist materialist conception of history (the belief that historical development is driven by economic and social conditions), which, he asserted, provided a tool that would 'not only [...] help us to explain past history, but it will enable us to make it in the future'.[17]

Starr's readership was largely confined to CLC students, but his assumptions were nevertheless broadly shared by several generations of historians on the left of British politics. The narratives offered by activist-historians offered a clear alternative to those of the Fabians: rather than gradual evolution towards reason, their driving force was class conflict.[18] By the end of the 1930s, a grand synthesis was available in the form of A.L. Morton's *A People's History of England* (1938). A Cambridge graduate and *Daily Worker* journalist, Morton viewed the past as a series of transformations driven by class conflict. Beginning in prehistory, sweeping through the rise and fall of feudalism, the Reformation and the industrial revolution, the book ended in 1938 with capitalism in crisis, class struggle intensifying and the world on the brink of war. Morton's people's history located its readers at the culmination of a grand Marxist narrative. It also represented a broadening of labour history into a wider people's history, and in this sense it both reached back to the work of writers such as Green and Rogers and pre-empted post-war developments in historiography. However, although the people were centre stage in Morton's narrative, they were also trapped within the determinism of the Marxist conception of history, subject to massive, impersonal economic and material forces that circumscribed their freedom of action.

The first half of the twentieth century, then, saw the foundations of British labour history established from two distinct building blocks: Fabianism and Marxism. These two views of history diverged sharply in many senses. One was moderate, drew comfortably on the resources of the academy, viewed progress as resulting from gradual improvement and celebrated the role of sensible, compromising, respectable working-class leaders; the other was militant, rejected the academy, viewed progress as arising from class conflict, and celebrated confrontation. Despite these differences, the two schools were united by some essential common aims. Central to the concerns of both was the desire to recover the past of the working class. Moreover, both understood class primarily in terms of its structures – trade unions and political parties – rather than as inherited tradition or lived experience. In other words, both focused on the economic and political aspects of class, rather than on its cultural manifestations. Likewise, both focused almost exclusively on active, politicized workers; there was little place for the apathetic, reactionary or unorganized in either narrative. They also shared some of the same basic prejudices. Both schools were Anglocentric, presented history from an overwhelmingly male perspective and were largely celebratory. They rejoiced in the 'Forward March of Labour' – a concept that was to be scrutinized more critically by labour historians in the second half of the twentieth century.

From labour history to people's history

The Second World War was a powerful force for social reform. The demands of the 'People's War' led to a 'People's Peace'. The Labour electoral landslide of 1945, the nationalization of key industries and the creation of the

National Health Service and welfare state seemed to justify the belief that a socialist utopia had been realized. In post-war Britain, the celebratory nature of labour history seemed appropriate. Labour historians now made the inexorable rise of the Labour Party, the movement that had built the New Jerusalem, central to their heroic historical narratives.[19] The period thus witnessed considerable growth in labour history. As increasing numbers of working-class students entered university, labour history secured a firmer foothold within the academy. The growing strength of the discipline was reflected in 1960 by the foundation of the Society for the Study of Labour History. In some respects, this growth confirmed the major outlines of pre-war labour history. In other ways, though, the scholarship of the post-war years began to transform the scope and nature of the field.

One important agent in this process was the Communist Party, which from 1946 exerted influence upon the writing of history in Britain through its Historians' Group (CPHG). In its heyday, the CPHG fused the study of history and political activism with considerable intellectual intensity. Eric Hobsbawm (1917–2012), one of its most prominent members, later described the energy behind the group's philosophy:

> History is the core of Marxism [...] For us and for the Party, history [...] had put our struggles on its agenda and guaranteed our final victory. Some of us even felt that it had recruited us as individuals. Where would we, as intellectuals, have been, what would have become of us, but for the experiences of war, revolution and depression, fascism and anti-fascism, which surrounded us in our youth? Our work as historians was therefore embedded in our work as Marxists, which we believed to imply membership of the Communist Party. It was inseparable from our political commitment and activity.[20]

Galvanized by political commitment, Hobsbawm and other members of the CPHG made a major contribution to the development of working-class history. In 1952, the group was instrumental in launching the journal *Past & Present*, which quickly became an influential forum in which Marxist and non-Marxist historians could engage. Seeing themselves as 'part of a general movement against "old fashioned" politico-constitutional or narrative history', the CPHG influenced historical writing in two main ways. First, for example, in Christopher Hill's work on the English Revolution of the 1640s, they extended the chronological reach of labour history, which had traditionally focused on the period from the late eighteenth century onwards. Secondly, in work such as George Rudé's writing on the crowd in history, they shifted focus away from the structures of the labour movement towards an understanding of the wider working class, including its social and cultural experiences.[21]

Arguably, then, it was through the development of historical understanding that communism made its most important contribution to British life. In this endeavour, the historians of the CPHG, and their fellow contributors to *Past & Present*, were inspired by the work of the French *Annales* school. Since the late 1920s, scholars such as Marc Bloch, Lucien Febvre, George Lefebvre and Fernand Braudel had sought to develop historical interpretations focusing upon the totality of social development, scorning narrow political history in favour of wide-ranging histories which borrowed approaches and methods from geography, anthropology, literature and psychology. By the 1960s, their influence upon left-wing British historians was palpable. In 1966, E.P. Thompson (1924–93) adopted in English a term originally used by George Lefebvre: 'history from below'. The 'engaged tradition' of labour history, he argued, had concentrated too heavily on 'filling the blank spaces and correcting the outlines of the maps left by the Webbs and G.D.H. Cole', and was in danger of becoming conservative. To revive labour history, attention must be shifted from the classic institutions of labour to such topics as the popular culture of labouring people. This would make labour history 'more dangerous to the established constitutional and parliamentary-political Thing, because more pervasive'.[22]

Thompson's recently published *The Making of the English Working Class* (1963) had already made a definitive contribution to this process. Written while he was working in adult education in Yorkshire, the work narrates the evolution of working-class politics from the years immediately following the French Revolution up to 1832. Thompson's agenda was to rescue the 'lost myriads of eternity' – the generations of workers who lived through the industrial revolution – from 'the enormous condescension of posterity'. In so doing he offered an interpretation that transformed the existing assumptions of labour history. An emphasis upon the historical role of class had been a defining feature of labour history since its foundations, but prior to Thompson historians had tended to see class as a category or a structure, and to see individuals within classes as involuntarily subject to the workings of external, economically driven material forces. *The Making of the English Working Class* effectively turned this understanding upon its head. Thompson presented class not as a structure, but as an experienced relationship that 'is defined by men as they live their own history'.[23] He thus put individual human agency and lived experience at the centre of historical understanding. No longer was it sufficient merely to chronicle and celebrate the growth of working-class institutions. Rather, the whole lived experience of the working class had become a necessary field for historical investigation.

The movement to history from below was part of a wider post-war growth in local and social history. Nevertheless, Thompson's book gave the politically conscious, bottom-up study of working-class history a phenomenal boost. One indication of this was another important development at Oxford's Ruskin College: the History Workshop movement, described by its leading protagonist Raphael Samuel (1934–96) as a 'loose coalition of worker-historians and full-time socialist researchers'.[24] Like the earlier Plebs League, it sprang from opposition to the control of the college authorities.[25] The philosophy behind History Workshop was to encourage students to take education into their own hands, engage in their own primary research and bring their life experience to bear upon historical understanding. From 1976, the movement published the *History Workshop Journal*. A manifesto-style editorial in the first issue proclaimed that the journal would have a 'strong grounding in working-class experience' and champion the role of history within 'the battle of ideas'. Explicitly socialist, it would seize history from the hands of the academics and place it in the hands of ordinary people:

> The journal is dedicated to making history a more democratic activity and a more urgent concern. We believe that history is a source of inspiration and understanding, furnishing not only the means of interpreting the past but also the best critical vantage point from which to view the present. So we believe that history should become common property, capable of shaping people's understanding of themselves and the society in which they live.[26]

The emergence of history from below, and the wider development of the new social history of which it was a part, amounted to a revolutionary transformation in historical studies. It demanded a fundamental reassessment of the relationship between the historian and historical sources, encouraging interest in sources previously considered marginal. Oral testimony, folk ballads, local government records, diaries of ordinary people, the landscape itself: all these and more were accorded new prominence, as the focus of study shifted from the national to the local.[27] New sources also implied new ways of reading: 'We cannot be positivists', reflected Eric Hobsbawm, 'believing that the questions and the answers arise naturally out of the study of the material. There is generally no material until our questions have revealed it'.[28] This logic demanded the adoption of new interrogative methodologies drawing upon disciplines beyond history, which in turn implied the dissolution of disciplinary boundaries and a redefinition of history itself. The new scholarship, commented one *History Workshop Journal* editorial, 'asks the philosopher to look at history, the economist at politics, the sociologist at art'.[29]

This methodological diversification reshaped the representation of the past. Even Thompson's work was not immune from the critical re-writing that it encouraged. It was soon made clear, for example, that a primary area of neglect in the work of traditional labour historians was the role and experience of women. By the 1970s, a generation of female historians deploying the methods of the new social history had begun to redefine the past by recovering the experience of the half of society that had been all but invisible to their male antecedents. Sheila Rowbotham's *Hidden from History* (1973) presented a new narrative, around which feminist historians began to elaborate a more inclusive view of the past. The work of Barbara Taylor and Anna Clark restored the role of women to Thompson's classic narrative, fundamentally reshaping it in the process.[30] Others began to focus their studies on the experience of women entirely outside of the labour movement, and indeed outside of the working class.[31] People's history was, for the first time, beginning to represent more than half of the people.

Geographically too the scope of people's history became more inclusive. In 1961, a Scottish committee of the Society for the Study of Labour History was established, which by 1966 had evolved into the autonomous Scottish Labour History Society. Wales too established its own independent labour history society, Llafur, in 1970. Both launched their own journals, which encouraged a level of understanding of the labour and social history of parts of Britain that had been all but absent in earlier analyses.

By the 1980s, then, labour history had dissolved into a wider, more inclusive people's history, which explored the world beyond organized labour and ventured into all areas of working-class existence. Social class, although still a central concern, was supplemented by other means of understanding human relationships, including the importance of gender and place in forming identities. This shift of understanding profoundly enriched the discipline of history. It nevertheless offered a fundamental challenge to the very concepts upon which labour and people's history were based – a challenge that was soon intensified by a changing social and economic climate.

Crisis and resilience

By the end of the 1970s, some on the British left were becoming concerned by what they perceived to be the diminishing vitality of the labour movement. In his 1978 Marx Memorial Lecture, Eric Hobsbawm argued that the Forward March of Labour had halted. Economic and social change since the 1950s had made the world familiar to traditional labour historians a thing of the past.[32] By the end of the next decade, after the onslaught of Thatcherism, one historian was even beginning to doubt that Labour's Forward March had ever happened at all.[33] With the decline of the labour movement, a force that had underpinned the study of working-class history for over a century was waning. The 1990s also witnessed setbacks in the world of adult education, as funding changes led to the closure of some adult education institutions and circumscribed the activities of others.[34] Thus, two of the wellsprings of people's history threatened to run dry.

Historians of the late twentieth- and early twenty-first centuries also had to contend with the intellectual influence of postmodernism (a movement related to poststructuralism, discussed in Siobhan McGurk's chapter in this volume). The central idea of the so-called linguistic turn in historical studies was that reality is structured by language.[35] This encouraged a refocusing of interest from lived experience to the way in which power is exerted, mediated and challenged in society – a tendency anticipated by Raphael Samuel in the 1980s as a shift in attention 'from the reservoirs of revolt to the structures of social dominance'.[36] This was arguably an appropriate intellectual response to the dominance of capitalism's ideological power. However, the iconoclasm of the postmodernists was so thorough that it threatened to dissolve the whole basis of working-class history. Class was already losing its historiographical centrality to other aspects of identity, such as gender, race, sexuality, disability, occupation and locality. The influence of postmodernism further marginalized class as a category of historical analysis by shifting the focus of historical study to representation. The view that historians can never access the reality of the past, and can do no more than deconstruct linguistic systems of meaning, denied even the possibility of the historical study of material, embodied experience. This development, then, not only marginalized class as a historical framework, but denied the ultimate reality of class experience and its recoverability. The very idea of working-class history was itself becoming a part of history.

By the mid-1990s, labour historians were contemplating what they perceived to be a crisis. The collapse of the Soviet Union portended the death of academic Marxism, which, alongside the dominance of neoliberal, free-market politics at home, led labour historians to adopt either a 'bunker mentality' or to engage in open soul-searching.[37] The confusion of the period was expressed in the wider sphere of people's history by a retreat from political commitment, a tendency that was confirmed in 1995 when *History Workshop Journal* dropped reference to socialism from its subtitle.[38] Arguably more serious was the growing detachment of people's history from the people whose history it sought to represent. The field had won respectability within the academy, but as it did so, the involvement of those outside had become less evident. The language of the linguistic turn was exclusive, rarefied and inaccessible to those not trained in its terminology. People's history was becoming the property of a professional elite of middle-class historians.

People's history – and even traditional labour history – has however proven to be a resilient creature. For a start, the much anguished 1990s 'crisis of labour history' was not universal. Labour historians in Scotland and Wales, for instance, were less influenced by postmodernism than those in England, and labour history has continued to thrive on the 'Celtic Fringe'.[39] Indeed, devolution and a growing sense of national consciousness in 'outer Britain' offer to be a revitalizing force within people's history, inviting new narratives, such as that presented in Chris Bambery's *A People's History of Scotland* (2014). More generally, narrative history, once pronounced dead, has found new advocates. Malcolm Chase's *Chartism* (2007), for example, is a major work that successfully integrates narrative history with individual experience in a way that suggests new and compelling directions for working-class history. Even the concept of class seems to be rising Lazarus-like to reassert itself in the work of a new generation of historians. The work of Katrina Navickas, for example, combines class, place and mythology to breathe new life into such classic themes of labour history as Luddism and popular protest, while historians such as Selina Todd are making a concerted effort to restore class to an understanding of British social history.[40] A conference at the University of Essex in 2014 explored 'the resurgence of class in history', including contributions on topics as diverse as early modern oyster dredgers to the miners' strike of 1984–85, while in virtual space the 'many-headed monster' blog tackles the theme of class in the early modern period from a clearly Thompsonian perspective.[41] On a local level too, groups such as the Bristol Radical History Group testify to a grass-roots resurgence of labour and people's history.[42] All are signs that the historiographical wheel is turning full circle.

This should not surprise us. People's history is, to borrow George Orwell's memorable words from another context, 'an everlasting animal stretching into the future and the past, and, like all living things, having the power to change out of recognition and yet remain the same'.[43] Harder to define than labour history, it is, as E.P. Thompson suggested, potentially more challenging. If it has been more prone to lose its way, it has also reflected acutely its own contemporary conditions. In the post-crash world of austerity and food banks, in which social inequalities are more obvious than they have been for generations, surely it is appropriate that one of the defining features of the history of the people – their existence and experience in class terms – is restated. That this is done with a sense of political commitment – another defining feature of people's history – is also apposite. As the American historian Howard Zinn put it, in 'a world of conflict, a world of victims and executioners, it is the job of thinking people [...] not to be on the side of the executioners'.[44] If people's history is to be potent, though, it must reinvigorate another of its defining features: its roots in the world beyond the academy. People's history must exist in two senses: it is not enough for it to be merely a history *of* the people; it must also be created and owned *by* the people.

STUDY QUESTIONS

- When and why did labour history emerge?
- What were the main ideological influences upon the development of labour and people's history?
- Is people's history still important in the twenty-first century?

Notes

1   D. Frank (1999) *J.B. McLachlan, A Biography: The Story of a Legendary Labour Leader and the Cape Breton Coal Miners* (Toronto, ON: Lorimer), p. 416.

2   T. Paine (1969) *The Rights of Man (Part II)* (Harmondsworth: Penguin) [1791], p. 190.

3   For the wider context, see R. Samuel (1981) 'People's History', in R. Samuel (ed.), *People's History and Socialist Theory* (London: Routledge and Kegan Paul), pp. xv–xxxix.

4   J. R. Green (1960) *A Short History of the English People*, Vol. 1 (London: Everyman) [1877], p. xi.

5   T. Rogers (1949) *Six Centuries of Work and Wages* (London: George Allen and Unwin) [1901], pp. 574–5.

6   R. Fieldhouse (1998) *A History of Modern British Adult Education* (London: National Institute of Adult Continuing Education).

7   K. Gentry (2013) 'Ruskin, Radicalism and Raphael Samuel: Politics, Pedagogy and the Origins of the History Workshop', *History Workshop Journal*, 76, p. 190.

8   Whig history, deriving its name from the British Whig Party, asserted a natural and inevitable progression in the direction of liberty and enlightenment.

9   G. M. Trevelyan (1944) *English Social History* (London: Longmans, Green and Company), p. vii.

10   A dialectical process of social development: the concept, derived by Marx from the German philosopher Hegel, that society evolves through the recurrent opposition and synthesis of opposing social forces.

11   M. Beer (1919–20) *History of British Socialism*, 2 vols (London: G. Bell and Sons); Mark Hovell (1919) *The Chartist Movement* (Manchester: Manchester University Press); J. L. and B. Hammond (1911) *The Village Labourer*, (1917) *The Town Labourer*, (1919) *The Skilled Labourer*, (1930) *The Age of the Chartists* [all (London: Longmans, Green and Company)]; G. D. H. Cole (1925) *The Life of William* Cobbett (London: Collins); G. D. H. Cole and R. Postgate (1938) *The Common People* (London: Methuen); M. Cole (1948) *Makers of the Labour Movement* (London: Longmans, Green and Company).

12   H. M. Hyndman (1883) *The Historical Basis of Socialism in England* (London: Kegan Paul, Trench and Company); E. B. Bax (1890) *The Story of the French Revolution* (London: S. Sonnenschein).

13   James Griffiths Papers, A1/15, National Library of Wales.

14   W. W. Craik (1964) *The Central Labour College 1909–29* (London: Lawrence and Wishart), p. 82.

15   R. Lewis (1993) 'Mark Starr (1894–1985), Workers' Educationalist', in J. Bellamy and J. Saville (eds), *Dictionary of Labour Biography* (Basingstoke and London: Palgrave Macmillan), Vol. 9, pp. 274–81.

16 M. Starr (1918) *A Worker Looks at History, Being Outlines of Industrial History Especially Written for CLC – Plebs Classes* (Sheffield: Plebs League) [1917], p. 6.

17 Starr, *A Worker Looks at History*, p. 14.

18 R. Postgate (1923) *The Builders' History* (London: Labour Publishing Company Limited); T. Rothstein (1929) *From Chartism to Labourism* (London: Dorrot Press Limited); S. Dutt (1939) *When England Arose* (London: Fore Publications); R. P. Arnot (1934) *William Morris: A Vindication* (London: Martin Lawrence Limited), (1949) *The Miners: A History of the Miners Federation of Great Britain 1889–1910* (London: Allen and Unwin).

19 F. Williams (1949) *Fifty Years March* (London: Odhams); H. Pelling (1954) *Origins of the Labour Party* (Oxford: Clarendon).

20 E. Hobsbawm (1978) 'The Historians' Group of the Communist Party', in M. Cornforth (ed.), *Rebels and Their Causes* (London: Lawrence and Wishart), p. 26.

21 Hobsbawm, 'The Historians' Group'.

22 E. P. Thompson, 'History from Below', *Times Literary Supplement*, 7 April 1966.

23 E. P. Thompson (1968) *The Making of the English Working Class* (London: Victor Gollancz) [1963], p. 11.

24 R. Samuel, 'History Workshop, 1966–80', in Samuel (ed.), *People's History and Socialist Theory*, p. 410.

25 Gentry, 'Ruskin, Radicalism and Raphael Samuel'.

26 Editorial (1976) *History Workshop Journal*, 1.

27 J. Burnett (1974) *Useful Toil: Autobiographies of Working People from the 1820s to the 1920s* (London: Allen Lane); R. Samuel (1976) 'Local History and Oral History', *History Workshop Journal*, 1, p. 1; P. Thompson (1978) *The Voice of the Past* (Oxford: Oxford University Press).

28 Positivism is the view that the only authentic knowledge is scientific knowledge, and such knowledge can only be affirmed through the scientific method of gathering observable, empirical and measurable evidence. E. Hobsbawm (1997) 'On History From Below', in Eric Hobsbawm, *On History* (London: Weidenfeld and Nicolson), p. 205.

29 Editorial (1977) *History Workshop Journal*, 4:1, p. 4.

30 B. Taylor (1983) *Eve and the New Jerusalem: Socialism and Feminism in the Nineteenth Century* (London: Virago); A. Clark (1995) *The Struggle for the Breeches: Gender and the Making of the British Working Class* (Berkeley, Los Angeles, CA, and London: University of California Press).

31 L. Davidoff and C. Hall (1987) *Family Fortunes: Men and Women of the English Middle Class, 1780–1850* (London: Hutchinson).

32 E. Hobsbawm (September 1978) 'The Forward March of Labour Halted', *Marxism Today*.

33 D. Howell (1990) 'When Was "The Forward March of Labour"?', *Llafur*, 5:3.

34   M. Wright (April–May 2005) 'The Strange Death of Liberal Adult Education',
      Planet, 170.

35   See, for example, G. S. Jones (1983) *Language of Class: Studies in English
      Working Class History 1832–1982* (Cambridge: Cambridge University Press);
      P. Joyce (1991) *Visions of the People: Industrial England and the Question of
      Class 1848–1914* (Cambridge: Cambridge University Press).

36   Samuel, 'History Workshop 1966–80', p. 412.

37   Editorial (1995) *Labour History Review*, 60:1, p. 2: Debate (1995), *Labour
      History Review*, 60:3; N. Kirk (2010) 'Challenge, Crisis and Renewal?
      Themes in the Labour History of Britain, 1960–2010', *Labour History
      Review*, 75:2.

38   Editorial (1995) *History Workshop Journal*, 39, pp. iii–iv.

39   A. Croll (2000) 'People's Remembrancers in a Post-Modern Age:
      Contemplating the Non-Crisis of Welsh Labour History', *Llafur*, 8:1.

40   K. Navickas (2011) 'What Happened to Class? New Histories of Labour
      and Collective Action in Britain', *Social History*, 36:2; S. Todd (2014) *The
      People: The Rise and Fall of the Working Class 1910–2010* (London: John
      Murray).

41   The Many-Headed Monster: https://manyheadedmonster.wordpress.com.
      Accessed 16 January 2016.

42   Bristol Radical History Group: http://www.brh.org.uk/site/. Accessed
      16 January 2016.

43   G. Orwell (1982) *The Lion and the Unicorn: Socialism and the English Genius*
      (London: Penguin) [1941], p. 70.

44   Zinn adapted this phrase from the French philosopher Albert Camus (1913–
      1960). H. Zinn (1995) *A People's History of the United States, 1492 – Present*,
      rev. edn (New York: Harper Perennial), p. 10.

Further Reading

A. Croll (2000) 'People's Remembrancers in a Post-Modern Age: Contemplating
   the Non-Crisis of Welsh Labour History', *Llafur*, 8:1, pp. 3–17.

K. Gentry (2013) 'Ruskin, Radicalism and Raphael Samuel: Politics, Pedagogy and
   the Origins of the History Workshop', *History Workshop Journal*, 76, pp. 187–
   211.

E. Hobsbawm (1978) 'The Historians' Group of the Communist Party', in M.
   Cornforth (ed.), *Rebels and Their Causes* (London: Lawrence and Wishart),
   pp. 21–47.

E. Hobsbawm (1997) 'On History from Below', in E. Hobsbawm, *On History*
   (London: Weidenfeld and Nicolson), pp. 201–16.

N. Kirk (2010) 'Challenge, Crisis and Renewal? Themes in the Labour History of
   Britain, 1960–2010', *Labour History Review*, 75:2, pp. 162–80.

K. Navickas (2011) 'What Happened to Class? New Histories of Labour and
   Collective Action in Britain', *Social History*, 36:2, pp. 192–204.

R. Samuel (ed.) (1981) *People's History and Socialist Theory* (London: Routledge and Kegan Paul).

E. P. Thompson (1963) *The Making of the English Working Class* (London: Victor Gollancz).

Websites

Bristol Radical History Group: http://www.brh.org.uk
Irish Labour History Society: http://www.irishlabourhistorysociety.com
Llafur, The Welsh People's History Society: http://www.llafur.org
Scottish Labour History Society: http://www.scottishlabourhistory.org.uk
Society for the Study of Labour History: http://www.sslh.org.uk
The Many-Headed Monster: https://manyheadedmonster.wordpress.com

6

Identities

Siobhan McGurk

In 2006, I encountered a fascinating set of black and white photographs. These images, of an androgynous-looking woman in a variety of poses, clothes and costumes, turned out to be self-portraits by a French artist called Claude Cahun (1894–1954). They were strange photographs – uniquely complex, hauntingly beautiful and intriguing for the way in which the subject used her own camera as a means of self-interrogation. Although they looked like very modern explorations of gender, identity and the self, they were taken between 1915 and 1939. I was captivated. Who was this individual? What prompted her to create these self-portraits? What were her thoughts, beliefs and opinions? I spent the next six years trying to answer precisely these questions.

All present-day historians, to greater or lesser extents, ask similar questions about their own subjects. Whether they want to know about great leaders, working-class activists, military manoeuvres or the development of popular culture, historians ask about those involved. Who were they? Who did they think they were? What were their beliefs? In other words, historians want to know how historical actors thought about themselves in relation to others, as well as how wider society identified, grouped and positioned individuals. Historians are interested in identities.

Since the 1960s, historians have explained and explored identity in many different ways, and with varying degrees of urgency. Their analytical choices have been directly connected to broader disciplinary changes, most especially the shift from social to cultural history between the 1970s and 1990s. This chapter traces these changes with a particular focus on scholars of gender, who led the way in transforming how historians conceptualize human identity. Their work continues to provide the foundation for studying other kinds of identities too, including race and class. In the latter half of this chapter, I use my own research on Claude Cahun to illustrate how current theoretical approaches to identity work in practice, what opportunities they present and what constraints remain. In doing so, I make reference to ongoing debates among historians about the tensions and problems inherent in current modes of theorizing 'identity'. I hope to show how and why historians make different analytical choices, how these choices affect their understanding of what it meant to be female, working class, black or gay at different points in history, and where future scholarly work might take us.

From social history to the 'new' social history

'Social history', a broad term used to describe the study of societies in the past, emerged after the Second World War and occupied the centre ground of the historical discipline until the 1980s. It was a heterogeneous branch of history, which included a wide variety of different approaches to the past: Marxist economic determinism, American modernization theory, labour history, feminist history and the social science-orientated French *Annales* group. Differences aside, social historians shared certain aims and practices. They all rejected the idea that society's rulers and leaders were the only historical subjects of importance and sought instead to recover the actions and experiences of ordinary people (for a further discussion of these ideas, see Martin Wright's chapter in this volume). Some focused their attentions on society's structures and institutions and put forth theories about how each component worked together, or even against one another, to sustain life and drive change.

For most social historians, human identity was directly linked to an individual's position within the social structure. For example, to a Marxist historian, nineteenth-century factory workers were automatically 'working class', and their particular relationship to economic production gave them a shared understanding of politics. However, in *The Making of the English Working Class* (1963), E.P. Thompson developed a new version of the relationship between social structure and social identity.[1] According to Thompson, eighteenth-century English male artisans formed a sense of collective identity not only through their social position, but also through inherited English culture *and* shared experiences of exploitation. Thompson argued that class identity was not simply a static and transparent description of social position, but a dynamic process formed by and through experience and relations with others. After Thompson, historians could no longer take identity for granted; it had to be found and pieced together by the experiences and relationships of historical subjects.

In the late 1960s and 1970s, labour historians and feminist historians took up this 'new social history', which explored the links between experience, identity and politics. For feminist historians, the practice of history was an urgent political matter born out of 'discussions in women's liberation [...] about the situation of women in contemporary capitalism'. The new social history seemed to provide tools capable of challenging the fixity and naturalness of inequality between the sexes.[2] The more scholars learned about the history of women, the more they uncovered problems with existing ways of 'doing history'. Most famously, in 1977 American historian Joan Kelly asked 'Did Women Have Renaissance?' as a way to show that traditional chronologies of progress and periodization are not universal and do not always apply to women.[3] As they uncovered more about women of the past, these scholars also increasingly struggled to explain how the category of 'women', predicated on sameness, contained an extremely diverse mixture of individuals. Why had specific physical differences come to take precedence over other kinds of differences? And how did certain characteristics come to be perceived as 'feminine' or 'masculine'? Women's historians thus proved that scholars lacked the means to fully get to grips with the origins and consequences of the gender hierarchy. Their work was a vital part of the new social history, which valued the transformative power of histories from below and suggested that the production of identities was a process of negotiation between dynamic economic, cultural and social factors, rather than predetermined by nature.

Initially speaking and writing from the peripheries of the academy, socialist-feminist historians began to transform the concept of gender from biological fact into social construct. They challenged the idea that biology underwrote social disparity, because this suggested gender inequality was both inevitable and acceptable. They maintained that in itself, biology could not explain the specific characteristics of gender identities and dynamics. Drawing on the theoretical approaches of the new social history and focusing on labour, socialist-feminist historians argued that capitalism, not nature, produced patriarchy and gender inequality. For example, in the late 1970s feminist historians and economists argued that during the industrial revolution women were gradually removed from the labour market and moved into a position of domestic servitude and dependence within the home. Heidi Hartmann argues this movement occurred because wage-earning women, created by free-market capitalism, threatened to undermine traditional male superiority. The sexual division of labour reasserted patriarchal control.[4]

Whereas earlier kinds of social history considered human identity as either natural or a transparent reflection of a person's place in the social structure, the new social history suggested that identity was constantly negotiated, and tied to economic and social power. For example, instead of taking for granted that homemaking is a feminine task, historians now argued that women *became* more concretely associated with the domestic sphere in the nineteenth century because men's superiority was threatened by capitalism and they wanted to reassert their power. Identities were therefore no longer to be taken for granted, and they were neither apparent nor inevitable. Scholars of the new social history insisted that rather than approach the past with predetermined notions of their subjects' identities, historians must *discover* their origins and particular forms among interactions, experiences, conflicts and practices.

Through this transformation of the concept of 'identity', the new social history restored a degree of agency to historical actors. E.P. Thompson and others did not believe that human beings were completely free to choose their own identities; people *were* born into a particular socio-economic position which shaped their life experiences. However, these historians reasoned that despite certain socio-economic restrictions, people also *chose* how to use culture and ideas to make sense of their lives. In the new social history, people were consciously present at the making of their own identities.

A 'cultural turn'

Conventional narratives claim that social history and the new social history declined during the late 1980s when historians turned away from economic interpretations of history towards cultural interpretations. In reality, there was no such clear break. As we have seen, British Marxists like E.P. Thompson, socialist-feminist historians, labour historians and those writing histories of other marginalized groups such as racial and social minorities paid much attention to the history of culture and how it shaped identity. Moreover, between the 1950s and 1980s, there were many cross-disciplinary exchanges between historians, sociologists, literary theorists and anthropologists, which produced new ideas about the role of culture in human life. Instead of one decisive 'cultural turn' then, 'new' social historians had taken lots of small steps towards rethinking the importance of culture and viewed it as more than an ephemeral reflection of 'serious' socio-economic and political events. However, in the 1980s, two particular cross-disciplinary conversations sparked a much more dramatic shift that irrevocably marginalized social history and the new social history, in favour of more purely cultural analyses. This shift had enormous consequences for the ways in which historians thought about identity.

The first of these conversations was with anthropology, a discipline that studies humans in the past and present. Anthropologists often studied non-Western societies which had little or no written culture, and had to develop innovative techniques to decode cultural meaning beyond written texts. These techniques were adapted by historians to understand past groups, societies and cultures which had left few written records.

Two anthropological techniques proved especially productive for historians who studied the lives of groups that had left few written accounts of their own perspectives, such as women, the colonized, certain racial/ethnic minorities and the working classes. The first technique, 'reading against the grain', is a form of subversive reading, best described as reading between the lines, or against the writer's intentions, in order to uncover deeper truths. In *Recreating Africa* (2003), James Sweet reads records from the Portuguese Inquisition as a way to uncover the lives, loves and fears of African slaves owned and traded by the Portuguese. In analysing slave testimony about learned beliefs and everyday practices, Sweet determines how they remembered and related to African traditions.[5] The second technique, described as 'thick description' by anthropologist Clifford Geertz in 1973, seeks to uncover the multiple hidden meanings in symbols, images, practices and gestures.[6] This form of reading was used by the historian Robert Darnton to analyse an old French tale about a group of Parisian apprentices who massacred their master's cats in the 1730s, seemingly for their own entertainment.[7] Darnton asks why we don't 'get' the joke – what are we missing? By exploring the depth and complexity of various symbols and images within the story, such as the multiple meanings associated with cats, Darnton argues that the massacre was a form of social protest against the artisans' master, and not meaningless cruelty. These forms of reading broadened what counted as historical sources, and opened up new realms of discovery, especially in the worlds of ordinary people and the oppressed.

The second conversation was with the disciplines of linguistics and literary criticism. In the 1970s and 1980s, a group of linguists called poststructuralists argued that language does not simply reflect reality but is a tool used to understand and give meaning to the world. For example, same-sex acts and desires have existed throughout recorded history, but only in the nineteenth century did these begin to be viewed as integral aspects of identity. Over the course of the 1800s, physicians, scientists, politicians and social reformers developed a new kind of language around homosexuality. By 1920, there were multiple available labels to describe those people who engaged in same-sex acts: homosexuals, inverts, uranians, lesbians, pederasts. Developments in language thus moulded the way in which we think about sexuality, moving it from being about acts to being about fixed identities.

When we think about language in this way, it becomes clear that systems of words are also systems of power. If we think about homosexuality as a fixed identity, this authorizes all kinds of new actions and institutions, some of which are oppressive (diagnosing homosexuality as a mental disorder in need of treatment), and some of which are empowering (the formation of gay rights groups such as Stonewall).[8] In order to differentiate this kind of language – a powerful sociopolitical force – from more conventional usages, scholars renamed it 'discourse'. Discourse is best imagined as a group of statements, symbols and/or arguments that create meanings about specific concerns. One need only think about the variety of current messages about homosexuality to understand that discourses are never coherent; they are frequently full of contradictions, and compete and overlap with other discourses.

So how did poststructuralism change the practice of history? For many historians, it suddenly seemed as though no one could ever truly 'know' the past because language is not transparent, and therefore written sources did not reflect an objective reality. The poststructural critique threatened to turn the study of history into the writing of fiction. However, for others, poststructuralism suggested exciting new avenues of discovery. Even if a real, objective world was inaccessible, studying discourses could show how historical subjects formed and articulated meaning from and about their surrounding world. Furthermore, because discourses were ways of creating knowledge and exercising power, historians could pull them apart in order to find competing voices. Ultimately, poststructuralism offered remedies for what many perceived to be some of social history's most serious flaws, especially the way economic determinism merely replaced biological determinism as the primary explanation for historical change and human difference. It completely transformed the study of human identities, into an inquiry about how labels like 'woman' are a form of meaning-making and power, rather than productions or reflections of biological or economic reality.

Towards a history of gender

In 1986, historian Joan Scott's article 'Gender: A Useful Category of Historical Analysis' systematically brought together diverse strands of thinking about 'difference' in poststructuralism, anthropology and socialist-feminism to present a new theory of gender.[9] Scott's article is a classic of cultural history and it remains the basis for how many cultural historians approach questions of identity, especially those of gender, but also race and sexuality.

Scott, like many of her contemporaries, believed other disciplines could offer historians previously unconsidered perspectives, which would help solve some of social history's inherent theoretical difficulties. Of particular concern was that social historians always argued that economics drove change. Even when scholars such as E.P. Thompson elevated the importance of traditions and experience, these remained of secondary importance and never fully possessed their own causal power. What, then, explained the existence of economics? Did it somehow give birth to and sustain itself? In essence, by the 1980s it had become increasingly difficult for many historians to support the idea that economics, or indeed anything, lived outside discourse. In other words, they wondered if culture had in fact created economics rather than vice versa. Could, for example, the very notion of profit be just as much a cultural idea as inherited English traditions?

With regard to human difference, social history had assumed that experience could take place apart from culture, and led directly and transparently to political and social identity: for example, labour exploitation unproblematically created working-class identity and politics. The new social history – best exemplified by Thompson's work – did not separate experience and culture, but rather imagined that the latter gave meaning to the former. Nevertheless, in both cases, people could experience life first and give meaning to it later. But if the working classes felt as one because of their experience of exploitation, then what explained the initial exploitation? If women felt as one because they were subordinated to men, what had caused this subordination in the first place? Social history could only ever answer with 'economics' or 'nature'. Poststructuralism, however, convincingly argued that humans understand *everything* through language. In simple terms, we cannot experience life separately from thoughts and knowledge, which are in turn shaped by language. Suddenly, labour exploitation is no longer a self-evident experience. Instead historians need to ask questions like 'how might religious, regional or gendered ideas and identities determine the initial structures of wage labour?' 'which ideas and identities shaped workers' experience of demands on their labour?' and 'how did culture determine what workers experienced as exploitation, and how they experienced it?'

Joan Scott's essay drew heavily on poststructuralism to jettison the causal power of economics and nature in favour of the idea that discourse created difference and identities. In simple terms, gender history rests on a crucial distinction between sex and gender: sex is biological, and refers to physical differences between men and women, while gender is socially constructed and has no basis in nature. Clothes, colours, behaviours, jobs and intellectual abilities are not naturally male or female, but become gendered through discourse. History is full of examples of how concepts of gender have changed throughout time. For example, in the eighteenth century, men wore high heels, and in medieval Europe ale brewing was predominantly a female trade.

Scott argued that although gender is actually a cultural construction, we tend to understand it as our natural essence, and this makes it a powerful tool. Gender also functions as a binary system and as a hierarchy in which female characteristics are always subordinate: men are perceived as rational, strong, competitive and proactive; women as emotional, weak, shy and passive. Crucially, Scott argued that gender structures *all* social relations, not just relations between men and women. For example, class relations have often been understood and spoken about in gendered ways. In early nineteenth-century America, the middle classes described the working classes as feminine because they were dependent on a financial elite, less educated and more emotionally spontaneous. A century later, this narrative flipped, and the middle classes began to worry that their own lack of physical activity made them effeminate.[10]

Finally, Scott insisted that gender discourses structured *all* kinds of relations that involve power, including conventionally 'masculine' domains such as politics, diplomacy and economics. For example, during the Second World War, American government and army propaganda portrayed France as a feminine country in need of rescue by a strong, male United States. At times, the liberation of France was even characterized as a sexual conquest.[11] Scott's most influential contribution was perhaps her insistence that we stop thinking gender only operates in kinship networks, and look at how it signifies power in every domain of life. Ultimately, perceptions of gender difference and hierarchy as biologically based, rather than socially constructed, help to normalize all kinds of systems of power and difference. For example, between the time that Jewish French military officer Alfred Dreyfus went on trial for treason in 1894 and his acquittal in 1906, his supporters and detractors hurled gendered insults back and forth across the divide.[12] In accusing their male opponents of effeminacy, they actually labelled them as unnatural, perverse, unworthy citizens.

Gender history in practice

In practice, how do historians apply gender theory in their work? What kinds of new stories does it produce about the past? What gaps does it fill and how does it transform existing narratives? On the flip side, what are some of gender history's constraints? What about other kinds of non-gender identities? Where do they fit in?

Some of the challenges and rewards in answering these questions can be illustrated by returning to my own work on Claude Cahun. My discovery of Cahun's photographic self-portraits threw up a long list of questions. What did these images mean? Why did Cahun take them? Who did she think she was? Who did others think she was? Answering these questions involved understanding what it meant to be a woman in France between 1915 and 1939, when Cahun created her self-portraits. Political writings, wartime propaganda, medical books, and images from art and popular culture all constructed and communicated discourses about gender. At the time, women in France were expected to conduct wifely and maternal duties: to marry, run their husbands' households and raise their children to be good republican citizens.[13] However, French politicians, who ran a secular state, feared that the Catholic Church took advantage of women's emotional and intellectual vulnerabilities to seduce them away from republican duties towards irrational spirituality. At the same time, doctors and psychologists debated whether or not women's physiological characteristics bore traces of intellectual inferiority and emotional instability, including a predisposition to hysteria.[14] Playwrights and novelists participated in discourses about gender in all kinds of ways. During the interwar years, there was an explosion of plays and novels about the damaging (and exciting) dangers of *la garçonne*, the French flapper. These usually attacked her as a selfish, self-obsessed and infertile young woman who endangered the health of the French nation by refusing traditional motherhood.[15]

This was the context in which Cahun lived. Gender identity was continually being *constructed* using binary opposites based on perceived natural differences between men and women. Men were constructed as rational beings suitable for political participation, and women as their subordinate opposites whose smaller brain size and wombs made them irrational, and more suited to childcare than politics. In this context, what did it mean for a French woman to take photographs and to make art? At this time, *creativity* was linked to action and intelligence, and consequently gendered masculine. Although there had been a small handful of respected female artists, including Surrealists Leonora Carrington (1917–2011) and Meret Oppenheim (1913–85), they never achieved the same level of success as their male counterparts. Indeed, Surrealism admitted women largely because its politics was predicated on a rejection of traditional bourgeois standards. As a woman who did not marry or have children, but instead created artwork, Cahun lived a life that rejected dominant ideas about what it meant to be a woman.

After I understood how discourses of gender functioned in reference to social relations, and also as a way to underpin access to creativity, I turned back to Cahun's own images. Because Cahun wrote little that forthrightly explained her work, I had to employ reading techniques derived from other disciplines, such as anthropology and visual culture studies. Figure 6.1 is a self-portrait taken in 1928, which shows the artist standing before a mirror wearing a striking chequered jacket, her head turned towards the camera. A surface reading might suggest this is a meaningless snapshot of an androgynous-looking woman, caught unawares examining herself in the mirror. However, if we take the time to understand what meanings were attached to clothes, objects and gestures in interwar France – as Darnton did with the cat massacre – we begin to uncover a more complex narrative which tells us something about the artists' intentions and audience reception.

Paintings and photographs of women studying their reflection in mirrors were commonplace at the turn of the twentieth century, and signified their sexual objectification under the male painter's or photographer's gaze. In turning her face away from the mirror and confronting her own camera's lens, which was probably operated by her female partner, Cahun refuses objectification by the male subject. This becomes an even more dramatic refusal when we remember that women were supposed to be passive, dependent and not creative. Cahun's cropped hair symbolizes a certain chosen masculinity, but crucially her jacket is a piece of women's designer clothing. The photograph thus starts to read as a patchwork of gendered symbols, out of sync with dominant ideas about how gender should operate. This suggests that individuals are capable of drawing on existing discourses, such as the symbolic meanings of the mirror, as a way

FIGURE 6.1 *Claude Cahun (1894–1954), untitled (self-portrait, reflected image in mirror with chequered jacket) 1928. Courtesy of the Jersey Heritage Collections.*

to shape and re-shape their sense of self and create their own identities, perhaps even against those foisted upon them from outside. This raises some important questions about how much freedom people have in the face of discourse. To what extent can people choose their gender? To what extent is it constructed and controlled by linguistic systems?

Agency versus discourse

Discourses are not consciously made or controlled by individuals or groups, because no one ever stands in a position entirely outside language. In other words, all human beings are trapped within and controlled by discourse.

As previously discussed, discourses are systems of thought – ideas, actions, beliefs and practices – that we use to understand the world, and that unconsciously emerge and reproduce over time, for example, the 'knowledge' that gender is natural, or the 'knowledge' that homosexuality is an aberration. These discourses possess power. This power is not necessarily wielded consciously by any one group, but rather inevitably emerges in all social relations and often happens without us realizing it. For example, nineteenth-century French men wielded power over women by virtue of a discourse of gender, but they were not conscious of this fact. It was simply how they made sense of the world through learned cultural and social knowledge.

If, then, human beings are trapped within discourse, how does anyone ever challenge discourse and pressure it to change? If culture creates everything, what creates culture and what forces it to change? To return to our example, how then did Cahun challenge dominant ideas? If not from outside discourse, from where did her challenge emerge?

Historians disagree on the extent to which human beings can achieve agency within dominant discourses. This is no small problem for a discipline that exists primarily to explain change over time. Some historians who reject poststructuralism do so precisely because it seems to have no engine of change. Others use poststructuralist theories selectively while holding on to the idea that economics drive history. Many more are primarily troubled by the way in which poststructuralism seems to remove all sense of human agency, and creates worlds in which everything is swallowed by language. This latter critique is the most troubling. Discourses cannot operate unless humans speak and enact them. As Cahun's photographs show us, individuals *are* able to challenge dominant discourses in certain ways. Historians need a productive way of conceptualizing human agency and its relationship to change.

In turning to Figure 6.1, we can think about how to conceptualize human agency without abandoning poststructuralism and gender history. In this self-portrait, Cahun rearranges gendered symbols in unexpected ways in order to challenge dominant narratives about what it means to be a woman. However, all the symbols she uses are drawn from dominant French culture, and her challenge to gender rests on rearranging the binary, not getting rid of it. In other words, there is nothing in her challenge that comes from outside the discursive system. In that case, perhaps we might think of change as something that happens when people find contradictions in discourses, and creatively rearrange them. Human agency exists, but it is not limitless; it is constrained by culture.

Mind and body

Cahun's photographs raised further questions. How did she self-identify? Her challenge to conventional notions of gender suggested a gap between social expectations of French women and what she thought about her identity. As I read, researched and thought more, I encountered another problem: gender history guides us to understand how discourse creates and controls gender, but struggles to tell us how those messages might be experienced at the level of the psyche and the body. Evidently, something within Cahun's person resisted and rearranged dominant messages, even if she only ended up recreating a new version of the old discourse. But what prompted her challenge?

In the last ten years, gender history and poststructuralism have been criticized for removing the body and the psyche from conversations about identity and subjectivity. Even if gender is a social construct made through language, it is *experienced* on a physical level, especially because gender seems to attach itself to our bodies. Cahun struggled with her body, which she described as 'badly constructed, full of graceless mutinies'.[16] I began to wonder if her internal conflicts arose from feeling that her body and gender did not fit notions of acceptable French womanhood. This led me to consider if her aesthetic challenges to gender discourse were born out of embodied and psychic experiences. Gender history, however, offers few tools with which to understand how and where discourse meets bodies.

Among historians, there is little consensus on how to approach the body. Strong poststructuralism forces it to exist only in language, while on the other end of the spectrum some scholars think that physical experiences – especially of sexual difference – *fully* determine experience and identity. Recently, some historians have tried to find centre ground, and argue that humans experience their bodies physically *and* through language. In other words, women might feel biologically different than men but culture frames this felt difference as *the* most important essence of humanity. Kathleen Canning and Elizabeth Grosz have suggested the potentially useful idea of 'embodiment' to describe how humans live in and with their bodies on a daily basis, being both shaped by discourse and defying it. They argue that although we understand our bodies through discourse, our physical selves are also uniquely positioned as tools of resistance. We can act upon our bodies, which therefore provide us with the means of defying discourse.[17]

If Cahun's anxieties about her body signal that physical sensations and embodiment shaped her relationship to identity, then spells of emotional instability suggest another possible dimension – the psychic. Many historians, particularly those who draw on psychoanalytical theories, argue that historians must pay greater attention to individual 'psychic make-up', which includes the unconscious, fear and fantasy.[18] Can we really understand how people relate to one another and to themselves without considering our irrational impulses and drives? When we consider the psychic we realize that historians must always differentiate between subjectivity and identity. The former is our sense of self, which includes our embodied experiences and our psychic impulses. The latter emerges when discourse gives meaning to our sense of self. If we imagine that these processes occur simultaneously and are intertwined, then we might suppose that Cahun's psychic and physical dimensions came into conflict with the gender ideals of the time.

Claude Cahun and her multiple, intersecting identities

No one possesses just one identity. Claude Cahun was a woman but she was also middle-class, Jewish and in a same-sex relationship. In my initial research, I focused closely on her identity as a woman rather than on any other ways she self-identified or was identified by others. In choosing to direct my focus in this way, I implicitly suggested that 'woman' was Cahun's most important identity. However, my sources strongly implied otherwise. Although it was unusual for middle-class women to forge careers in journalism, literature and art, these paths opened to Cahun because her uncle and her father were part of these worlds. Her first published article appeared in *Le Phare de la Loire*, a Nantaise publication owned and managed by her father. Religion also played a part in her life. In the 1920s, Cahun photographed herself in profile, emphasizing the shape of her facial features. These images echo those taken around the same time by French anthropologists and criminologists as they sought to identify and catalogue Jews, criminals and the mentally insane.[19] Furthermore, in choosing the pseudonym Claude Cahun (the French equivalent of Cohen), she explicitly embraced her Jewish heritage. How should historians deal with the fact that all individuals possess more than one identity? Should these identities be studied separately? Or should historians consider how different identities relate to and affect each other?

On this matter, work by US historians of race has proved particularly instructive. During the late 1980s and early 1990s, those who studied the lives of African Americans before and after slavery accused gender historians of finding 'little to say about race', even though history clearly showed that black women's experiences of gender differed greatly from those of white Anglo-Americans.[20] Indeed, in the late 1960s and 1970s, black feminists in the United States and Britain had split from mainstream feminist organizations and founded their own movements. They argued that white women were unable to understand that despite certain common experiences, white women and women of colour also experienced gender very differently.

History helps bring this political altercation to life. In nineteenth-century America, women were supposed to become mothers and guardians of the home. As such, it was not considered appropriate for them to take part in manual labour. As slaves, however, black women were expected to work as much as their male counterparts, as well as produce children. Post-slavery, many black women worked as domestic servants because wages for African Americans were so low that few could afford to stay at home and care for their own children.[21] In the 1960s and 1970s, black feminists therefore had no interest in pursuing rights for women to work outside the home because for centuries they had been forced to work alongside men. Furthermore, African-American women had a long history of being oppressed by white men *and* women. During the 1940s, 1950s and 1960s a large number of black women suffered ritualistic sexual assault at the hands of white men, but few white Americans – whether male or female – believed their accusations. Rather, it was thought that African-American women were sexually aggressive and had invited male advances, or even prostituted themselves.[22]

As these examples show, gender and race affect one another: they *intersect*. Representations and experiences of femininity are different for black and white women. Furthermore, class and gender also affect one another. For example, in nineteenth-century Europe, prostitutes drawn from the lower classes were considered a necessary evil because they provided the chance for young middle-class men to expend sexual energy before marriage, thus protecting the purity and virginity of middle-class women. Class also dictates attitudes towards sexuality.

It is therefore a mistake to speak of Cahun's gender identity as separate from her racial and class identity. In the years during and following the Dreyfus Affair, rising anti-Semitism changed Jewish men and women's lives. Over the course of the nineteenth century, bourgeois Jews had increasingly integrated into French society and internalized French bourgeois gender ideals.[23] However, during the Dreyfus Affair, anti-Semitic articles, books and cartoons began to call into question, among other things, Jewish masculinity and femininity. In fact, in 1907, at the age of thirteen, Cahun moved schools because of anti-Semitic incidents. To understand Cahun's identity then we must, at the very least, understand the intersection of race, gender and class in the French Third Republic. And what about Cahun's sexuality?

From about the age of sixteen until her death, Cahun was in a same-sex relationship with her stepsister Suzanne Malherbe (1892–1972). Just as gender historians caution against fixed meanings, historians of sexuality try to approach their work without preconceived ideas. Instead of labelling either woman as a 'lesbian', I explored the various and competing meanings of same-sex desire and relationships in early twentieth-century France. At the time, doctors, social reformers and sexologists debated whether homosexuality was genetic or acquired, and puzzled over what same-sex desire meant about gender. This was also the same period in which homosexuality was being reconceptualized as an identity. In an effort to understand and contain the pathology, health professionals and social reformers obsessively tried to categorize different kinds of homosexuals.[24] Cahun took an interest in these developments. She was particularly attracted to 'inversion' and 'uranism' as concepts. These words referred to the idea that a homosexual's body and soul were mismatched; women with same-sex desires possessed male souls, and men with same-sex desires possessed female souls. Clearly then, sexuality intersected with gender. Perhaps Cahun experienced her body as 'badly constructed, full of graceless mutinies' because it did not match her soul.[25]

Conclusion

Historians no longer take for granted that biological make-up, social position, or place of birth determines identity. Instead, they try to approach their sources with a more open mind, both to uncover how discourses determine identity, and how individuals and groups might use and transform these same cultural discourses to make sense of their worlds. Historians now apply techniques such as 'reading against the grain' and 'thick description' to unconventional sources including magazines, advertisements, letters, court records, theatre reviews and even music in the effort to understand how individuals make sense of, and articulate, beliefs about themselves and others. Many recent works of cultural history focus on complex questions of *intersectionality*, and seek to uncover how multiple identities – such as race, class and gender – affect one another. Most recently, scholars of gender and race have tried to conceptualize identity without jettisoning the body; and particularly interesting analysis is currently taking place within the domains of performance studies and disability studies.[26] Once again, then, conceptual inspiration and theoretical breakthroughs might come, not from inside the discipline of history, but through valuable interdisciplinary conversations.

STUDY QUESTIONS

- Why is it important for historians to understand identity?
- How have historical approaches to questions of identity changed since the 1960s?
- Why does the concept of discourse simultaneously offer rewards and pose challenges to historians?
- Why is the concept of 'intersecting identities' so essential to the practice of history?

Notes

1   E. P. Thompson (1963) *The Making of the English Working Class* (London: Victor Gollancz).

2   S. Rowbotham (1977) *Hidden from History: 300 Years of Women's Oppression and the Fight Against It*, 3rd edn (London: Pluto Press), p. ix; L. L. Downs (2010) *Writing Gender History*, 2nd edn (London: Bloomsbury Academic), pp. 21–3.

3   J. Kelly (1977) 'Did Women Have a Renaissance?', in R. Bridenthal and C. Koonz (eds), *Becoming Visible: Women in European History* (Boston, MA: Houghton Mifflin).

4   H. Hartmann (1976) 'Capitalism, Patriarchy and Job Segregation by Sex', *Signs*, 1; see also S. Alexander (1976) 'Women's Work in Nineteenth-Century London: A Study of the Years 1820–1850', in J. Mitchell and A. Oakley (eds), *The Rights and Wrongs of Women* (New York: Penguin Books); J. Humphries (1977) 'Class Struggle and the Persistence of the Working Class Family', *Cambridge Journal of Economics*, 1.

5   J. Sweet (2003) *Recreating Africa: Culture, Kinship and Religion in the African-Portuguese World, 1441–1770* (Chapel Hill, NC: University of North Carolina Press).

6   C. Geertz (1973) *The Interpretation of Cultures: Selected Essays* (New York: Basic Books), pp. 3–30.

7   R. Darnton (1985) *The Great Cat Massacre and Other Episodes in French Cultural History* (Harmondsworth: Penguin), pp. 79–104.

8   I. Hacking (1986) 'Making Up People', in T. C. Heller, M. Sosna and D. E.Wellbery (eds), *Reconstructing Individualism: Autonomy, Individuality and the Self in Western Thought* (Stanford: Stanford University Press); I. Hacking (1995) 'The Looping Effects of Human Kinds', in D. Sperber, D. Premack and A. J. Premack (eds), *Causal Cognition: A Multidisciplinary Debate* (Oxford: Clarendon Press).

9   J. Scott (1999) 'Gender: A Useful Category of Historical Analysis', in J. Scott, *Gender and the Politics of History*, rev. edn (New York: Columbia University Press).

10 G. Bederman (1995) *Manliness and Civilization: A Cultural History of Gender and Race in the United States, 1880–1917* (Chicago, IL: Chicago University Press), pp. 10–20.

11 M. L. Roberts (2013) *What Soldiers Do: Sex and the American GI in World War II France* (Chicago, IL: Chicago University Press).

12 In 1894, Dreyfus, a French army officer of Jewish descent, was falsely accused of providing military secrets to the Germans. The Dreyfus Affair precipitated a major political crisis in France, provoking intense debate on militarism and anti-Semitism over the course of Dreyfus's trial, imprisonment and retrial. He was eventually officially exonerated in 1906. C. Forth (2004) *The Dreyfus Affair and the Crisis of French Manhood* (Baltimore, MD: Johns Hopkins University Press).

13 J. McMillan (1981) *The Place of Women in French Society 1870–1940* (New York: St. Martin's Press); J. Scott (1996) *Only Paradoxes to Offer: French*

Feminists and the Rights of Man (Cambridge, MA: Harvard University Press); M. L. Roberts (2002) *Disruptive Acts: The New Woman in Fin-de-Siècle France* (Chicago, IL: Chicago University Press).

14   F. Gordon (1990) *The Integral Feminist: Madeleine Pelletier, 1874–1939: Feminism, Socialism and Medicine* (Oxford: Polity).

15   M. L. Roberts (1994) *Civilization Without Sexes: Reconstructing Gender in Postwar France, 1917–1927* (Chicago, IL: Chicago University Press).

16   C. Cahun (2007) *Disavowals*, trans. S. de Muth (London: Tate Gallery Publications), p. 77.

17   E. Grosz (1990) 'Inscriptions and Body Maps: Representations and the Corporeal', in T. Threadgold and A. Cranny-Francis (eds), *Feminine, Masculine and Representation* (Sydney: Allen and Unwin); K. Canning (1999) 'The Body as Method? Reflections on the Place of the Body in Gender History', *Gender & History*, 11:3.

18   M. Roper (2005) 'Slipping Out of View: Subjectivity and Emotion in Gender History', *History Workshop Journal*, 59, p. 58.

19   D. Pick (1989) *Faces of Degeneration: A European Disorder, 1848–1918* (Cambridge: Cambridge University Press); G. Didi-Huberman (2004) *Invention of Hysteria: Charcot and the Photographic Iconography of the Salpêtrière*, trans. A. Hartz (Cambridge, MA: MIT Press).

20   E. Higginbotham (1992) 'African-American Women's History and the Metalanguage of Race', *Signs*, 17:2, p. 251.

21   T. Hunter (1998) *To Joy My Freedom: Southern Black Women's Lives and Labors after the Civil War* (Cambridge, MA: Harvard University Press); Higginbotham, 'African-American Women's History and the Metalanguage of Race'.

22   D. McGuire (2011) *At the Dark End of the Street: Black Women, Rape, and Resistance – A New History of the Civil Rights Movement from Rosa Parks to the Rise of Black Power* (New York: Vintage Books).

23   Forth, *The Dreyfus Affair and the Crisis of French Manhood*.

24   R. Nye (ed.) (1999) *Sexuality* (Oxford: Oxford University Press), pp. 115–202.

25   Cahun, *Disavowals*.

26   S. Kienitz (2002) 'Body Damage: War Disability and Constructions of Masculinity in Weimar Germany', in K. Hagemann and S. Schüler-Springorum (eds), *Home/Front: The Military, War and Gender in Twentieth-Century Germany* (New York: Berg Publishers); B. Gottschild (2002) *The Black Dancing Body: A Geography from Coon to Cool* (London: Palgrave Macmillan).

Further Reading

G. Bederman (1996) *Manliness and Civilization: A Cultural History of Gender and Race in the United States, 1880–1917* (Chicago, IL: Chicago University Press).

K. Canning (1999) 'The Body as Method? Reflections on the Place of the Body in Gender History', *Gender & History*, 11:3, pp. 499–513.

L. L. Downs (2010) *Writing Gender History*, 2nd edn (London: Bloomsbury Academic).

C. Forth (2004) *The Dreyfus Affair and the Crisis of French Manhood* (Baltimore, MD: Johns Hopkins University Press).

E. Higginbotham (1992) 'African-American Women's History and the Metalanguage of Race', *Signs*, 17:2, pp. 251–74.

J. Kamensky (1996) 'Talk Like a Man: Speech, Power, and Masculinity in Early New England', *Gender & History*, 8:1, pp. 22–47.

A. Najmabadi (2006) 'Beyond the Americas: Are Gender and Sexuality Useful Categories of Analysis?', *Journal of Women's History*, 18:1, pp. 11–21.

M. L. Roberts (2013) *What Soldiers Do: Sex and the American GI in World War II France* (Chicago, IL: Chicago University Press), pp.57–84.

J. Scott (1999) *Gender and the Politics of History*, rev. edn (New York: Columbia University Press).

T. Stovall (2003) 'Love, Labor, Race: Colonial Men and White Women in France during the Great War', in T. Stovall and G. van den Abbeele (eds), *French Civilization and Its Discontents: Nationalism, Colonialism, Race* (Lanham, MD: Lexington Books), pp. 297–323.

Examples of 'reading against the grain' and 'thick description'

I. Clendinnen (1999) 'Yucatec Maya Women and the Spanish Conquest: Role and Ritual in Historical Reconstruction', in A. Green and K. Troup (eds), *The Houses of History: A Critical Reader in Twentieth-Century History and Theory* (New York: New York University Press), pp. 183–203.

N. Z. Davis (1983) *The Return of Martin Guerre* (Cambridge, MA: Harvard University Press).

PART TWO

The Historian's Craft

Introduction:
The Historian's Craft

Tracey Loughran

Few historians have demonstrated such commitment to the ideal of historical objectivity as Samuel Rawson Gardiner (1829–1902), author of numerous multi-volume histories of early modern England. As an acolyte of the German historian Leopold von Ranke (1795–1886), often identified as the 'father' of the modern historical profession, Gardiner sought to study the past on its own terms, and to strip all vestiges of present-mindedness from his investigations. In the effort to avoid contaminating his conclusions with hindsight, Gardiner adopted a peculiar research technique: he conducted bursts of research on short historical periods, and did not read any documents dealing with later events until he had completed earlier sections. It has even been said that he refused to examine sources for 1654 until he had finished writing a section on 1653.[1] This approach did not achieve the desired effect, and not only because Gardiner could not entirely expunge his own political sympathies from the text. More importantly, he could not obliterate his prior knowledge of the events he researched. When Gardiner – a descendant of Oliver Cromwell's daughter, no less – started writing his multi-volume *History of the Great Civil War* (1886–93), he already knew how the war ended, and that it was a major turning point in British political history. From the moment the idea for this new project began to form in his mind, long before he consulted his first document, and very much against his conscious aims, Gardiner began the process of selection and interpretation. It could not be otherwise.

Writing four decades after Gardiner's death, the French medievalist Marc Bloch (1886–1944) offered a very different account of the historian's working procedures. Bloch criticized the 'extraordinarily simplified notion' many people held of historical research:

First, as they are only too eager to tell you, there are the documents. The historian collects them, reads them, attempts to weigh their authenticity and truthfulness. Then, and only then, he makes use of them. There is only one trouble with this idea: no historian has ever worked in such a way, even when, by some caprice, he fancied that he was doing so.

In Bloch's view, documents 'speak only when they are properly questioned', and the skill of the historian lies in knowing how to conduct this cross-examination. Any inquiry always 'has a direction at the very first step', and so there is no distinction between preparing for historical research and its practice.[2] Like Gardiner, Bloch believed that history should aspire to scientific status, but he also acknowledged that the discipline had not yet attained that status. Crucially, he conceived historical knowledge as dynamic, 'something progressive which is constantly transforming and perfecting itself' through new discoveries, improved research techniques and the generation of new questions.[3] Bloch described his own disquisition on historical methods not as a scientific treatise, but as 'the memorandum of a craftsman who has always liked to reflect over his daily task, the notebook of a journeyman who has long handled the ruler and the level, without imagining himself to be a mathematician'.[4]

This vision of history as both craft and incipient science captures its dual essence. History is a discipline which employs quasi-scientific methods (commitment to empiricism, documentation of proofs and hypothesis-testing) and aspires to a scientific ideal of objectivity (even if most historians now accept that this ideal cannot be attained). It also trains through apprenticeship: students learn through contact with practitioners (in seminars, lectures and by reading their works), and through actual practice (beginning with essays and working up to independent research dissertations). The critical factor which separates history from the natural or physical sciences, however, is human. The history on the printed page is always an expression of the individuality of the historian. As Sir Keith Thomas (b. 1933), one of the elder statesmen of the discipline, puts it, 'When writing history, there are rules to be followed and evidence to be respected. But no two histories will be the same, whereas the essence of scientific experiments is that they can be endlessly replicated'.[5] Armed with the same equipment, any physicist can repeat Ernest Rutherford's experiments in atomic energy and achieve exactly the same results, but access to the endnotes of Thomas's *Religion and the Decline of Magic* (1971) would not enable an aspiring historian to write exactly the same book.

The bald declaration that the history is inseparable from the historian begs an urgent question: if the human factor defines the discipline of history, what makes history more than a matter of individual opinion, and how can we judge the relative worth of different histories? The answer has already been given: 'there are rules to be followed and evidence to be respected'. There might be some disagreement on the exact content of these rules, but all practitioners agree that history is an evidence-based discipline, and that evidence must be respected (that is to say, not fabricated, deliberately neglected or intentionally misconstrued). These convictions define the historical profession, and to reject them is to move outside its bounds. Within these boundaries, approaches might diverge considerably. Gardiner and Bloch had very different views on what history could ultimately achieve, and on how historians should go about their work. Nevertheless, the bedrock of the practice of both men was close examination of historical sources. Careful use of historical evidence is what separates historical research from mere opinion. This position is worked out in most detail in Kevin Passmore's chapter, 'Evidence and Interpretation', but it is the aim of this entire section to demonstrate how historians use evidence, and to equip you to approach different kinds of sources with sensitivity and discrimination.

The identification and interpretation of historical evidence is never straightforward, whether the historian is working with written documents such as transcripts of parliamentary proceedings, oral testimony solicited through interviews with living people or material objects such as clothes or jewellery. In part, this is because interpretation depends on the questions historians ask of evidence. But it is also because historical evidence is always fragmentary (we only have access to the limited survivals of past cultures), partial (produced by a particular individual or organization, with a particular purpose in mind) and resists immediate comprehension (we might grasp the basic meaning of individual phrases, or how particular objects were used, but without understanding exactly how they fitted into the fabric of vanished societies). In Simon Schama's words,

> historians are left forever chasing shadows, painfully aware of their inability ever to reconstruct a dead world in its completeness, however thorough or revealing their documentation [...] We are doomed to be forever hailing someone who has just gone around the corner and out of earshot.[6]

Historians ask questions and put forward provisional answers, but certainty will always elude us. We have no choice but to accept this. This does not make historical research a pointless endeavour. Rather, it is all the more important that we understand what evidence is available, how to access it and how to read it: otherwise our histories slide from incompleteness to mere stories about the past. It is easy to be intimidated and dejected by what it is impossible to know, but that is no excuse for neglecting the knowledge that is possible or the interpretation that is probable. We owe the dead this much.

An understanding of how historians use evidence is crucial even when writing essays based entirely on secondary scholarship. At university, you are expected to read widely rather than relying on a single textbook. This requirement reflects the conviction that no single historian can put forward an absolutely authoritative version of events. Interpretations will always differ: historians ask different questions, consult different kinds of evidence and sew their material together into different shapes. The ability to adjudicate between different versions of the past and assess their reliability is integral to the practice of history, whether you are consulting original documents or articles and monographs produced by historians. This section aims to give you confidence in assessing the worth of other historians' work. Chapters by Helen Nicholson and Keir Waddington discuss some of the different kinds of primary and secondary evidence you are likely to encounter, from document readers to websites, and explain how to approach these sources with a critical and enquiring spirit. Federica Ferlanti demonstrates the role of selection and interpretation in determining the survival and retention of documents in archives, and shows that documents can reveal a variety of 'truths'. These chapters provide practical guidance on using sources, but also establish that it is essential to know exactly how each source ended up in front of you, in this specific form, in order to effectively analyse it.

Historians do not only deconstruct evidence. They also construct new arguments and interpretations. Non-historians rarely share this view, but history is an intensely creative discipline. Historians are tied to the evidence but also have the freedom to decide what stories to tell, and how to tell them. If not quite a playground, the past nevertheless offers more possibilities than can be tackled in one lifetime. Every time you read the words of someone long dead, you enter a lost world. The experience of glimpsing past worlds is joyous, even when what we witness is tinged with pain. The ability to bear witness is a privilege which few can access. As the historian Gillian Beer reminds us, 'These people were as alive as we are. And writing allows some of that experience and that thinking to survive, close up to the present reader.'[7] This power to speak on behalf of those who can no longer explain themselves is a responsibility which cannot be shirked. History is not simply reading about the past: it is communicating understanding about the past to different audiences. For this reason, this section is bookended by chapters showing how historians transform the raw materials of history into coherent accounts of the past: my own discussion of reading and writing history at undergraduate level, and Garthine Walker's chapter, 'Historical Research', which demonstrates that an undergraduate history degree trains students in the same skills professional historians employ when conducting research and writing for publication.

Like any craft, history requires practice, concentration and dedication for the practitioner to produce objects which are both beautiful and useful. A fine work of history is both: it holds the past in front of us, so we can marvel at something previously unseen or unimagined, and in this way teaches us about the infinite variety of human experience. This might seem very far from what you are doing when you write essays, but the first creations of any craftsman are only resemblances of what *might* be achieved. Do not be daunted at all there is to do. A working understanding of the past, which is all any of us can ever achieve, is attainable to anyone driven by the desire for immersion in the past. As Keith Thomas explains,

> Historians are like reliable local guides. Ideally, they will know the terrain like the backs of their hands. They recognise all the inhabitants and have a sharp eye for strangers and imposters. They may not have much sense of world geography and probably can't even draw a map. But if you want to know how to get somewhere, they are the ones to take you.[8]

For now, you need guides such as your tutors and this book, but by the end of your undergraduate career, you will be equipped to read the terrain of the past for others. It is an inspiring thought.

Notes

1   L. Bowen (2005) 'Political History', in G. Walker (ed.), *Writing Early Modern History* (London: Hodder Arnold/Bloomsbury), pp. 184–6.

2   M. Bloch (1998) *The Historian's Craft*, trans. Peter Putnam (Manchester: Manchester University Press), pp. 53–4. [First English publication 1954].

3   Bloch, *The Historian's Craft*, p. 48.

4   Bloch, *The Historian's Craft*, p. 16.

5   K. Thomas, 'Diary', *London Review of Books*, 32:11, 10 June 2010, p. 37.

6   S. Schama (1991) *Dead Certainties (Unwarranted Speculations)* (London: Granta), p. 320.

7   'The Greatest Pleasure I Know', *Guardian*, Review Supplement, 22 September 2012.

8   Thomas, 'Diary', p. 37.

7

Historical Research

Garthine Walker

The purpose of this chapter is to encourage students to reflect upon the processes involved in historical research. We shall explore how practising historians formulate, research and write up new projects. Crucially, we shall consider the similarities between the steps taken by professional historians in producing books and articles and how students research and write history essays. Students might understandably not immediately see the connection between these endeavours. Explanatory texts on how to study history often deal with either one or the other, and even books that cover both usually treat them separately. On the one hand, we have discussions of historiography and of methods, theories and approaches to history where the object of study is how and why historians research and write in particular ways. On the other hand, there is guidance on the practical study skills that history students will find useful in approaching their own studies.[1] This book takes a different approach. It is concerned with practical issues that attend to both the writing and studying of history, and is committed to considering the relationship between the two. Remember, your history lecturers and the authors of the books and articles on your reading lists were once undergraduate students. Their training as professional historians began when they arrived at university as first-year undergraduates, just like you. Their first attempts to produce historical writing were the history essays they wrote, just as yours are.

This chapter begins with the 'building blocks' of historical research. We will start with why historians choose certain topics, and move through the steps from the initial selection of a topic, through engaging with what others have written and undertaking primary research, to developing and refining the argument. Some of these features are dealt with in greater detail elsewhere in this volume. In the second part of the chapter, I shall exemplify how this works in practice with instances of my own research on rape in early modern England and Wales. The point is not to teach you about the history of rape or how to research it but rather to give you a flavour of how research projects are conceived and carried out.

The building blocks of historical research

Whether we are writing our very first undergraduate history essay or a book based on twenty years of research, the building blocks of historical research are the same. Figure 7.1 presents these blocks in a linear fashion. In practice, the steps between choosing a topic and writing up one's findings do not necessarily unfold precisely this way, but may involve much going back and forth. These building blocks also form the foundations of an undergraduate history degree.[2] You may well find yourself enrolled on modules that introduce you to a range of concepts, theories and methods that historians use. You might take modules where you investigate in detail particular historiographical debates or controversies. You will have the opportunity to analyse primary sources – documents, images or artefacts from the historical period and place you are studying. The pinnacle of a history degree is usually a sustained piece of your own original and independent primary research: the final-year dissertation. Although we often teach these elements separately in order to facilitate your development of the historian's skills,

- We choose a topic: What do we find interesting?

- We investigate the historiography: What has already been written on the topic? How convincing is it?

- We refine our question(s) and we form hypotheses: In the light of our reading, what do we want to know? What do we expect to find?

- We identify and select appropriate sources: What sorts of historical sources may have the answers to the questions we wish to ask?

- We test our hypotheses by analysing primary and secondary sources and developing our argument: What is our contribution to the knowledge and understanding of the past?

- We present our findings in writing to others: student essays and other assignments are marked; academic books, chapters and articles undergo a process of peer review.

FIGURE 7.1 *The building blocks of historical research.*

historical research and writing involves each of them, and in your final-year dissertation you will have the opportunity to draw on them together to produce your own research. They also encompass ways of thinking and doing that tend to be referred to as 'transferable skills'. An enquiring mind, the ability to gather relevant information, intellectual maturity, an ability to evaluate critically and respectfully the arguments of others, an ability to modify one's own position in the light of new information, as well to present one's own argument cogently all make history graduates popular with employers in a range of fields.

Choosing a topic

The essay question we (as students) choose to answer or the subject of our research (as academics or as students undertaking dissertations) depends on what we personally find interesting. Any individual will be fascinated by some topics and find others less appealing. Historians specialize in the things that interest them most. However, we must not assume that the personal interests and political positions which inform historians' questions necessarily dictate their conclusions. If that were true, there would be little debate and controversy among historians working in similar fields. You will learn during your study of history at university that there is much disagreement between historians who are interested in related topics, and that understanding the roots of those specific differences is a complex business and not reducible to broad generalizations (so-and-so is a Marxist, or feminist, or German historian, and therefore they argue such-and-such).

Sometimes historians reveal the connections between their research interests and their personal lives. Pat Hudson, the historian of industrialization, linked her love of economic history to her post-war childhood experiences of growing up in the industrial town of Barrow in north-west England: 'ship yard cranes dominated the skyline and the buzzer marked out the working day', at which thousands of working men walked and cycled home from work. Economic history, she says, was all around her.[3] Others have traced the allure of the past to a specific encounter. Roderick Floud, Professor of Modern History at Birkbeck, University of London, from 1975 to 1988, remembers 'the excitement of discovery', which never left him, upon winning as a school prize an illustrated children's historical novel set in the medieval period, Cynthia Harnett's *The Wool-Pack*.[4]

Personal circumstances can also lead to historians' research taking an unexpected direction. In 1952, Natalie Zemon Davis, who was to become a path-breaking cultural historian, faced a huge setback to her doctoral research on Protestant print workers in sixteenth-century France. The US State Department confiscated her passport after she wrote a political pamphlet criticizing the activities of the House Un-American Activities Committee as unconstitutional.

I was devastated, heartsick, by the loss of my passport. I had counted on getting back to the archives in France not only to finish the research for my thesis, but for any future work I hoped to do on my new path of social history. (Remember in those days there was no web, no digitization, and not even microfilms of most documents.)

Unable to travel to France for eight years, Davis had to rethink her research. She investigated the holdings of libraries in the United States, and discovered that many rare book collections contained sixteenth-century French books in which she was able to find traces of printers, other artisans and women. Even when she was again free to visit French archives, Davis continued to combine research on early printed books with manuscripts in archives.[5] We rarely know why historians study one thing and not another. It is therefore unhelpful for students to speculate about historians' personal motives. It is far better to analyse what they have written.

While we might take heed of E.H. Carr's advice to his students in 1961 to 'study the historian before you begin to study the facts', and '[b]efore you study the historian study his [sic] historical and social environment', we should not make crude assumptions about individuals' perspectives and arguments. Such assumptions might be based on our own naivety or unwitting prejudices. For instance, one might wrongly assume that a female historian writing women's history must be a feminist and therefore not be objective, and that a male historian writing about women in the past is not a feminist and therefore will be objective. If this were true, then all female historians writing about women would agree with each other and disagree with all male historians. Clearly, this is far from the case! Carr was right, however, to stress that the historian's perspective, methods and the context in which their historical sources were produced all inform the kind of history we write.[6] This is why history degrees nowadays almost always include modules that focus on historiography and/or historical methods.

Historiography

When we are interested in a topic, we read what others have written about it. It is while surveying the work of other scholars that historians define or refine their topic. Professional historians do two things when reading academic books and articles. One, we read for information relevant to our topic. Two, we analyse and evaluate the author's argument.

Analysing historians' work in this way involves identifying the intellectual and historiographical perspectives from which they write. This is a key skill that you will develop during your study of history at university. Thus, for example, in an essay on changes in the nature of marriage between the seventeenth and nineteenth centuries, you might consider that even historians who argued that family relationships 'modernized' with industrialization could have differing perspectives. Compare Lawrence

Stone's negative characterization of the early modern family as lacking in affection, for instance, to that advanced by Peter Laslett. Whereas Laslett argued that industrialization shattered the previously close emotional bonds of early modern families, Stone assumed that 'traditional' cold and uncaring family relationships were necessarily replaced by more loving 'modern' ones. Both of these historians' histories of the family were part of the turn to social history in the 1960s and 1970s; Stone's previous work saw the family in terms only of its political importance, while Laslett had originally been a scholar of political theory. Thus, we can see historians' interests also changing over time.[7] If you were writing an essay on this topic, your reading around the subject would demonstrate too that the history of the family was not unrelated to larger historical processes or the preserve of 'women's history' or written only by feminists. You might nonetheless acknowledge that historians of women and gender in the 1980s and later hugely advanced our understanding of the nature and significance of the family in the past.[8] When we survey any historical field, then, we need to be aware of *when* as well as *what* historians have written in order to gain a sense of how the field has developed.

When students read secondary literature, they sometimes focus on the first of these ways of reading (searching for 'the answer' to an essay question) at the expense of the second (analysing and evaluating the author's argument). Like most seemingly daunting activities, the latter becomes more manageable if one breaks it down into smaller tasks. For instance, one might ask the following questions: What are the author's expressed aims in the article or chapter in question? What kind of historical problem have they identified? What assumptions underlie their question and approach? How is their argument structured? How do they make each point of the argument? Is it convincing? Do they provide a solution to the problem raised? By approaching the secondary literature like this, and by noting examples as you go along, you will effectively create an abstract of everything you read.

This is how historians read and engage with each other's work. If you aim to do this too when reading for essays or seminars, you will hone the analytic skills of the historian (see Tracey Loughran's chapter in this section for further hints on reading academic articles and monographs). As Patrick Rael says,

> Just as the scholar you are reading uses evidence and analysis to make his/her case, so too your summation (or critique) of that scholarship requires evidence and analysis. There is no such thing as mere summary; you are, in fact, making an argument about what the argument is in a piece of historical writing.[9]

Reading critically what other scholars have written as well as reading their work for information allows us to refine our own research questions.

We can identify where gaps exist in knowledge and understanding, or where explanations remain problematic, partial, or unconvincing. Such critical reading does not necessarily focus on what others have done badly. We must also acknowledge their positive contribution. As the American Historical Association, the largest professional society for historians in the world, stressed in its 'Statement on Standards of Professional Conduct', 'Practicing history with integrity means acknowledging one's debts to the work of other historians'.[10] Integrity does not only mean avoiding plagiarism but also speaks to the nature of historical writing as a collective endeavour.

Historians are engaged in an ongoing, communal and collaborative exercise whereby we seek to understand more about the past by research, interpretation and argument. We each rely on and build upon what others have written. Even historians who vehemently disagree with each other produce research that is based on much common ground.

Given the emphasis on historiography, theory and method in most history degrees, history students sometimes focus far more on how historians disagree than they do on the ways in which historians overcome their differences. This is partly because few historians explicitly state in print that they have changed their minds or that their critics were right. It does sometimes happen. The historian of American slavery, George Rawick, admitted in 1972 that he no longer accepted the characterization of negro slaves as 'Sambos' – passive, childlike buffoons – because he had been convinced of the concept's 'implicit racism and elitism'.[11] Others have admitted that criticisms of their work exposed real shortcomings which required them to rethink their entire argument. Michael Ignatieff, for instance, explained that critical responses to his book *A Just Measure of Pain: The Penitentiary in the Industrial Revolution* had persuaded him that it 'contained three basic misconceptions'. He subsequently sought to develop a new explanation for the ways that prisons and other sorts of institutions, such as asylums, developed that avoided the pitfalls both of his own former view and of his adversaries, an endeavour which he nonetheless described as 'an exercise in self-criticism'.[12] David Halperin similarly drew attention to Eve Kosofsky Sedgwick's 'brilliant critique' and 'just' criticisms of his *One Hundred Years of Homosexuality*, which led him to modify his approach and ultimately produce an entirely new book. 'It has taken me nearly ten years to get my mind round Sedgwick's objection, to absorb it into my own thinking', he explained. Crucially, his response to the criticisms made against him was not simply to adopt her views in place of his own, but rather to engage critically with his own work and hers and 'to integrate Sedgwick's critique' into a new, more sophisticated approach to the history of homosexuality.[13] In all these examples, initial criticism and disagreement led to re-evaluation of the author's position and formulation of new arguments. Resolution of differences among scholars rarely takes the simplistic form of one being wholly wrong and one wholly right. The process is frequently subtle and difficult to discern.

Historians spend much of their working lives reading and thinking. Some of what we read is bound to tacitly or explicitly disagree with or challenge our own work. It is not always possible to identify precisely how and when our ideas shifted. We come to a new or modified position not necessarily in a moment of revelation but often over a considerable time of mulling things over. This is why historians sometimes seem to contradict themselves – it is worth considering whether such apparent contradictions are evidence of the development of someone's thinking rather than their lack of it! James Oakes, Distinguished Professor of History at the City University of New York, explains that:

> I try not to be overly committed to anything I've put into print. Print captures my thinking at the moment of publication. Sometimes all it takes is evidence, new or newly persuasive evidence, to get me to change my mind. At other times I become aware of dubious premises I had unconsciously assumed, and so back away. Occasionally I'm impressed by what Jürgen Habermas calls 'the unforced force of the better argument'. And there's always something new to learn. The more documents I read the more nuances I'm likely to notice in the next one I read. It's like learning a language I didn't even know existed. It's hard to figure it out, but it's also fun; serious, but joyful. It's why I love what I do. Because every day the past seems just a little bit different to me than it seemed the day before.[14]

The best historians are rarely stubborn, combative and insistent that theirs is the last word on any given topic. There are of course individuals who may feel defensive when others disagree with them, but that is a personality trait and not the consequence or reflection of historical training!

Questions, sources and developing an argument

On the basis of our reading the historiography, we refine our questions and we form hypotheses. By 'hypothesis', I mean what we imagine the answer to our questions might be. We must not only seek evidence that supports our hypothesis. On the contrary, we must ensure that our questions are framed in a way that allows us to be proved wrong as well as right. We have to be able to change our views as we go along.

In many respects, a historian's research is only as good as the questions he or she asks. As Hugh Trevor-Roper, Regius Professor of Modern History at Oxford University between 1957 and 1980, noted, the 'function of genius is not to give new answers, but to pose new questions'. As we cannot all be geniuses, Trevor-Roper conceded that the questions thus posed should be those 'which time and mediocrity can resolve'![15] Actually, the most significant and exciting new research does not always pose entirely new questions on topics that no one has ever worked on before – something that students sometimes mistakenly believe is meant by 'originality'. Reformulating old questions, asking them from a different perspective, posing the same questions of different sources or posing different questions of the same sources can all produce as brilliant analytic history as asking something entirely novel. Similarly, the way that students problematize the questions they answer has a huge impact on their potential to develop an argument which can be awarded the highest marks. Just as a good book, chapter or article sets out the questions to be addressed, so too a good student essay identifies issues which arise from the question, which they will then explore.[16]

In order to test our hypotheses, we identify and select primary sources – original historical evidence in the form of documents, images, artefacts and so on – which we believe may hold clues to the answers we seek. Crucially, this means acknowledging the limits of our sources, being aware of what our primary sources *cannot* tell us as well as what they can. Sometimes historians find that their research fails to confirm what they expected. Students might suppose this to be horribly worrying. On the contrary, it can be very exciting when our research fails to produce exactly the results we expected, for we are thereby forced to consider *new* possible explanations. Similarly if when you are writing an essay you find exception after exception to the view you start off with, think about how you might modify that argument rather than ignoring the evidence that does not fit.

This applies equally to the secondary literature you read. When students come upon something that is ambiguous, or seems contradictory, or lacks coherence in the books and articles they read, they tend either to worry that they are not clever enough to understand the author's point or to think that the historian in question is being 'hypocritical'. What you should do, however, is ask yourself why the point is difficult to understand, what is really going on there. Sometimes one has to read a particular piece of work more than once, especially if you are new to the topic or if the argument is especially complex. Many pieces of historical writing repay a second, or even a third, reading. However, sometimes the matter that causes us concern is an issue that itself requires serious thinking about and which might lead you to develop a convincing argument of your own, one that shows an independent engagement with your secondary sources. Perhaps what you have identified is not your inability to understand but a problem in the author's argument.

The final parallel I wish to make between student essay writing and academic writing for publication concerns the issue of feedback. Constructive feedback is essential for us all. A postgraduate student recently confided to me that she felt demoralized when, having given her supervisor a draft chapter of her MA dissertation, the supervisor returned it with many suggestions for improvement and a list of queries. Yet as Tracey Loughran emphasizes in her chapter in this volume, feedback of this nature is a crucial – and positive – element in the process of historical research and writing, not just for students but for academics, too. Just as your lecturers provide feedback on your work, so academic historians receive feedback on their published work *before* it is published (as well as afterwards in the form of book reviews). If you look at the acknowledgements page of an academic monograph or the first footnote in a journal article, you will very often find the names of persons to whom the author is grateful for reading all or part of the manuscript. The point of these helpful souls reading the manuscript was to comment on it, effectively to provide feedback and suggest ways in which it might be improved. In addition, many academics present their research at seminars and conferences in order to receive feedback from an informed audience before they commit their ideas to print.

Most books and articles are also subject to formal feedback as part of the peer review process. This is when publishers and journal editors send manuscripts to scholars in related fields, who evaluate the contribution to our knowledge and understanding of the topic, recommend publication or not, and provide comments and suggestions for improvement to the author. This process is usually double blind – neither the author nor the peer reviewers are informed of each other's identity. Generally speaking, the more prestigious the publication, the greater the degree of peer review. An article in a journal such as *Past & Present* has to be approved by as many as five or more peer reviewers before a decision is taken to publish it; articles published in *Gender & History* are each read by two editors, one additional member of the editorial collective and two external peer reviewers. The feedback created in this process is almost always useful, even when authors disagree with some of its content. Indeed, the place where academic historians are most likely to resolve differences in a literal sense is through this process of peer review that remains invisible to the reader, as the final manuscript is one that is acceptable to both author and editor, informed by the peer reviewers.

Historical research in practice: Writing the history of rape

I suggested earlier that the research process does not always unfold in a linear manner in the order outlined in Figure 7.1. In practice, as Carr said, historical enquiry is 'a continuous process of interaction between the historian and his [*sic*] facts, an unending dialogue between the present and the past'.[17] This interaction might best be imagined not as dialogue but in a trialogue between (a) our own ideas, which we reframe and reformulate as we go along, (b) the ideas and arguments of other scholars and (c) primary evidence from the period of study. I shall illustrate how this works in two examples of my own work on the history of rape in early modern England

and Wales, one published early in my career and one more recently. While these articles are connected by their subject matter, they each arose from specific engagements with primary and secondary sources, from which emerged particular research questions that shaped my subsequent work.

Example 1. Rereading rape

'Rereading Rape and Sexual Violence in Early Modern England' (1998) was written in response to an article by Miranda Chaytor on the same topic. Both articles were published in *Gender & History*.[18] Chaytor's article appeared in 1995, shortly after I completed my PhD. My doctoral thesis on gender and crime in early modern society had arisen from interests and issues I had identified as an undergraduate. During my undergraduate studies, I had observed that crime historians largely ignored women's criminality except for 'female' offences like witchcraft, infanticide and scolding. Such historians explained that women were less likely than men to commit other sorts of crimes because women were naturally more passive. It seemed to me that such arguments were based on assumptions about gender difference rather than on historical evidence. These historians' own figures showed that supposedly 'female' offences were a tiny proportion of actual crimes prosecuted. If one counted the numbers of women prosecuted for common offences like theft or assault, one might find a far greater number of women being prosecuted for 'male' crimes than for supposedly female ones like witchcraft or infanticide. This was, in other words, a hypothesis. My PhD project tested that hypothesis, and my primary research showed that that was, indeed, the case.[19]

It was as a historian of crime, then, that I engaged with Chaytor's article about rape with such interest. Chaytor discussed rape victims' and witnesses' pre-trial statements, which were recorded by magistrates when women made accusations of rape. Chaytor noted, correctly, that women's descriptions of rape included little about the sexual act. They provided greater details about other things: their clothes being torn or soiled, or the rapist's violence. Yet Chaytor's interpretation of this material seemed unconvincing. She argued that in these documents, the non-sexual violence – the bleeding, the physical pain – indicated 'thoughts which cannot be spoken directly, which cannot even by consciously known'. Such sources therefore reveal to historians 'the failure, the repression, of memory': 'what could be remembered, must be remembered, [and] what was forgotten [was] repressed'. According to Chaytor, the sexual aspect of rape was absent from the primary sources because women were repressing their memories of it. Chaytor interpreted the sources in the light of a psychological theory of traumatic repression: that is, that in order to cope with an extremely stressful or traumatic experience we unconsciously block all memory of it.

Chaytor's approach can itself be situated historically. The Freudian notion of repression – that when something awful happens, we unconsciously block it out rather than deal with it – was not new. But in the late 1980s and early 1990s, when Chaytor was researching and writing her article, there was a great deal of popular media attention to what seemed to be a new phenomenon: cases of adult women uncovering 'repressed' memories of sexual abuse during psychotherapy. Within academic psychology, the issue was controversial. Most psychologists argued that such 'memories' were false: that they were not memories of events that had occurred but rather were imagined constructs.[20] This contemporary interest in repressed memory of sexual abuse informed Chaytor's questions and her interpretation of sources. It seemed to me that even if it were possible to recover repressed memories of sexual abuse through therapy in the present, it was very doubtful that seventeenth-century pre-trial examinations and depositions could be interpreted in such a way. Chaytor asserted that every point she made about rape depended upon the nature of the primary sources: the informations (allegations of rape by the victims) and depositions (witness testimony) that were given verbally and then written down by magistrates' clerks. Every such document, she said, 'is the product of its context, a response to a specific event, everything it includes must at some level (though not necessarily consciously) be about that event, be a commentary on it and a way of bearing its pain'. Chaytor's assertions were problematic because the documents she referred to were not verbatim transcripts of what people said in full. They were rather summaries of answers to questions put to them by magistrates, questions that themselves related to points of law and not what people felt about their experiences.[21] Moreover, it seemed to me impossible to discern which bits of legal testimony were conscious and which unconscious. Such a method, I argued, promoted over-interpretation – conclusions that the evidence could not support. In order to investigate the matter further I conducted my own research. First, I read all the testimonies that Chaytor had cited. Then I identified and analysed many more. I found, for instance, that Chaytor's imaginative description of cases reflected her approach and assumptions rather than the content of the primary sources.

Take, for example, Chaytor's discussion of Issabell Moorhouse's complaint against John Wood in 1653. Chaytor asserted that this was a false accusation. Issabell, she claimed, 'had caught a glimpse' of John Wood, a man whom she did not know, and 'had started to daydream about him – about how as she walked home in the dark from the evening's milking he would meet her in the churchyard, and would kiss her, and they would begin to make love'. Issabell's information was 'a reverie of very great tenderness' that had 'a slow, sensual, dreamlike quality'. But the actual record tells a different story. Chaytor quoted the first part of Issabell's information: that as she was coming home from milking the cows, John Wood 'did meet [her] near St Nicholas church. And he put his hand about my neck and kissed me. And then he took up my coats and put his hand to my secret parts [genitals]'. Chaytor neglected to mention what Issabell said happened next.

Wood 'struggled with [her] for a quarter of an hour' in an attempt to rape her. Although she managed to get away briefly, he caught up with her,

> and struggled with her again and took down her milk, and threw her down and by force did ravish [rape] her, and she cried out but the said John Wood laid his hand on her mouth and stopped her from crying out …

I could not find anywhere in this source anything that evoked Chaytor's tender, dreamlike fantasy. It was a tale of a violent rape. The victim was groped and assaulted, fought off the rapist for fifteen minutes, managing to escape before being caught again, thrown to the ground, and raped.[22]

My first article on rape thus arose from what I found problematic in secondary reading and my knowledge of the primary sources. This does not mean that Chaytor's article makes no worthwhile contribution to our understanding of early modern rape or attitudes towards it. Historians rarely disagree with *everything* someone else has said, just something in particular. If you read my article, you will see that on several occasions I positively acknowledge Chaytor's work in my endnotes. This example serves also to illustrate the ways in which historians' research develops in unexpected ways. For my dissatisfaction with Chaytor's theoretical and interpretative framework led me also to investigate in detail the strengths and weaknesses of psychoanalytic theory for historians,[23] and afterwards to produce a book about historical approaches to the early modern period,[24] neither of which I had previously intended to do. I also developed further my views on what early modern legal testimony can and cannot tell us about the experience of individuals in the past.[25] What historians choose to write about arises from our engagement with what others have written as well as from that with primary sources.

Example 2. Acquittals and culpability

My second example – an article about the ways in which seventeenth- and eighteenth-century rape trials were reported, published in *Past & Present* in 2013 – demonstrates how unexpected findings in primary sources can lead to new research questions and interpretations.[26] Rape is problematic for historians because it seems to be transhistorical, a phenomenon that is unchanging and ever-present in human history. Studies of rape in many historical periods tend to show that rape trials almost always ended in acquittal. This similarity in the outcomes of trials has reasonably led historians to assume that 'not guilty' verdicts in any given period had the same explanation: that judges and juries believed that women lied about rape and accused men were innocent. However, my research suggested that in the late seventeenth and early eighteenth centuries, acquittals could not be primarily explained in this manner.

The chief sources I explored in this context were the cheap, printed reports of trials held at the Old Bailey, the main criminal court for London and Middlesex, and newspapers which reported Old Bailey trials and those held at the provincial Assizes. The *Old Bailey Proceedings* were printed with the court's approval and thus justified verdicts rather than suggesting that justice had not been served. Newspapers were subject to little censorship. I expected both sources to contain evidence that men were acquitted of rape because juries thought women had fabricated the charges or brought the rape upon themselves. Yet this was not what I found. It was true that most trials ended in acquittal. But in neither the *Proceedings* nor newspapers were acquittals understood to be synonymous with innocence.

Acquitted men were rarely said to be innocent. In fact, they were frequently said to have been guilty. '[A]lthough the fact appeared very foul against' one defendant, the Proceedings declared in 1675, 'yet the Circumstances thereto *not being so direct as to prove a Rape according as the law directs* [...] he was brought in not guilty'.[27] In other words, *legal* criteria for rape could not be met, even where judges and juries were convinced that the man in question was guilty. Newspapers and *Proceedings* regularly lamented that acquittals resulted from 'the evidence not being clear enough' or 'not being strong enough' to convict. For a rape trial to result in conviction, 'carnal knowledge' had to be proven. This was difficult in a period without modern forensic science and where 'carnal knowledge' was understood to mean not only penile penetration of the vagina but also ejaculation inside the body. If a man ejaculated outside the body, it did not constitute rape in law. Child rape was even harder to prove as the age at which one could give sworn testimony (that is, testimony given under oath) in a trial for felony (where conviction resulted in capital punishment) was fourteen. Although the courts listened to the evidence given by little girls, they were technically unable to convict a man (and thus sentence him to death) on unsworn testimony. The article explores in detail these and other issues relating to the legal criteria for rape, how they were applied and what people thought about them. My research thus developed in a way that I had not anticipated, as a direct result of my hypothesis being disproved by the primary sources. In addition to the argument that I proposed in this article, this research led to my developing new questions and hypotheses about when and why the victim-blaming narratives that we are now so familiar with entered the courtroom; this is the subject of my current research.

Conclusion

In practice, historical enquiry is a trialogue between the historian, the historiography (the secondary literature) and the evidence (the primary sources). It is the relationship between these three things that keeps producing new questions and keeps the discipline of history moving forward. This is also how you should approach your essays: not passively to look for ready-made answers in what historians have written, but in a spirit of curiosity. By participating in the scholarly process, you will develop your creative and critical skills and become researchers in your own right.

STUDY QUESTIONS

- In what ways is writing an undergraduate history essay similar to writing for publication?
- What role does engagement with other scholars play in the formulation of new historical hypotheses?
- Do historians need to find new sources to formulate a genuinely 'original' interpretation?

Notes

1   For example, M. Abbott (2009) (ed.) *History Skills: A Student's Handbook*, 2nd edn (Abingdon: Routledge); J. Black and D. M. MacRaild (2007) *Studying History*, 3rd edn (Basingstoke: Palgrave Macmillan); W. H. McDowell (2002) *Historical Research: A Guide* (Abingdon: Routledge).

2   See the QAA Subject Benchmark Statement for History: http://www.qaa.ac.uk /en/Publications/Documents/SBS-history-14.pdf. Accessed 16 January 2016.

3   P. Hudson (2001) 'The Economic History of Life', in P. Hudson (ed.), *Living Economic and Social History* (Glasgow: Economic and Social History Society), p. 157.

4   R. Floud (2001) 'In at the Beginning of Cliometrics', in Hudson (ed.), *Living Economic and Social History*, p. 86; Cynthia Harnett (1951) *The Wool-Pack* (London: Methuen).

5   N. Z. Davis, 'How the FBI Turned Me On to Rare Books', NYRBlog, 30 July 2013: http://www.nybooks.com/blogs/nyrblog/2013/jul/30/fbi-turned -me-on-to-rare-books/. Accessed 16 January 2016.

6   E. H. Carr (2001), *What Is History?* 2nd edn (Basingstoke: Palgrave Macmillan) [1961], pp. 17 and 38.

7   L. Stone (1977) *The Family, Sex and Marriage in England, 1500–1800* (New York: Harper); P. Laslett (1965) *The World We Have Lost* (London: Methuen). See also G. Walker (2005) 'Modernization', in G. Walker (ed.), *Writing Early Modern History* (London: Hodder Arnold/Bloomsbury).

8   For example, L. Davidoff and C. Hall (1987) *Family Fortunes: Men and Women of the English Working Class, 1780–1850* (Chicago, IL: University

of Chicago Press); K. Harvey (2012) *The Little Republic: Masculinity and Domestic Authority in Eighteenth-Century Britain* (Oxford: Oxford University Press).

9 P. Rael (2005) 'What Happened and Why? Helping Students Read and Write like Historians', *The History Teacher*, 39:1, p. 27.

10 American Historical Association (2011), 'Statement on Standards of Professional Conduct (updated 2011)': http://www.historians.org/jobs-and-professional-development/statements-and-standards-of-the-profession/statement-on-standards-of-professional-conduct. Accessed 16 January 2016.

11 G. P. Rawick (1972) *From Sundown to Sunup: the Making of the Black Community* (Westport, CT: Greenwood), n. 2, cited in C. N. Degler (1976) 'Why Historians Change Their Minds', *Pacific Historical Review*, 45:2, pp. 176–7.

12 M. Ignatieff (1978) *A Just Measure of Pain: the Penitentiary in the Industrial Revolution, 1750–1850* (London: Macmillan); M. Ignatieff (1981) 'State, Civil Society, and Total Institutions: A Critique of Recent Social Histories of Punishment', *Crime and Justice*, 3.

13 D. M. Halperin (2002) *How to Do the History of Homosexuality* (Chicago, IL: University of Chicago Press), pp. 10–12; Halperin (1990) *One Hundred Years of Homosexuality* (London: Routledge).

14 J. Oakes (2012) 'On Changing My Mind', *Perspectives on History: the Newsmagazine of the American Historical Association*: https://www.historians.org/publications-and-directories/perspectives-on-history/september-2012/on-changing-my-mind. Accessed 16 January 2016.

15 H. R. Trevor-Roper (1957) *Man and Events: Historical Essays* (New York: Harper), p. 238.

16 Rael, 'What Happened and Why?' pp. 24–5.

17 Carr, *What Is History?* p. 24.

18 G. Walker (1998) 'Rereading Rape and Sexual Violence in Early Modern England', *Gender & History*, 10:1; M. Chaytor (1995) 'Husband(ry): Narratives of Rape in the Seventeenth Century', *Gender & History*, 7:3.

19 See G. Walker (2003) *Crime, Gender and Social Order in Early Modern England* (Cambridge: Cambridge University Press); G. Walker and J. Kermode (1994) 'Introduction', in J. Kermode and G. Walker (eds), *Women, Crime and the Courts in Early Modern England* (London and Chapel Hill, NC: UCL Press and University of North Carolina Press).

20 E. F. Loftus and K. Ketcham (1994) *The Myth of Repressed Memory* (New York: St. Martin's Press).

21 Chaytor, 'Husband(ry)', pp. 379, 381.

22 The National Archives, Assizes: Northern and North-Eastern Circuits: Criminal Depositions and Case Papers [ASSI 45] 4/3/113, Information of Issabell Moorehouse, 27 October 1653.

23 G. Walker (2003) 'Psychoanalysis and History', in S. Berger, H. Feldner and K. Passmore (eds), *Writing History: Theory and Practice* (London: Hodder Arnold/Bloomsbury).

24   Walker (ed.) *Writing Early Modern History*.

25   G. Walker (2003) 'Telling Tales of Infant Death in Early Modern England', in M. Mikesell and A. Seeff (eds), *Culture and Change: Attending to Early Modern Women* (Newark: University of Delaware Press).

26   G. Walker (2013) 'Rape, Acquittal and Culpability in Popular Crime Reports in England, c.1670–c.1750', *Past & Present*, 220.

27   Old Bailey Proceedings Online (www.oldbaileyonline.org, version 7.1, April 2013), January 1675, trial of Edward Coker, t16750115-3; my italics.

Further Reading

P. Burke (2002) *History and Historians in the Twentieth Century* (Oxford: Oxford University Press).

A. Burton (2006) *Archive Stories: Facts, Fictions, and the Writing of History* (Durham, NC: Duke University Press).

A. Curthoys and A. McGrath (2011) *How to Write History That People Want to Read* (Basingstoke: Palgrave Macmillan).

G. Eley (2005) *A Crooked Line: From Cultural History to the History of Society* (Ann Arbor, MI: University of Michigan Press).

M. Pallares-Burke (2002) *The New History: Confessions and Conversations* (Oxford: Blackwell).

P. Rael (2005) 'What Happened and Why? Helping Students Read and Write like Historians', *The History Teacher*, 39:1, pp. 23–32.

K. Thomas, 'Diary', *London Review of Books*, 32:11, 10 June 2010, pp. 36–7.

8

Evidence and Interpretation

Kevin Passmore

When tutors ask new students what they think is different about studying history at university, they sometimes respond that they are no longer able to rely on teachers and textbooks and that they have to give their own opinions. This expectation might be reinforced by the still common requirement that students read E.H. Carr's *What Is History?* (1961). This classic is best known for its contention that historians cannot simply rely on facts and that bias is unavoidable. Perhaps also a tutor will criticize a student's first essay for relying too much on 'description' or 'narrative', for merely recounting 'facts' rather than developing an 'interpretation' and 'argument'. The tutor might urge the writer to explore the 'debates' or to include 'the historiography' in their essay. Yet the same tutor might also criticize the essay for 'factual mistakes' and failure to back up arguments with 'evidence' and footnotes. It is hardly surprising that students are perplexed. How can facts matter if history is all about opinion? If bias is inevitable, then how can we say that one historical interpretation is any better than another?

Much hinges on our understanding of loaded terms such as 'objectivity', 'opinion' and 'interpretation'. Students often arrive at university believing that historians should be 'objective' – that is, they should put forward neutral accounts of the past, free from their own perspectives, opinions or beliefs. Yet for at least half a century, historians have known very well that backgrounds and interests influence historians' writings, and that objectivity, in the sense of a completely disinterested perspective on the past, is impossible. It follows that doing history at university cannot be about becoming *objective*, for nobody can completely set aside their background and personal ideas. Yet neither is history as practised in a university just about giving an 'opinion'. Indeed, it is better to avoid using the word 'opinion' in historical writing altogether, because in everyday language it denotes speculation in the absence of knowledge, or political or moral judgement of what is good or bad. In both these senses, 'opinion' is incompatible with good historical practice. 'Interpretation' is a better term for historians to use because it implies two things. First, just as we translate from an unknown foreign language into one we can understand, interpretation means translation of unfamiliar things in the past into terms that we can understand now. Secondly, interpretation, unlike opinion, depends on the supporting *evidence*, and on the citation (in footnotes) of relevant facts. Proper use of evidence allows us to distinguish valid from invalid interpretations of the past. Historical interpretation, then, depends on both perspective and facts, and becoming a historian means learning to bring the two together.

In this chapter, I explore the relationship between historical interpretation and evidence. All historians begin with preconceptions, but the key point is whether these ideas can potentially be changed by confrontation with evidence. If our ideas were fixed, there would be no point in doing history, as research into the past could not possibly alter our initial preconceptions. Likewise, it is pointless to say that a source is 'biased', because all sources are biased: *all* sources are produced using preconceived ideas for particular purposes. The historian's task is to work out what these preconceptions and purposes were, and what consequences they had for whom.[1] I shall show that this task raises a whole range of questions about bias, moral judgement, the status of facts and indeed the place of history in society.

Interpretation

Students are not alone in their confusion about the difference between facts and opinion. The following example comes from a university tutor's blog on common mistakes made by students.

Here's an example of how *not* to represent a fact, via CNN:

> Considering that [Hillary] Clinton's departure will leave only 16 women in the Senate out of 100 senators, many feminists believe women are underrepresented on Capitol Hill.

Wait. Feminists 'believe'? Given that women are 51% of the population, 16 out of 100 means that women *are* underrepresented on Capitol Hill. This is a social fact, yeah? Now, you can agree or disagree with feminists that this is a *problem*, but do not suggest, as CNN does, that the fact itself is an opinion. This is a common mistake, and it is frustrating for both instructors and students to get past. Life will be much easier if you know the difference.[2]

Let us say that a fact is a statement that we believe beyond reasonable doubt to be true (as in a court of law). A reasonable person could not deny that women are underrepresented in the Senate relative to their presence in the population as a whole. It is not just an 'opinion', because the statement is backed by evidence.

Opinion enters when we think about moral right and wrong. Anyone who believes in the equal rights of men and women will see underrepresentation of women in the Senate as morally unfair. Any member of society may express their views on such matters, and historians have the same right to do so as anyone else. Yet historians' views on moral issues are no more *valid* than anyone else's, and when historians comment on moral issues, they do so without engaging their special training as historians.

There are some sinister examples of what can happen when historians appoint themselves as judges of right and wrong. In early twentieth-century Germany, professional historians were highly committed to scholarly standards, which they thought guaranteed their ability to know the truth about the past. Yet they also confused what they thought was scientifically right with what they thought was morally right. They believed that history was a story of the struggle of 'advanced' nations to increase their power over backward people, a contention that is in fact more political (racist, we could say) than historical. When Hitler came to power, these historians carried out research that justified colonization of Eastern Europe on the grounds of the 'mission' of the German people, defined in racial terms.[3] Historians were just one of several professional groups in Hitler's Germany to believe that their scientific training entitled them to adjudicate moral problems and even to decide who had the right to live. Historians in democracies have also made simplistic links between politics and history. Since the nineteenth century, historians and other academics have cited the need to spread democracy as justification for imperial conquest.[4] Interpreting the past in the light of one's own values is bad history. It leads historians to deliberately select facts and evidence that fit with the development of what they happen to believe in. Of course, historians have the right to express their political views, but when they do so, it is as private persons, not as historians.

If historians are no more or less qualified than anyone else to judge right and wrong, then what *does* their training qualify them to do that others cannot? To develop our earlier example, they can show the historical position of women in society, for instance, their underrepresentation in positions of power, unequal pay and denigration of their intellectual abilities. But no self-evident moral position arises from these facts, and historically they have supported opposed moral positions. Feminists nowadays differ enormously in their political conclusions. In other times and places both antifeminists and feminists have argued that unequal pay was necessary because women's primary duty was care of the home and children. Moral or political judgement is separate from documented historical facts.

However, although historians have no special insight into morality, they can still do more than *only* establish facts. Their training qualifies them to interpret: they can explain *why* women have occupied unequal positions in society, pointing, for instance, to the prevalence of gender prejudice among religious groups or to the capitalist economy's requirement for cheap labour. Again, these interpretations are not 'opinion', because they are based on evidence. *Historians endeavour to explain and understand.* Their interpretations are based on evidence and facts, which differentiates them from mere opinion. However, historical writing cannot just rely on facts either, as some early practitioners erroneously thought it could. We know that historians disagree about many things, which suggests that history is not just about facts any more than it is about opinion.

Facts and evidence

The historical profession as we know it today is still influenced by the methods of Leopold von Ranke (1795–1886). The iconic Prussian urged historians to show the past 'as it really was'. They should always *begin with facts*, which meant studying original documents, establishing their origin, authorship and authenticity. Historians would then arrange proven facts in sequence as a historical 'narrative'. Footnotes – references to the documents – would allow other historians to check the validity of the work. In seminars, historians would pass on their skills to students, who would ultimately produce a piece of research of their own (the 'doctorate' or 'PhD', or 'DPhil'). Training produced *professional* historians, who were uniquely qualified to understand sources. Rankeans also established new journals, such as *Historische Zeitschrift* (1859), *Revue historique* (1887), *English Historical Review* (1886) and *American Historical Review* (1895), in which 'peer review' (anonymous reading by experts in the field) ensured adherence to the aforementioned scholarly standards. Ranke used as his model the scientific experiment, which assumed that any scientist who repeated it exactly would achieve the same result. Likewise, Ranke assumed that anyone who approached a given source using his methods would interpret it in the same way. The footnote guaranteed the replicability of historical 'results'. Ranke's innovations remain essential to the historical profession. However, we shall see that they are used differently now, for Ranke's conviction that historians can begin with facts – that facts can speak for themselves – is problematic.

One difficulty is that Ranke did not allow for disagreement among historians. Contrary to his expectation, historians did not always reach the same conclusions, even when they used the same sources. In *What Is History?* E.H. Carr argued that it was actually impossible for historians first to establish the facts and then interpret them, for in reality *interpretation was present from the beginning*. He gave three reasons.[5] First, the historian cannot simply list everything that happened on a given topic. There are an infinite number of facts about the French Revolution, for instance, and the historian cannot include all of them. The selection of material for inclusion in a history is also an act of interpretation, for the historian must use some method to determine which facts are relevant. Secondly, in deciding what to include and exclude the historian's background and purpose necessarily matters. Ranke and his followers were unwittingly good examples of that difficulty, for they thought that the development of the state and nation were the most important facts of history, and so they tended to write political and diplomatic history. As shown elsewhere in this volume, since the 1960s historians have challenged these assumptions and instead produced histories exploring many different aspects of the identities of 'ordinary' people. Thirdly, Carr pointed out that 'facts' were not intrinsically trustworthy. The documents which survive were often pre-selected by certain groups in the period in question. For example, monks produced many surviving medieval documents. Even modern historians have more sources produced by the state than, say, factory workers. Furthermore, there is also an element of chance in determining which documents survive the vicissitudes of the ages, and in what form, as Helen Nicholson's chapter in this volume demonstrates. We may add a fourth reason, which is implicit in Carr's discussion: even if historians had just one source, they would still need to decide which questions to ask of it. For instance, court records have traditionally been used to ask questions about crime and the operation of the criminal justice system. Only recently have historians thought of using these sources to understand gender or ecological history. Indeed, we cannot know what new meanings people in the future will discover in old sources. This point confirms Carr's key point that we cannot first give the facts and then interpret them – interpretation is present from the start.

Nowadays, historians generally agree with Carr that bias (understood as 'point of view') inevitably shapes historical writing, and affects interpretation and the use of sources. Since Carr wrote – indeed partly because of his work – historians have given a new meaning to the old term 'historiography'. It once meant the techniques used to analyse sources, as Ranke understood them. It now means studying the historians rather than the history, uncovering their acknowledged and unacknowledged biases, and analysing the influence of different political, social and cultural circumstances on how they have interpreted the past. Since the 1960s, many history degrees have included courses on 'historiography'. By the time they finish their degrees, students are now usually expected to recognize differences between Rankean, Marxist and postmodern approaches, among others, and to be aware of the strengths and weaknesses of their own ways of doing history. History graduates know that understanding history involves a point of view.

Choosing a topic: Frames and conceptual choices

Interpretation is, then, an inevitable part of historical research and writing. Yet this does not mean that history is just a matter of 'opinion', or that all histories are equally valid (a position known as 'relativism'). No history degree is organized on the principle that historical writing is *only* a story, and students who invent essays rarely flourish. Even those professional historians who are most sceptical of the possibility of 'objectivity' write about the past as if they can say something meaningful; they use sources, original documents and other evidence, and they reference these with footnotes. So how can historians acknowledge the inevitability of perspective and still produce worthwhile interpretations? Although perspective enters historical writing in several ways, it does not follow that we can say whatever we like about the past, or that we cannot adjudicate between competing historical interpretations. Historians begin with particular interests and write from specific perspectives, but they must shape this starting point into a question that they can test against evidence.

Perspective is inevitable because any historian must first *choose* a subject. Understandably, historians opt for the topics in which they are most interested, for example, political, military or religious history. They may also have particular ideas about government, war or the Church that they want to develop. Inevitably, these ideas and preconceptions derive from their background and experience, perhaps in ways of which they are not aware. Interests and perspective enter historical investigation from the beginning. Historians who are interested in the military are no more and no less biased than those who want to know about the roles of women or different ethnic groups in past societies. Everybody has to choose a starting point. What really matters is *whether the ideas that form this starting point can potentially be changed or modified through research, debate, critique and confrontation with evidence.*[6] That depends on learning how to frame a topic and a question open to such modification.

Each starting point for research is a choice. As Carr argued, definition of the limits of the topic or object of study is a form of bias intrinsic to historical writing. We must be clear about how our choices affect what we write about the past. Take the question, 'Why did the Second World War break out in 1939?' This apparently uncontroversial question involves a judgement on when the Second World War actually began, with which people living in different countries at the time might have disagreed. Others might argue that the war began with the Japanese invasion of Manchuria (1931), the Italian invasion of Abyssinia (1935), the British and French declarations of war on Germany (1939), the German invasion of the Soviet Union (June 1941) or with the Japanese attack on Pearl Harbor (December 1941).This choice shapes the focus of research, and therefore the answer. If we take 1931 as the starting point, we might emphasize imperial interests; if we begin with 1939, we might be more concerned with the European balance of power.

The question of boundaries is all the more important because some historical debates are not about fact, or perhaps even interpretation, but about where limits should be set and how a topic should be defined. For instance, in an important article published in 1989, Paula Schwartz argued that previous historians had underestimated the role of women in the French Resistance. She showed that a few women *had* been involved in combat, but more importantly, argued that women's activity looked more important if the definition of resistance was extended to include transporting weapons and messages, food riots and more. Schwartz's argument depended on re-defining resistance to include more activities, rather than contradicting existing knowledge, for both new and old interpretations agreed that physical combat had been almost exclusively the province of men. While in principle some historians might have objected that 'real resistance' was military, in practice they largely accepted the new definition and incorporated women into their stories. Consequently, the two views were able to live together. However, Schwartz also presented further arguments that were less widely accepted. She argued that prejudices about gender roles – that men's natures were best suited to combat and women's to support roles – explained different male and female patterns of resistance. She thus challenged the assumption that the Resistance fought for equal human rights for all people against Nazi oppression, for it did not treat men and women equally. While some historians modified their accounts to incorporate this view, others rejected it and some simply ignored it.[7]

Framing a topic entails other conceptual choices. Answering any historical question involves taking a position in relation to ideas about how society works and humans behave. No historian, even the most opposed to the use of 'theory', can avoid doing this, and historians often use casually terms such as 'unconscious' that originally were highly theoretical, but have now passed into 'common-sense' language. Assumptions of this type can make an enormous difference to specific interpretations. Take for instance the role of propaganda in society. Some social theorists assume that if slogans are constantly repeated, ordinary people will unwittingly absorb them and become vulnerable to manipulation. Others think that whether propaganda influences people depends on circumstances and that people may sometimes misunderstand, criticize or even resist it. It is easy to see that a historian's stance on such a question influences interpretation of topics from the role of the Church in the medieval world through fascist dictatorship to the place of advertising in contemporary society.[8] It is important to stress that these conceptual decisions are not mere opinion or bias. These concepts have themselves been subject to rigorous academic investigation and testing, and the best historians will be aware of where they stand in relation to such theories.

Historians must, then, make clear how they are framing their topic, and perhaps show that they are aware that this framing affects their answer.

Choice of framing will always rule out things that others might consider important, and so historians should beware of making exaggerated claims for their contributions. Historians must be as clear as possible on where their arguments contradict and where they complement other interpretations. Indeed, most topics have been explored by previous historians. Consequently, in their introductions, historians should indicate the state of play in the field, so that they can explain how their own research confirms, contradicts or modifies other interpretations (this positioning is sometimes called 'situating work historiographically'). Footnotes acknowledge that the historian's own contribution depends on many other contributions.

Provisional hypotheses and evidence

To sum up so far, perspective is intrinsic to historical writing because we must begin with interests, choose from many possible ways of framing a topic and conducting research, and select from a potentially immense body of evidence. Yet if our starting point is a choice, it does not follow that our conclusions are simply biased. Rather, the historical method depends on turning our interests and perhaps hunches into *questions*. The point about questions is that we ask them because we are not sure of the answer, and so whatever ideas we start with could *potentially* be changed through reason, research and confrontation with evidence. What would be the point of researching the past if discovering new knowledge could not possibly modify our existing ideas? Asking a question that can serve as a starting point for research is possible only if it is properly framed. That is why initially students usually have to select essay questions from a list provided by the tutor. Gradually, as they progress though to masters and PhD levels, they acquire greater room to choose their questions. Learning to frame an answerable question is an essential part of training as a historian.

An answerable question is one which contains a *hypothesis* about the reasons for a specific historical event – a provisional explanation that research will reveal to be right, partially right or wrong. It is also a *perspective* in that the historian could choose other angles from which to investigate this event, and so any answer can never be a complete account of the topic. Moreover, people in the future will ask questions about the topic that have not occurred to us, just as Paula Schwartz asked questions about the role of women in the Resistance from a perspective which previous historians had not considered. As this example suggests, all histories are provisional, no matter how thorough the research, as all histories could be modified through asking new questions or consulting new evidence.

Thinking about framing answerable questions helps us to see why history is not just opinion. We begin with questions, or provisional hypotheses, but our answers must be supported by evidence. If they are not, the hypothesis must be discarded. This 'hypothetico-deductive method' is associated with the philosopher of science Karl Popper (1902–94). Popper's major contribution was to suggest that as we embark on research we must think of potential ways that evidence and research might *disprove* our hypothesis. This might sound counterintuitive, but the point is actually quite easy to understand. If we asked a question that could not be in principle disproved, there would be little point in doing research. We would know the answers before we started and history really would be just opinion. It is necessary to frame a hypothesis which might be disproved because *confirmation* of a proposition is deceptively easy. Take the contention that all cats have tails. We would likely see any number of cats with tails as we walked about the city, but in fact the proposition would never be proven. We could never be certain that the statement is true, for it could be falsified by spotting just one tailless cat. Translating that into historical terms, Paul Kennedy, in a book that had great resonance outside the world of professional historians, claimed that since the sixteenth century, the relative political power of nation-states has depended on their economic power. He provided many examples to confirm his hypothesis, but just one example of a politically powerful state with a weak economy would oblige him to abandon or at least modify his interpretation.[9] This is Popper's principle of *falsification*: historians attempt to disprove interpretations and they retain those that best stand up to this process.

As Figure 8.1 shows, the principle that we must begin with a provisional hypothesis has consequences for how we use evidence. Clearly, we cannot just collect evidence in the hope that it will be relevant. Rather, our question dictates what evidence is relevant and how we should use it. The example of Schwartz's research on resistance is relevant here. Historians who defined resistance in military terms did not look for evidence of women's role in food riots, because it seemed to be outside their realm of enquiry. Historians working with an expanded definition of resistance look for different kinds of evidence because they are asking different questions. Questions shape the research process as well as the final argument. This 'selection' of evidence has nothing to do with 'bias', or with choosing evidence that fits our argument. On the contrary, a properly framed question obliges us to choose evidence that might actually falsify our starting point, and cause us to modify our argument.

Testing hypotheses about the past can be complex. There is always much room for debate, for the use of evidence and ways of dealing with it are never straightforward. There are three potential complications to bear in mind. The first is that historical interpretations rarely consist of single statements that can be tested against a clear set of evidence. For example, the question of economic motivations in the decision to go to war involves complex hypotheses about the links between military and civil power in a democracy, the nature of capitalism, and even more general questions such as the relationship between ideas and material interests. Falsifying

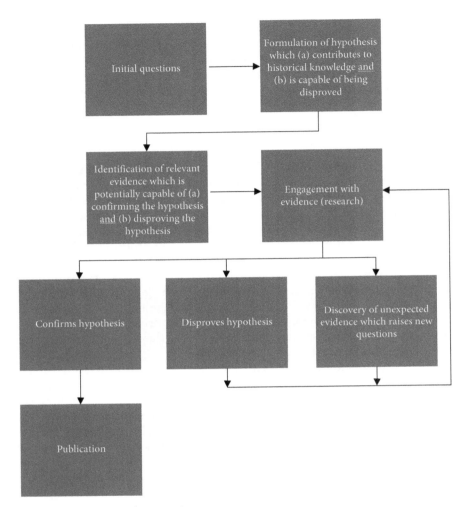

FIGURE 8.1 *Hypothesis testing.*

one contention might not undermine the whole interpretation. The second problem is that we must treat our evidence with caution. As Carr points out, evidence is not intrinsically reliable. The statistics on which historians rely for British population estimates before the nineteenth century are notoriously untrustworthy, for instance. Sometimes, the evidence, not the hypothesis, might be wrong. Historians can obviate some of the problems around reliability of evidence by consulting the widest possible number of relevant sources, comparing these sources to determine the probable reliability or individual perspective of each, and acknowledging both the limits and possibilities of these different kinds of sources in their published works. However, because they cannot be certain of their evidence, historians have to work with *probabilities*. That is one of the (many) ways in which Holocaust deniers fail to meet scholarly standards: it is simply not probable that the millions of original documents, physical remains and other evidence of the extermination of the Jews could have been fabricated.[10] A third problem is that historians are never (can never be) wholly aware of their own perspective and biases, and so they are not perfectly placed to test their own ideas. They will have blind spots and inconsistencies in their arguments. That is why mutual criticism is so important in the historical profession, and it is one reason why historians have not abandoned the professional structures that Rankeans invented all those years ago – the critique of sources, footnotes and peer review.

Conspiracy theories, critique and debate

The importance of falsifiability, probability and mutual criticism in historical writing emerges from comparison with conspiracy theories, such as the conviction that Lee Harvey Oswald did not kill John F. Kennedy or that American astronauts did not land on the moon. Conspiracy theories are not provisional hypotheses that research could modify or contradict. They are unshakeable convictions that work along the following lines: the perpetrators, 'they', are powerful, hidden forces that 'obviously' have a motive to carry out the conspiracy in question and therefore must have done it. Conspiracy theorists select evidence that fits the theory and, as we have seen, it is all too easy to find apparent confirmation of a theory. Conspiracy theorists are not open to falsification – in fact, they are sceptical about everything except their own theories. If evidence apparently contradicts their theory, the conspirators must have fabricated it. If evidence is missing, 'they' must have hidden it, for 'they' supposedly have the power to do that. Conspiracy theories are also improbable. While it is theoretically possible to cover up one of the conspiracies in question, it is improbable, given the number of accomplices required. Is it really likely that none of the huge number of people who would have had to have been involved in fabricating evidence of the moon landings have not come forward with some solid evidence?

In contrast to conspiracy theorists, historians do modify their arguments in the course of debate with other historians and of confrontation with evidence. Historians do not stick blindly to their starting points or indeed their conclusions. To be sure, many debates are not resolved. Some never could be, for they involve moral questions that are not the province of historians. Other controversies simply come to seem irrelevant. For instance, from the 1950s to the 1970s, historians were greatly interested in the origins of the French and Russian revolutions, and debates were particularly controversial because they were entangled with political divisions between left and right during the Cold War. In the 1990s, the topic fell out of fashion, partly because the political climate changed and partly because of methodological developments including the turn to cultural history.

Other disagreements turn out on close inspection to be false controversies, in which the competing positions are actually different perspectives that are compatible with each other. To illustrate this point, Steve Rigby uses the example of a long-running historical controversy about the origins of capitalism in medieval Europe, known as the Brenner debate. Some historians argued the decline of the population was crucial, while others emphasized struggles between peasants and landlords concerning rent payments. Rigby argues that the two views were actually compatible, and that historians agreed without realizing it.[11]

Most often, debate, critique and research modify views. Schwartz's research on women's role in the French Resistance, which caused other historians to adjust their arguments in the light of her new methods and data, is a good example of this process of revision. In some cases, historians might even make so many concessions to each other that in practice their positions end up as indistinguishable. For example, Steve Rigby argues that between the 1960s and the 1980s, historiographical Marxism 'died the death of a thousand qualifications'.[12] Sometimes opponents may even come to agree – after all, historians write in the hope of persuading others. They also try to anticipate the criticisms from others, and that can open the way to compromise. Indeed, the development of an argument involves negotiation, agreement and disagreement with many other historians. For students, this process takes place through lectures, seminar debates, reading published books and sources, and via feedback from tutors. For professional historians, it also involves peer review. In some cases, historians quite explicitly accept that they were wrong. As it happens, I did so in the second edition of a book that I wrote about fascism, in which I conceded that my conviction that studying fascism depended on producing a correct definition (or model) was erroneous. I did so after direct and indirect debate with critics, through reading, participation in conferences and peer review.[13]

Professionalism and objectivity today

Today, Ranke's conviction that professionalism, facts and footnotes guarantee the scientific objectivity of historical writing is untenable. The emphasis now is on perspective and provisional knowledge. Yet much of what the Rankeans established remains central to the discipline, even if contemporary historians use these methods and approaches differently. For instance, we no longer agree with Rankeans that footnotes underpin objectivity, but footnotes remain an essential protection against plagiarism and a safeguard against simply inventing interpretations. Present-day historians also see footnotes as recognition that histories are partial perspectives that rely on a whole web of work by other historians; they show some of the many other interpretations on which a particular historian relies and perhaps indicate some of their conceptual assumptions. Footnotes are part of a continuing dialogue between the author of a work and previous and future historians in a constantly revised history, based on agreement and disagreement.[14] Historians know that others will follow up their footnotes in their own research and use the same sources in different ways.

Seminars have changed, too. No longer are they a means for the tutor simply to pass on his or her techniques and conclusions. Students must develop their own ideas, with increasing autonomy. At undergraduate level, the tutor helps students to formulate their own interpretations and skills. At the other end of the professional history structure, established academics present papers to their peers in research seminars and invite criticism (so history is always a collective endeavour). Similar principles apply in students' written work, in that tutors help students to formulate their ideas. Tutors know that there is not a single answer to a question, and do not expect students to rehash their own view. They ask how coherently students have formulated their own ideas, how widely they have read, how convincingly they have positioned their essay in relation to other work on the subject, and how well they use evidence and reference it. Likewise, the anonymous peer review to which professional historians are subjected is meant to ensure that their publications are coherent, that they have formulated their questions properly and are clear on what they contribute, and have provided evidence to support their arguments.

Conclusion: Open interpretations

I began this chapter by discussing the common assumption among undergraduates that history at university is all about giving one's own opinion. Historical writing certainly cannot be objective or give us complete or definitive answers, but the term 'opinion' may not be the most helpful. It has the disadvantage of being used in contexts that do not (rightly) require the sort of rigorous analysis that is incumbent upon historians. Historians are better advised to use terms such as 'interpretation', 'explanation' and 'understanding'. Rigorous analysis means consciously paying attention to the definition of the subject and the methods used, and asking questions that can be tested against evidence and potentially modified or falsified. Indeed, one mark of a good interpretation is that it allows for other perspectives, so long as they too depend on a proper historical method, and do not claim to be *the* interpretation. That is the basis on which historians assess both students' and each other's work, and it is the basis on which histories are judged to be valid, if not definitive, complete, or incontestable.

Acknowledgements

I would like to thank the following Cardiff University History students who kindly agreed to comment on an early draft of this chapter: Sophie Adams, Daniel Bear, Peter Budd, Dan Jewson and Jordan Rees.

Study Questions

- What is the difference between 'opinion' and 'interpretation'?
- What is the difference between an 'objective' and a 'valid' history?
- What is the relationship between evidence and interpretation in historical research and writing?
- Why do most historians nowadays believe that all histories are provisional?

Notes

1   L. Jordanova (2006) *History in Practice*, 2nd edn (London: Hodder Arnold), pp. 87–104; Mary Fulbrook (2002) *Historical Theory* (London and New York: Routledge), pp. 31–49.

2   L. Wade (2014) 'Professors' Pet Peeves': http://thesocietypages.org/socimages/2014/08/25/professors-pet-peeves/. Accessed 16 January 2016.

3   S. Berger (1997) *The Search for Normality: National Identity and Historical Consciousness in Germany since 1800* (New York and Oxford: Berghahn); M. Burleigh (1988) *Germany Turns Eastwards: A Study of Ostforschung in the Third Reich* (Cambridge: Cambridge University Press).

4   For an example of a somewhat political approach to empire, see N. Ferguson (2004) *Empire: How Britain Made the Modern World* (London: Penguin).

5   E. H. Carr (1961) *What Is History?* (London: Macmillan), pp. 1–31.

6   M. H. Beales (2014) 'This Source Is Accurate, That Source Is Bias(ed): A Re-examination of Historical Pedagogy': http://mhbeals.com/teachingblog/this-source-is-accurate-that-source-is-biased-a-re-examination-of-historical-pedagogy/. Accessed 16 January 2016.

7   P. Schwartz (1989) 'Partisanes and Gender Politics in Vichy France', *French Historical Studies*, 16:1.

8   See, for instance, the approaches of D. Welch (1993) *The Third Reich: Politics and Propaganda* (New York: Routledge); and Claudia Koonz (2003) *The Nazi Conscience* (Cambridge, MA: Harvard University Press).

9   Paul M. Kennedy (1988) *The Rise and Fall of the Great Powers: Economic Change and Military Conflict from 1500 to 2000* (London: Random House).

10 K. Passmore (2010) 'Poststructuralism and History', in S. Berger, H. Feldner and K. Passmore (eds), *Writing History: Theory and Practice*, 2nd edn (London: Bloomsbury).

11 S. H. Rigby (1995) 'Historical Causation: Is One Thing More Important than Another?', *History*, 80.

12 S. H. Rigby (1997) 'Marxist Historiography', in M. Bentley (ed.), *Companion to Historiography* (London: Taylor & Francis).

13 K. Passmore (2014) *Fascism: A Very Short Introduction*, 2nd edn (Oxford: Oxford University Press).

14 A. Grafton (1997) *The Footnote: A Curious History* (London: Faber and Faber).

Further Reading

J. Arnold (2000) *History: A Very Short Introduction* (Oxford and New York: Oxford University Press).

E. H. Carr (1961) *What Is History?* (London: Macmillan).

R. J. Evans (1996) *In Defence of History* (London: Granta).

M. Fulbrook (2002) *Historical Theory* (London and New York: Routledge).

K. Jenkins (1991) *Re-Thinking History* (London: Routledge).

L. Jordanova (2006) *History in Practice*, 2nd edn (London: Hodder Arnold).

P. Lambert (2010) 'The Professionalization and Institutionalization of History', in S. Berger, H. Feldner and K. Passmore (eds), *Writing History: Theory and Practice*, 2nd edn (London: Bloomsbury), pp. 40–58.

S. Okasha (2002) *Philosophy of Science: A Very Short Introduction* (Oxford: Oxford University Press).

S. H. Rigby (1995) 'Historical Causation: Is One Thing More Important than Another?', *History*, 80, pp. 227–42.

M. Stanford (1994) *A Companion to the Study of History* (Oxford: Blackwell).

J. Tosh (2008) *Why History Matters* (Basingstoke: Palgrave Macmillan).

J. Tosh (2015) *The Pursuit of History: Aims, Methods and New Directions in the Study of History*, 6th edn (London and New York: Routledge).

9

Archives

Federica Ferlanti

A long time ago (*BI*, before the Internet) while taking an MPhil in Cambridge I encountered the peculiar fixation historians have with archival materials. My supervisor was obsessed with archival sources, as became evident during never-ending sessions of translating Chinese early Republican archival documents into English. My two classmates and I ploughed through published collections of Chinese documents trying to make sense of the structure, vocabulary, meaning and context. Despite spending hours and hours preparing for those sessions, I often felt utterly miserable when in class we compared translations and I realized that I had misunderstood the text, or struggled to link it to the broader context. Our supervisor also lectured us about the archives in China and more specifically how and where to look for primary sources. I had never been to an archive, let alone to a Chinese archive!

This apprenticeship turned out to be crucial. Ironically, I too became 'addicted' to the thrilling experience of unearthing material in the archives. I still enjoy ploughing through Chinese documents that I have collected and continue to collect in archives around the world. Visiting archives is central to my research, because this is what historians do. This chapter explains the nature and purpose of archives, including what is not preserved and why. I explore issues around access to archives in the United Kingdom and abroad, with a specific focus on the People's Republic of China (PRC). Finally, I consider how archival documents can tell different 'truths' depending on how historians read and interpret them.

The nature and purpose of archives

Archives are places where various records are kept: documents, photographs, sound recordings, maps, newspapers, journals and now digital media are stored and catalogued according to systems that researchers need to understand and navigate. The type of documents held in a given archive depends on the nature of the archive. National archives, which every country maintains, contain documents concerning the State which are issued by different administrative bodies such as the Cabinet, ministries and specific committees, with records of government and politics, and material relating to diplomacy and the conduct of international affairs. These materials can be organized around specific collections and arranged according to geographical areas, time periods, topics and individuals. Archives do not contain everything, and the records collected in the archives consist of a selection of material; documents are kept because an individual or a government committee has made that very decision. The process of selecting what is kept in any given archive is therefore highly subjective and is based typically on the 'usefulness' of the material for the general public – individuals may need to refer to it for personal reasons such as in the case of title deeds, the census and so on.

The UK's National Archives, previously known as the Public Record Office, is located at Kew in west London. Counterparts can be found abroad: Les Archives Nationales in Paris (France), the Archivio Centrale dello Stato in Rome (Italy) and the Second Historical Archive in Nanjing (PRC), to name but three. There are archives which are devoted exclusively to specific subjects, such as the Imperial War Museum in London whose collections 'cover all aspects of twentieth and twenty-first century conflict involving Britain, the Commonwealth and other former empire countries'.[1] The British Library Newspapers Collections is another example of a specialized archival collection,[2] and if you happen to be interested in Italian visual history, the Archivio Storico Istituto Luce (Luce Institute Historical Archive) in Rome is the place to visit in order to access film and photographic records.[3]

Regional archives are also important places to explore. In Britain, these are customarily county archives, such as the Glamorgan Archives in Cardiff, which often hold material going back centuries, as well as more recent documents such as local newspapers, maps and posters.[4] There are also hidden gems in the archival collections of university and college libraries, such as the SCOLAR collection held in the Cardiff University Arts and Social Studies Library;[5] archives of individual companies and institutions at Cambridge University Library;[6] and family collections and personal papers held at Leeds University Library.[7] There are boundless possibilities and potential combinations for historians to pursue in archival research.

Archives devise systems to keep all their material in order. Typically, they list holdings in an electronic catalogue (although some archives may have only a printed version of their catalogue), and every item is given a reference number. Sometimes, not all the material has been catalogued. Often understaffed and short of funds, archives might be unable to keep up with the cataloguing process, and this may result in single items or whole groups of records not being catalogued. Historians need the reference number in order to request the records they wish to consult, but perhaps even more importantly they need to include this reference number and other relevant information in their footnotes to indicate from where they have taken a particular piece of information. The straightforward way to reference an archival source is by presenting it as it appears in the catalogue, and when in doubt staff can clarify issues surrounding the archives' referencing policy. Archives may require researchers to ask for permission before citing material, particularly when personal papers are involved, or request that they use a fixed turn of phrase. For example, the National Archives has a section on its website on how to cite and reference its records.[8] As a general rule, referencing of archival records should contain the name of the archives, location, the document's reference number, title and date: for instance, 'Second Historical Archives of China, Nanjing, PRC, 116/107 "Report to the Relief Committee on June 16th 1940 at 9pm" (報告二十九年六月十六日下午九時與賑濟委員會), June 1940'. In this example, the Archives use number 116 to identify the collection of documents grouped under the body of the Relief Committee, and 107 indicates the folder in which the record is kept.

Students are expected to reference both secondary works and primary sources thoroughly in their essays and dissertations. This is not only a matter of accuracy. By identifying where the source comes from, other historians can verify it and possibly use it to challenge or suggest a different interpretation of the source cited by colleagues. Sloppy referencing undermines the reliability of the research.

What is *not* preserved, what is made available, and why

Having established that archives may not contain an accurate or updated record of what they hold, we must turn our attention to the issues of what archives do *not* keep, and what historians *can* access. Historians need to weigh carefully what has been left out from any archival holding, and why. Material is routinely thrown away by archives because it is considered unimportant or without intrinsic historical value, and is also routinely destroyed by institutions before it even reaches the archives. The holdings of any archive are determined by these decisions. Someone has made, and others continue to make, judgements about what is valuable, and to throw away documents that at least in theory could still be of interest to historians. The MI5 website contains a section about retention and destruction of files which confirms that files identified as having historical interest are kept permanently and after thirty years transferred to the National Archives. It also acknowledges that the destruction of 175,000 files between 1909 and the early 1970s hampered some of MI5's investigative activities in the late 1960s.[9] One cannot help but wonder whether any of the destroyed documents might, under different circumstances, be deemed of historical value.

Even when historians make it as far as the archives, there is no guarantee that they will be allowed to see everything they want. Some materials are classified; the Public Records Act 1958 stipulated that British Cabinet papers could be transferred to the National Archives and made available to researchers or accessible to the wider public only after fifty years had elapsed. This was amended to thirty years in a second Public Records Act of 1967. A more recent piece of legislation, the Freedom of Information Act 2000, specifies that individuals can place a request to see a closed record, although the request can be denied on the basis of exemptions listed in the Act.[10] The restrictions applied to the Cabinet Papers have to do with sensitiveness and security. More broadly, the information contained in any archival record may be still politically sensitive, or is not disclosed to protect the reputations of institutions or individuals.

The political and historical context plays a fundamental part in the selection of materials which can now be accessed in the archives. Materials can be deemed compromising or dangerous at a specific point in time because they reveal activities which governments, institutions or individuals wish to keep secret. The destruction of documents following regime changes is a frequent occurrence. Following the fall of the Berlin Wall in 1989, the personnel of the Ministry of State Security (Stasi) in the German Democratic Republic destroyed large amounts of documents. As a result of this, the archives of the Stasi records in Berlin are not complete and there is an ongoing project to manually and visually reconstruct torn documents.[11] Even when regime changes are not involved, warfare and political upheavals may result in partial holdings in today's archives. The Second Historical Archives in Nanjing (PRC) is a national archive which holds the records of the central government in China between 1912 and 1949 (the Republican period). In this period, China experienced extreme internal and external conflict, including the War against Japan (1937–45) and the Civil War between the Nationalists and the Communists (1945–49). Although records concerning the wartime period are kept in this archive, historians who research this period are aware of the scale of destruction that took place at the time and therefore are mindful that records kept at the Second Historical Archives may provide a partial picture of the activities of the government in power. In addition, the Communist takeover in 1949 and the Cultural Revolution in 1966 which explicitly attacked the 'Four Olds'[12] have resulted in a further loss of historical records beyond the wartime context of the Republican period. Hence, whenever historians set foot in an archive, they are acutely aware that its records are by definition subjective and limited. The materials collected in archives must be evaluated and corroborated, and the findings combined with other sources.

The political context may also influence *when* records are made available to the public. This raises questions about the environments in which historians conduct their research. The highly publicized 'release' of wartime files from the Jilin Provincial Archives, for example, shows that the delay or release of archival records can serve purposes other than historical research. The Jilin Provincial Archives is located in the city of Changchun in the PRC. This north-east province, following the invasion of Manchuria by the Japanese in 1931, became part of the Manchurian State (Manzhouguo) set up by the Japanese government with its capital in Changchun. In recent times, the holdings of the Archives have captured the media's interest. In 2014, the English *People's Daily Online* reported the news issued by Xinhua (State Press Agency) that eighty-nine documents relating to the War against Japan from the Jilin Provincial Archives had been made public, among them twenty-five files related to the issue of 'comfort women'.[13] In a follow-up based on China's Newscom (Zhongxinguang), the *People's Daily Online* focused on the specific aspect of wartime 'atrocities' committed by the Japanese Army:

> The Jilin Provincial Archives has just released the latest research into 450 wartime documents. These documents, including 45,000 letters written in Japanese, were from the monthly postal review reports to the Japan's Kwantung Military Police Headquarters. Letters exchanged between Japanese people account for more than one half. The letters reveal Japanese army atrocities, strategic bombing, and plots to invade the Far East, and prove that the Japanese army also conducted chemical warfare and bacterial warfare in China. Based on the research, the Jilin Provincial Archives has published the first two of a series of books named The Monthly Postal Review Reports in the Jilin Provincial Archives during Japan's War of Aggression against China in Changchun, northeast China's Jilin Province. (Chinanews.com/Zhang Yao)[14]

This extract tells us that researchers at the Jilin Provincial Archives have conducted research on the War against Japan and have started publishing a multi-volume collection of documents. It is not specified whether the volumes can be purchased, but many archives publish edited volumes of sources, which are sold typically at the archives or in academic bookshops. An article on Reuters' US online edition published at the same time indicated that '[t]he publication comes during a fraught period in Japan-China relations'.[15] The first article on the Chinese media outlet was even more direct and explained that some files were made public 'as a response to Japan's right-wing politicians' denial of its wartime crimes in China'.[16]

It is highly unlikely that the volumes were prepared in a short amount of time simply to 'respond' to the contemporary political context. However, the existence of archival documents on 'comfort women' was framed publicly along the lines of a current political debate. In recent years, China's relations with Japan have been tense, and the War against Japan and its consequences are still felt strongly by the wider population. Given the context, it is unlikely that the timing of the announcement was coincidental, and this also explains the media's keen interest in the story. As this example shows, although all historians are pleased when new materials are released, after a natural frisson of excitement they need to ascertain the criteria used by researchers in selecting documents for publication (why some and not others?), and more crucially, whether the original files will also be open for consultation.

Access to archival material and archives

The Internet and modern technology have changed how researchers use archives, and have greatly benefitted them. The majority of archives have an online presence. Their websites are vital for gathering information about policy and regulations concerning access and use. More importantly, historians can do a great deal of preliminary work, such as establishing if the archives' holdings are relevant to their research topic, just by searching online catalogues. For instance, the 'Archives Hub' enables researchers to access descriptions of archives held at 250 Institutions in the UK, and the 'Discovery' search engine hosted by the National Archives website allows them to search records both in the National Archives and over 2,500 British archives.[17]

Moreover, many archives have digitized at least some of their records, driven by the need to preserve original records and the lack of storage space. Some records can be downloaded directly to one's computer either for free or upon paying a fee.[18] This is an invaluable gain for historians, as visiting a distant archive can be a costly experience. Paying a fee to download documents can be an effective and less expensive way to conduct research. However, it is rare for archives to digitize everything they hold and once again, there is a process of selection involved. The National Archives has so far digitized only around 5 per cent of its records. Some of these collections have been digitized in partnership with commercial publishers.[19] This is an important aspect of digitization of records and subsequent access to these holdings. In addition to their own papers, microfilms and digitized records, university libraries typically purchase digitized collections from archives, which can be accessed and downloaded for free by students and researchers through the university library network. This is nothing new; although the technology has changed and the quality of digitized documents tends to be superior to the microfilm form, university libraries have been developing collections of reproduced archival records for years. A case in point is Cardiff University Library's SCOLAR Collection, which includes sets of Cabinet papers of the UK Government on microfilm covering the period between 1920 and 1974.[20] A quick search through the SCOLAR online catalogue saves Cardiff-based researchers who are interested in British politics time-consuming and costly trips to the National Archives. Such collections are replicated at university libraries throughout the UK, and university library databases are an excellent starting point for students working on their undergraduate dissertations.[21]

In the PRC, where changing attitudes towards access and consultation keep historians well on their toes, communication through the Internet about recent visits to archives is an excellent way for researchers to stay on top of the latest developments, and can enhance their general knowledge and understanding. Information can be found by surfing academic websites and blogs. The *Dissertation Review* website with its section *Fresh from the Archives* is a fitting example.[22] The section circulates 'reviews' of archives or specific archival collections in the world and across fields of history. These reviews are written by academic researchers on the basis of first-hand experience.[23] The detailed review about the Shanghai Municipal Archives is an invaluable piece of 'intelligence' concerning access, holdings and retrieval policy for anyone planning a visit there. A further sub-section of *Recent Comments* provides researchers with the chance to chip in and offer updates, such as changes concerning access policy, and opens a window onto wider issues such as the latest widespread 'tightened access' to archives in the PRC.[24]

However, the amount of information and sources available on the Internet can be overwhelming and must be unpicked carefully. Web-based resources are arrows on the researcher's bowstring, but a direct visit to the archives often provides historians with a chance to uncover neglected or overlooked records. Figure 9.1 is a list of questions to consider before visiting an archive. Access to British archives is fairly straightforward. The National Archives requires a 'reader's ticket' in order to consult original documents, but archival material available online, on microfilm and on microfiche can be accessed without prior registration or a reader's ticket. Registration can be completed online six weeks prior to one's visit or at a computer terminal available in the reader registration room. In order to obtain the ticket two forms of identity, one proving name and the other proving address, must be produced.[25] Collections held at the Imperial War Museum which are not available online can be viewed by appointment after submitting an online form.[26] Students and academic staff can access for free the Archives and Special Collections at the School of Oriental and African Studies (SOAS) after obtaining a library card.[27]

- Does the archive hold the records I need to consult?

- Do I need to make an appointment to visit the archive?

- Do I need to take proof of identification or affiliation (such as a letter from my university) in order to access the archives?

- Are the records I need to consult held on-site, or will I need to order them in advance of my visit?

- What am I allowed to take into the archive? Are certain items, such as pens or digital cameras, restricted?

- How long will it take to read the relevant documents? Is more than one visit necessary?

- Is it possible to photograph or to photocopy documents, and is there a charge for these services?

FIGURE 9.1 *Preparing to visit the archives.*

Each country has different policies when it comes to accessing its archives, and there are also regional variations. As such historians in different places may enjoy different access rights, or lack research tools that we take for granted in British archives. Historians need flexibility and a great deal of patience to adapt to different sets of circumstances. Even though few of the readers of this volume will end up doing research in the PRC, it is likely that at least some will pursue research abroad in the future. The case study below illustrates how researchers who visit foreign archives need to make extra efforts to navigate the system, and explains how their ability to conduct research work can be affected by the history and political context of the country in which archives are held.

Archives in the People's Republic of China

The opening of archival records for consultation is celebrated by historians all over the world. However, few of us have an understanding of the extent and significance of the 'archival revolution' that has taken place in the PRC since the 1990s. Although archives were open to foreign researchers even before the 1990s, to a greater or lesser degree depending on the location and nature of the archives, the presence of foreign researchers gaining admission to the archives has grown exponentially as China has continued on the road of economic development and interaction with the outside world.

Chinese national archives are state archives, and formally there is no difference between the PRC's archives and those in any other country.

Archives exist at different administrative levels (national, provincial, municipal, county and sometimes district), and access varies greatly depending on their location and on the research topic one wishes to pursue.[28] If historians wish to see records concerning the Great Leap Forward in the Chinese Communist Party Archives in Beijing, it is likely that they will experience difficulties in accessing them. At provincial level and further down, much depends on local leadership and administrative personnel and, overall, on the capacity of individual researchers to build bridges at all levels with academic and institutional partners that may (or may not) facilitate the paperwork.

As in archives elsewhere, in the PRC what is kept in the national and local archives is the result of a selection decided upon by a limited number of people over time. However, the existence of a political and administrative system characterized by a one-party state offers additional challenges. If what is kept in the archives is a selection, then in a country ruled by one party the sources kept in the archives and the writing of its history are disproportionately affected by the party's ideological disposition rather than the variety of forces which typically influence the selection process. Since 1949, the state has controlled archival preservation and access to the archives, but state domination in the preservation of archival records and the 'greater interest in controlling than in preserving the historical records' preceded the Communist government and can be traced back to imperial China and the Republican period.[29] Nonetheless, the Chinese Communist Party had great interest in keeping under control channels of information, and the ideological change brought forth by the Communists in 1949 lent itself to a new approach in the writing of history and its use.

In the PRC, access to archival materials has been limited and closely vetted, particularly at times of political upheaval and international crisis. Having spent years doing research in Chinese archives since the 1990s, I witnessed the changes which occurred in this period, and have experienced a great deal of variation in accessing national and regional archives. The paperwork can vary. In some archives only a passport and a form filled upon arrival is needed; in other cases, the archives require a letter of introduction from one's home university; in yet other cases the scholar is required to produce a letter of invitation or, for a lengthy period of research, an affiliation to a central or local organization (for instance, a university or the Chinese Academy of Social Sciences and its local branches). At times, even when the paperwork was duly provided and with a central or local affiliation in place, I found myself with limited access to provincial archives, whereas in municipal archives I was granted unlimited access; other colleagues of mine have experienced the opposite. All of this shows that no one can be sure of what can be accessed until arrival in the archives.

A great deal of groundwork is needed to understand how different systems work, and it is good practice to prepare thoroughly before setting foot in any archives. Some central and regional archives may have a complete and accessible website, and in some instances catalogues can be searched online or in the archives, but in others it is time-consuming to establish what records an archive holds. Consulting printed guides to archives available in libraries or in the archives themselves is good place to start; in addition, collaborative staff can make a huge difference in determining whether a visit to the archives is fruitful. A diligent daily presence over an extended period of time is often needed to achieve good results. But even so, entire folders containing files can be deemed 'not open' without further explanation, and if it is necessary to see *those records* the only option is to be very flexible and even creative. Frustration, though understandable, does not get you anywhere. One approach is to work around *those records* by retrieving, for instance, a set of records issued on the same topic by different bodies and produced during the same time period. This is easier said than done, especially when, as I have experienced, archives do not grant access to the electronic catalogue. When this is the case, even a basic keyword search becomes impossible and all that is left are handwritten volumes of said catalogue which list the archival holdings. At this point, one may ask whether *those records* are after all kept somewhere else.

It is also important for historians to remember that the collection, classification and organization of archives are the result of historical processes, and this has a bearing on the research process. Following the defeat in the Civil War and Mao Zedong's proclamation of the founding of the PRC in October 1949, Chiang Kai-shek and the Nationalists left China and retreated to Taiwan. They took with them a bulk of documents concerning the Nationalist Party (Guomindang) and government which subsequently formed the archival collection on the Republican period in Taiwan. The diaspora of Republican documents must be taken into account when trying to locate records. For instance, historians conducting research in the Second Historical Archives in Nanjing may come across draft copies of a document which is held at the Academica Historica in Taipei (Taiwan). This allows historians to dig deeper even when some documents appear to have been lost, destroyed or are closed to access in one place, as with luck they may be available outside the PRC. In 2004, redacted copies of the Chiang Kai-shek Diaries (and Chiang Ching-kuo Diaries)[30] were loaned by the Chiang Kai-shek family to the Hoover Institution at Stanford University (USA), and made available for consultation. There are of course restrictions to access in place, and researchers are asked to sign an agreement before consulting them.[31] The Diaries draw researchers from all over the world and offer a valuable insight into individuals and events in China during the Republican period. Incidentally, Hoover has been involved lately in a lawsuit among Chiang's descendants concerning the deposit ownership.[32] This demonstrates that records held in archives are not inert objects consigned to a distant past, and their very existence can have unexpected repercussions in the present day.

Working in a high-pressure environment can be unsettling. Historians are not immune from developing idiosyncrasies which might be described as 'paranoid', and I count myself in this category. When conducting research abroad, I never pack copies of the documents I have collected in the archives in hold luggage, and always keep receipts from the archives in case I am asked to explain where the materials come from. Most hard copies are stamped by the archives, but digital ones may not carry this stamp, and after spending six months cooped up in an archive the last thing one wants is to lose those precious records. But sometimes unforeseen complications emerge. A couple of years ago, I purchased in Nanjing a number of academic books about the Nationalist Party and the Republican period, and proceeded to send the parcel home from the post office nearest to my hotel. The parcel was left open for the customary inspection and I was surprised by the reaction of the clerk who, after looking at the titles, explained that he needed to get authorization from the line manager. One book in particular – a guide to local archives – had raised strong interest. I had sent books from several post offices across China over a period of ten years and I had never before experienced this level of scrutiny. I realized, however, that I had mostly sent books from post offices located in university compounds where, it stands to reason, the personnel are accustomed to visiting scholars sending books. In the end, the parcel was authorized and started its long journey to the UK. The experience left me a touch self-conscious and has taught me to be more discerning in my choice of post offices!

Doing research outside the comfort of one's own country can be challenging, but also extremely rewarding. Researchers need to find out how the system works and how to navigate it. In some cases conditions may change abruptly due to the political context and, despite there being a central system in place, there is a degree of variation between archives and accessibility to records. Although a great deal of information can be gathered from publications and the Internet, personal experience is key to understanding the breadth and nature of the archival records we, as historians, require in order to pursue original research. Flexibility, patience, people skills and humility can often enhance the chances of retrieving records.

Do archival documents tell historians the 'truth'?

The process of analysis and interpretation of archival documents is central to the historian's work. Novices tend to have a reverential respect towards documents and often assume that, because they are kept in archives and issued by official bodies, the information or data they contain is 'truthful' and impartial. This assumption is mistaken. Archival materials ought to undergo the scrutiny one applies to all historical sources.[33] Questions about authorship, contextualization, audience and possible omissions (intentional and unintentional) are in order. As Garthine Walker and Kevin Passmore show elsewhere in this volume, even though historians may ask identical questions, their understanding and interpretation of the sources can lead to different conclusions. Often, historians ask different questions of the sources, and what questions are asked depends on the historian's perspective. This explains why historians often differ in the way they approach, read and build arguments from sources. Take for instance the debate surrounding the Great Leap Forward and its consequences.

The Great Leap Forward (GLF) was part of the Second Five-Year Plan and was launched by Mao Zedong in 1958. Its main objective was to boost the Chinese economy by mobilizing the masses. Peasants were organized into communes with the aim of increasing agricultural production to support a strong growth in industrial production. The GLF saw the mobilization of millions in the countryside with tragic consequences; the famine which followed claimed the lives of millions of people.[34] Issues surrounding the extent of the death toll triggered by the GLF and the famine, the chain of command (who knew what?) and the impact of party policies are still sensitive. As a result, historians have often encountered difficulties in gaining access to relevant archival documents, in particular at central government level.

Recently, Frank Dikötter has provided an in-depth analysis of the consequences of the Leap and has argued 'that at least 45 million people died unnecessarily between 1958 and 1962'.[35] Dikötter's *Mao's Great Famine: The History of China's Most Devastating Catastrophe, 1958–62* (2010) is unique because it is based on sources gathered from archives at central and provincial levels in the PRC. These include not only official documents, but also records of 'letters from ordinary people', 'investigations into cases of corruption' and 'general reports on peasant resistance'.[36] In addition, Dikötter has made use of archival materials from other countries and interviews.[37] Overall, the range of sources is remarkable, and Dikötter has been praised for his extensive work in the archives. However, he has been criticized for drawing certain conclusions on the basis of these archival sources. Cormac Ó Gráda, an economic historian with expertise in the study of famines, has found faults with Dikötter's aggregation and interpretation of data. Ó Gráda argued that a number of factors significant for determining the causes of famine and interpreting the data (including China's poverty and economic conditions, causes of death, the unreliability of data concerning birth and death rates and other demographic patterns, weather conditions, and lack of data) from the worst-hit provinces had not been taken into account in Dikötter's analysis.[38] Who are we to 'believe'?

These historians approach the topic of famine during the GLF from different perspectives. Dikötter focuses on the bigger picture of the man-made catastrophe which hit China, its consequences and Mao Zedong's personal responsibilities in perpetuating the famine. Cormac Ó Gráda focuses on the methodology which famine historians should adopt when collating and interpreting data. They diverge on how to understand and use the sources. In the end, the differences in their approaches show that the sources can be read in many ways. There is no self-evident meaning in any source; it is the historian's interpretation that builds an argument. Historians challenge each other's interpretations and they reach different conclusions. Archival documents can potentially tell us a variety of 'truths': the 'truth' elected by the individuals or bodies who have written them, and the 'truth' elected by historians who analyse them.

Conclusion

Archival documents are an excellent source of raw materials on which to base original historical research, but there are also intrinsic limitations to the records kept in the archives and their nature. A limited number of records are kept in the archives and what *is* kept is the result of a process of selection decided upon by individuals, dictated by political context and subject to historical events that may cause materials to be excluded or even destroyed. Furthermore, historical events such as wars or regime changes may lead to further loss of materials. State archives are particularly dependent on government decisions; documents remain classified if they contain information which is politically sensitive for institutions or individuals. The fact that a document is kept in an archive does not make its content any more 'true' than a source gathered elsewhere, and it should undergo the same process of scrutiny as any other kind of document by the historian who wishes to use it. Archival documents present us with a wide range of information, but what they can tell us is always dependent on the historian's interpretation. Ultimately, this is what makes the historian's work so precious, fulfilling and exciting.

STUDY QUESTIONS

- What types of documents do archives hold?
- Why is it important to reference sources accurately?
- Does the political and historical context play a part in what is kept in the archives and made available to historians?
- What are the potential challenges of conducting research in the archives?

Notes

1   Imperial War Museums: Collection and Research: http://www.iwm.org.uk/
     collections-research. Accessed 16 January 2016.

2   British Library: Newspaper Collections: http://www.bl.uk/newspapers.
     Accessed 16 January 2016.

3   Archivio Storico Istituto Luce: http://www.archivioluce.com/archivio/#n.
     Accessed 16 January 2016.

4   Glamorgan Archives/Archifau Morgannwg: http://www.glamarchives.gov.uk/.
     Accessed 16 January 2016.

5   Cardiff University Information Services: Special Collections and Archives
     (SCOLAR): http://www.cardiff.ac.uk/insrv/libraries/scolar/. Accessed
     16 January 2016.

6   Cambridge University Library: Jardine Matheson Archive: http://janus.lib.cam.
     ac.uk/db/node.xsp?id=EAD/GBR/0012/MS%20JM. Accessed 16 January 2016.

7   Leeds University Library: Liddle Collection Guide (personal papers from First
     and Second World War): http://library.leeds.ac.uk/special-collections-liddle-
     collection. Accessed 16 January 2016.

8   The National Archives: Citing Documents in the National Archives:
     http://www.nationalarchives.gov.uk/records/citing-documents.htm. Accessed
     16 January 2016.

9   Security Service MI5: Managing Information: https://www.mi5.gov.uk
     /managing-information. Accessed 24 May 2016.

10   The National Archives: Cabinet Papers 1915–1986: http://www.
     nationalarchives.gov.uk/cabinetpapers/cabinet-gov/meetings-papers.htm; The
     National Archives: Freedom of Information Act 2000: http://www.legislation.
     gov.uk/ukpga/2000/36/contents. Both accessed 16 January 2016.

11   Federal Commissioner for the Records of the State Security Service
     of the Former German Democratic Republic: The Reconstruction
     of Torn Documents: http://www.bstu.bund.de/EN/Archives/
     ReconstructionOfShreddedRecords/_node.html. Accessed 16 January 2016.

12   The 'Four Olds' were 'old customs, old habits, old culture, and old thinking'.
     See J. D. Spence (1999) *The Search for Modern China*, 2nd edn (New York:
     W.W. Norton), p. 575.

13   'Archives Reveal "Comfort Women" Official Actions of Japan', *People's Daily
     Online*, 26 April 2014: http://english.peopledaily.com.cn/90785/8610818.
     html. Accessed 16 January 2016. The expression 'comfort women' indicates
     girls and women forced into sexual slavery by the Japanese Imperial Army in
     occupied territories.

14   'Jilin Releases New Research on Japan's War of Aggression against China',
     People's Daily Online, 7 July 2014: http://english.people.com.cn/n/2014/0707/
     c98649-8751864.html. Accessed 16 January 2016.

15   A. Harney, 'China Releases Japanese Wartime Documents: State Media',
     Reuters US, 27 April 2014: http://www.reuters.com/article/2014/04/27/us-
     china-japan-war-idUSBREA3Q02220140427. Accessed 16 January 2016.

16 'Archives Reveal "Comfort Women" Official Actions of Japan'.

17 Archives Hub: http://www.archiveshub.ac.uk/ and The National Archives: Discovery: http://discovery.nationalarchives.gov.uk/. Both accessed 16 January 2016.

18 See, for instance, the British Library: British Newspaper Archive: http://www. britishnewspaperarchive.co.uk/. Accessed 16 January 2016.

19 The National Archives: Our Online Records: http://www.nationalarchives.gov. uk/records/our-online-records.htm. Accessed 16 January 2016.

20 Cardiff University Information Services: Cabinet Papers (20th C.): http:// www.cardiff.ac.uk/insrv/libraries/scolar/special/cabinet.html. Accessed 16 January 2016.

21 Undergraduates and postgraduates enrolled in British universities can gain access to participating libraries nationwide through SCONUL Access. SCONUL: SCONUL Access: http://www.sconul.ac.uk/sconul-access. Accessed 16 January 2016.

22 Dissertation Reviews: http://dissertationreviews.org/. Accessed 16 January 2016.

23 Dissertation Reviews: Fresh from the Archives: http://dissertationreviews.org/ fresh-from-the-archives. Accessed 16 January 2016.

24 M. Cunningham, 'Denying Historians: China's Archives Increasingly Off-Bounds', *The Wall Street Journal*, 19 August 2014: http://blogs.wsj.com/ chinarealtime/2014/08/19/denying-historians-chinas-archives-increasingly-off-bounds/. Accessed 16 January 2016.

25 The National Archives: Will I Need a Reader's Ticket?: http://www. nationalarchives.gov.uk/visit/readers-ticket.htm. Accessed 16 January 2016.

26 Imperial War Museums: Our Research Facilities: http://www.iwm.org.uk/ collections-research/research-facilities. Accessed 16 January 2016.

27 SOAS Library: Access to Archives & Special Collections: http://www. soas.ac.uk/library/archives/services/access-to-collections/. Accessed 16 January 2016.

28 For a detailed discussion on the history and organization of archives in the PRC, see W. Ye and J. W. Esherick (1996) *Chinese Archives: An Introductory Guide* (Berkeley, Los Angeles: University of California Press).

29 Ye and Esherick, *Chinese Archives*, p. 5 and p. 12.

30 Chiang Ching-kuo was Chiang Kai-shek's son.

31 See the overview, inclusive of restrictions and agreement for Chiang Kai-shek Diaries, at Online Archive of California: Inventory of the Chiang Kai-Shek Diaries: http://www.oac.cdlib.org/findaid/ark:/13030/kt438nc7np/?query=Chiang+%28Kai-shek%29+diaries. Accessed 16 January 2016.

32 See, for instance, the Hoover Institution, Stanford University, Chiang Kai-shek Diaries: http://www.hoover.org/library-archives/collections/chiang-kai-shek-diaries; 'Stanford Seeks Court Help to Solve Ownership Claims of Chiang Diaries', *University Herald*, 26 September 2013: http://www.universityherald. com/articles/4673/20130926/stanford-university-courtownership-claims-chiang-diaries.htm#ixzz3eFwsP7Uf, and 'Inheritance of Chiangs' Diaries

Sparks Dispute', *Taipei Times*, 2 December 2010: http://www.taipeitimes.com/
News/taiwan/archives/2010/12/02/2003489938. All accessed 16 January 2016.

33   For a detailed discussion about source interpretation, see J. Tosh with S. Lang
     (2006) *The Pursuit of History: Aims, Methods and New Directions in the
     Study of Modern History*, 4th edn (Harlow: Pearson Longman), pp. 60–3.

34   Spence, *The Search for Modern China*, pp. 548–50 and p. 553.

35   F. Dikötter (2010) *Mao's Great Famine: The History of China's Most
     Devastating Catastrophe, 1958–62* (London: Bloomsbury), Preface, p. x.

36   Dikötter, 'Essay on Sources', in *Mao's Great Famine*, p. 342.

37   Dikötter, 'Essay on Sources', in *Mao's Great Famine*, pp. 345–6.

38   C. Ó Gráda (2011), 'A Review Essay: Mao's Great Famine: The History
     of China's Most Devastating Catastrophe, 1958–1962 by Frank Dikötter',
     Population and Development Review, 37:1; see also F. Wemheuer (2011) 'Sites
     of Horror: Mao's Great Famine [with Response]', *The China Journal*, p. 66.

Further Reading

J. H. Arnold (2000) *History: A Very Short Introduction* (Oxford and New York:
    Oxford University Press), pp. 35–57.

A. Burton (ed.) (2005) *Archive Stories: Facts, Fictions, and the Writing of History*
    (Durham, NC and London: Duke University Press).

M. Donnelly and C. Norton (2011) *Doing History* (London and New York:
    Routledge), pp. 65–82 and 117–36.

R. Harrison, A. Jones and P. Lambert (2004) 'Methodology: "Scientific" History
    and the Problem of Objectivity', in P. Lambert and P. Schofield (eds), *Making
    History: An Introduction to the History and Practices of a Discipline* (London
    and New York: Routledge), pp. 26–37.

L. Jordanova (2006) *History in Practice*, 2nd edn (London: Hodder Arnold),
    pp. 150–72.

J. Tosh (2010) *The Pursuit of History: Aims, Methods and New Directions in the
    Study of Modern History*, 5th edn (Harlow: Pearson Education), pp. 88–146.

10

Documents, Editions and Translations

Helen J. Nicholson

Historians usually draw their evidence from written documents of some sort. Since ancient times, scholars have accepted that contemporary, preferably eyewitness records provide the most reliable source of evidence for past events. This means that all historians must base their work on original documents from the historical period that they are studying. Very often, however, they will rely on published documents that have been edited or even translated, rather than the originals. As historians, we need to ask what impact using such edited documents has on the accuracy of our work.[1]

In historical terms, a document is a written record, but it need not be written on paper. Before the invention of the typewriter, most documents were not printed, so historians must learn their subjects' handwriting as well as their language. These original documents were written in the language of their creators, following the conventions for writing then in use. Sometimes they were created as a temporary record and were never intended for later generations to decipher.

As many of the published documents studied by students at university have gone through a process of editing and possibly translation, what the student sees on the printed page has already been partially interpreted, even before the student lays eyes on it. It can be difficult to work out what is from the original document and what has been introduced by the editor. So students must not take documents at face value, but what *is* the face value of a document?

Documents

Professional historians find many of the original documents for their research in archives, which have been discussed in the previous chapter. Many others are in libraries, having already been published – perhaps centuries ago. Having got her hands on an original document, the first thing for the historian to consider is the document as a physical object. She should examine the material of the document (paper? parchment? cloth? clay? wood? stone?). This could indicate the significance of the document to its creator: whether it was intended to be kept, or was a temporary record. So, fourteenth-century English legal records were generally recorded on parchment, which lasts for centuries; while personal letters sent by members of the garrison of the Roman military camp at Vindolanda were written on wooden tablets, and intended to be temporary. On the other hand, this could simply indicate what was available to the document's creator: for example, novels published in Britain during the Second World War were printed on cheap paper because paper was scarce in wartime.

The historian should also look at the physical context of the document: that is, what other documents are with this one. Has it been filed or bound with other documents? Bindings may be contemporary, but often documents were rebound by later collectors. The binding gives an indication of how the document was used at some point in its history, but not necessarily how it was used when it was first created. For example, a modern archive might group documents relating to the same estate together, but originally those documents were produced at different times by different people for different purposes. A modern library may bind series of weekly magazines together, but few of the original readers would have read successive issues side-by-side. A 1920s publisher might have issued several best-selling novels together under a single binding, giving a modern historian an insight into the expected readership of those novels.

Having examined the physical shape and context of the document, the historian can start to read it – or at least try to read it. An old document may have been damaged by water, mice or poor storage, so that parts are no longer legible. Handwritten documents from any period of history can be extremely difficult to read. An early twentieth-century letter-writer writing to a friend did not need to produce a document that an outsider could read, and the resulting scrawl might be almost undecipherable to a stranger. Thirteenth-century English government records were written in a characteristic record-keeping script, which was heavily abbreviated in order to save time and parchment. Virtually illegible to the casual eye, like modern shorthand this is easy to read when you have learnt the code – but first you must learn it.

Battling with old shorthand or modern scrawl is all very well for the professional researcher, but students at university normally study published works, on paper or online. If the document was originally unpublished, this published text will have been edited by a skilled researcher, to make it readily available to other scholars and students. Even works that were originally published, such as the publications of William Caxton (c. 1415x24–92, the first Englishman to print books), may be re-published in modern format and with a modern commentary to make them more accessible to modern readers.

Editions

An edited text is intended to produce an accessible version of a historical document, so that researchers can consult a printed text rather than the inaccessible, indecipherable original. It may combine several versions of a document, showing how they relate to each other and how the final versions of the document were developed. A published edition also allows the original documents to be preserved, rather than researchers repeatedly handling these unique or rare and fragile historic artefacts.

However, the production of an edited text involves a process of interpretation and analysis by the editor. When you read a printed edition of a historic text, you are reading the editor's interpretation of how that text should be read and used. Any interpretations you then put upon that printed edition are to some extent dependent on decisions already made by the editor.

The first decision an editor makes is that a certain document should be made more widely available. But which document should be selected? The catalogue of any archive contains thousands, even millions, of unpublished documents, of which only a handful will ever be published. It may appear easy to point out the 'bias' in a text, which reflects the original author's own views. Yet the chance which leads to one document being published while another is not can skew future students' view of events in the past more effectively than any biased author.

Editors select documents on the basis of their apparent significance for the study of history. They might select important diplomatic records, the writings of significant persons, representative records of taxation, records of significant legal cases, accounts and analyses of important events written by contemporaries of those events, the archives of influential national and international institutions, personal letters, diaries, personal wills, popular novels – in fact any document that casts significant light on a particular area of history.

Of course, researchers differ in what they regard as significant. Researchers who are interested in the development of Parliament are unlikely to regard the court records from a small village in Northamptonshire (for example) as significant. However, the gender historian Judith Bennett used the court records from the Northamptonshire village of Brigstock to re-create the life of

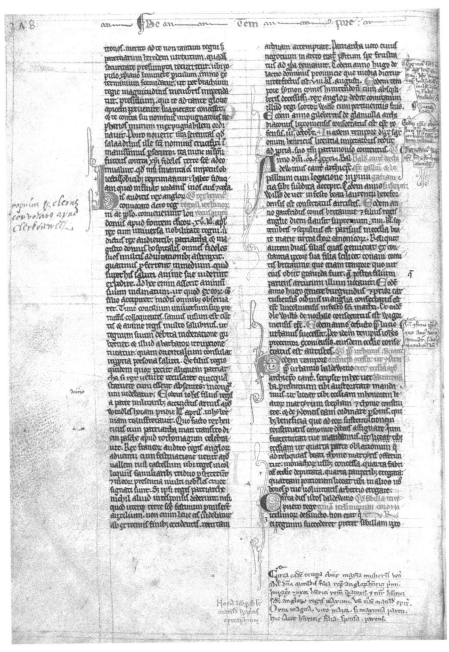

FIGURE 10.1a and b *The famous medieval monk-commentator Matthew Paris (d. 1259) enlivened his work with marginal illustrations of the events he described. He crammed his illustration of the Battle of Hattin (1187) in his* Chronica Majora *into the bottom right-hand corner of his folio, but modern reproductions generally present it as if it were placed in prime position on the page, giving a false impression of its importance in the original volume.*

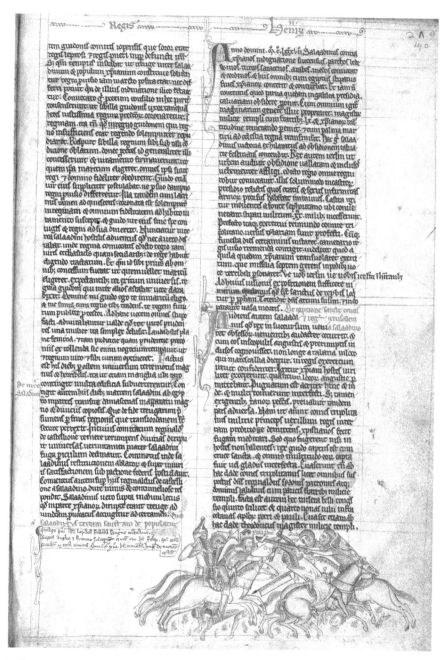

Parker Library, CCCC MS 26 folios 139v and 140r: reproduced with permission of The Master and Fellows of Corpus Christi College, Cambridge.

Cecilia Penifader (c. 1295–1344), a non-noble medieval woman – a member of a section of society which is virtually unmentioned in contemporary historical accounts.[2] Would-be editors' selection of documents is a personal choice, reflecting their own research interests: but other researchers would probably have made a different selection. As the majority of documents remain unread and unknown, we cannot be certain that those which have been chosen are representative of the rest.

Having chosen the documents, the next question is how they should be published. Some documents can be satisfactorily reproduced in photographs, which can be published in printed form or in digital form online. Photographs are a good means of reproducing and distributing a document if it is short and the text is easy to read, and if the document is readily understandable without additional information. However, many documents are not, perhaps because they are not in a modern language, or are difficult to read, or because additional information is required to interpret them. What is more, if there are several different versions of the document, photographs will only allow the reader to compare them; it will not show the reader how the various versions relate to each other. A published edition will involve analysis of the original documents to establish how they link together.

Having decided that an edition is needed, how does the original document become a published text? The answer might seem obvious – copy what is there! But this can be easier said than done.[3]

If the original document includes diagrams or drawings, how should the editor deal with these? If they are not integral to the text, editors usually leave them out, perhaps indicating in a footnote that there was a picture in the original. This means that highly illustrated documents, such as the works of the famous medieval monk-commentator Matthew Paris (d. 1259), shown above in Figure 10.1a and b, or Guillaume Caoursin's eyewitness account of the Ottoman Turks' siege of Rhodes in 1480, are generally published without their illustrations, or with only a select few. The illustrations may be published in a separate part of the book, or in a separate volume.[4] Yet, without the context of the text, it is difficult to appreciate how the original readers would have interpreted them. In such cases, online publication of the original document can allow modern readers to see what the original looked like, while the printed edition allows them to read it. However, for long documents or large collections of documents it is impractical to include photographs of the complete original text in the printed book, although it may be possible to reproduce these online.[5]

Sometimes the illustrations are such a key part of the text that it is incomprehensible without them. The Bayeux Tapestry is a document that includes text, but the text makes little sense without the images on the tapestry. The correspondence of the Scottish scientist Joseph Black (1728–99) contains calculations, lists of figures from scientific observations, accounts and diagrams to illustrate his points. The published edition of his letters includes all these details, carefully positioned in relation to the text so that the modern reader sees something like the original form of the letter.[6] However, the cost of producing such an edition is enormous, and so the purchase price is correspondingly high.

Whether or not the original text has illustrations, the editor will have to decide how far she is prepared to amend the original to make it easily understood by modern readers. If the text does not make sense, should she 'correct' it? Should she fill in gaps? Modern editors prefer to keep 'corrections' to a minimum.

If the text is repetitive, should she simply summarize it? On the other hand, if the text is abbreviated, should the editor resolve the abbreviations, or leave the text as it was originally written? For example, each letter of the text of *Domesday Book* (1086), as shown in Figure 10.2 below, is clear, but each entry is very heavily abbreviated. If the editor leaves the abbreviations as they stand, non-experts will need some guidance to understand the text, such as notes in the margin or at the bottom of the page. Most scholars agree that it is easier to resolve all abbreviations and present readers with a complete text. Normally this is easily done, although sometimes it is not clear what the complete word should be! But resolving the abbreviations raises another problem.

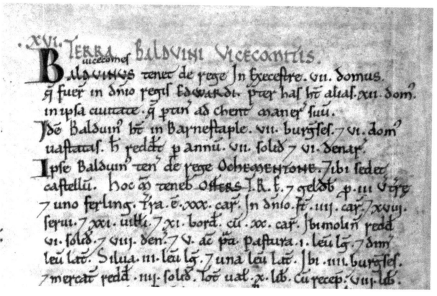

FIGURE 10.2 *The entry in* Domesday Book *for Okehampton illustrates the heavily abbreviated nature of the text: The National Archives E 31/2/1 fol. 105v.*

Where the text is heavily abbreviated, producing a complete text without any abbreviations gives readers a false impression of the document. They certainly see the information that was in the document, but not as it was originally presented. To take a modern example, consider these two sentences:

'Shall I or sh'an't I?' – 'Don't do it'.

If we resolve the abbreviations, this reads as:

'Shall I or shall I not?' – 'Do not do it'.

Resolving the abbreviations changes the tone of the text from casual banter to a formal conversation. Similar issues could arise with any historical text.

The editor could try to get around this problem by indicating where she has resolved abbreviations; if readers can see how the text has been changed, they can imagine how the original readers would have seen it. The drawback is that the printed words become difficult to read.

A similar problem arises over spelling and capitalization. Modern readers prefer consistent spelling, and they expect all personal names to have a capital letter and other nouns to start with a lower-case letter. But when the document was written, conventions may have been completely different, using different spelling of names each time they appeared, or with all nouns capitalized or none. Should the modern editor follow modern conventions or those in use when the document was created? Should the editor of a new edition of Jane Austen's novels (for example) modernize the spelling? Changing the text to match modern conventions may make it easier for modern readers to understand, but it also creates a false impression of the past.

Even twentieth-century documents can present challenges to a modern student's expectations. A modern reader studying the autobiography of Guy Gibson, *Enemy Coast Ahead* (1944), may be shocked by the name of the wartime hero's dog, a black Labrador whom Gibson called by a colloquial form of the Latin word for black. As that word is now highly offensive, should a modern editor remove it?

Clearly, these editorial decisions can make a considerable difference to the final text. So in the introduction to the edition the conscientious editor will set out the conventions she has followed, to allow readers to understand how the text has been amended. Not all editors provide this information, but readers must remember that some amendments will have been made. The editor should also point out what has been omitted from the published edition, such as illustrations in the original document, or additions in the margins (marginalia). She may also mention aspects of the document which cannot be reproduced on the printed page, such as where the document has been heavily worn (this might indicate that a particular part of the document has been read more than the rest).

The editor will also have to decide how much additional information to include with the text to enable readers to interpret it for themselves. Should he identify every person named, every place and every allusion which will not be immediately familiar to the reader? He must decide what he can assume as standard knowledge and what a non-expert will not know. This information may be included in the introduction to the edition, or put into footnotes or endnotes. If the editor gives too much information, he will find that some of his notes fill a whole page – but if he does not give enough information, readers will be confused. Readers must also bear in mind that the information that the editor provides will reflect his own interpretation of the text.

Critical editions

What if there is more than one version of the original text?[7] If the document is a personal letter, or a government record – for example, a tax return – there is probably only one copy. But before the invention of the printing press in the fifteenth century, every copy of a book had to be copied out by hand, and each scribe wrote slightly differently. Sometimes scribes added or removed information. Sometimes they made mistakes, such as accidentally leaving out a few lines of the text they were copying. The modern editor has to compare the various surviving versions, analysing them to decide which variant of the text to prefer, and producing a *critical edition*.

The aim of a critical edition is often to reconstruct the original text as written by the original author. However, texts which began in an oral form may not have had an identifiable original author, and as texts were copied and recopied they developed new forms to meet the requirements of new generations, which may be just as interesting to historians as the non-existent 'original' text. If a text clearly went through several formative stages, the editor may decide to print more than one version: so when William Roach produced a critical edition of three of the continuations of Chrétien de Troyes's adventure-romance *Perceval* (c. 1191), he printed three quite different versions of the first continuation.[8]

It is easy to understand why many critical editions are of texts that survive in just a few manuscripts. Locating every surviving manuscript of a text is a time-consuming business. The editor has to copy the manuscripts, often from photographs, then compare them, and so decide which version of the text to print as the main text and which versions are subsidiary. Where a text was frequently copied and circulated widely, it is so difficult and time-consuming to produce a comprehensive critical edition that it may be impossible for a single scholar to complete the work in a lifetime. As a result, there is no critical edition of many of the books which were best known in the middle ages. Instead, scholars rely on early printed versions, or printed editions based on just one or two manuscripts. But of course these editions only represent one version of the text that medieval people knew.

For example, in the second half of the twelfth century Archbishop William of Tyre wrote a history of the crusader kingdom of Jerusalem which covered the period from the First Crusade (1095–99) to 1184. He wrote in Latin, the language of the educated elite, but in the early thirteenth century his history was translated into French and circulated widely: it has been estimated that nearly every castle and major town in Western Europe would have known this work.[9] Later writers added to his history, and over seventy manuscripts survive of the French translation with different continuations. Clearly, this was the version of the history of the crusader states familiar to thirteenth-century Europeans – it would have influenced their view of the Crusades, of Islam and of the Middle East as a whole. However, because the work was so widely read and so many different versions survive in manuscript form, producing a modern critical edition is a difficult task. In the meantime, scholars refer to nineteenth-century editions, based on just a handful of manuscripts. And even when a critical edition is published, as the text is in medieval French students will ask for a translation: which brings us to the next problem.

Translations

The translator's lot is not a happy one. She must produce a text which a modern reader finds accessible and interesting, without losing the meaning of the original text. That original was the product of a very different society and culture, with expectations very different from those of a modern readership. The translator must be familiar with the society from which the original text came, and able to translate its concepts and concerns into language which modern readers will understand. She must try to understand what the original author intended to say and then render that intention into modern English.

To make matters more difficult, the original language of the text may not be amenable to straightforward translation. To take the case of the Old French translations of William of Tyre, thirteenth-century French was still developing into a literary language. It was not yet well suited to sophisticated narratives; its vocabulary was limited and its users struggled to express complex theological or scientific concepts. The modern translator must decide whether to translate using the same limited vocabulary and stilted style, or whether to use the wider range of vocabulary and lucid style that modern English offers. Most readers would prefer the latter, but they will then miss the direct simplicity of the original prose.

Translators also have to decide whether to retain the sentence structure of their original, or to use a modern sentence structure. Medieval writers piled phrase upon phrase, so that a sentence could be as long as a modern paragraph. Modern readers would prefer shorter sentences, but – yet again – some of the character of the text is lost when the flowing phrases are cut up.

The translator must also beware of 'false friends'. Many words have changed their meaning over the centuries. Translators need to read widely in literature written at the same period as the text they are translating, to learn the idiom of the time and how words were used. Dictionaries and a thesaurus are essential tools.

With all this in mind, it is not surprising that no two translators agree on the best translation of a text. Many students are disturbed to find how much translations of the same text can differ, and assume that one must be 'right' and the others 'wrong'. Every translator knows that there is no 'right' translation of a text; every translation is 'wrong' to some degree. The question is – how much is it wrong? Because only an expert in the original language can answer that question, the best way to find out the accuracy of a translation is to learn the original language and then translate it yourself!

Conclusion

Primary sources are historians' raw material, on which our analysis of the past is based. Through studying primary sources historians develop their own interpretation of past events, rather than being reliant on other scholars' work. Yet, as this chapter has shown, the printed historical documents that students analyse at university have already been through many stages of interpretation. They have been selected from a vast number of other possible documents and then converted into a form suitable to read on a printed page. Illustrations and annotations from the original document have probably been removed. The printed document may be a combination of several surviving versions of the document, which have been critically analysed by the editor and assembled to produce the 'best' text. Documents may have been further interpreted through being translated, or through supporting analysis by the editor.

With all this in mind, students may decide that they would prefer to go back to the original documents, rather than relying upon the judgement and guidance of the unseen editor. Of course, they will then have to learn editorial skills for themselves. Alternatively, they may read the editor's introduction critically, note what the editor tells them about the editorial process and then analyse the edition as thoroughly as they would analyse an original document. In doing this, they will develop their own skills as historians.

STUDY QUESTIONS

- Why is it important for students to understand the processes of selection and interpretation involved in producing collections of documents, critical editions and translations?
- What kinds of historical skills must editors and translators deploy when producing such collections?
- What kinds of historical skills must students deploy when interpreting sources taken from such collections?

Notes

1   Much of this chapter is based on my research for my edition of *The Proceedings against the Templars in the British Isles*, 2 vols (Farnham: Ashgate, 2011).

2   J. M. Bennett (1999) *A Medieval Life: Cecilia Penifader of Brigstock, c. 1295–1344* (Boston, MA: McGraw-Hill College).

3   For further discussion of some of the problems set out below, see P. D. A. Harvey (2001) *Editing Historical Records* (London: British Library); R. F. Hunnisett (1977) *Editing Records for Publication* (London: British Records Association).

4   See, for example: R. Vaughan (1994) *The Illustrated Chronicles of Matthew Paris: Observations of Thirteenth-Century Life*, new edn (Stroud: Sutton); S. Lewis (1987) *The Art of Matthew Paris in the 'Chronica Majora'* (Berkeley: University of California Press); J.-B. de Vaivre and L. Vissière (eds) (2014) *Tous les deables d'enfer: relations du siege de Rhodes par les Ottomans en 1480* (Geneva: Droz): illuminations, integral to the original text, are published as plates separately from the text.

5   For example, D. Munro (ed.) (2013) *A German Third Crusader's Chronicle of His Voyage and the Siege of Almohad Silves, 1189 AD/ Muwahid Xelb, 585 AH: De Itinere Navali* (No place: Antimony), includes black and white photographs in the printed book, and a colour reproduction of the sole manuscript in the e-book.

6   R. G. W. Anderson and J. Jones (eds) (2012) *The Correspondence of Joseph Black*, 2 vols (Farnham: Ashgate).

7   For further discussion see, for example, R. B. C. Huygens (2000) *Ars Edendi: A Practical Introduction to Editing Medieval Latin Texts* (Turnhout: Brepols).

8   W. Roach (ed.) (1952–1983) *The Continuations of the Old French* Perceval *of Chrétien de Troyes*, 5 vols (Philadelphia, PA: American Philosophical Society), vols 1–3. The *Continuations* were composed between c. 1191 and c. 1230.

9   R. H. C. Davis (1973) 'William of Tyre', in D. Baker (ed.), *Relations between East and West in the Middle Ages* (Edinburgh: Edinburgh University Press), p. 71.

Further Reading

R. G. W. Anderson and J. Jones (eds) (2012) *The Correspondence of Joseph Black*, 2 vols (Farnham: Ashgate).

J. M. Bennett (1999) *A Medieval Life: Cecilia Penifader of Brigstock, c. 1295–1344* (Boston, MA: McGraw-Hill College).

R. H. C. Davis (1973) 'William of Tyre', in D. Baker (ed.), *Relations between East and West in the Middle Ages* (Edinburgh: Edinburgh University Press), pp. 64–76.

P. D. A. Harvey (2001) *Editing Historical Records* (London: British Library).

R. F. Hunnisett (1977) *Editing Records for Publication* (London: British Records Association).

R. B. C. Huygens (2000) *Ars Edendi: A Practical Introduction to Editing Medieval Latin Texts* (Turnhout: Brepols).

S. Lewis (1987) *The Art of Matthew Paris in the 'Chronica Majora'* (Berkeley: University of California Press).

D. Munro (ed.) (2013) *A German Third Crusader's Chronicle of His Voyage and the Siege of Almohad Silves, 1189 AD/ Muwahid Xelb, 585 AH: De Itinere Navali* (No place: Antimony).

W. Roach (ed.) (1952–1983) *The Continuations of the Old French* Perceval *of Chrétien de Troyes*, 5 vols (Philadelphia, PA: American Philosophical Society).

J.-B. de Vaivre and L. Vissière (eds) (2014) *Tous les deables d'enfer: relations du siege de Rhodes par les Ottomans en 1480* (Geneva: Droz).

R. Vaughan (1994) *The Illustrated Chronicles of Matthew Paris: Observations of Thirteenth-Century Life*, new edn (Stroud: Sutton).

11

The Good, the Bad and the Ugly: Sources for Essays

Keir Waddington

You have to write an essay on the Black Death or the 'Hitler myth', but what sources should you use? You will have written essays before, but essays at degree level demand different skills from the other essays you will have written. One of these skills is understanding what sources to use for your essays. Where is the best place to start? A textbook? A monograph? An article in an academic journal? Will the Internet help or hinder you?

As an undergraduate history student, you will need to show that you can draw on existing scholarship to provide your own answers to problems on the basis of independent analysis. This independence comes with rewards, but also potential risks: the freedom to conduct your own research and develop your ideas in essays but also the liberty to write weak essays based on dubious sources and the ideas they contain. Some of the risks of using certain sources for your essays are obvious. If you are writing an essay on the relations between Scotland and England in the eighteenth century and want to pass, you will not rely on Simon Schama's TV series *A History of Britain* (2000–02). A TV series that covers 5,000 years of history in fifteen episodes cannot provide the kind of detailed analysis of specific historical questions which is expected from undergraduate history essays. Moreover, on television, historians are not required to cite their sources or to acknowledge differing interpretations. These are both skills you are expected to demonstrate in your own essays. Other risks are less obvious, especially when it comes to the Internet.

Crucial to avoiding problematic sources is evaluating the material you come across and determining its use and value for writing essays. This chapter encourages you to think critically about the sources you use, and provides tips on finding useful sources. To help you avoid some potential pitfalls of historical research, it explains how to distinguish between helpful sources for essays and those that are of questionable quality. The strongest starting point for writing good essays is the identification of sources that engage constructively with the existing academic literature, that are based on sound methods of research and that present an argument supported by evidence that can be verified. The chapter also covers why some sources can be considered unreliable, and how using such works can be highly problematic. The ability to critically navigate the large amount of historical information and resources upon which essays might be based, and to think about why some sources are better than others, will lead you to write more sophisticated essays.

The Internet, Google and Wikipedia

It might be tempting to turn to the web as your first port of call when researching an essay. The Internet is useful for both general and more specific searches for information on a topic: these days many historians use Google in this way. However, there are problems with using the Internet indiscriminately. The number of results is often bewildering. Moreover, no matter how you define your search, Internet search engines are promiscuous: they use complex algorithms to find results, but do not judge their 'value', merely rank them. The top results are the most popular, or those most relevant according to the formula of the algorithm (which might be very different to your definition of 'relevant'). More precise search terms (avoiding searches such as 'early modern crime') or Boolean searches (using words such as AND, OR, NOT) can produce better results, but search engines still do not focus on academic resources. A considerable amount of information from your searches will be irrelevant or at worst misleading. For example, if you are writing an essay on race and the Whitechapel murders, you will find links to Ripper tours, speculations on the identity of Jack the Ripper, contemporary news stories and so on, but little academic work. Furthermore, search engines only respond to your queries: are you asking the right questions in the first place?

Often the top-ranked result in many searches is Wikipedia. With over 31 million articles, Wikipedia is an online encyclopaedia that can help you identify basic information. However, much of the material included is rudimentary. Wikipedia articles only weakly reflect historical scholarship. Wikipedia has a 'no original research' policy and its guiding principles are to make knowledge free and maintain a neutral point of view. As we have seen at several points in this volume, history can never be neutral. This makes an uncomfortable fit with the ethos behind Wikipedia and you will find little on the site to help you construct a sophisticated essay on, for example, the nature of the French Revolution. There are other problems with Wikipedia. Entries do not conform to accepted standards of academic rigour: many are written collaboratively by largely anonymous volunteers. Anyone with Internet access can write or make changes to articles. The inclusion of references in Wikipedia articles can be misleading, as these will only direct you to published sources. Wikipedia considers unpublished sources (a category which includes many primary sources) as 'unreliable', but views mainstream newspapers as 'reliable' sources of information. This can lead to dubious judgements, as seen in the Wikipedia material on the Knights Templar, which includes a History Channel documentary and books by film directors as 'reliable' evidence. Encyclopaedias like Wikipedia should only be used to acquire basic facts or background information, a view shared by Wikipedia founder Jimmy Wales.[1]

It is important to remember that the Internet has significant limitations when it comes to academic history. There is an extensive amount of scholarship not accessible on the Internet, or not indexed in such a manner that you can come across it easily. For example, if you are writing an essay on the city and health in nineteenth-century Britain and want to research the history of pollution, Internet search results will be dominated by popular histories or journalistic accounts, not academic histories. Just as with other sources, you need to consider critically the authority, reliability, integrity and usefulness of the websites you access. It is important to ask questions, such as those outlined in Figure 11.1, about the authority of websites.

As we shall see in a later section, the Internet can be a remarkable resource for research, but you need to remember that it is an unregulated space where anyone can claim anything. The information you find always needs to be filtered and assessed. You need to guard against blindly using websites as if they were fact, and importantly avoid the temptation to cut-and-paste content from the web directly into your essay – this is one of the main causes of plagiarism. You need to recognize that the Internet is only a means to an end, not an end in itself, and that uncritical or injudicious use of online resources will lead you into dangerous territory. To ensure that you are able to effectively use the Internet as a research tool, you should use one of the tutorials directed at historians written for the Intute Virtual Training Suite.

Primary and secondary sources

If the Internet is a potentially problematic research tool, what about basing your essay on primary sources? At GCSE and A-level, you will have discussed the differences between primary and secondary sources. Your undergraduate history modules will introduce you to ways of reading primary and secondary sources, as well as the sources themselves. Yet navigating this

- Who is providing the information, and can you trust them?
  - What is their level or nature of expertise?
  - Is the information from a higher education institution (identified by the .ac, .uk or .edu domain for UK and US universities) or a recognizable organization?

- Is the website accurate and reliable?
  - Is the information complete or providing one point of view?
  - Does the website have an explicit or implicit agenda?
  - Is the website simply expressing an opinion, or putting forward distorted or exaggerated views? For example, David Irving's website contains information about Auschwitz, but as a controversial Holocaust denier, most historians would argue that Irving puts forward erroneous views based on flawed interpretations.

- What kind of the evidence does the website contain?
  - Does the source come from an individual or political organization interested in a particular topic, be it Winston Churchill or the Civil Rights movement in the USA?
  - If so, are the judgements supported by references that you can check?
  - If not, why trust their statements or views?

- Who is the website aimed at?
  - Is it aimed at academics, GCSE students, supporters of a particular organization or some other group?
  - Is the website likely to simplify discussion, or to fail to acknowledge opposing views, because it aimed at a particular audience?

- How recent is the information?
  - Is the information outdated or disproven?

FIGURE 11.1 *Checking the authority of websites.*

evidence can be problematic. Where do you start? This is a difficult question to answer, even for experienced historians: defining what sources to use in historical research is seldom straightforward. As Garthine Walker shows elsewhere in this volume, the type or range of sources historians can use depends on the questions they ask, and on how they want to approach these questions. Finding sources and making decisions about how to read and use them is an important skill. To help undergraduates negotiate what can be a bewildering array of sources, tutors often produce document packs for their modules. Some historians have published document collections, particularly for European topics where students may not be able to read the sources in their original language.[2] Such collections bring together key documents that you can analyse for yourself, and also offer interpretations of the evidence. They can be a good place to start.

At a later stage in your degree, you may conduct more in-depth original research. University libraries, record offices and specialist archives hold a wealth of primary sources, much of which remains untapped. As Federica Ferlanti shows in her chapter, 'Archives', archival research offers joys and possibilities which all history students should sample at some point in their undergraduate careers. However, it may be comforting to know that you can include primary sources in your essays, even as a first year, without visiting the archives. The last decade has seen an incredible expansion of digitized sources.[3] Digitization provides historians with online access to a growing range of printed, manuscript and other types of sources – for example, through the Internet Archive – which previously could only be consulted in a research library or archive. Historians have responded to these developments with cautious enthusiasm, acknowledging both the practical benefits of digitization and drawbacks such as problems with the accuracy of optical character recognition (OCR) or loss of materiality, which can alter our understanding of a source. Not all historical periods or areas have been equally well served by digitization – copyright issues, for example, restrict the digitization of twentieth-century newspapers. Moreover, the limitations of OCR mean that large parts of online collections can be inaccessible via keyword searches. Nevertheless, one of the key benefits of digitization is the opportunity to write evidence-based studies on many more topics using online sources.

Using primary sources in your essay is never simply a question of searching for an example, quotation or extract that suits your needs. It requires deep engagement with the source and understanding of its wider context. Just using keyword searches to find a source will bypass this context. For example, if you are writing an essay on attitudes to Victorian crime, a basic search for 'murder' on the British Library 19th Century British Newspapers database yields over 100,000 results. But just picking one example to support your point, without asking further questions of the source (about authorship, purpose, language and so on) and its context within these results, will almost certainly lead you to misinterpret the evidence. Researching primary sources enriches your work and allows you to develop original arguments, but to fully understand any source you also need wider knowledge of the topic it covers and period in which it was produced. Historians do not reinvent the wheel each time they write a book or article: they start with the secondary literature.

Most undergraduate history essays rely on this secondary literature. It forms the starting point for thinking about a topic, and provides the evidence and interpretation to support your arguments. However, as with primary sources, using secondary literature is never a case of relying on one book or article. You need to read widely for your essays, and to avoid simply repeating ideas found in the secondary literature. Instead, engaging with this literature critically provides the essential foundations from which to develop your own interpretations.

Textbooks, monographs and articles

Not all the secondary literature on a topic, even if produced by reputable historians, is of equal value or sophistication. There is a significant difference between a short piece written by a historian on the First World War for the *BBC History Magazine*, and the same person's research published as an academic journal article or monograph which explores similar territory in much greater depth. Articles in history magazines such as *History Today* and popular histories (published by general presses and often lacking footnotes, or only providing minimal documentation) are highly accessible, but they can only act as introductions to a topic. Likewise, relying on textbooks will not produce the type of essays your lecturers are looking for. Textbooks provide accessible and considered introductions to a period, topic or field of study: concise overviews that survey the state of the field, synthesize debates or key themes, and sometimes generate new ideas and questions. The very best textbooks, such as Ian Kershaw's *The Nazi Dictatorship: Problems and Perspectives of Interpretation* (first published 1985), are recognized as important contributions in their own right, while others, such as the Oxford Handbook series, bring together leading scholars to evaluate current thinking on specific topics. Textbooks can offer effective routes into a subject because they summarize and evaluate the state of scholarship, but their accessibility is usually dependent on a degree of simplification, which means they can also smooth over historical differences, debates and nuances. Relying on even very good textbooks will lead you to further simplification in your essays. Textbooks cannot give you the complex treatment that your lecturers are looking for in your essays.

Publications such as *History Today* or textbooks offer introductions to topics, but must always be followed by sustained reading of specialist literature produced by professional historians. As discussed in Kevin Passmore's chapter, 'Evidence and Interpretation', professional history follows a series of practices, such as use of footnotes, designed to ensure the critical use of evidence and the possibility of verification by tracing claims back to the original evidence. This approach, combined with depth of knowledge, sophistication, and complex and coherent argument, is only found in research monographs, peer-reviewed journal articles and edited collections. Monographs arise from sustained original scholarship, and usually take the form of case studies based on extensive research and engagement with primary sources. They offer important new approaches, evidence or a fresh look at existing problems. You only have to think of examples such as E.P. Thompson's *The Making of the English Working Class* (1963) to see how research monographs have advanced the discipline in extraordinary ways. Articles in academic journals, such as the *American Historical Review* or *Past & Present*, and chapters in edited collections are also based on original research but are even more specialized, usually addressing a particular historical problem or debate. Because these academic publications focus in some depth on specific historical topics, with full documentation of their sources and attention to competing interpretations, they help you to engage with historical questions in more sophisticated ways than if you drew your ideas solely from textbooks. Such academic work may be daunting at first. Consulting abstracts of articles or book reviews in academic journals can help you to assess whether particular works will be useful for your essay, although these should never be a substitute for reading the work itself.

Most lecturers will provide lists of essential reading from academic journals, edited collections or monographs. You should read these recommended items first. Why do these forms of academic work make more valuable contributions to historical knowledge than popular forms of history? Why should you use them extensively in your essays? The answer is not just in the depth of research which characterizes academic publications, but also in the academic scrutiny involved in the anonymous peer review process (discussed more fully in Garthine Walker's chapter). Peer review ensures that before publication, historical research is scrutinized by professional historians with extensive knowledge of the field. Peer review is a form of feedback, much the same as students receive on essays, used to improve academic work before it is published. While the peer review process is not perfect – mistakes and flawed interpretations still slip through in published work – it represents a form of academic quality control to ensure that the highest standards of scholarship are maintained. Because of this peer review process, not all research gets published. This does not mean that published research is the definitive word on any topic. Rather, to be worthy of publication in a peer-reviewed forum, the research has been judged by experts to be an original contribution to knowledge, based on sound methods of research, with an argument supported by evidence. It is the process of peer review which ensures that academic publications such as monographs, journal articles, and edited collections contain rigorous or sophisticated research, and therefore form the essential basis for any essay. However, be aware that you can disagree with peer-reviewed work. Your lecturers will expect you to read this work critically, to evaluate the claims made, and take issue with it where appropriate.

Libraries, e-journals, e-books, and finding secondary literature

Your lecturers expect you to start research for essays in a university library, drawing on references in your reading lists. However, be prepared to be adventurous in finding relevant items for essays. Your university library catalogue is an essential research tool; searching it will produce other books and articles to consult. You can also use bibliographies or footnotes in academic works to identify other sources, look through academic journals to see what else might be relevant or explore what is shelved near the books on your reading list. No matter how extensive your module reading list, there is always scope to extend your reading.

Your university library not only provides many of the books and journals you need, but also holds online resources to find and access academic scholarship. The resources contained on these sites are often not found through general Internet searches. Access to them depends in part on what subscriptions your university has, as subscriptions to these resources are expensive and not all universities can subscribe to every resource you may want. The most commonly used online resource for electronic versions of printed journal articles is JSTOR. JSTOR allows you to search these digital versions and download them as PDF files. However, JSTOR is neither complete nor comprehensive in its coverage. Some e-journals are only available on publishers' subscription sites. Additionally, journals on JSTOR have moving firewalls. For example, JSTOR has *The Historical Journal* from 1958, but not the most recent five years of the journal; to access recent issues you have to use the Cambridge University Press digital archive. It is worth remembering these gaps. To make access easier, many universities have invested in e-journals or electronic journal portals, which allow you to access and search thousands of online journals. However, search tools and catalogues are not perfect. You need to persevere, checking both e-journals *and* the physical holdings in your university library before you tell your lecturer that you 'can't find X'.

There are also online scholarly resources, again usually subscription-only, through which you can access e-book versions of general academic works. For example, Cambridge Histories Online covers over 300 volumes published by Cambridge University Press. These subscription services are more extensive and reliable than non-specialist resources available for free on the web, such as Google Books. Google Books is useful for highlighting texts in which particular topics and subject areas arise and for suggesting what books might be useful. However, search results on Google Books return the opinions of self-published amateurs next to academic publications, making it difficult to assess the academic merits of different works. Errors exist in the bibliographic data held by Google, which means Google Books will not direct you to all relevant works, and some books have pages missing or pages with bits left off. Furthermore, while books published in Europe before 1865 can be accessed in full, copyright restrictions mean works published after this date can only be viewed in snippets. You must avoid relying on such extracts if you cannot access other parts of the volume: other sections might modify or extend what is said in the part you can access, and you will get a distorted view of an argument if you only read a small part of it. Google Scholar is more useful: it searches research content, e-journals and specialist databases. While it can provide an overview of what published material exists on a topic, as a resource it still needs to be used with caution. This is because it does not cover everything and the algorithm that produces the results does so largely on the basis of citations. Less-cited articles, which are perhaps more appropriate for your essays, might not make it onto the first ten pages of results.

To go beyond your reading lists, you can use a range of subscription-only online databases, again available via your university library, to find academic publications. The most important tools for finding secondary literature are the Bibliography of British and Irish History, Historical Abstracts, the International Medieval Bibliography, and the Web of Knowledge. These bibliographical search engines will help you identify academic literature which might be of use in your research. Using these resources is essential for your dissertation and for essays where independent research is required.

Online research resources

It requires skill to avoid potential problems in using the Internet as a research resource for your essays, but the web also offers a wealth of useful scholarly resources. These include excellent online resources for primary source material, from the collections housed by national museums such as the Science Museum, to portals for accessing sources such as the European History Primary Sources website or the Library of Congress American Memory collection. Other key resources include the Institute of Historical Research's British History Online, which includes primary and secondary sources from the Middle Ages to c. 1900, and its History in Focus project, which provides free resources for teaching and learning on popular themes, such as slavery, war or 'what is history?'

More and more historians are turning to social media and blogs to present some of their research findings. Facebook, Flickr or Pinterest might seem unlikely places to find scholarly research, but some historians use them to share information, while blogging is seen as a way of making research findings accessible to a wider audience. For example, the Institute of Historical Research's Digital Facebook page has links to academic papers and new resources. You need to be aware, however, that research published on blogs and social media is often work in progress, and sometimes not aimed at scholarly audiences. It is not peer-reviewed or necessarily of the same level of sophistication as monographs, articles or edited collections. You need to be just as critical in your engagement with this online scholarship as you are with other academic work. Above all, remember to reference it appropriately so that you do not appear to be trying to pass off other people's ideas as your own.

Conclusion

The Internet is a potential resource of good information about where to look for an answer to your essay question, or to access a wealth of primary sources, but it cannot write the essay for you. There is no substitute for using your university library, reading books and scholarly articles, and thinking. Just as historians disagree because of the kinds of perspectives, approaches or sources they use, there is room for you to contribute your own interpretations. It is your interpretation that your lecturers are interested in. To present your interpretation you need to base your ideas on a solid foundation: this means reading widely and reading reputable, dependable sources which make sophisticated arguments based on a rigorous, professional approach to the evidence. Google or other search engines can reveal the surface features of a topic or debate, but you can only develop sophisticated arguments by reading and engaging creatively with what professional historians have written. Other types of history – such as those found in television programmes, popular magazines or amateur websites – do not develop ideas in as much depth, or explicitly call on as much evidence. You can use textbooks as a route into subjects, but you should always supplement them with more detailed, specific and challenging material from monographs, journal articles and edited collections. The nature of the discussion found in these academic works will help you to make arguments, offer alternative positions and engage with the question in more sophisticated ways.

STUDY QUESTIONS

- What makes the difference between a reliable and unreliable piece of evidence for your essay?
- What is the difference between a textbook and a research monograph?
- What are the main dangers associated with using the Internet as a research tool or resource for essays?

Notes

1   'Wikipedia: "A Work in Progress"', *Business Week*, 13 December 2005: http://www.businessweek.com/stories/2005-12-13/wikipedia-a-work-in-progress. Accessed 13 August 2014.

2   An excellent example of this kind of document collection is J. Noakes and
    G. Pridham (eds) (2004) *Nazism 1919–1945. A Documentary Reader*, 4
    vols (Exeter: University of Exeter Press). See Helen Nicholson's chapter in
    this volume for further discussion on the role of selection, interpretation and
    editing in the compilation of document collections.

3   To find archival and manuscript sources in the UK, you can use the National
    Archives' Access to Archives (see 'Research Resources' for further details).

Research Resources

British History Online, Institute of Historical Research: http://www.history.ac.uk/
    projects/digital/british-history-online
British Library: http://www.bl.uk/
Cambridge Histories Online: http://universitypublishingonline.org/cambridge/
    histories/
European History Primary Sources: http://primary-sources.eui.eu/
The Faculty of History, Cambridge, has an excellent site for electronic resources:
    http://www.hist.cam.ac.uk/seeley-library/online-resources/e-resources
History in Focus, Institute of Historical Research: http://www.history.ac.uk/
    projects/digital/history-in-focus
Internet Archive: https://archive.org/
Intute Virtual Training Suite: http://www.vtstutorials.co.uk/tutorial/history
JISC Digital content: http://www.jisc.ac.uk/content
Library of Congress: http://www.loc.gov/
National Archives, Access to Archives: http://apps.nationalarchives.gov.uk/a2a/
Web of Knowledge: http://wok.mimas.ac.uk/

Further Reading

T. Hitchcock (2013) 'Confronting the Digital; or How Academic Writing History
    Lost the Plot', *Cultural and Social History*, 10:1, pp. 9–23.

12

Reading and Writing History

Tracey Loughran

By the time I finished my undergraduate degree, my essay-writing routine was perfectly honed. Forty-eight hours before the deadline I went to the newsagents, armed with a short shopping list: six cans of Coke, one tub of ice cream and sixty cigarettes. Back home, I barricaded myself into my bedroom, with no plans to eat a solid meal or sleep until I had finished writing. Fortified by caffeine, sugar and nicotine, I typed up notes from all the articles and books I had read in the preceding weeks. As I typed these notes, themes relevant to the essay question eventually emerged, although usually not before tears of frustration had filled my eyes more than once. I then reorganized the notes under appropriate headings. At some point, I turned these notes into paragraphs on each identified theme. As time ran out and panic hit, I wrote the introduction and conclusion to the essay. Finally, I printed the essay and emerged wild-eyed from a fug of smoke to embark on the train journey to my university, praying that the rail network would not let me down after these heroic efforts. With the essay safely submitted, I attempted to collapse in relief, but unfortunately the caffeine usually kept me awake for more hours than ideal. In retrospect, this is not a routine I would recommend to undergraduates.

I can't speak to the state of my heart or lungs after all the cigarettes and sugar, but for now I am living proof that it is possible to write good undergraduate essays with lots of reading and virtually no organization. That doesn't mean it's a good idea. At best, my working practices wasted time, induced unnecessary panic and resulted in lower marks than I might otherwise have achieved. At worst… well, see the opening sentence of this paragraph. Of course, I didn't *want* to end up stressed, tired, hoarse and manic every time I wrote an essay. I identified essay and examination questions I wanted to answer early in the academic year, read voraciously for every essay and thought about little else in the weeks leading up to the deadline. In short, I wanted to write excellent essays: in fact, I wanted this so badly that I ended up paralysed with fear every time I even thought about putting words on paper, and so I delayed, and delayed, and delayed, until once again, I found myself walking to the newsagents, steeled for an all-nighter (or two). I evolved an essay-writing routine which required a government health warning not because I was a bad student, but because I didn't know any better. Of course, I never picked up a book like this when I was an undergraduate. In reading this chapter, whether you end up agreeing with the contents or not, you've already displayed more common sense than I managed to acquire until I was a university lecturer, with responsibility for running a skills module. That's not a bad start.

Reading academic history

The most unexpected and daunting aspect of undergraduate study is the *amount* and the *type* of reading required. Most students arrive at university used to studying major topics through one or two key textbooks. At university, you are expected to read scholarly articles and monographs. As Keir Waddington discusses in the previous chapter, these are very different beasts to textbooks, and at first they might seem utterly untameable. Unfortunately, academic writing is often laden with jargon, and makes few concessions to the inexperienced academic reader. Even more unfortunately, there is no short cut to getting used to this kind of writing. Reading even a short academic journal article takes much more time than reading chapters of a textbook, and at first you may not understand a great deal of what you read. Eventually, you will become accustomed to the conventions of academic writing and the process will become quicker and less painful. Crucially, the more you read, the more you will understand. It is important not to despair at an early stage, or to blame yourself for initial difficulties. You would not expect to fully master driving a car by the end of your first lesson, so accept that learning to understand academic writing is another skill which requires time, effort and practice.

There are some techniques which make it easier to read and understand academic writing. Above all, always read with a clearly defined purpose in mind: what are you trying to find out, and why? Sometimes, you require general understanding of a topic. Most reading lists explicitly recommend some books as overviews of a period or topic. Try to commit to reading at least one such text in its entirety over the course of a module, with no other purpose than understanding the broad outlines of the topic. However, most of the time, you do not need to know absolutely everything about a topic. Module handbooks might provide a short description of the contents of lectures and seminars, or set out questions for discussion. In turn, essay and examination questions should be related to the topics covered in teaching sessions. Use the information provided in all these arenas to guide which items you select to read, and how you read them. Before you read an article or book chapter thoroughly, scan the abstract, introduction, section headings and conclusion to check if it is definitely relevant to your question(s). If you intend to read an entire book – an increasingly rare decision among undergraduates, and therefore one which will impress your tutors – look up book reviews online to gauge its scope and main arguments.

When you have selected reading material, try to read each item through once without making any notes. Although this might seem like a waste of time, it is important to *understand* what you read. Tutors want you to read widely, but it is far better to demonstrate thorough understanding of ten scholarly articles than to pad out footnotes with superficial reference to twenty items. Expect to be flummoxed by some scholarly jargon, and be prepared to use a dictionary to look up unfamiliar words. Read for argument rather than for 'facts'. What is the author trying to say, and why does she think her argument is a valuable contribution to the debates? Authors usually sum up the purpose of their arguments in the opening and closing paragraphs of an article or chapter, even if in an oblique manner. To identify an argument, look for key words, such as 'proves', 'demonstrates' and 'shows', as well as how the author positions his own work in relation to that of other historians. Does he name other historians in the text? If so, why? Does he agree or disagree with them? Does he use other historians' work to show that he achieves something different and if so, what is this difference? These questions will help you to understand the nature and purpose of specific historical arguments – *one of the most crucial aspects of research at undergraduate level*. Your tutors expect you to attend to argument, to explain disagreement among historians and to create an independent argument out of your reading.

Understanding and analysing academic argument

When you are reasonably confident that you understand *what* argument the author wants to make, look for *how* she makes it, and assess whether it is a convincing argument. Students often find it difficult to conduct this kind of detailed analysis of published work, but once again, the more you read, the more you will understand. Consider what kinds of question the historian is trying to answer, as the historian's aims at least partially shape the evidence consulted (Garthine Walker's chapter in this volume discusses this problem in detail). It is not always easy to identify why a historian has used particular sources, much less to work out whether these sources provide the most suitable kinds of evidence for the questions the historian has asked. Figure 12.1 suggests some questions about the use of evidence which will help you to assess whether a particular historian's argument is compelling.

- **What evidence is produced to support the claims?** What kinds of sources are used – legal, political, religious? Is the evidence published or unpublished – does the footnote state that it is from an archive, or is a publisher or place of publication mentioned? You might not recognize certain kinds of evidence at first (for example, few students realize that *Hansard* records parliamentary debates), but get into the habit of looking at footnotes.

- **Whose perspective is the author attempting to uncover, and does the aim match up with the evidence?** For example, if he is making claims about the views of voters in the 1951 general election, are these adequately conveyed by political speeches?

- **Does the evidence bear the weight put on it?** If the historian attempts to explain individual motive, is it sufficient to assume that an individual must have thought or felt a particular way without producing evidence? On the other hand, if he is talking about broad cultural trends, does the diary of one highbrow writer such as Virginia Woolf (1882–1941) tell us anything about what the bulk of people thought and felt?

- **If the author's argument seems speculative in some respects, is there any evidence which *would* satisfactorily back up the point?** For example, a politician's speech might not tell us about the views of voters, but opinion polls would provide some indication of these views.

FIGURE 12.1 *How does the historian use evidence?*

As an undergraduate student, you are not expected to be familiar with all the published and unpublished works a historian might consult. But as you read more widely, consider whether historians use the same or different kinds of evidence to make similar arguments; whether they use the same evidence to make different arguments; and whether some historians consult a wider array of sources than others, and how this affects their arguments. These are difficult problems to grapple with, but your tutors will certainly be impressed if you try.

Making notes on academic history

Once you have read, understood and dissected an author's argument, you should take notes. (Some students may find it easier to take notes, and then dissect an argument, or to conduct these tasks simultaneously – through trial and error, find out what works for you.) A good set of notes is the foundation for confident essay writing, and makes every other step of the process much easier. Figure 12.2 provides guidance on how to take good notes, and how to make the most of them.

- **Set up workable information retrieval systems.** Make sure you can always find your notes, and the relevant information within them. Always keep your notes for a particular project in one clearly labelled file.

- **Make sure you include relevant information.** Always head your notes with all the information needed for referencing; always record page numbers for key arguments, evidence and quotations.

- **Take account of whether you will be able to retrieve the text itself at a later date or not.** If you have easy access to a text, instead of taking full notes you can simply jot down the page number with a short comment on what is discussed.

- **Concentrate on argument and key pieces of evidence.** Don't attempt to record absolutely everything an author says. It is more important to understand these points of a scholarly text than to gather 'facts', not least because it is usually not too difficult to run your eye down a page and look for dates, statistics and quotations at a later stage, when piecing your argument together for essays.

- **If you find yourself writing everything down, stop!** Instead, try to distil the author's argument at every step by summarizing the key *argument* of each paragraph in no more than one sentence, and then briefly noting the *evidence* used to support this claim, e.g., 'discusses evidences from medical journals stating that hysteria was perceived as a feminine illness'.

- **Paraphrase (put the author's argument into your own words).** Your notes will be far more useful as a learning tool if you consistently paraphrase. Paraphrasing helps you to digest the meaning of a scholarly text, to avoid repeating words or phrases that you do not understand and to ensure that you do not unwittingly plagiarize another historian's work. It is an integral aspect of understanding the author's argument.

- **Make notes on each item as soon as you have finished reading, when it is still fresh in your memory.** It is daunting to end up with a pile of articles and books from which you must take notes before you even start writing an essay.

FIGURE 12.2 *Rules for taking notes.*

As you conduct more reading on the same topic, and areas of consensus among different authors emerge, your notes on each item will become shorter: you don't need to record uncontroversial facts or accepted arguments more than once. If you keep the purpose of reading and making notes in mind as you go along, you will also find that your own argument and interpretation start to form long before you begin formally planning your essay. When deadlines loom and you feel under pressure, it is tempting to skip the note-taking stage. However, any task is easier if you first make sure your tools are in order. Every cook knows that sharpening the knife before starting to chop saves a great deal of effort.

Essay plans

A timetable is the most basic stage of planning. Assume that you will encounter unexpected problems, and factor into your timetable how long these might take to resolve. One of the most common difficulties students face is accessing material. When all the students on a module want to use the same books for their essays, the library seems woefully understocked. Lack of familiarity with academic libraries and online research materials compounds these difficulties in accessing material. It takes time to learn how to use an unfamiliar system. Don't be scared to talk to librarians: it's the quickest way to find out where you might be going wrong. You can also circumvent some of these problems by getting to the library before everyone else. Essay deadlines and questions are usually available as soon as a module starts. At an early stage, make a shortlist of questions which most interest you. As you read for lectures and seminars on a week-by-week basis, keep this shortlist in mind. It will help to focus your reading on the essay question, and ensure that you do not have to double your labour by reading the same material from a different angle later on. It will also allow you pick your final question sooner, and therefore to clear out the library before everyone else does.

When you have selected your question and conducted some initial reading, make an essay plan. Many students dislike this stage and try to skip it, perhaps because they assume that a proper plan presupposes knowledge of the final answer. In fact, as Garthine Walker shows elsewhere in this volume, research is a to-and-fro process. It starts with a question; initial research provides some answers, but also prompts other questions; more research is needed; this process could go on forever, and often it ends only because the deadline is fast approaching. The good researcher is always dissatisfied with provisional answers, but this thirst for knowledge can prevent the production of good historical writing. A scholar aware of the inadequacy of her knowledge in the face of everything which still remains to be understood often puts off writing until she can formulate a complete answer. Unfortunately, that day will never come. The most likely end result of this way of thinking is a hastily-written essay with no coherent argument, which not only fails to adequately display depth of scholarship, but actually obscures it.

How, then, to balance the demand for a high level of research with the need for a carefully crafted and coherent piece of writing which acknowledges, but is not mired in, the complexities of the topic? The solution lies in an altered approach to both planning and writing. Think in terms of making several consecutive essay plans rather than one all-encompassing plan. Select your question; jot down some notes; do some reading; add to and reorganize your notes; do some more reading; revise your plan again; and so on. Every time you stop to plan, no matter how hastily, you consciously reassess your views and stagger the difficult process of formulating a final answer. Likewise, think of writing as a process that happens alongside planning and research, rather than an all-in-one heroic effort. The ideal time to start writing is when you have conducted some research, but before you feel ready to start writing. You will never be ready, so you might as well start as soon as possible. It doesn't matter *what* you write, or even if you don't know what you want to say when typing your first word. You can start in the middle, or only write about one aspect of the question at first. The important point is to write *something*, then go back to reading, and planning, and then start writing again. Your ideas will only take coherent shape when you consciously try to mould them. Expect the whole process to be difficult. Eureka moments are rare among historians.

Constructing an argument

If all the wisdom of tutors through the ages could be distilled into one pithy proverb, it might be this: a question demands an answer. In other words, whatever else you do in an essay, *answer the question*. Most questions pose a problem for you to discuss. You therefore need to limit your material and frame your argument accordingly. A good essay argues from start to finish. It starts by giving an indication of the problem to be addressed, and how you will address it. Every single statement, quotation and piece of information thereafter should contribute to the argument, either by supporting it, or showing what objections could be made to it. At every stage of the essay, make it clear why you are producing a particular piece of evidence or line of argument. At the end, summarize your reasons for reaching this conclusion, and restate your argument.

Marking criteria often use words such as 'independent' or 'original', which seem to imply that to get the best marks, you need to come up with an argument no one else has ever put forward. This is not the case. All you need to do in a history essay (and this is more than enough) is create your own argument through assessing the merits of different historical interpretations, and showing why you support a particular argument. You must clearly state this argument in your introduction and conclusion, and construct the argument throughout the essay by selecting and organizing evidence gleaned from a variety of secondary (and perhaps primary) sources. This element of selection and interpretation makes your argument original. You may be using evidence another historian has collected, but you are using it as part of *your* argument.

How is this different from 'opinion'? The role of evidence is crucial here. 'Opinion' is defined as 'a view or judgement formed about something, not necessarily based on fact or knowledge'. 'Opinion' is close to 'prejudice' ('preconceived opinion that is not based on reason or actual experience'). As a historian, you should not state opinion, but argue a case based on evidence. A balanced argument demonstrates awareness of competing arguments, but also adjudicates between them. It makes a judgement as to which argument is most convincing, based on the historian's deployment of evidence (for example, whether the historian uses an appropriate range and type of sources to back up his interpretation).

There are some simple tricks which show markers that an argument is your own without resorting to statements of opinion. Avoid phrases which suggest that an entirely subjective point follows, such as 'I think', 'In my opinion' or 'It seems to me'. Instead, actively follow the historian's practice of arguing a point and backing it up with evidence through use of phrases such as 'As this demonstrates', 'The evidence shows' and 'This proves'. Distinguish your own argument from those of other historians through careful statements of argument in the introduction and conclusion, as well as in the main body of the essay. Each paragraph should tackle a single point or argument, with supporting evidence for the central argument of the paragraph. It should begin and end with a sentence indicating the overall argument of the paragraph, such as 'Another limitation of the Marxist view of fascism is that ....' These sentences show what *your* argument is. Even if the same evidence and argument are used by other historians, the combination of these bracketing sentences with the relevant evidence demonstrates that you have reached an independent judgement on the value of this evidence and argument.

Attention to essay structure is essential in building a compelling argument. It is best to structure an essay around successive paragraphs on particular themes, such as political leadership, economic factors, popular protest and international pressure. This approach allows you to assess the arguments for and against each factor over one or two linked paragraphs, before moving on to the next factor; to maintain an argument throughout the essay rather than introducing it at the end; to analyse each factor in more depth; and to independently formulate an answer rather than making a list. Before submission, read over your essay and attempt to summarize the main point of each paragraph in one sentence. If you cannot summarize the main point of the paragraph in one sentence, it is likely that you are trying to do too much in the paragraph. On the other hand, if three paragraphs all seem to make exactly the same point, then you are probably waffling or have not structured the essay very well.

Strong introductions and conclusions make a great deal of difference to the overall effectiveness of the argument. The introduction is the first part the marker reads, and it should act as a map or key which makes sense of everything that follows. It tells the reader what your argument is and allows him to put the rest of the evidence you produce into a wider context. Introductions should state the problem the essay explores; demonstrate awareness of debates on the topic (perhaps summarizing how historians have approached it and where they disagree); if relevant, define key terms; and indicate the argument. It might seem odd to state the argument at the outset, but remember that this is a history essay, not a murder mystery. Your aim is not to maintain suspense as you masterfully lead the reader through the twists and turns of your arguments, but to construct an argument which makes sense to the reader at every stage of the essay. Your aim is to convince the reader, not to impress him: or, at the very least, it is only possible to impress once you have convinced.

In many ways an introduction is like an essay plan written out in expanded form. The same applies to the conclusion. This is the final part the marker reads, and it is your chance to ensure that the essay leaves the right impression on her mind. A poor conclusion can undo lots of good work; a good conclusion can help to make up for flaws elsewhere. The conclusion should restate the argument, draw the evidence together, and match up with the introduction – it should demonstrate that you have followed the map set out in your introduction. In fact, if you are struggling to begin writing, you can even start with the conclusion – this will make you get straight to the point. If you have already produced a draft, and you have attempted to summarize each paragraph in one sentence, you should be able to string these sentences together to make a decent conclusion. You may need to rewrite these sentences slightly so that it is more stylish, but the contents should be accurate.

Style

Good writing is integral to constructing an effective argument. No response will convince if it is not comprehensible. There are many excellent guides to improving your writing (some are listed at the end of this chapter), and it is worth investing in at least one of these works. However, there are some very basic principles of good writing which anyone can implement. Above all, keep it simple. Think about the worst academic article you have ever read. It probably used technical jargon you did not understand, did not state the argument clearly or did not present the argument in a logical fashion. All these flaws hinder both understanding and enjoyment. Now think about the best academic article you have ever read. You probably didn't even notice the prose style, which means it must have been easy to understand. As the great essayist George Orwell said, 'Good prose is like a window pane'.[1] Aim for an unobtrusive prose style, and remember that the primary purpose of writing is to communicate meaning to the reader. Concision and precision are the watchwords of the good academic writer. Figure 12.3 provides some tips on achieving these qualities in your writing.

- **Avoid passive sentences that begin with 'it':** 'It was thought that …' or 'It was considered that …'. Ask yourself who thought or considered whatever it is: Everyone? Legislators? Priests? Landowners? Paupers? On reflection, you may find that the view you are writing about was expressed only by certain groups in particular contexts. If you provide the correct information on 'what', 'where' and 'who', you have a much better chance of convincingly explaining 'how' and 'why' an event occurred. It is much better to write active sentences, in which it is clear who is performing the action.

- **Use short and common words instead of long, obscure or pretentious ones.** Never include a long sentence if you can make the same point using less words.

- **Only use a word when you are certain that you understand its meaning.**

- **Read your work out loud.** If it sounds odd, convoluted or confused, then it probably is, so work out exactly what you are trying to say and rewrite accordingly.

- **Ask someone else to read your work.** Ideally, this will be someone who is not taking the same module, who is comfortable criticizing you and whose criticism you will listen to.

- **Be prepared to spend time redrafting your work.** It takes time and effort to achieve a simple and effective prose style.

FIGURE 12.3 *How to achieve concision and precision in academic writing.*

It is absolutely essential that you spend time redrafting your essay. Read your work carefully to see where you can make points more simply and clearly. Use the tips on effective note-taking in the first part of this chapter to ensure that your own argument is easily identifiable; apply your skills as an academic reader to critiquing and improving your own writing. No academic ever submits a first draft for publication: the chapter you are reading now has been through at least four redrafts. Your essays are not for publication, but each piece of coursework does contribute to your overall degree classification, so take similar care.

What next?

Handing an essay in is not the end of the story. For each essay submitted, you should receive both a mark and written feedback, perhaps including annotations on the essay itself. Make sure you understand the feedback. Read the tutor's comments carefully and check that you understand where you went wrong. If anything is unclear, contact your tutor for a feedback tutorial. When you have completed the first draft of your next essay, read the previous feedback again: this will stop you making the same mistakes twice. Make a note of what you did right, as well as what you got wrong. Writing a good essay is about developing your strengths, not just avoiding errors. Above all, don't be disheartened or embarrassed by criticism. Every single historian has tales of harsh comments and rejection from editors of journals or monograph series. In the past, different anonymous reviewers have described my own work (deep breath) using the phrases 'intellectual posturing', 'I don't know why any of this matters' and 'it is the kind of article that leaves me cold'. I have a colleague who says that he could paper his office in rejection letters, and another who claims to have received the quickest rejection e-mail for a book proposal ever (under three minutes). We all keep on publishing. If you receive critical feedback, cry if you want to, but then dust yourself off and start thinking about how you might do better next time.

Like research itself, learning to read and to produce good academic writing is a to-and-fro process. It involves looking backwards and forwards: thinking carefully about what you (and other historians) have done in the past, and about what you can or should do in the future. Evolving effective study techniques is partly a matter of trial and error, and finding what works for you. There are some tips which make essay writing easier, but no one-size-fits-all solution. It can be immensely liberating to realize that the search for perfection is doomed to end in failure, because this realization leads to the formulation of a goal which *is* always achievable: improvement. If you consistently focus on enhancing your understanding of history, and are open to learning from both experience and the guidance of others, you will get better at all kinds of tasks which seemed near-impossible at the start of your undergraduate degree. Every single one of your lecturers started out in the same place you are now. They made mistakes and suffered criticism, but perhaps more importantly they all continue to do so, and to hone their skills through further research and writing. The process of becoming a good historian never ends.

Acknowledgements

I am very grateful to Lloyd Bowen, Dan Jewson, Lisa Mitchell, Catherine Prescott, Jordan Rees and Stephanie Ward for their comments on earlier drafts of this chapter.

Notes

1   G. Orwell (2004) *Why I Write* (London: Penguin) [1946], p. 10.

Further Reading

M. Abbott (2008) *History Skills: A Student's Handbook*, 2nd edn (London and New York: Routledge).

S. Cottrell (2013) *The Study Skills Handbook*, 4th edn (Basingstoke: Palgrave Macmillan).

G. Orwell (2013) *Politics and the English Language* (London: Penguin Classics) [1946].

J. Peck and M. Coyle (2012) *The Student's Guide to Writing: Grammar, Spelling and Punctuation*, 3rd edn (Basingstoke: Palgrave Macmillan).

W. K. Storey (2012) *Writing History: A Guide for Students*, 4th edn (Oxford and New York: Oxford University Press).

R. Stott, A. Snaith and R. Rylance (eds) (2001) *Making Your Case: A Practical Guide to Essay Writing* (Harlow, Essex: Pearson Education).

PART THREE

History in Public

Introduction: History in Public

Tracey Loughran

It's a rainy day, and I'm bored. What should I do? I might turn to the book I'm currently reading, Siddhartha Mukherjee's *The Emperor of All Maladies: A Biography of Cancer* (2010). Despite the depressing subject matter, many agree that this history of cancer treatment and research is a good read: it appeared on the *New York Times* Bestseller List. But maybe I'm not in the mood for reading. What's on TV tonight? BBC2 is showing *The Scandalous Lady W*, a drama based on the late eighteenth-century divorce case of Lady Worsley. BBC4 offers its usual diet of highbrow programming: I can choose between a documentary on the British Renaissance, broadcaster Andrew Marr's investigation of Churchill's paintings, historian David Reynolds's examination of Stalin's response to the German invasion of the Soviet Union in 1941 or an exploration of 1950s British war films. If I fancy something lighter, perhaps I could watch the ITV comedy *Plebs*, a show about three young men in ancient Rome chasing sex and money in the big city, or catch a repeat of the modern-day re-imagining of the exploits of Victorian hero Sherlock Holmes on BBC1.

No: I want to get out of the house. My local cinema is showing director Guy Ritchie's reboot of 1960s TV show *The Man from U.N.C.L.E.*, or perhaps I could see *The Diary of a Teenage Girl*, a coming-of-age film set in 1970s San Francisco. Instead, I might just go for a walk in Castle Park, close to my home in Colchester, Essex: past the Roman wall at the end of my road, loop round the monument marking the site of the execution of Royalist leaders in the 1648 siege of the town and back up past the First World War memorial. I could even pop into Colchester Castle, a largely complete Norman keep, or if I'm not feeling flush, I could take advantage of free entry to the Colchester Natural History Museum or the Hollytrees Museum, an eighteenth-century house converted into a museum showing life in Colchester in bygone times – all within ten minutes' walking distance.

History is everywhere in the world around us.[1] Trade publishers profit from the perennial popularity of historical topics; TV channels and film directors cannot resist the appeal of costume dramas or shows in which historians walk around in fields, wildly gesticulating to the ghosts of the past; and the number of visitors to heritage sites run by organizations such as the National Trust and Cadw seems to increase year-on-year. Moreover, the public do not simply engage with history for entertainment. Local history societies, founded and maintained by community members, and representing diverse constituencies, thrive across the United Kingdom.[2] Archives are populated not only by professional historians, but members of the public keen to find out more about their family's history.[3] Many people who have not formally studied history since their early schooldays find the subject interesting and believe that it is important to know about the past. And of course, these popular forms of history all play a part in encouraging students to study the subject at university. In England, between 10,000 and 12,000 students take up places to read history at university each year.[4] Inspirational teachers keep applications buoyant, but so too do the *Horrible Histories* books and television series, the *Civilization* suite of computer games and stories told by grandparents.

It can be quite a shock to arrive at university only to find that tutors hold completely different conceptions of where the interest and importance of the subject lies. It is dispiriting to be told that the approaches and skills fostered during secondary and further education – the same approaches which motivated you to choose history as a degree subject, the same skills which gained you a place at university – will not be sufficient to see you through undergraduate study. It is bewildering to be informed that Simon Schama's TV series *A History of Britain* (2000–02), still often shown in secondary school classrooms, is not a suitable source to cite in essays. Most of all, it is disorienting to discover that lecturers believe that 'real' history is found in dry academic articles and monographs, and not in the world beyond the university walls.

In part, this dissonance arises from the special status of history. As historian Richard Overy points out, 'history is everyone's property in a way that advanced research in the natural or social sciences is not'.[5] We do not expect complex research in chemistry or mathematics to be accessible to non-specialists, but we hold history to a different standard. Having grown up with history all around us, it is sometimes difficult to appreciate that professional historians work with sophisticated methods and technical vocabularies that can make their scholarship appear 'arcane, theoretically driven and undramatic'.[6]

Of course, there is some shared ground between non-academic and popular historians. Professional historians and the producers of popular history rely on each other. Academic historians need non-professional practitioners of history to stoke interest in the subject; when the number of applicants to study history at university falls, it is likely redundancies will follow. On the other hand, without research conducted in universities, there would be little material out of which to generate popular histories. If the relationship between professional historians and other producers and consumers of history is sometimes fraught, this is because codependency imposes strains that both sides rub against.

What are the differences between academic and non-academic history? Any summary will be contentious, but I argue that what distinguishes professional from other forms of history is the *combination* of certain features: the requirement to conduct original research and to employ the scholarly apparatus that allows this research to be verified, rather than relying entirely on secondary scholarship which is not cited in footnotes; the commitment to deepening historical knowledge through asking and answering questions, rather than treating the past primarily as a curiosity or source of entertainment; the belief that specialized research on small areas is necessary to illuminate broader historical questions; and the ability to communicate with specialist audiences through shared understanding of disciplinary approaches and methods. Of course, division between the approaches and methods of different practitioners is not always clear-cut in practice. Professional historians sometimes communicate with non-specialist audiences through sparsely documented narrative histories or television programmes, while history teachers and curators seek to educate rather than entertain. Nevertheless, to claim the title of professional historian, scholars must at some point in their careers produce research which combines all of the above features, whereas except in exceptional cases, non-academic history will meet at most two or three of these criteria. Professional historians therefore use specialized research techniques, present their findings in accordance with specific disciplinary conventions and perceive the primary audience for their original research as composed of other scholars.

The advantages and potential frustrations of professional history are intertwined. For example, take the footnote. Professional historians love footnotes. In scholarly articles and monographs, meticulous referencing performs the essential function of allowing readers to verify the claims put forward. When David Irving brought a libel case against Deborah Lipstadt and Penguin Books in 2000, Lipstadt defended herself by claiming that Irving's statements about the Holocaust were false. The defence asked historian Richard J. Evans to comb through Irving's footnotes and re-examine the documents on which his case rested; Evans found that Irving had misrepresented these documents, and Lipstadt won the case. In using Irving's own footnotes to show that he had flouted the accepted standards of scholarly practice, the defence 'weakened the plausibility of Holocaust denial'.[7]

It is because footnotes hold such power that university tutors spend so much time exhorting students to get to grips with referencing. Conversely, it is because referencing is an attribute of academic studies, rather than more familiar popular forms of history, that students find this so difficult and frustrating. Trade publishers discourage non-fiction authors from including too many references, pleading that they prevent readers immersing themselves in the text. This argument has some famous supporters: the playwright Noel Coward (1899–1973) protested that having to read footnotes was like being forced to answer the front door in the middle of making love.[8] Nevertheless, disparagement of the footnote shows that no matter how excellent the popular history, its makers are not subject to the same restrictions as academic historians. We would all switch off our TV sets if, at the end of an episode of BBC1's *Who Do You Think You Are?*, a solemn voiceover listed every source consulted. This should warn us to attend to the different aims and methods of popular and professional histories. Rigorous documentation interferes with the popular historian's primary aim of effectively communicating to a wide audience, and so it is jettisoned. For the professional historian, not including such documentation undermines the trustworthiness of the history, and cancels out efforts to make a convincing argument. Each method is appropriate to the form, but consumers of history should not confuse one kind of history with another.

This section helps you to avoid such confusion by considering how best to approach different forms of non-academic history. Lloyd Bowen shows that the teaching of history in schools always reflects interests that operate outside the education sector, while Matthew Grant demonstrates how the relationship of policy-makers to history can affect how historians engage with different publics. My own chapter on historical novels compares the practice of historical novelists and professional historians, and considers the power of historical fiction to subvert conventional historical narratives. In her exploration of history and heritage, Stephanie Ward tackles the thorny question of who 'owns' the past, and lays bare the power relations embedded within the creation and management of heritage. The final two chapters reveal the benefits to be accrued when historians step outside the academy. Jane Hamlett reflects on her own experience of communicating historical research to wider audiences through co-curating an exhibition at the Geffrye Museum, while David Wyatt makes an impassioned plea for students to take history into the wider world.

These chapters deal with disparate topics, reflecting the diversity of non-academic forms of history, but they all further understanding of the nature of history by probing the aims, methods and achievements of different forms of historical practice. Whether we are professional historians, producers of non-academic history or newly minted history undergraduates, our understandings of the past are formed out of an accretion of obvious and unrecognized influences, from the world around us as well as books read and time spent in seminar rooms. Analysis of works by professional historians requires understanding their perspectives, because the questions they ask determine research methods and the contour of their histories. To engage with popular history in an informed and responsible manner, we must apply the same analytic skills to television programmes, historical novels and museum exhibitions. Critical reflection on the differences between academic and popular history enables deeper understanding of the purposes of the historical discipline, the stances of different producers of history and how different audiences make meaning out of history.

Notes

1   On the manifold forms of popular engagement with history, see J. de Groot (2009) *Consuming History: Historians and Heritage in Contemporary Popular Culture* (London and New York: Routledge).

2   The many activities and groups listed on Local History Online demonstrates the vibrancy of local history: http://www.local-history.co.uk/. Accessed 16 January 2016.

3   See, for example, The National Archives' audio and video materials for family historians: http://media.nationalarchives.gov.uk/index.php/category/family-history/. Accessed 16 January 2016.

4   Higher Education Funding Council for England, 'Time Series of Undergraduates in Higher Education Subjects': http://www.hefce.ac.uk/analysis/supplydemand/ug/. Accessed 16 January 2016.

5   R. Overy, 'The Historical Present', *Times Higher Education*, 29 April 2010, p. 32.

6   Overy, 'The Historical Present', p. 32.

7   J. Tosh (2008) *Why History Matters* (Basingstoke and New York: Palgrave Macmillan), p. 108; Richard J. Evans (2002) *Telling Lies about Hitler: The Holocaust, History, and the David Irving Trial* (London: Verso).

8   A. Grafton (1997) *The Footnote: A Curious History* (London: Faber and Faber), pp. 69–70.

13

History in Schools

Lloyd Bowen

On 26 September 2014, the *Guardian* newspaper reported a dispute which had flared up in Jefferson County, Colorado. A new school board had recently been elected, and one of its members angered parents and pupils by a proposal to review the local schools' history curriculum. She argued for new criteria to be employed in this review which should 'promote citizenship, patriotism, essentials and benefits of the free enterprise system … [and] should not encourage or condone civil disorder, social strife or disregard of the law'. She defended this approach saying, 'I don't think we should encourage our kids to be little rebels'.[1] A large number of staff and students protested against this intervention and proposals were formulated for pupils to dress up as 'rebels' including Eleanor Roosevelt, Rosa Parks and Martin Luther. The story prompted the newspaper to ask, 'What is American History?' and it canvassed US readers on their experiences of an important historical holiday, Columbus Day, which celebrates the 'discovery' of America in 1492. The published responses included one from 'Paul' of Massachusetts who said his teachers in the 1960s and 1970s were of the World War II generation who 'proclaimed American exceptionalism', and hailed Columbus as a 'great explorer' bringing civilization to a land of 'savages'. Ken Bridges, a Cherokee respondent from Oklahoma, maintained that he was 'taught like every other elementary student, from a textbook that misrepresented history in favour of the victors' and was 'Eurocentric'. 'Joan', meanwhile, spoke of her differing experiences in New Jersey, where she was exposed to a traditional celebratory history of Columbus, and South Dakota, a centre for indigenous populations, where 'Native American Day' was celebrated instead; indeed, the name had recently been changed by the state legislature there.[2]

The Colorado episode and the discussion of Columbus Day highlight the often controversial and contested nature of history teaching in schools. Such disputes illustrate how questions about the 'correct' way to interpret the past often spill beyond the province of education policy and touch upon issues of citizenship and belonging. History is often seen as a discipline which speaks to the present as much as to the past. As a result, the teaching of history is often an area for government intervention and public conflict because different interests within the state often have distinct versions of history they wish to promote and sponsor in line with their own ideological predilections. These competing visions of the past are often the product of rival political affiliations, but they can also result from the influence of new methodological and intellectual developments within the higher education (HE) sector that 'filter down' to the instruction of younger age groups. History teaching in schools, then, is important to understand because it helps shape the public contexts in which professional historians and students of history at university operate. It also profoundly influences the broader historical culture of a society, and thus the context within which historians' opinions are formulated as well as the audiences to which they address works like textbooks, public lectures and, in an increasingly marketized HE sector, undergraduate courses, too. The vast majority of history lecturers and students will have had their interests shaped in part by their exposure to historical topics and methods in their primary and secondary education. Part of the reason why the global historical community is so diverse is because of the different backgrounds, interests and preconceptions which emerge from the constellation of varied educational establishments and historically informed publics. The natures of these constituencies vary from place to place, of course, but are themselves products of particular historical circumstances and developments and are thus also the subject of debate, discussion and reinterpretation by historians and their students.

This chapter considers the nature of history teaching in schools by examining the ways in which the regimes of Soviet Russia, post-independence Zimbabwe and the United Kingdom have sought to shape the presentation of the past to their youth through their respective school systems. Passions are often inflamed, as in the example covered in the *Guardian*, because history is seen as a vital element in framing and understanding the present and for constructing versions of identity and belonging. Was Columbus an intrepid explorer bringing civilization to the New World, or a plunderer who decimated indigenous populations? What role should history education play in promoting a particular set of moral values and qualities among a population?[3] If children cannot be taught the entirety of history, which bits should be included and which bits left out? The ways in which such questions are framed in schools reveal a good deal about the priorities and attitudes of the educational establishment, its political masters and the historical cultures of the populations being educated.

History schooling and the state

Policymakers have long believed that the importance of history instruction in schools lay in its ability to teach the state's citizens about their collective past, and that this would in turn help foster their allegiance to the nation (itself understood as a historical artefact) and to their fellow citizens. This is partly a legacy from the golden age of nation and empire building in the nineteenth century, when the development of history as a discipline was intimately connected to the project of making the nation.[4] In 1898, David Salmon's (1852–1944) *The Art of Teaching* claimed that 'History fosters patriotism. It fills the student with admiration for his forefathers' wisdom, heroism and devotion to duty, which have made the nation what it is'.[5] In France, meanwhile, Ernest Lavisse (1842–1922) held a particular sway over the teaching of history through his writing of influential school textbooks in the late nineteenth and early twentieth centuries which promoted pride in the nation's praiseworthy past. In one work designed for use in teacher training programmes in the mid-1880s, Lavisse observed that French patriotism was 'at the same time a sentiment and a sense of duty. All sentiments are susceptible to cultivation, and all such senses can be taught. History needs to cultivate the sentiment and specify the duty'.[6] This connection between patriotism and the past provides an important thread running through many of the debates about the teaching of history in schools in the modern era.

While writers like Lavisse and Salmon were keen to stress the connections between history teaching and patriotism, their approach to school curricula was moderate and restrained compared with many revolutionary and totalitarian regimes of the twentieth century which viewed history schooling as a key ideological prop for the state. History (or at least a suspect history) was potentially corrosive to the interests of a revolutionary polity which looked to wipe time's slate clean and start again. This was seen most radically in the institution of 'Year Zero' by the Communist Khmer Rouge in Cambodia in 1975. Hailing the end to 'two thousand years of Cambodian history', the revolutionary Khmer leader, Pol Pot (1925–98), proudly stated his desire to 'do away with all vestiges of the past'.[7] Other revolutionary regimes like Soviet Russia and Communist China looked to remake the past in their own image rather than simply try to eradicate it, instructing their citizenry in approved forms of memorialization, historical method and practice.[8] In these societies schools were seen as vital engines of production, shaping the raw materials of the state's future citizenry. What they were taught and how was thus a vital concern for governing elites, and this led to some very heavy-handed interventions in schooling, particularly in the kinds of history schoolchildren were taught. The following section considers how this process played out in Soviet Russia, a society with a deep ideological commitment to a specific view of the past and of the path and nature of history itself.

Teaching radical subjects: History in Soviet schools

The foundational Marxist ideology of the Soviet Union was particularly historical in its principles and elaboration. This ideology became an integral part of all elements in the state's apparatus, so it is unsurprising to discover its directing influence in the educational sector. The role of education in Soviet Russia was to support the Communist regime, which in turn claimed the 'sole authority to interpret the present, the past and the future'.[9] As a result, Soviet leaders were concerned that the people should learn an agreed history curriculum but also an agreed approach to the past so that they would become serviceable and valuable Communist citizens who inhabited a common interpretative universe. History was viewed as a potentially subversive subject unless it could be 'domesticated' by following a single narrative. As Nikita Khrushchev (1894–1971), the leader of the Soviet Union, remarked in 1956, 'Historians are dangerous people. They are capable of upsetting everything. They must be directed.'[10]

The aftermath of the Bolshevik Revolution and Civil War saw a good deal of disruption to the established school system, while an emphasis on social sciences and abstract Marxist theory meant that history as a separate subject all but vanished from the Soviet curriculum.[11] However, the political developments of the late 1920s saw the reintroduction of history as a discrete discipline.[12] But the subject was only allowed to develop within strict boundaries of what was acceptable to the Communist Party and a patriotic brand of Soviet Communism. The Soviet state was seen by its leaders as moving towards a kind of perfection; they believed that it had developed in line with the trajectory outlined by Karl Marx, who maintained that history would move through particular stages, from feudalism through capitalism to the rule of the proletariat, with revolutionary change marking off these transitions. This was precisely how the history of Russia, its satellite states and indeed the rest of the world was to be taught to the schoolchildren of the Soviet Union. The state influenced particular control in the classroom through its production of official textbooks and its role in appointing approved teachers. For example, in 1948 the educationalist M.A. Zinoviev published a manual for secondary school teachers which observed that 'the correct teaching of history must create in the students the conviction that capitalism will inevitably perish', and argued that using approved textbooks would be the best means to achieve this.[13] The Soviet leadership could not allow historians to deviate from its interpretation of the past because that would delegitimize not only their own positions at the top of the political tree, but the entire Soviet system which was ultimately seen as a historical project.

In the 1930s, Josef Stalin (1878–1953) was sufficiently concerned about this to assist personally in the writing of a very influential textbook for use in Soviet schools: the *History of the Communist Party of the Soviet Union (Bolsheviks): Short Course*, which was published in 1938 and had 30 million copies distributed over the following decade.[14] This was a political text as much a historical work, however, and was indicative of the ways in which Stalin subordinated the study of history to a form of party propaganda which placed himself at the heart of an heroic history. In this work, Stalin's role in the 1917 Revolution was falsely exaggerated, while the actions of his mortal enemy and onetime ally, Leon Trotsky (1879–1940), were dramatically downplayed; the latter was vilified in the text as a pawn of foreign capitalist powers. Trotsky for his part rubbished this approach as the 'Stalin school of falsification'. However, through interventions such as the *Short Course*, history in Soviet schools was rigorously controlled and policed. One state report of 1959 maintained that history in secondary schools 'must develop in them [students] a conviction about the inevitable victory of communism, while revealing the role of the popular masses as the true makers of history'.[15]

We should be wary, however, of seeing the presentation of history within the Soviet system as one-dimensional. Officially sanctioned histories for schools would shift along with what was acceptable or not in the upper echelons of the ruling Politburo. Just as Stalin changed the nature of acceptable historical enquiry in the 1930s, so Khrushchev modified Stalin's approved historical curricula in the 1950s. Only one 'official' interpretation of history prevailed in schools at any one time and, as one Russian commentator remarked following the fall of the Soviet state in 1989, it was 'a country with an unpredictable past'.[16] Moreover, there is ample evidence that this heavy-handed intervention in the presentation of school history largely failed to achieve its desired goals. The repetitive nature of the curriculum and its obvious distortions wrought by the history-as-politics approach produced little enthusiasm or concrete results among a populace which was largely sceptical of the authorized versions fed to them.[17] However, the pervasiveness of a single interpretation of historical development and the absence of alternative viewpoints, and the educational materials to provide them, certainly had a profound influence on public understandings of history in the USSR.

Historical battlegrounds: Ukraine and Russia

Although the USSR is a rather extreme example, it does suggest the ways in which school histories connect with, and are influenced by, broader political contexts and concerns. One of the defining characteristics of the fall of Communism in 1989 was the revelatory recovery of aspects of a national past which had been denied or distorted previously.[18] Students now had the opportunity to argue about and interpret facts, and not simply to trust the authority of the state-sponsored version. This also had a profound influence on the teaching of history in countries which escaped the grip of the Soviet empire, as states like Ukraine rediscovered (or reinvented) separate national stories.[19] Often these countries implemented new school curricula which presented a picture of their long fight against the repression of an over-mighty Russia and their desire to forge a new, independent, path.[20] In 2006 the government of the recently independent Ukraine established the Ukrainian Institute of National History with the aim of publicizing the path to the country's independence, partly through producing school textbooks which were to be 'filled purposefully with the historical information useful for the development of the state'.[21] One such text presented the country as a historically European rather than Asian (i.e. Russian) state. It described Ukrainian culture as more advanced than that of its former political master, characterising Ukraine as the 'air-way through which Moscow society learned about the cultural achievements of West European civilization…culture in Russia was developed by Ukrainian books'.[22] Such historical legacies were more than grist to the educational mill, however, as can be seen in the tensions between Ukraine and Russia which erupted into armed conflict in 2014 and Russia's annexation of Crimea. The arguments deployed by both sides in their political and diplomatic propaganda offensives centred on issues of language and ethnicity, but of history too.[23] Doubtless, these conflicts will have their echoes in the future history classes of the respective states which will present the conflict to its young citizens in line with prevailing political orthodoxies.

Independent minds? History schooling in modern Zimbabwe

A different but highly illuminating example of the changing face of history in schools can be seen in Zimbabwe, the former British colony of Rhodesia. The country achieved independence in 1980 under the Marxist nationalist revolutionary who still rules at the time of writing in 2016, Robert Mugabe (b.1924). The history textbooks used in the country's schools during the era of colonial rule were blatantly racist tools of colonial repression. Children of all races were told that white men held the land and black men worked on it because of the 'very great difference between the energetic, skilful and ambitious white employers and the raw and ignorant black labourers'.[24] School history was thus used to legitimate the rule of the colonial master and indoctrinate the black majority with a sense of their own inferiority. Moreover, the view of indigenous tribes as constantly warring before the coming of colonial rule provided a justificatory narrative for the controlling hand of the 'civil' European, and an argument against extending the franchise to peoples who, as history purportedly showed, were incapable of governing themselves.

After independence, things changed markedly in history classes. A new syllabus was developed and new textbooks written which rejected the old colonial narratives and stressed the opportunities presented by black African socialism. Thus the view of the white colonizer as bringer of civilization and development was rejected in favour of a history that stressed the vitality and viability of indigenous cultures, and described the destruction or subjugation of these by white settlers.[25] Mugabe's government introduced a new 'O' Level history syllabus in 1990 which drew upon Marxist ideas to explain social and political change. Zimbabwean and African perspectives now had a central role in the syllabus, unlike previously when the histories of Britain and Europe predominated. Schoolchildren were also told that their history (and that of other places) should be understood in Marxist terms of class conflict, industrialization, progress, social history and revolution. There was a racial element to this which inverted the older colonial stereotypes to provide support for the ruling party's nationalist agenda. Whites (who were portrayed as a uniform group) were presented as opposed to African advancement and were implicated in the exploitation of indigenous people and resources, while blacks (again treated uniformly) were heroic freedom fighters who sought universally to end settler rule. This was an 'us and them' view of history (and indeed of the present) which reflected nationalist perspectives, and chimed with the kinds of narratives the government promoted in newspapers, in radio programmes and on television. There was little space given in the classroom, or indeed in society more generally, for different perspectives or any degree of complexity in historical interpretation.[26]

In 2002 a more radical syllabus was introduced which placed an even greater emphasis on African and particularly Zimbabwean history, sometimes to the exclusion of all else. It also moved further away from older formats of discussion and debate in history teaching to a kind of rote learning about the past which glorified the independence movement and hence its current incarnation, the ruling ZANU-PF party.[27] As one academic has observed, it is 'difficult to escape the conclusion that the introduction of a new syllabus was related to a desire on the part of the state to concentrate young minds on a more legitimizing narrative for the status quo and the ruling party, faced as it was with vigorous political opposition'.[28] Shortly after this new syllabus was introduced, the government began setting up youth militia camps in which young men were taught a decidedly non-academic 'patriotic history'.[29]

In both Zimbabwe and Soviet Russia, we can see how the teaching of history in schools became closely connected to legitimizing the ruling powers in the state. Partly this involved producing a citizenry which was politically pliant and not given to questioning received ideas about a past which supported the political structures of the present. Although these are rather interventionist examples of state influence in history teaching, they nevertheless are suggestive of the manner in which governments of all stripes concern themselves with the nature of education generally, and history education in particular. No one would argue that the Mugabe regime and the Colorado Board of Education operate in comparable ways, but they nevertheless reside on a continuum of state involvement in history education which can be found in most nations; the difference is a question of degree. Academics, students and informed publics in all countries variously adopt, modify or challenge the historical orthodoxies endorsed by the structures of authority in their education systems. This dialogue between the history taught in schools and the ideological preferences of those in authority will now be considered in a concluding section that brings us closer to home: recent debates over school history in England.[30] This illustrates how the involvement of the state in history teaching is not simply the preserve of the totalitarian past or 'distant' countries like Zimbabwe, but is also noisily present in our mature democracy with its long traditions of free speech and unfettered enquiry.

Historical subjects? The politics of history teaching in England

The last quarter of the twentieth century saw important changes in the nature of history teaching in England which had a profound effect on the shape of the discipline and of historical culture more broadly. Down to the 1970s, history in schools was often seen as a very 'dry' subject, taught as a succession of monarchs and great men, battles and constitutional turning points which constituted a national story – usually that of England. History in the classroom was often presented as a litany of events, dates and personalities to be remembered and reproduced in an examination. History was believed to be about chronology, recall and detail, not interpretation and argument. One commentator in 1968 argued that in many schools the subject had become 'excruciatingly, dangerously dull'.[31] The social, political and cultural developments of the 1960s and 1970s helped usher in significant change to this approach, and this was driven in part by shifts in the kinds of historical research being undertaken in universities.[32] We should remember, of course, that secondary school teachers in England, for the most part, receive an education at university or some comparable institution of higher education. They are thus exposed to new historical methods and subjects of enquiry which influence their approach to the subject, the topics in which they are interested, and the kinds of questions they are disposed to ask. This in turn is reflected in the kinds of history they present in their classrooms and the methods they employ in their teaching. The 'new history' which emerged in British universities in the 1960s and 1970s was more concerned than previously with groups which had been neglected and marginalized, such as the working classes, women, and the subjects of empire as well as the perpetrators of it. This also fed into a changing approach to the teaching of history in schools, which saw an increasing emphasis on argument and debate about the past rather than simply its memorization. There was also a new emphasis on creative engagement with a range of sources as a means of accessing the complex realities of the past rather than the rehearsal of an agreed national story told through the actions of kings, prime ministers and parliaments. As people of this era challenged received ideas about gender roles, class structures and political authority, so this influenced approaches to what the past meant, what history should be taught to children, and what kind of historical awareness the citizenry should have.[33]

The development of this 'new history' in schools during the 1970s and 1980s, however, was not without its strident critics. There was concern among many, often on the political right, that its emphasis on themes, skills and historical empathy was potentially destructive of national unity and the idea of a shared past which had prevailed in older methods of teaching. Some argued that the new directions in history teaching could undermine one of the central elements of cohesion in the United Kingdom: a common history.[34] The Conservative prime minister from 1979 to 1990, Margaret Thatcher (1925–2013), was attached to the traditional story of the growth of British liberty, and believed that history should contribute to individuals' sense of national pride. In concert with her intellectual mentor and Secretary of State for Education, Sir Keith Joseph (1918–94), she embarked on a long path of implementing reform in the teaching of history in England which culminated in the introduction of the National Curriculum in History in 1990.

There was a passionate debate between the political parties as to what the content of the history syllabus under this National Curriculum should be, particularly as it was now being made compulsory for children between the ages of 11 and 14. In the House of Commons, Thatcher argued that 'children should know the great landmarks of British history and should be taught them at school'.[35] Her supporters claimed that the 'flight from British history' in recent educational practice had '[left] our young people distrustful and confused', and that an 'emphasis on gender or ethnic perspectives' would allow pupils to grow up 'knowing next to nothing about the Gunpowder Plot, Trafalgar, Waterloo or Winston Churchill. And everything about the experiences of black peoples in the Americas or the lifestyle of the Ancient Egyptians'.[36] Those who opposed the proposed history curriculum were much more suspicious of a syllabus that seemed to privilege the structures of authority rather than investigate those over whom that authority was exercised. One participant in this debate, the socialist historian Raphael Samuel (1934–96), argued that 'a constitutional history which took as its vantage point the rights of the subject rather than the rhetoric of the lawmakers would be an altogether more chequered affair than that of Mr [Kenneth] Baker or Sir Keith Joseph' (both Conservative education ministers).[37] There was also a feeling on the political left that the vision of history championed by Thatcher and her successive ministers for education excluded groups who were not white, male, English and powerful.

The debates which swirled around what history was to be taught to schoolchildren under this new National Curriculum reflected anxieties about what it meant in the late 1980s and early 1990s to be British; how that was to be defined, how its history was to be taught, and thus how future generations would understand the historical foundations of this political construct. Conservatives were worried that a 'new history' approach would undermine traditional perspectives and dissolve the bonds of citizenship and society, while those on the left were anxious that justice be done to the stories of people outside of royal courts and parliaments; the disenfranchised and those without much money or power. People like the average target Labour voter, in fact.

The syllabus which ultimately emerged in fact reflected a pluralist approach that allowed teachers to cover a wide range of topics and themes, and rather undermined the Tory wish list for a history of great British leaders and great British events.[38] It examined a range of periods and approaches, and considered monarchs and ordinary people alike. There was a mix of British, European and world history which reflected recent developments in the historical profession as well as a society which was more aware, and perhaps more at ease, with its multicultural status, unsavoury colonial heritage, and declining post-war influence. The emphasis in this teaching was on skills, interpretation and argument, and not on memorization and recall.

However, introduction of this syllabus did not lay the issue to rest, and arguments over the teaching of history in English schools sprang to life once more with reforms suggested by the Coalition Government that was elected in 2010. The Conservative Education Secretary, Michael Gove, argued for a review of history teaching which he claimed, in an echo of the arguments made by Thatcher and her supporters in the 1980s, had become too heavily based on skills and interpretation, and insufficiently focused on key information, dates, events and the national narrative. It was argued that attempts to reform history teaching in schools in the previous decades had left it fragmented, difficult to interpret and lacking a cohesive approach or structure. Gove picked up on these criticisms at the Tory Party Conference in October 2010, maintaining:

Children are growing up ignorant of one of the most inspiring stories I know – the history of our United Kingdom. Our history has moments of pride, and shame, but unless we fully understand the struggles of the past we will not properly value the liberties of the present. The current approach we have to history denies children the opportunity to hear our island story. Children are given a mix of topics at primary, a cursory run through of Henry VIII and Hitler at secondary and many give up the subject at 14, without knowing how the vivid episodes of our past become a connected narrative. Well, this trashing of our past has to stop.[39]

Several commentators reacted with alarm that this was a programme for building nations rather than making historians. There were claims that an emphasis on the kinds of political history and key events Gove favoured would sideline the histories and experiences of minority groups, place too much emphasis on Britain (or, more accurately, England) to the exclusion of elsewhere, and privilege factual recall and narrative over analysis and discussion.[40] The curriculum which eventually emerged in September 2013, to little fanfare, took on board some of these criticisms and included more non-British history, but retained the chronological spine of enquiry.[41] Although the debate will rumble on, politics again provides a critical context within which to interpret this intervention in history schooling because this curriculum will not apply in Scotland or Wales where education matters are devolved, nor even to much of England, for the expanding body of academy schools, championed by the Coalition Government, are not compelled to follow its directives.

Conclusion

This chapter has chosen to concentrate on the ways in which history as taught in schools is often constructed in a complex relationship with structures of authority, particularly national governments. There are other dimensions to this topic which are worthy of investigation but are more elusive to explore and more difficult to quantify: how do history teachers implement or circumvent the curricula provided to them? What is the impact of these histories on schoolchildren, and how do they adopt or react against this knowledge as adults? How far does the history studied in schools influence the interests of the public at large? What is the relationship between historical developments in higher education and the teaching of the subject in schools? All of these are important elements to consider in the round, but the emphasis on the relationship between knowledge and power, as detailed in the cases discussed in this chapter, indicates how history is always taught within contexts that condition freedom of enquiry in sometimes subtle and sometimes obvious ways. As the discipline of history has become more reflexive and aware of its own origins, biases and limitations in recent times, so it is useful to reflect on the ways in which school history has been constrained and shaped by the politics of the present as well as that of the past.

STUDY QUESTIONS

- Why should children be educated about their national history at school?
- Do governments always involve themselves in the history curricula of the schools they supervise or control?
- Is it correct to discuss the close supervision of history in schools under totalitarian regimes alongside that of modern Britain? Are the examples comparable?
- Is the history taught at higher education institutions like universities free from government interference and control?

Notes

1   N. Woolf, 'US "Little Rebels" Protest against Changes to History Curriculum', *Guardian*, 26 September 2014: http://www.theguardian.com/world/2014/sep/26/-sp-colorado-ap-history-curriculum-protest-patriotism-schools-students. Accessed 16 January 2016.

2   S. Galo, 'In 1492, Columbus Sailed the Ocean Blue ... and Slaughtered the Indigenous Peoples He Found', *Guardian*, 13 October 2014: http://www.theguardian.com/commentisfree/2014/oct/13/christopher-columbus-slaughter-indigenous-people-history. Accessed 16 January 2016.

3   J. A. Diorio (1985) 'The Decline of History as a Tool of Moral Training', *History of Education Quarterly*, 25; K. E. McNeil (1993) 'The Role of Moral Education in the Teaching of History in Secondary Schools' (Durham University, MEd. thesis): http://etheses.dur.ac.uk/5545/. Accessed 16 January 2016; S. Wright (2012) 'Citizenship, Moral Education and the Elementary School', in L. Brockliss and N. Sheldon (eds), *Mass Education and the Limits of State Building 1870–1930* (Basingstoke: Palgrave).

4   S. Berger, M. Donovan and K. Passmore (eds) (1999) *Writing National Histories: Western Europe since 1800* (London and New York: Routledge).

5   Quoted in S. J. Heathorn (2000) *For Home, Country, and Race: Constructing Gender, Class and Englishness in the Elementary School, 1880–1914* (Toronto, ON: University of Toronto Press), p. 41.

6   Quoted in T. Baycroft (2013) *Culture, Identity and Nationalism: French Flanders in the Nineteenth and Twentieth Centuries* (Woodbridge: Boydell & Brewer), p. 105. See also P. Nora (1962) 'Ernest Lavisse: Son Rôle dans la Formation du Sentiment National', *Revue Historique*, 228.

7   T. Clayton (1998) 'Building the New Cambodia: Educational Destruction and Construction under the Khmer Rouge, 1975–1979', *History of Education Quarterly*, 38.

8 For Russia, see below, and for China, see C. T. Hu (1969) 'Orthodoxy over Historicity: The Teaching of History in Communist China', *Comparative Education Review*, 13; S. Weigelin-Schwiedrzik (1996) 'On *Shi* and *Lun*: Toward a Typology of Historiography in the PRC', *History and Theory*, 35; A. Jones (2005) 'Changing the Past to Serve the Present: History Education in Mainland China', in E. Vickers and A. Jones (eds), *History Education and National Identity in East Asia* (London and New York: Routledge); A. Jones (2007) 'Changing the Past to Build the Future: History Education in Post-Mao China' (University of Leeds, PhD thesis): http://etheses.whiterose.ac.uk/308/1/uk_bl_ethos_436447.pdf. Accessed 16 January 2016.

9 N. H. Gaworek (1977) 'Education, Ideology and Politics: History in Soviet Primary and Secondary Schools', *The History Teacher*, 11, p. 56.

10 Quoted in B. D. Wolfe (1964) 'Party Histories from Lenin to Khrushchev', in J. Keep (ed.), *Contemporary History in the Soviet Mirror* (London: Allen & Unwin), p. 43.

11 S. Fitzpatrick (1979) *Education and Social Mobility in the Soviet Union, 1921–1934* (Cambridge: Cambridge University Press), pp. 230–3.

12 D. Dorotich (1967) 'A Turning Point in the Soviet School: The Seventeenth Party Congress and the Teaching of History', *History of Education Quarterly*, 7.

13 M. A. Zinoviev (1952) *Soviet Methods of Teaching History*, trans. A. Muin-Pushkin (Ann Arbor: Edwards Brothers), p. 84.

14 R. D. Marwick (2001), *Rewriting History in Soviet Russia* (Basingstoke and New York: Palgrave), p. 42.

15 Quoted in Gaworek, 'Education, Ideology and Politics', p. 65.

16 A. B. Kamenskii (1997) *The Russian Empire in the Eighteenth Century: Searching for a Place in the World*, trans. D. Griffiths (Armonk, NY: M.E. Sharpe, Inc.), p. 6.

17 Gaworek, 'Education, Ideology and Politics', pp. 66–9.

18 This is charted with a journalist's vivid immediacy in D. Remnick (1993) *Lenin's Tomb: The Last Days of the Soviet Empire* (London: Vintage).

19 T. Kuzio (2002) 'History, Memory and Nation Building in the Post-Soviet Colonial Space', *Nationalities Papers*, 30; T. Kuzio (2005) 'Nation Building, History Writing and Competition over the Legacy of Kyiv Rus in Ukraine', *Nationalities Papers*, 33.

20 E. Levintova (2010) 'Past Imperfect: The Construction of History in the School Curriculum and Mass Media in Post-Communist Russia and Ukraine', and Karina Korostelina (2010) 'War of Textbooks: History Education in Russia and Ukraine', *Communist and Post-Communist Studies*, 43; K. Korostelina (2011) 'Shaping Unpredictable Past: National Identity and History Education in Ukraine', *National Identities*, 33; K. Korostelina (2013) 'Constructing Nation: National Narratives of History Teachers in Ukraine', *National Identities*, 15.

21 Korostelina, 'War of Textbooks', p. 131.

22 Korostelina, 'War of Textbooks', pp. 135–6, quote at p. 135.

23 C. Emmerson, 'Ukraine and Russia's History Wars', *History Today*: History Matters, 4 March 2014: http://www.historytoday.com/blog/2014/03/ukraine-and-russia's-history-wars. Accessed 16 January 2016.

24 Quoted in C. Harber (1989) *Politics in African Education* (London and Basingstoke: Macmillan), p. 106.

25 S. McGrath (1993), *Changing the Subject: Curriculum Change and Zimbabwean Education since Independence* (Edinburgh: Centre for African Studies), pp. 16–21.

26 T. Barnes (2007) '"History Has to Play Its Role": Constructions of Race and Reconciliation in Secondary School Historiography in Zimbabwe, 1980–2002', *Journal of Southern African Studies*, 33:3.

27 Barnes, '"History Has to Play Its Role"'; T. Ranger (2004) 'Nationalist Historiography, Patriotic History and the History of the Nation: The Struggle over the Past in Zimbabwe', *Journal of South African Studies*, 30.

28 Barnes, '"History Has to Play Its Role"', p. 649.

29 Ranger, 'Nationalist Historiography'.

30 I concentrate on England, because the devolution settlements of the 1990s make it difficult to discuss concisely history education policy in Northern Ireland, Wales and Scotland under the rubric of the 'United Kingdom'.

31 M. Price (1968) 'History in Danger', *History*, 53, p. 345.

32 N. Sheldon (2012) 'Politicians and History: The National Curriculum, National Identity and the Revival of the National Narrative', *History*, 93.

33 D. Cannadine, J. Keating and N. Sheldon (2011) *The Right Kind of History: Teaching the Past in Twentieth-Century England* (Basingstoke: Palgrave), pp. 156–80.

34 K. Crawford (1995) 'A History of the Right: The Battle for Control of National Curriculum History, 1989–1994', *British Journal of Educational Studies*, 43; R. Phillips (1998) 'Contesting the Past, Constructing the Future: History, Identity and Politics in Schools', *British Journal of Educational Studies*, 46; Sheldon, 'Politicians and History', pp. 256–71.

35 Quoted in L. Russell (2006) *Teaching the Holocaust in School History: Teachers or Preachers?* (London and New York: Continuum), p. 86.

36 Quoted in Crawford, 'A History of the Right', p. 442.

37 R. Samuel (1998) 'History's Battle for a New Past', in his *Island Stories: Unravelling Britain. Theatres of Memory, Volume II* (London and New York: Verso Books), p. 199.

38 Cannadine, Keating and Sheldon, *The Right Kind of History*, pp. 197–200.

39 Quoted in R. J. Evans, 'The Wonderfulness of Us (The Tory Interpretation of History)', *London Review of Books*, 33:6, 17 March 2011, p. 9.

40 For one example, see K. Bradley, L. Bowen, A. Mackillop, S. Middleton and N. Sheldon (2012) 'History in the UK National Curriculum: A Discussion', *Cultural and Social History*, 9.

41   United Kingdom Department of Education (2013) History National
     Curriculum in England Programmes of Study: https://www.gov.uk/
     government/publications/national-curriculum-in-england-history-programmes-
     of-study/national-curriculum-in-england-history-programmes-of-study.
     Accessed 16 January 2016.

Further Reading

'History, the Nation and Schools', *History Workshop Journal Online*: http://www.
   historyworkshop.org.uk/history-the-nation-and-the-schools/.
T. Barnes (2007) '"History Has to Play Its Role": Constructions of Race and
   Reconciliation in Secondary School Historiography in Zimbabwe, 1980–2002',
   Journal of Southern African Studies, 33:3, pp. 633–51.
D. Cannadine, J. Keating and N. Sheldon (2011) *The Right Kind of History:
   Teaching the Past in Twentieth-Century England* (Basingstoke: Palgrave).
K. Korostelina (2010) 'War of Textbooks: History Education in Russia and
   Ukraine', *Communist and Post-Communist Studies*, 43:2, pp. 129–37.
R. Phillips (1998) *History Teaching, Nationhood and the State: A Study in
   Educational Politics* (London: Cassell).
N. Sheldon (2012) 'Politicians and History: The National Curriculum, National
   Identity and the Revival of the National Narrative', *History*, 97, pp. 256–71.
E. Vickers and A. Jones (eds) (2005) *History Education and National Identity in
   East Asia* (Abingdon: Routledge).
T. Volodina (2005) 'Teaching History in Russia after the Collapse of the USSR',
   The History Teacher, 38:2, pp. 179–88.

14

History and Policy

Matthew Grant

In their advertising literature, designed to encourage prospective students to apply, history departments use a range of inspirational quotations. I vividly remember one used by the department in which I studied as an undergraduate. It was a statement Winston Churchill apparently made to an American schoolboy: 'Study history! In history lie all the secrets of statecraft'. There is a common belief that history can, and should, be used in the service of the present, and that it is the role of history to provide 'lessons from the past' for the politicians and civil servants who make up today's 'policy-makers'. The idea that history can help guide policy is an alluring prospect for historians and policy-makers alike: it suggests that there are patterns to events, which could become discernible in the present if only we paid attention to the past. But this grand idea is predicated not only on the basic assumption that we can learn from the past, but also on the idea that policy-makers and historians can communicate with each other: that policy-makers are willing to learn from history, and historians are willing – and able – to speak effectively to the concerns of policy-makers. As we shall see, this assumption is often far from the reality. In general, policy-makers and historians have passed each other like ships in the night: thinking about common issues, seeking solutions to similar problems, but all the while oblivious to what the other group is doing. This is now changing, and a growing number of historians are communicating with policy-makers more successfully. This is partly because recent changes to how research conducted in universities is funded have encouraged historians to engage with the policy-making process. The extent to which we can learn from the past, however, is still disputed.

Policy and history

At a basic level, 'policy' is inseparable from history. Politicians use history to justify themselves and their actions, or to score party-political points, as mistakes or supposed mistakes are held against opponents. Often, this political use of the past transcends history and shades into myth, as in the continued use, well into the mid-1990s, of the industrial unrest in the 'Winter of Discontent' in 1978–79 to suggest the Labour Party could not be trusted to run the country. In other ways, history is ever-present. It is no exaggeration to say that the entire direction of economic and social policy for the first three decades after 1945 was determined at least in part by the historical experience of Britain in the 1930s and 1940s – an age of both deep economic depression and total war.

History has shaped United Kingdom government policy in profound ways. Perhaps the best example of this is the British Government's foreign policy of the 1930s. The failure of the policy of appeasement to prevent the outbreak of the Second World War has been a central touchstone for British governments ever since, to the extent that 'Appeasement' or 'Munich' (after the German city which hosted the key 1938 meeting between Hitler and Neville Chamberlain) have become shorthand warnings against overconciliatory policies towards foreign powers. The 'lesson' of the 1930s was apparently that aggressors could not be 'appeased' with concessions, but would be emboldened by such 'weakness' into more violent actions. Chamberlain's failed policy cast a long shadow, and its memory has certainly influenced policy multiple times since 1945. It shaped the 'peace through strength' policy of nuclear deterrence in the Cold War, and has given British Prime Ministers a readymade tool for justifying military action against supposed aggressors, as seen in military actions in Suez (1956), the Falklands (1982) and Iraq (2003). It is no exaggeration to say that the history of appeasement has shaped British foreign policy and political attitudes to British power ever since the 1930s.[1] Appeasement, however, is a unique case of history scarring the national imagination, with the memory of an intensely felt humiliation always raw and at the forefront of the collective memory. This is an example of how history can influence policy because it is part of a general public discourse on the past and present status of the nation. The historical aspects of the discourse result from many different narratives, of which academic history is only a part – and a small part at that.

Policy-makers rarely engage with academic history in any sustained fashion, such as regularly reading books and articles written by professional historians. A recent study has suggested that politicians deploy research produced in universities in a 'symbolic' way – that is, to substantiate policy decisions and legitimize existing views, rather than to actively drive policy change.[2] Another summary of historians' critiques of political uses of the past concluded that history was 'opportunistically' exploited to justify policy decisions.³ Often when politicians *have* consulted historians, these have been chosen for their ideological affinity with the government in question, rather than solely for their professional expertise. For example, when Margaret Thatcher (1925–2013) was formulating policy towards the Soviet Union in the early 1980s, she organized a seminar of experts which included Robert Conquest (1917–2015), the noted historian of the Stalinist Terror of the 1930s. Conquest's views on the nature of Soviet politics and ideology, which greatly influenced Thatcher, were clearly both historical and political in nature; he was certainly an ardent supporter of her government.⁴

When it comes to using understandings the past to create or implement policy, the British political class has struggled. This is partly because of the belief, apparently inherent in politicians, that the pressing issues of the present – so important in their daily work – have no relationship to the issues faced by the generation before them. A related assumption is that the history of what we can call 'pre-watershed' political moments is redundant. To many in the political world, anything which occurred before the election of Tony Blair in 1997 is the distant past, while anything that predates the election of Margaret Thatcher is barely history at all, and like the building of Stonehenge or the functioning of the feudal economy can be consigned to the category of the politically negligible. This political bias against anything that smacks of a more distant past has had important consequences for how Britain has been governed. Political scientists Anthony King and Ivor Crewe have detailed a range of major policy blunders by British governments since 1979, caused by a variety of personal and institutional failings, but linked by a basic disconnect between policy *making* and policy *implementation*. King and Crewe argue that awareness of previous failings, and therefore the ability to learn from past mistakes, could radically improve the quality of government in Britain.⁵

The key lesson of history for policy-makers is perhaps that the failings of past governments need to be acknowledged and understood to ensure better government in the present and in the future. Of course, this requires the political class in Britain to engage directly with history. Peter Hennessy, a contemporary historian who sits in the House of Lords as Baron Hennessy of Nympsfield, has argued that there are two main ways in which the government could engage more seriously with history.⁶ The first is through the appointment of a 'Chief Historical Adviser' to Whitehall Departments, tasked with 'speaking truth unto power'. Hennessy hopes such a post would provide 'swiftly produced and easily digestible road map[s]' for policy-makers confronting live issues.⁷ This proposal assumes that knowledge of history (and previous policies) will help politicians to avoid the mistakes of the past. Yet the suggestion also raises the question of how such advisers would avoid becoming too close to their political masters, and whether they would actually provide a 'government-sanctioned' version of events. Would such an adviser be listened to and respected, both within government and the historical community?

Hennessy's second proposal also provokes anxieties about the relationship between history and government. He suggests that a renewed emphasis on 'official histories' (histories commissioned by the government to investigate and make public aspects of past policy) could correct the present-mindedness of many politicians. In Britain, official histories were published as early as 1908, but there was a step-change in the production and perceived value of this form of history from 1966, when a 'Peacetime Series' was commissioned to 'help both policymakers and historians'.[8] Hennessy believes official histories are valuable for 'policy-makers, Parliament and the reading public alike'.[9] In his view, a proliferation of official histories would benefit policy-makers by sustaining a 'collective memory' of the complexities of previous discussion, acknowledged as relevant to contemporary issues. Historians, on the other hand, would benefit from access to records closed to non-official historians. However, the privileged access 'official' status brings is not without its drawbacks. Official histories have to be cleared by the authorities before publication, and there are fears that historians can become 'institutionalized' by close collaboration with the government. The tensions involved can be seen from the fraught process leading up to the publication of Christopher Andrew's *The Defence of the Realm: the Authorized History of MI5* (2009). In his introduction, Andrew makes it clear he had 'unrestricted' access to secret files, and that 'no attempt' was made to influence his findings. Yet he also believes some excisions he was required to make to his original manuscript for reasons of 'national security' were overly stringent. One in particular, Andrew tells us, was 'hard to justify' (for obvious reasons, he cannot state which one!).[10] This rather absurd position, complaining of a decision which in itself is secret, highlights the basic tensions of researching and writing 'official' history. Increased access is traded for compromises in the final project, and the silencing of the historian's voice in some, unnamed, parts of the history can lead to charges of general censorship. One reviewer in a British national newspaper, for example, accused both Andrew and the Security Service of covering up unwelcome episodes in its history.[11] This raises the broader question of what the point of official history is for policy-makers. If what the historian is allowed to publish is limited, then policy-makers will lose the benefit of training the historical spotlight on vital areas, rather negating the whole point of the exercise.

Historians and policy

So far, this chapter has dealt with how various governments have used (or have failed to make use of) history, and how policy-makers might establish closer relationships with historians in future. In recent years, however, the relationship between history and policy has shifted to one in which increasingly historians actively seek to engage with policy-makers. In Britain, the most sustained attempt of historians to engage with policy debates is the History & Policy initiative, jointly run by the Institute of Contemporary British History at King's College, London, and the University of Cambridge. The initiative is based on the assumption, expressed in the run up to the 2010 election, that 'history is currently an under-used resource, but historical research and the input of expert historians could help shed light on current policy problems and the options available to manage them'.[12] The most innovative aspect of History & Policy is its attempt to promote the use of history by policy-makers. Rather than rely on the happenstance of politicians and policy-makers reading their books, History & Policy takes a more active approach to ensuring dialogue between historians and policy-makers. When the initiative was first set up in 2002, it relied heavily on free-to-access online policy briefings produced by historians to provide historical context on live political issues. This approach proved popular with historians, with over 150 such briefings produced by mid-2014, but the mere existence of these papers is not enough to actually influence policy: unsolicited policy advice is rarely picked up. More recently, the initiative has expanded its avenues for interested historians to influence policy-making by staging workshops and seminars where historians can speak directly to civil servants in government. The aim of these events is to connect 'historians, departments and journalists'.[13] The initiative also provides media training to historians who want their research to reach policy-makers or the press, recognizing that traditional academic skills do not help historians to present their findings in the brief, bite-sized chunks desired by media or Whitehall 'consumers'. Certainly, in retrospect my own policy paper of 2009 now appears far too focused on academic findings, rather than their policy implications, to be of interest to any potential policy-maker.[14] History & Policy has been a trailblazer for attempts to use historical research to improve policy. Its efforts now seem particularly important given the new emphasis within the UK Higher Education (HE) sector on the ability of academics to prove that their research has 'impact' on the world outside the university system.

Indeed, in today's world the relationship between history and policy is inseparable from the financial context in which UK higher education operates. Universities in the United Kingdom have two main aims: to advance knowledge (Research) and to impart that knowledge to students (Education). The money which funds these multi-million-pound institutions likewise comes mostly from Research and Education. Education income derives largely, and increasingly, from tuition fees raised from students. Universities in England now receive no direct government funding for teaching students in arts and humanities subjects such as history, although more cost-intensive science, medicine and engineering subjects continue to receive a hefty grant per student to enable universities to continue teaching in these areas. Research income, however, is still very much reliant on government funding. Historical research receives government money in two ways. The first is through assessments run by each of the four UK Higher Education Funding Councils,[15] currently called the Research Excellence Framework (REF), which evaluate the quality of research produced in each discipline ('Unit of Assessment') in each University, and allocate research money accordingly (most recently in REF 2014). The second is through research funding awarded to historians, as individuals or teams, through competitive schemes run by government-funded Research Councils, usually either the Arts and Humanities Research Council (AHRC), or the Economic and Social Research Council (ESRC). It is important to emphasize that the discipline's reliance on funding from government sources does not compromise research independence. Far from it; as we shall see, historians are always willing to attack the faulty reasoning of governments.

Academic freedom may continue unfettered, but changes to how research 'quality' is measured both by REF 2014 and the Funding Councils has, for the first time, instituted direct financial benefits to engaging with policy for historians in the UK. Within REF 2014, 20 per cent of the research quality score for each Unit of Assessment was determined by 'Research Impact'. Likewise, the Research Councils assess the quality of applications according to their potential 'impact' as well as the overall worth of the proposed programme in 'pure' research terms. 'Impact' in this sense is not sharply defined. Indeed, the different Research Councils define 'impact' differently, and the Funding Councils also instituted their own definition for REF 2014. Put broadly, 'impact' is the beneficial effects of research for government, society and culture outside of higher education. The new financial incentives for demonstrating 'impact' are transforming how historians engage with the public, and with social and cultural actors and institutions. Universities understand their financial health now requires them to pursue the 'impact' agenda, and so staff are now encouraged to apply their research to wider audiences.

The new obsession with 'impact' has attracted much criticism. When the plans for REF 2014 were first outlined in detail, the historian Stefan Collini mounted a powerful assault on the concept of 'impact'. He pointed out that what constitutes 'impact' is very vague, and there are problems with how it is measured. The REF makes a hard-line distinction between those 'inside' and 'outside' higher education, discounting the most obvious and profound way academics influence the world: through teaching students. The REF definition also conflates 'impact' with 'benefit', assuming that if the research has 'affected' people, then that is beneficial to society at large. 'Impact' as defined by the REF also has to derive from *direct* efforts to engage 'outside users'. In the example Collini gives, the Anglo-Saxon historian whose work influences a museum director to develop a new exhibition, but who did not actively seek this outcome, cannot be described as part of her department's 'efforts to exploit or apply the research findings'.[16] Finally, Collini laments that far from promoting research quality, the obsession with 'impact' could serve to promote 'meretricious and vulgarising treatments' of topics, in the hope of generating popular media coverage of research findings, rather than the nuanced argument which the very best research provides.[17]

Influence on policy was only one aspect of how 'impact' was measured in REF 2014. The results of this exercise showed that although a majority of departmental 'impact case studies' mentioned 'policy', this often only provided context for social or cultural 'impacts'. Only a relatively small number of these case studies claimed that historical research had directly influenced policy – although these did provide rich examples of the potentially far-reaching practical applications of historical investigations, from research on biological and chemical weapons,[18] to guidance on ethnically appropriate health provision.[19] Quite apart from 'impact' on policy, these case studies showed that cultural and social 'impact' was widespread, diverse and genuinely important. It is clear that Collini's fears about his Anglo-Saxon historian ended up wide of the mark, as several examples of 'impact' highlighted the work of historians with galleries, museums and archives, helping them develop new displays, change their historical narratives or curatorial practice, or put on new exhibitions. Such collaboration could lead to dramatic increases in visitors to the museum. Moreover, it is clear from how REF 2014 was assessed that these forms of 'impact' often scored the very highest grade.

The 'impact' agenda means that never before has so much importance been attached to active engagement with policy-makers. Historians have seized this opportunity and, perhaps more importantly, universities have also sought to create opportunities for academics (who are, after all, their employees) to do so. 'Impact' has become central to the landscape of academic research mainly because the government believes that the HE sector needs to contribute more directly to national economic and social well-being – to escape from the ivory tower and justify the large amount of money it receives from the state. Universities and Research Councils have had little option but to adapt to the priorities of those holding the purse strings. For individual academics, the new emphasis on 'impact' has created a dilemma. Some believe it is a dangerous imposition on academic freedom. Others see it as an unfortunate development which has to be lived with. However, many see it as a continuation of the genuine desire to engage with the world beyond universities and to make a difference in the world – as the History & Policy initiative proved long before 'impact' was enshrined within REF 2014. Countless historians believe that their insights into the past can make a valuable contribution to contemporary debates over a wide field. This is not new: some historians have always interacted with broad publics, but 'impact' has given fresh impetus to these efforts, providing time and money to help those with a passion for public engagement to shape the world around them.

A dangerous partnership?

Although it is difficult to judge, so far it seems as though the 'impact' agenda has had broadly positive effects in encouraging academic engagement with the world outside universities. However, commentators such as Collini were right to suggest that historians must be alert to the *potential* effects of the 'impact' agenda. In 2010, an argument erupted about the influence of the Conservative-Liberal Democrat Coalition Government's 'Big Society' initiative on how research was funded. This initiative was founded on the view that through bottom-up volunteering, local groups were better able to develop community-based services than those run by national or local government, who were often detached from the real needs of areas they controlled. Critics argued that the policy was mere cover for a series of planned cuts to local services, with Conservative leader David Cameron dressing up an attempt to row back the boundaries of the state as social and civic renewal. Whatever the ideological basis of the plan, the Big Society was heavily promoted by the new Government after it came to power in May 2010.[20]

The Big Society attracted the critical attention of historians from the beginning. A general consensus emerged, arguing that the Big Society initiative was mistaken in its basic assumptions: the Government had overestimated the ability of the voluntary sector to drive social change without support from the state, and had miscalculated when arguing that voluntary action was in decline.[21] As earlier historians had shown, many charities were not community-led, bottom-up transformers of society, but were instead almost entirely reliant on government grants.[22] Of course, critics argued, these grants were being cut by the Coalition Government in the name of the Big Society.

This intellectual antipathy to the Big Society helps us to understand the anger following a shift by one of the Funding Councils which appeared to prioritize research into the Big Society. In December 2010, the AHRC announced a new 'Delivery Plan', which discussed how it could 'contribute' to the Big Society in a range of ways, primarily through its Connected Communities programme. Historical research funded within this programme, the AHRC declared, might include 'the evolution of civic institutions mediating between the citizen and the state and the role of these institutions in developing (or frustrating) engagement (e.g. schools, churches, GP practices, the voluntary sector)'. Such research would have been important to formulating Big Society policy. The tone of the Plan further suggested that the Connected Communities programme would help, rather than merely investigate, or even critique, this controversial government policy.[23] A few months later, at the end of March 2011, the *Observer* alleged that the Department of Business, Innovation and Skills (BIS) had told the AHRC that naming research into the Big Society as one of its 'priority areas' was 'non-negotiable if it wished to maintain its funding'. The piece quoted historian Peter Mandler as arguing that such intervention directly contravened the Haldane Principle, which states that government-funded research must be conducted free from political interference.[24]

The same day the *Observer* article was published, the AHRC categorically denied any political influence over its choice of funding priorities: 'We did NOT receive our funding settlement on condition that we supported the "Big Society", and we were NOT instructed, pressured or otherwise coerced by BIS or anyone else into support for this initiative'.[25] This statement pointed out that the Connected Communities programme, *not* the Big Society, was an AHRC priority area, and had been from 2008, well before the election of the coalition. This denial did not convince everyone, and the episode resulted in a series of resignations from the AHRC's Peer Review College (the body of academics who, on an unpaid basis, read, comment on, and evaluate funding applications submitted to the Council), as well as calls for resistance to the politicization of academic research.[26]

The extent to which the AHRC was pressured by the government is difficult to gauge. One perceptive commentator has argued that there was almost certainly no *direct* pressure, but the closeness between the Council and the Government is perhaps even more troubling than direct interference.[27] It seems most likely that the AHRC, concerned about protecting its budget at a time of deep government cuts to public services, latched onto the government's obsession with the Big Society and attempted to underline the relevance of its existing research priorities to the government's agenda. In one sense this is perfectly understandable strategic reasoning. As the AHRC pointed out in its refutation of the *Observer*'s charges, there was clear overlap between the aims of the longstanding Connected Communities programme and the Big Society initiative.[28] However, the AHRC did embrace these similarities rather too enthusiastically for some people. Certainly, the 2010 Delivery Plan's promise to 'contribute' created the impression that the AHRC wished to support rather than to research the Big Society. Such references were noticeably absent when the AHRC published a new strategy in March 2013.[29]

It is easy to understand why so many academics were exercised by the issue. Government intervention in research agendas is repugnant to virtually all academics, who prize intellectual freedom above all; for the government to use academics as fig-leaves covering the ideological dismantling of the state borders on the obscene. In the end, the Big Society initiative died a discreet death, the victim of both lack of political capital to force the policy through and its own fundamental flaws. The AHRC's apparent bandwagon jumping, and certainly the language of its 2010 Delivery Plan document, now seems slightly ridiculous considering the ignominious end of the Big Society initiative. The Connected Communities programme, however, continues to flourish, and has funded a range of projects on the changing nature of communities and societies. It has been more successful than ideologically driven initiatives such as the Big Society could ever be, precisely because assumptions about the nature of (for example) social cohesion require interrogation outside the bounds of party-political discourse. This incident provides a salutary lesson for all academics who engage with policy: policy initiatives come and go very quickly, but academic concerns with the fundamental questions of our society and culture will always remain.

Learning from the past

If the furore over the Big Society showed the problems that can arise from the way higher education is now funded, there can be no doubt that those changes have had a part in inspiring historians to engage with the way we in the present can learn from the past. Few would now agree with Churchill that 'all' the secrets of statecraft, or indeed anything else, can be learned from the past. But historians do believe that *something* can be learned, and many stress that the process of engaging with and informing policy is essential to the discipline. John Tosh, in a powerful book on *Why History Matters* (2008), argues that historians need to be more active within political culture, combating the lazy historical assumptions of politicians and media alike. He gives the example of the misuse of history in the build-up to the Iraq war of 2003, arguing that the intervention of historians would have 'equipped' the public with 'the relevant historical material' to understand the issues. I suspect this way of engaging with policy, with the historian in the role of sage correcting the wrongs of the political elite, would attract many historians, and Tosh is surely right to argue that the role of history is to disrupt easy comparisons. However, more problematically, Tosh argues that history should be applied to policy 'in ways that are defined neither by politics or ideology'.[30] All interventions into political culture are 'political', and all of us bring 'ideology' to any discussion. Rather than try to push such things to one side, it is better for historians to recognize themselves as political and ideological subjects if they wish to be historically engaged activists in way hoped for by Tosh and, a long time before him, Max Weber.[31]

Taking a different approach, Jo Guldi and David Armitage's *The History Manifesto* (2014) confidently asserts history's ability to answer the big questions facing both policy-makers and society as a whole, and takes historians to task for failing to provide 'usable' histories which can tackle such questions as coping with climate change. For them, history's duty is to tackle the 'short-termism' which bedevils current political and social discourse. The discipline can only do this, they argue, if historians abandon the 'short-termism' of detailed small-scale histories in their own research and return to telling 'arching stories of scale'.[32] Guldi and Armitage provide an alluring vision of historians shaping the 'public future' by 'developing a *longue durée* contextual background against which archival information, events, and sources can be interpreted', and which will enable historians to help imagine alternative futures for the world.[33] In some respects, this follows John Arnold's belief that

Contemporary political ideology often grounds its authority through either a claim to radical novelty, or an assumption of what is 'natural' or 'traditional'. Only through a long view can these claims be successfully critiqued: for example, notions of what constitute a 'family' or the varying claims of nationhood or the disparate forms of collective social action through which many communities have prospered.[34]

Arnold highlights the need for historians to attack rooted assumptions and received ideas. In this view, medieval and early modern history are just as, if not more, important to policy than the histories of the recent past which so dominate the History & Policy website. *The History Manifesto*, however, is more proscriptive. It seems to blame historians for turning their backs on policy-makers in order to undertake research on ever-more concentrated past episodes, holding them to account for seeking to deepen knowledge of history itself. The book's privileging of grand-scale histories of the *longue durée* over 'micro' studies suggests a radical, and unacceptable, contraction of what the discipline should do, and it has been heavily criticized both for this argument and the evidence used to support it.[35] In the UK in particular, the evidence of REF 2014 suggests that historians *are* heavily engaged with the world around them, often on the basis of the sort of 'narrow' work Guldi and Armitage would have us jettison.

The crux of the matter is that history does not exist to provide simple answers to complex issues. It cannot supply quick or easy answers – any suggestion that it can ignores what it is to be truly historical – but it can suggest contemporary parallels with, and ways of approaching, the past. To suggest that a policy is directly and unproblematically 'rooted' in specific past events is teleological. Often, such suggestions neglect to consider the influence of intervening periods of time in shaping the immediate policy context. To claim that any policy issue of today is exactly the same as one from, say, 1962, is ahistorical. For example, the foreign policy deliberations of governments after 1945 were never simple re-runs of the 'Appeasement' issue. The political, economic and social contexts of each issue are necessarily completely different, and any lopsided emphasis on similarities does a disservice to both history *and* policy. In the same way, promising that the 'lessons of the past' can provide easy or unambiguous answers for the future, even if based on a '*longue durée*', does a disservice to both the future *and* history.

Conclusion

What history can and does do is highlight the contingent and uncertain nature of the world around us. Historians speak of 'the pastness of the past'. This is the very quality that makes history so exciting to study, but it is also what is most easily lost when historians attempt to engage with policy. All too often, the emphasis is on making the past look like the present. However, this is also exactly why history is relevant to policy-making. To put it another way, history can show policy-makers and the public that there are different choices to be made, that the assumptions which rule policy are just that – assumptions – not hard-and-fast laws. Traditions can be powerful shapers of policy, but traditions are often surprisingly recent.[36] History is there to show that there are unintended, often profound, consequences of any policy decision, but not to show what those consequences will be. History does this as effectively, perhaps more effectively, through closely reasoned small-scale studies as through long-term 'grand narratives'. What is needed, for historians and policy-makers alike, is the realization that history's influence on policy is far from certain, has often been negative and is best used not as a lamp illuminating the path ahead, but as a red man on a pedestrian crossing – requiring us to stop, look both ways and only proceed when safe to do so.

STUDY QUESTIONS

- Can we learn from the past?
- What are the potential benefits and problems of governments engaging more directly with history?
- Should historians attempt to make an 'impact' on policy-making, society and culture?

Notes

1   R. Gerald Hughes (2014) *The Postwar Legacy of Appeasement: British Foreign Policy since 1945* (London: Bloomsbury).

2   C. Boswell, 'Research Impact on Policy-Making Is Often Understood in Instrumentalist Terms, but More Often Plays Symbolic Roles', *LSE Impact Blog*, 17 July 2014: http://blogs.lse.ac.uk/impactofsocialsciences/2014/07/17/research-impact-policy-symbolic-instrumental/. Accessed 16 January 2016.

3   See M. Reiz, 'Past Mistakes', *Times Higher Education*, 15 October 2009: http://www.timeshighereducation.co.uk/408693.article. Accessed 16 January 2016.

4   A. Brown (2008) 'The Change to Engagement in Britain's Cold War Policy: The Origins of the Thatcher-Gorbachev Relationship', *Journal of Cold War Studies*, 10:3.

5   A. King and I. Crewe (2013) *The Blunders of Our Governments* (London: Oneworld Publications).

6   P. Hennessy (2012) *Distilling the Frenzy: Writing the History of One's Own Times* (London: Biteback Publishing), pp. 187–9.

7   Hennessy, *Distilling the Frenzy*, p. 187.

8   R. Lowe (2008) 'Official History', Institute of Historical Research: Making History: http://www.history.ac.uk/makinghistory/resources/articles/official_history.html. Accessed 16 January 2016.

9   Hennessy, *Distilling the Frenzy*, p. 188.

10 C. Andrew (2009) *The Defence of the Realm: the Authorized History of MI5* (London: Penguin), p. xx.

11 D. Leigh, '*The Defence of the Realm: The Authorized History of MI5 by Christopher Andrew*', *Guardian*, 10 October 2009: http://www.theguardian.com/books/2009/oct/10/defence-of-the-realm-mi5. Accessed 7 November 2014.

12 M. Porter and A. Reid (3 May 2010) 'Today's Toughest Policy Problems: How History Can Help', *History & Policy*: http://www.historyandpolicy.org/policy-papers/papers/todays-toughest-policy-problems-how-history-can-help. Accessed 16 January 2016.

13 History & Policy (no date) 'What We Do': http://www.historyandpolicy.org/about-us/what-we-do. Accessed 16 January 2016.

14 M. Grant (2009) 'Upgrading Britain's Nuclear Deterrent: From V-Bombers to Trident Replacement', *History & Policy*: http://www.historyandpolicy.org/policy-papers/papers/upgrading-britains-nuclear-deterrent-from-v-bombers-to-trident-replacement. Accessed 16 January 2016.

15 There is a Higher Education Funding Council for each nation of the UK, although Northern Irish funding is dealt with by the Northern Ireland Department for Employment and Learning.

16 S. Collini (2012) *What Are Universities For?* (London: Penguin), p. 174.

17 Collini, *What Are Universities For?* p. 172.

18 University of Kent (2015) 'Cold War at Porton Down: Medical Ethics and Legal Dimensions of Britain's Biological and Chemical Warfare Programme, 1945–1989', REF 2014 Impact Case Studies: http://impact.ref.ac.uk/CaseStudies/CaseStudy.aspx?Id=951. Accessed 16 January 2016.

19 University of Warwick (2015) 'Ethnicity, Health and Medicine in Postcolonial Britain: The Value of History in Improving the Delivery of Ethnically Appropriate Health Research, Services and Policy', REF 2014 Impact Case Studies: http://impact.ref.ac.uk/CaseStudies/CaseStudy.aspx?Id=23552. Accessed 16 January 2016.

20 Cabinet Office (2010) *Building the Big Society*: https://www.gov.uk/government/publications/building-the-big-society. Accessed 16 January 2016.

21 M. Hilton and J. McKay (eds) (2011) *The Ages of Voluntarism: How We Got to the Big Society* (Oxford: Oxford University Press); A. Ishkanian and S. Szreter (eds) (2012) *The Big Society Debate: A New Agenda for Social Policy?* (Cheltenham: Edward Elgar Publishing).

22 See G. Finlayson (1994) *Citizen, State and Social Welfare in Britain, 1830–1990* (Oxford: Oxford University Press).

23   AHRC (2010) Delivery Plan, 2011–2015: http://www.ahrc.ac.uk/documents/strategy/arts-humanities-research-council-delivery-plan-2011-2015/. Accessed 16 January 2016.

24   D. Boffey, 'Academic Fury over Order to Study the Big Society', *Observer*, 27 March 2011: http://www.theguardian.com/education/2011/mar/27/academic-study-big-society. Accessed 16 January 2016.

25   AHRC, 'Important Statement', 27 March 2011. Press releases issued by the AHRC are only available on its website for three years.

26   P. Jump, 'AHRC Big Society Row Deepens as 42 Peer Reviewers Pull Out and Call for Mass Resignations', *Times Higher Education*, 27 June 2011: http://www.timeshighereducation.co.uk/416641.article. Accessed 16 January 2016.

27   P. Benneworth (2011) 'The AHRC Funding Debate Must Now Focus on What Is Really Important', *LSE Blog*: http://eprints.lse.ac.uk/35743/1/blogs.lse.ac.uk-The_AHRC_funding_debate_must_now_focus_on_what_is_really_important_ensuring_that_academics_retain_the.pdf. Accessed 16 January 2016.

28   AHRC, 'Important Statement'.

29   AHRC (2013) *The Arts and Humanities in Our Times: AHRC Strategy, 2013–2018*: http://www.ahrc.ac.uk/documents/publications/the-human-world-the-arts-and-humanities-in-our-times-ahrc-strategy-2013-2018/. Accessed 16 January 2016.

30   J. Tosh (2008) *Why History Matters* (Basingstoke: Palgrave Macmillan), p. x.

31   M. Weber (1999) 'Science as a Vocation', in H. H. Werth and C. W. Mills (eds), *From Max Weber: Essays in Sociology*, trans. Werth and Mills (London: Routledge) [1919].

32   J. Guldi and D. Armitage (2014) *The History Manifesto* (Cambridge: Cambridge University Press), pp. 7–8.

33   Guldi and Armitage, *The History Manifesto*, p. 117.

34   J. Arnold (2008) 'Why History Matters – and Why Medieval History Also Matters', *History & Policy*: http://www.historyandpolicy.org/policy-papers/papers/why-history-matters-and-why-medieval-history-also-matters. Accessed 16 January 2016.

35   See, in particular, D. Cohen and P. Mandler (2015) '*The History Manifesto*: A Critique', *American Historical Review*, 120:2.

36   E. Hobsbawm and T. Ranger (eds) (1983) *The Invention of Tradition* (Cambridge: Cambridge University Press).

Further Reading

S. Collini (2012) *What Are Universities For?* (London: Penguin).
J. Guldi and D. Armitage (2014) *The History Manifesto* (Cambridge: Cambridge University Press).
P. Hennessy (2012) *Distilling the Frenzy: Writing the History of One's Own Times* (London: Biteback Publishing).

R. G. Hughes (2014) *The Postwar Legacy of Appeasement: British Foreign Policy since 1945* (London: Bloomsbury).

A. King and I. Crewe (2013) *The Blunders of Our Governments* (London: Oneworld Publications).

M. Macmillan (2009) *The Uses and Abuses of History* (London: Profile Books).

J. Tosh (2008) *Why History Matters* (Basingstoke: Palgrave Macmillan).

M. Weber (1999) 'Science as a Vocation', in H. H. Werth and C. W. Mills (eds), *From Max Weber: Essays in Sociology*, trans. Werth and Mills (London: Routledge) [1919], pp. 129–55.

15

Historical Novels

Tracey Loughran

The room is dark. A subdued light emanates from an electrical battery. The doctor locks the door and tells his patient, a mute soldier, 'You will not leave this room until you are talking as well as you ever did; no, not before'. He inserts a tongue depressor into the patient's mouth to keep it open, and attaches electrodes to his pharynx. The initial application of electricity knocks the patient backwards, detaching the wires from the electrical battery. The doctor reattaches the wires and applies weaker doses of electricity, all the while exhorting the patient to speak, until eventually he produces a whisper. After more than ninety minutes of continuous effort and application of electricity, the patient becomes tired. The doctor walks him around the room to keep him awake. He prompts the patient to continue talking as he walks. Each whisper is hard-won. Every time the patient produces a sound, his neck muscles contract and his head violently jerks. He tries to escape more than once, but is unable to force the door open. At one point in the 'treatment', he breaks down in tears. The doctor continues to apply electricity until the patient can repeat vowels, letters of the alphabet, days of the week, months of the year and numbers. He continues to apply electricity until the patient can speak without stammering or going into spasms. As the spasms disappear from the patient's neck and jaw, his left arm develops a tremor. The doctor re-applies the electrodes and applies electricity to the arm until the tremor disappears, and then promptly reappears in the right arm. Before the tremor disappears altogether, it has to be chased from the left arm, right arm, left leg and right leg. The 'treatment' lasts four hours in all, before the patient is deemed cured and allowed to leave the room.

This is a true story. The 'treatment' was carried out in 1917 at the National Hospital for the Paralysed and Epileptic in London by the Canadian neurologist Lewis Yealland (1884–1954); we know his patient only as Case A1. But there are two potential endings to this narrative. In the first version, the patient is pleased to be cured. He exclaims, 'Doctor, doctor, I am champion'. Yealland replies, 'You are a hero'. In the second version, the doctor asks, 'Are you not pleased to be cured?' The patient smiles. Yealland objects to the smile, and attaches an electrode to the side of the patient's mouth. After a further dose of electricity, the patient does not smile again. Instead, he thanks the doctor and salutes him. The first ending is taken from a historical document, Yealland's medical text *Hysterical Disorders of Warfare* (1918), and, so far as we know, accurately describes what happened in that electrical room. The second is taken from Pat Barker's historical novel *Regeneration* (1991), and the events which conclude this narrative almost certainly did not take place.

It is tempting to say simply that one of these stories is true and the other is not. Yealland participated in the events he describes, and wrote his account shortly after Case A1's 'treatment'. Barker was not alive during the First World War. Her version, written nearly seventy-five years after the Armistice, takes advantage of the novelist's licence to embroider and embellish. Yet it is not as easy as it first seems to draw the line between history and fiction. If parts of Barker's story spring from the novelist's imagination, other parts are demonstrably based on historical evidence. The story of Case A1's 'treatment' told in the first paragraph of this chapter could have been adapted from either Yealland's or Barker's text. Until the ending, these accounts are virtually identical in substance and in detail. Barker's account is neither wholly true nor wholly false. To further complicate matters, the integrity of the historical evidence is itself questionable. We have only Yealland's word that Case A1 ever existed, and he clearly recounted this case history to show that his form of treatment worked. Even if Yealland's account is entirely faithful to the facts as he remembered them, Case A1 might have viewed these events in a very different way. Indeed, Yealland's report of the soldier's gratitude following extended and painful electrical 'treatment' is best read sceptically: here the text seems to slip into overt propaganda. Yealland's text is a historical document, but we do not know whether it is true, and parts of it ring false.

This chapter reflects on the aims, methods and achievements of historical novels as mediums for approaching the past. A historical novel is one which 'has as its setting a period of history and [...] attempts to convey the spirit, manners, and social conditions of a past age with realistic detail and fidelity (which is in some cases only apparent fidelity) to historical fact'.[1] Consideration of similarities and differences between history and historical novels furthers our understanding of both forms. Historical novelists have an explicit licence to fictionalize which academic historians lack, but in other respects their practice is similar. Both conduct research, use evidence (albeit in very different ways) to support their claims to authentic representation of the past, and attempt to deepen understanding of past lives and events. Both select and interpret evidence, use imaginative reconstruction to obviate gaps or deficiencies in the historical record, and construct narratives which attribute specific meanings to the past. As illustrated by the similar yet divergent accounts of Case A1's 'treatment', it is sometimes difficult to draw hard-and-fast boundaries between history and historical fiction. Precisely because this boundary is permeable and sometimes difficult to police, an exploration of the relationship between history and historical novels provokes complex questions about power, responsibility and authenticity, the construction of meaning, and the use of history to legitimate or challenge different versions of the past.[2]

History and the historical novel

In what does the difference between history and fiction reside? There are real and important differences between history and fiction, but these are not self-evident, and it is necessary to probe this boundary to fully appreciate the purposes and achievements of either form. History 'stands for the search for some kind of truth about the past', while fiction 'has to do with such claims, descriptions, explanations' which do not aspire to this kind of verifiable truth.[3] This is not a division between objective fact and subjective interpretation. As Kevin Passmore shows elsewhere in this volume, the kind of historical objectivity to which early professional historians aspired is a mirage. There is no part of the research process which is free from selection, interpretation, or the human perspective of the historian. History is never a matter of pure 'fact', and so this is not what separates history from the more overtly imaginative work of fiction.

There are further difficulties in drawing boundaries between history and fiction. Only fragments of the past survive in the form of evidence. The historian must knit these together into some kind of coherent shape, aware that large hunks will never be recovered, and that it is impossible to know for certain how the extant shards originally slotted together. Attempts at reconstruction are like trying to complete a jigsaw puzzle with no idea how many pieces the set originally contained, and only the haziest idea of what the picture is supposed to look like. Moreover, in organizing evidence into narratives which have a beginning, middle and an end, historians impose meaning and order on the chaos of potentially limitless evidence of past lives and events. This process involves implicit and explicit claims about causation (A led to B because of C) which can be argued, but never ultimately proved.[4] Some literary scholars and postmodernist historians claim that because historians create narratives out of incomplete and contestable evidence, there is no real distinction between the knowledge claims of history and fiction: history cannot tell a verifiable 'truth'; it is only one more story.[5] Many historians accept that objectivity is not possible and narratives are never innocent, but reject this radical conclusion. We maintain there is a difference between history and fiction.

This difference lies in fidelity to the historical evidence. As a character invented by the novelist and historian Wallace Stegner (1909–93) states, a novelist is permitted freely to 'invent within the logic of a situation', but the historian is constrained 'to invent within a body of inhibiting facts'.[6] Different rules govern the use of evidence in histories and historical novels. These rules centre on the degree to which it is permissible to deviate from the historical record, and accepted conventions for acknowledging the use of sources. Historians cannot provide definitive accounts of the past, but nevertheless aim to write *valid* histories. They test hypotheses against available evidence, and revise their claims in the light of these findings. Historians must work within the limits imposed by the available evidence. Speculation is only permitted where there are gaps in the documentary record. Even then, conjectures must arise out of the available evidence and the historian must clearly signal the provisional status of such claims. This is achieved through the scholarly apparatus of footnotes and bibliography, which demonstrates adherence to the documentary record, and allows historical claims to be verified. In practice, historians sometimes unwittingly deviate from these professional standards. It is even arguable that disciplinary conventions such as use of the impersonal voice actually work to disguise interpretation as fact, and to conceal the provisional status of all histories.[7] Yet these difficulties do not undermine the goal of treating evidence with integrity, and in an open manner. If scholars knowingly depart from these aims, they can no longer be described as historians.

'Authenticity', artificiality and the author's responsibility to the past

We might then ask a different question: what are the *similarities* between history and historical fiction? The historical novel is a hybrid form: it is fiction which also owes something to history. The fictional elements of historical novels make them 'not-history', but the historical elements also make them unlike other forms of fiction. Historical novelists often conduct substantial amounts of research. For example, Sarah Waters wrote a PhD thesis on historical fiction, and her own novels are meticulously researched. For *The Paying Guests* (2014), a crime story set in the 1920s, she consulted 'newspapers, diaries, letters, maps, photographs' and made extensive efforts to 'get to grips with police procedure, legal process, forensics, fashion, cookery and housework'.[8] The historical novelist is often 'an accumulator and sifter and sorter of facts, dates and research' as well as a storyteller in the more conventional sense.[9]

Historical novelists therefore operate somewhere in the space between absolute fidelity to the historical evidence and complete fabrication. However, there is no standard mode of negotiating the boundaries between fact and fiction. Ian McEwan, whose *Atonement* (2001) is set partly in the Second World War, categorically states that although the historical novelist 'may resent his dependence on the written record, on memoirs and eye-witness accounts [...] there is no escape: Dunkirk or a wartime hospital can be novelistically realised, but they cannot be reinvented'.[10] A marginally less forensic approach is to invent only what *cannot* be known, as does Hilary Mantel: 'I will make up the thoughts of a man's heart, but I will not make up the colour of his drawing room wallpaper. I had much rather move the action to his study, where I know what colour the wallpaper was'.[11]

A more overtly imaginative reconstruction is undertaken by Gaynor Arnold, whose *Girl in a Blue Dress* (2008) uses the fictional characters of Dorothea and Alfred Gibson to loosely re-imagine the lives of Charles and Catherine Dickens. Arnold created new characters, family relationships, scenes and dialogue but nevertheless insists that she 'attempted to keep true to the essential natures of the two main protagonists as I have come to understand them'.[12] This is different order of fictionalization again from Robert Harris's counterfactual novel *Fatherland* (1992), which imagines a world in which Germany won the Second World War. (Counterfactual novels explore alternate histories, using historical events which never happened as the point of departure.) Harris inserts into the text both genuine and fabricated historical documents relating to the Holocaust. Even here, he claims some kind of fidelity to the record: 'Where I have created documents, I have tried to do so on the basis of fact'.[13] There are different degrees and kinds of fictionalization, and the admixture of history and fiction in any historical novel cannot be neatly quantified or disentangled.

This is especially evident in a novel such as *Regeneration*, which contains an unusually high proportion of fact to fiction. The novel explores the relationship between the poet Siegfried Sassoon (1886–1967) and the psychiatrist W.H.R. Rivers (1864–1922) at Craiglockhart War Hospital in Edinburgh, where Sassoon was sent for psychological treatment following a highly publicized protest against the war. Other real-life figures feature in the novel, including the poets Wilfred Owen (1893–1918) and Robert Graves (1895–1985). Many of the patients treated in Barker's Craiglockhart are based on case studies in W.H.R. Rivers's works. The novel opens with the transcript of Sassoon's 'Soldier's Declaration', published in the *Times* in July 1917, and Barker directly cites or paraphrases numerous other historical sources, including memoirs, autobiographies and letters as well as psychiatric texts. One episode which seems highly contrived, when Sassoon helps Owen to redraft his famous poem 'Anthem for Doomed Youth' (1917), did actually happen: a manuscript of the poem, with amendments in Sassoon's handwriting, is the basis for Barker's imagining of the conversation between the two men.

Like many other historical novelists, Barker professes a sense of responsibility towards the past. She has emphasized that 'it was always very important to me that I didn't change anything about the historical characters, that they actually thought and said what I've said they thought and did on a particular day'.[14] Yet because Barker does not reference her sources in the same way as an academic historian, only a reader deeply immersed in the literature and history of the First World War could separate out fact and fiction in the novel. Barker instead adopts a common practice of historical novelists, and includes an 'Author's Note' at the end of the novel, to 'help the reader' understand 'what is historical and what is not'.[15] This supplies readers with the necessary information to find out more about the novel's historical elements, and therefore the rudimentary tools to assess the validity of the author's interpretation of the events and people described.

The Author's Note usually briefly sets out some historical facts, discusses the degree of departure from the historical record, and acknowledges specific primary or secondary sources. It serves as a partial replacement for the footnote in a work of academic history. Footnotes are not usually used in historical novels, partly because such intrusions would prevent immersion in the novel, but also because it is not always possible to draw the line between fact, fabrication and imaginative reconstruction. As Hilary Mantel points out, in her own work full documentation would require a footnote in 'every line' because there is 'an actuating cause a line, half a line, behind anything I make up'.[16] In the absence of full documentation, the Author's Note gestures towards the responsibilities of the historical novelist and tentatively suggests what is and is not permissible within the historical novel. It indicates that the author has invented, but within certain bounds; and a more reflective historical novelist can use it to acknowledge both the incompleteness of the historical record and the provisional status of her version of events, as 'a proposal, an offer' to the reader, rather than a definitive statement.[17] The Author's Note simultaneously conveys the authenticity and the artificiality of the historical novel as a genre.[18]

The explicit authorial interjection of the Author's Note has another important function. It highlights that the novel is 'a cooperative effort, a joint venture between writer and reader'.[19] The meaning of any text, fiction or non-fiction, is partially created by the reader's expectations, previous knowledge and mode of reading. A student who diligently reads the footnotes of a scholarly article has a deeper understanding of the author's intention and methods than one who scans it for 'facts'; a historian of the First World War responds to *Regeneration* very differently from a reader with no previous knowledge of the historical events related in the novel. The Author's Note claims authority through invoking the author's scholarly credentials, but it also admits and reinforces the reader's agency by assuming active reading strategies, including the possibility that the reader will want to undertake further research.[20] Historical novelists who use Author's Notes in this way demonstrate respect for the intelligence and discernment of their readers, who are assumed to be capable of understanding that the historical novel is a form of fiction.

Showing the workings and working in the gaps

Readers approach histories and historical novels with a set of assumptions that govern their responses to the text. These suppositions are rarely articulated, but formed out of inchoate beliefs about the historical discipline, prior knowledge of the period or topic, and expectations attached to each form. In turn, authors make working assumptions about what readers already know or what they will expect. The reader of historical novels is often 'presumed to have some historical knowledge and therefore gains a certain power over the narrative to the extent that the novel cannot shock or challenge events'.[21] For example, in a novel such as A.S. Byatt's *The Children's Book* (2009), which traces the lives of several families between 1895 and 1919, the reader knows there cannot be a happy ending for all the boys approaching maturity in 1914. This knowledge shadows innocent Edwardian summers: the reader understands these events in a way denied to the fictional participants, as a prelude to tragedy. The effect of the historical novel often depends on this collusion between reader and author.

Yet historical novelists can also exploit the reader's apparent foreknowledge to confound expectations. Hilary Mantel's *Bring Up the Bodies* (2012) tells the story of the months preceding the execution of Anne Boleyn in May 1536 from the point of view of Thomas Cromwell (1485–1540), Henry VIII's chief minister. The story of Anne Boleyn's fall, packed with intrigue, romance and betrayal, has been endlessly retold in academic and popular histories, historical novels, television programmes and films. If British schoolchildren learn nothing else about Tudor history, they know that Anne Boleyn's name comes early in the sequence of Henry VIII's six wives. Readers open *Bring Up the Bodies* with the reasonable belief that there will be no major plot twists.

Mantel breaks this pact. The most genuinely shocking moment of *Bring Up the Bodies* occurs about halfway through, when Cromwell is disturbed at his work by a messenger announcing that the king is dead. This is a feint, we think: Henry VIII did not die in 1536, Mantel's Henry cannot be dead. But then Cromwell runs, and sees the body; the great noblemen of England cluster round the corpse. Suspense is maintained for a few pages, until Cromwell notices that the king is breathing and sends for physicians. In the meantime, the reader has been jolted into an unexpected uncertainty. It is a clever trick on Mantel's part, but serves several serious purposes. Most immediately, it emphasizes the precariousness of Cromwell's own position, and the danger to his own life without the king's protection. It also, however, provokes awareness of how easily those familiar pasts might never have happened: with Henry's death in 1536, perhaps no sixteenth-century English Reformation and no first Elizabethan Age; certainly no childhood chant of *'Divorced, Beheaded, Died, Divorced, Beheaded, Survived'*. Suddenly, everything is flux. Mantel subverts the more usual method of the historical novelist, and instead of relying on the sense of inevitability to achieve her effects, emphasizes the contingent and provisional nature of history itself.

Mantel has described her territory as a historical novelist as the 'off-the-record area', the happenings 'on the back stair and the words behind a hand, that which cannot by its nature make its way onto the record'.[22] Like many historical novelists, she works 'in the gaps of history, in the spaces between knowledges, in the lacking texts, within the misunderstood codes'.[23] Where Mantel differs from many other historical novelists is in her belief that historical novels cannot be written in an 'unselfconscious manner [...] It seems to me we're best to show our workings, discuss our problems with the reader'.[24] *Bring Up the Bodies* is littered with asides on the problematic status of historical evidence, 'the silences of history, the erasures and the gaps'.[25] Mantel's account of Henry's 'death' imaginatively reconstructs the immediate aftermath of a jousting accident in which the king was injured in January 1536. In Mantel's version, Cromwell deliberately suppresses the truth about the seriousness of the accident; he emphasizes to those around him that a fiction must be maintained, that 'this never happened'. He destroys evidence relating to the king's injury, and reflects that in the future, it will only be known that 'on such a date, the king's horse stumbled'.[26]

This is fiction, but it is also a warning about the process of historical research: we cannot trust the evidence, because records can be manipulated, expunged or mislaid.[27] Some things are never written down at all, and as Mantel repeatedly reminds us, there is much which cannot be revealed by a written document: the formal score sheet for a jousting tournament records touches on the body,

> but the marks on paper do not tell you about the pain of a broken ankle or the efforts of a suffocating man not to vomit inside his helmet. As the combatants will always tell you, you really needed to see it, you had to be there.[28]

Any knowledge of the past is a subjective reconstruction, even when based on the available evidence, because that evidence is itself always partial and open to interpretation. A historical novel always plays with the provisionality of the past, but few historical novelists 'show their workings' in quite the same way as Mantel. However, it is equally true that although most historians are quite aware of the limitations of different forms of evidence, and agree that there is an unavoidable element of subjective reconstruction in their histories, it is still relatively uncommon to discuss problems of the nature of historical knowledge outside the pages of specialist works on historiography and historical theory.

Safety or subversion?

Because historical novels are set in the past, they come with a ready-made sense of difference, of something which is strange and other. To this extent, 'the subversive potential of the form is innate within it at all points'.[29] Yet this potential is not always realized. Critics argue that all too often, historical novels regurgitate 'safe' versions of history. One variant of this critique is that readers seek out recognizable pasts, which confirm their preconceptions about specific historical events, people or periods. A related argument is that historical novels often ignore the 'different mindsets, different morals, different values' of past ages, and put forward a version of the past as no more than the present dressed up in mutton-sleeves and hoop-skirts.[30] These criticisms can be usefully illuminated by a discussion of responses to two novels set in the First World War: Sebastian Faulks's *Birdsong* (1993) and Barker's *Regeneration*.

Birdsong is the story of a fictional character, Stephen Wraysford, at different points in his life before and during the First World War. An excerpt from one review, reproduced in the Vintage paperback edition, tells us that the novel tackles with 'unusual power' the 'grim horrors of trench warfare, the murderous first day on the Somme, the loony schemes of the general staff, the pains and fears of ordinary men and their officers, the letters to and from home, the incomprehension of the war back home'.[31] Readers' reviews on Amazon echo this view of the novel as a painful, compelling and essentially accurate representation of a futile war.[32] Historians of the myth and memory of the First World War argue this perception of authenticity is mistaken. Audiences primed by endless popular representations of the war confound easily assimilable images – 'poets, men shot at dawn, horror, death, waste' – with the definitive 'truth' of the war, to the exclusion of counter-narratives which might challenge these tropes. In this view, novels such as *Birdsong* tell readers nothing about history, but rather reflect and reinforce the 'dominant myths of the culture that produced them'.[33]

Different accusations are levelled at *Regeneration*. It is claimed that Barker's book is loaded with 'modern baggage', tells us more about '1980s "counselling culture"' than about the relationships of soldiers and psychiatrists in the First World War, and transposes 'the authentic whingeing note of the 1990s' onto wartime events.[34] Barker is viewed as projecting contemporary concerns onto her wartime protagonists. Yet it is possible to doubt *Regeneration*'s status as an absolutely faithful account of the events it describes, without accepting the substance of these criticisms. Siegfried Sassoon *did* embark on a well-publicized protest against the war in 1917; he *was* treated at Craiglockhart War Hospital by W.H.R. Rivers, a psychiatrist noted for his pioneering use of psychotherapeutic techniques; this relationship *did* cause both men to reappraise, in complex ways, their views on the legitimacy of the war.[35] All this is well documented. Barker tells a story which resonates with contemporary concerns about the traumatic consequences and ethical implications of war, but this is an act of selection – the story of Sassoon and Rivers, from all the other historical episodes which might be imaginatively reconstructed – as much as interpretation. The heart of the story is not a fabrication.

Far from anachronistically replicating present-day attitudes, for some audiences historical novels open up alternative ways of viewing familiar episodes. *Regeneration* offered perspectives notably absent from most popular representations of the First World War available at the time of its publication: it was set on the home front rather than in the trenches, it focused on the aftermath of battle rather than combat, and issues of class, gender and sexuality loom large for its characters. Barker writes *against*, as well as with, the clichés of First World War historical fiction. In doing so, she exploits the potential of the historical novel to provide a voice and a role for those marginalized in mainstream historical narratives, and therefore to challenge prevalent understandings of the past.[36] Barker did not take the lead in reinserting marginalized individuals and groups back into history: as her Author's Note demonstrates, she drew on the work of academic historians who had already charted this terrain. However, historical novelists are able to transmit new approaches to the past to wider audiences than academic historians, whose works are often read only by specialists. Moreover, the historical novelist's licence to fabricate allows Barker to do something which historians cannot: to make those silent in the historical records speak, even if imperfectly, and not with their own voices.

If the past survives into the present only in fragments, then these fragments disproportionately represent the lives and experiences of those with power. It is part of the condition of powerlessness to leave fewer traces on the world. Among marginalized groups, there is a hunger for knowledge of a past which must always remain incomplete, because the archive itself is near-empty. The fictional genealogies provided by historical novels are not substitutes for a documented past, but under such circumstances offer ways of imagining the past, of grounding an identity, which may not be readily available in other forms. This is a political rather than historical achievement, but then again, history itself is never neutral. Barker's political act is to invent a working-class officer, Billy Prior, who vocally challenges the class-based assumptions of early twentieth-century psychiatry in ways which few historians seem to have considered, or dared.[37] Along different lines but perhaps with similarly political intentions, Sarah Waters writes about past sexualities in ways which deny the ahistorical transposition of today's rigid sexual categorizations. This opens up the historical proliferation of different ways of being. Waters argues that historical fiction is most productive where it problematizes the very categories with which sex and gender are constructed.[38] Historical fiction can gesture towards the infinite potential of identities experienced in the past, and yet to be realized in the future.[39]

Conclusion

There are important and real differences between history and fiction, but there is no clear and self-evident boundary between historical 'truth' and historical fiction. The professional historian has a responsibility to represent the past as faithfully as possible: to consult an array of available evidence, to adjudicate between the claims of different sources and to leave a trail of footnotes for other scholars to follow in assessing the validity of specific interpretations and arguments. The historical novelist can alter the past, invent new characters and imagine different endings to familiar stories. Within the confines of the form, this does not mean an irresponsible attitude to the past, but operation within looser constraints, according to less well-defined rules, with an overt licence to fictionalize which is forever denied to the professional historian, and without the requirement to verify specific facts or interpretations. Consequently, professional historians and historical novelists claim different kinds of authority for their versions of the past, and readers approach their texts in very different ways. It also means, however, that historical novelists perhaps operate most effectively when they exploit the gaps in the historical record, and offer interpretations of what can never be known for certain. Historical novels might replicate stereotypical views of the past, or dress up the present in old-fashioned clothes, but they can also fulfil an important political function in imagining dissident histories, or bringing alternative perspectives on the past to new audiences.

With this in mind, let us return to the scene of the electrical room in 1917. This time, we are not ghost witnesses present at the actual scene. Instead, imagine yourself reading Barker's disturbing account of the torture of this mute patient, horrified by the brutal exercise of medical power over a traumatized soldier. Now imagine yourself some years later, equipped with the training of the professional historian, reading Yealland's dispassionate explanation of his treatment methods, couched in the language of scientific objectivity. What does the historian make of each version of events? One is, at best, only partially true; the other is, at best, a partial and polemical description of what happened. But these narratives do not have to be taken in isolation. Barker puts flesh on Case A1's bones: she gives him a name and the possibility of agency, of sullen resistance rather than abject gratitude. These imagined possibilities underline the injustice of Case A1's treatment: but it is the historical document which reveals the depth of his powerlessness, in its revelation of the extreme limitations of a historical record which will never give up his name, far less what he thought as he lived, suffered and died. This is the most shocking truth, and it speaks to the value of historical novels as an adjunct to historical research. Case A1 and all the other silent millions of history deserve imaginative reconstructions of their pasts, which cannot be recovered; but even more, they demand that historians never stop trying to halt the slide into oblivion, to tell the stories which might be told.

STUDY QUESTIONS

- What is the role of selection and interpretation in history and in historical novels?
- Why does it matter that historical novelists are not required to 'show their workings' in the same ways as professional historians?
- Is it fair to say that professional historians are 'objective', but historical novelists are not?
- In what ways do the aims and achievements of historians and historical novelists differ, and in what ways are they the same?

Notes

1   'Historical Novel', *Encyclopaedia Britannica*: http://www.britannica.com/
EBchecked/topic/267395/historical-novel. Accessed 26 May 2015. For an
alternative definition, see Richard Lee, 'Defining the Genre', Historical Novel
Society: http://historicalnovelsociety.org/guides/defining-the-genre/. Accessed
26 May 2015. There are many different types of historical novel. For reasons
of space, this chapter concentrates on literary fiction by authors who perceive
research as an important part of their remit as historical novelists.

2   For further discussion of some of these problems in relation to the history and
literature of 'shell-shock', see T. Loughran (2012) 'Shell Shock, Trauma, and
the First World War: The Making of a Diagnosis and Its Histories', *Journal of
the History of Medicine and Allied Sciences*, 67.

3   Adapted from B. Southgate (2009) *History Meets Fiction* (Harlow: Pearson
Education Limited), p. 190.

4   Southgate, *History Meets Fiction*, pp. 32–3. For an extended discussion of
these issues, see M. Fulbrook (2002) *Historical Theory* (London and New
York: Routledge), pp. 53–73.

5   See K. Passmore (2010) 'Poststructuralism and History', in S. Berger, H.
Feldner and K. Passmore (eds), *Writing History: Theory and Practice*, 2nd edn
(London and New York: Bloomsbury Academic).

6   Wallace Stegner (1971) *Angle of Repose*. Quoted in Southgate, *History Meets
Fiction*, p. 38.

7   H. Sword (2012) *Stylish Academic Writing* (Cambridge, MA and London: Harvard University Press), pp. 39–40.

8   S. Waters, 'I Wanted *The Paying Guests* to Be Sexy without Being a Romp', *Guardian*, Review Supplement, 6 June 2015.

9   H. Mantel (2010) 'A Kind of Alchemy: Sarah O'Reilly Talks to Hilary Mantel', in H. Mantel, *A Place of Greater Safety* (London: Fourth Estate) [1992], p. 4 [repaginated matter at end of novel].

10 I. McEwan, 'An Inspiration, Yes', *Guardian*, 27 November 2006. Quoted in J. de Groot (2010) *The Historical Novel* (London and New York: Routledge), p. 172.

11 H. Mantel, 'Hilary Mantel and David Loades in Conversation', *Novel Approaches: From Academic History to Historical Fiction Conference*, 17 November 2011: https://ihrconference.wordpress.com/2011/11/21/hilary-mantel-and-david-loades-in-discussion/. Accessed 16 January 2016.

12 G. Arnold (2008) *Girl in a Blue Dress* (Birmingham: Tindal Street Press), Afterword.

13 Robert Harris, *Fatherland* (1992). Quoted in de Groot, *The Historical Novel*, p. 172.

14 Pat Barker (2000) Interview in 'The Making of *Regeneration*', DVD extra, *Regeneration* (dir. Gilles MacKinnon, Artificial Eye). Quoted in de Groot, *The Historical Novel*, p. 104.

15 P. Barker (1992) *Regeneration* (London: Penguin) [1991], p. 251.

16 Mantel, 'Hilary Mantel and David Loades in Conversation'.

17 Hilary Mantel (2013) *Bring Up the Bodies* (London: Fourth Estate) [2012], p. 483.

18 For an extended discussion of this issue, see de Groot, *The Historical Novel*, pp. 6–9.

19 Mantel, *A Place of Greater Safety*, p. ix.

20 de Groot, *The Historical Novel*, p. 4.

21 de Groot, *The Historical Novel*, p. 8.

22 Mantel, 'Hilary Mantel and David Loades in Conversation'.

23 de Groot, *The Historical Novel*, p. 182.

24 Mantel, 'Hilary Mantel and David Loades in Conversation'.

25 Mantel, 'Hilary Mantel and David Loades in Conversation'.

26 Mantel, *Bring Up the Bodies*, pp. 206, 209.

27 Mantel, *Bring Up the Bodies*, p. 481.

28 Mantel, *Bring Up the Bodies*, pp. 194–5.

29 de Groot, *The Historical Novel*, p. 4.

30 Mantel, 'Hilary Mantel and David Loades in Conversation'.

31 Valerie Cunningham in *Country Life*, reproduced in S. Faulks (1994) *Birdsong* (London: Vintage), front matter.

32 D. Todman (2005) *The Great War: Myth and Memory* (London and New York: Hambledon and London), p. 121.

33 Todman, *The Great War*, p. 160.

34 B. Shephard (2002) *A War of Nerves: Soldiers and Psychiatrists, 1914–1994* (London: Pimlico), p. xx; Brian Bond (2002) *The Unquiet Western Front: Britain's Role in Literature and History* (Cambridge: Cambridge University Press), p. 77.

35 E. Showalter (1987) *The Female Malady: Women, Madness and English Culture* (London: Virago), pp. 178–89.

36 For an extended discussion of the dissonant space of the historical novel, see de Groot, *The Historical Novel*, pp. 139–82.

37 Barker, *Regeneration*, pp. 96–7.

38 L. Doan and S. Waters (2000) 'Making Up Lost Time: Contemporary Lesbian Writing and the Invention of History', in D. Alderson and L. Anderson (eds), *Territories of Desire in Queer Culture: Refiguring Contemporary Boundaries* (Manchester and New York: Manchester University Press).

39 de Groot, *The Historical Novel*, p. 151.

Further Reading

Rethinking History: The Journal of Theory and Practice (2005) 9:2–3, special issue on history and historical fiction.

L. Doan and S. Waters (2000) 'Making Up Lost Time: Contemporary Lesbian Writing and the Invention of History', in D. Alderson and L. Anderson (eds), *Territories of Desire in Queer Culture: Refiguring Contemporary Boundaries* (Manchester and New York: Manchester University Press), pp. 12–28.

J. de Groot (2009) *Consuming History: Historians and Heritage in Contemporary Popular Culture* (London and New York: Routledge), pp. 181–232.

J. de Groot (2010) *The Historical Novel* (London and New York: Routledge).

Institute of Historical Research, *Novel Approaches: From Academic History to Historical Fiction*: https://ihrconference.wordpress.com/

M. Margaronis (2008) 'The Anxiety of Authenticity: Writing Historical Fiction at the End of the Twentieth Century', *History Workshop Journal*, 65, pp. 138–60.

B. Southgate (2009) *History Meets Fiction* (Harlow: Pearson Education Limited).

16

History and Heritage

Stephanie Ward

Visits to heritage sites are one of the principal ways in which people engage with history and gain historical knowledge. In 2013 in the UK, museums, art galleries, castles, historic houses and religious buildings attracted 101 million visitors.[1] Indeed, unless prospective students keen to prove their history credentials greatly embellish their application forms for university, there is a good chance that your own academic interest in history developed out of visits to heritage sites. This fascination with heritage and its popular appeal is largely a post–Second World War phenomenon; by the end of the twentieth century, 95 per cent of museums in Britain had been established after 1945.[2] Membership of the National Trust, Britain's largest heritage charity, grew from 725 members in 1914, to 500,000 by 1975, and to 4 million by 2011.[3] David Lowenthal's point in 1998 that 'never before have so many been so engaged with so many different pasts' is still very relevant today.[4] Heritage sites and practices include: national, regional and local museums, now often with interactive displays; living history museums with character actors; heritage trails; monuments and memorials to everything from the slave trade, to soldiers of the First World War, to animals that have died in wars; re-enactment societies; protected landscapes; virtual online museums; countless internet websites for local and community histories; and dedicated history months for women, LGBT, black and Asian people. Engagement with heritage ranges from the actions of large institutionalized organizations on the one hand, to radical politicized groups on the other.

While it might be easy to find examples of heritage sites and practices, defining heritage and understanding its importance is a more difficult task. The purpose of this chapter is to explore why the meaning, significance and practice of heritage transform over time, are dependent on the values of those who engage with it and are shaped by power relations. The chapter begins with examination of the questions 'What is heritage' and 'Who owns the past?' before exploring national narratives and the issue of heritage and belonging. Finally, it examines the relationship between historians and the heritage industry, and argues that only collaborative approaches can challenge the hegemonic narratives still common to much heritage practice.

What is heritage?

There is no agreed understanding of heritage beyond that it involves objects (tangible heritage) or cultural traditions (intangible heritage) which are inherited. What makes some of these items heritage is the meaning we attach to them: objects or artefacts on their own do not have an innate significance. It is for this reason that Laurajane Smith has made the bold claim that 'there is, really, no such thing as heritage'. For example, without the cultural meanings we attach to the site, Stonehenge is just some rocks in a field.[5] Heritage should be viewed as a cultural practice with deep significance. Heritage gives us a sense of belonging through the connections we make with inherited objects or cultural practices and our family or community (including religious, ethnic or national) history. Although relating to objects from the past, heritage is 'present-centred' in that its worth is shaped and reshaped by the current values and concerns of a society.[6]

Understanding the ways in which heritage creates a sense of belonging and identity explains why, as one historian has put it, 'the protection of one's heritage has become a quasi human right'.[7] As such, the United Nations Educational, Scientific and Cultural Organization (UNESCO) has intervened to protect heritage through a series of international conventions. UNESCO believes heritage can help to 'build a lasting peace' because 'heritage constitutes a source of identity and cohesion for communities disrupted by bewildering change and economic instability'.[8] Most governments have some form of legislation to protect tangible and intangible forms of heritage because of the importance which is attached to the role of heritage within society. Such interventions show that what forms of heritage are preserved is not down to chance: what survives and the meanings taken from it reflect not only the values of a particular society, but the power relations within it.

Heritage as an industry is an incredibly important economic resource. Visits to heritage sites generate a Gross Domestic Product in the UK of around £5 billion.[9] By the 1980s, the exponential growth of heritage drew criticism from historians who were alarmed at the apparent commodification of the past. The idea that a dumbed-down 'Disneyfied' version of history was being marketed through theme parks for economic gain was seen as at best distasteful and at worst as an indication that the public were blinded by nostalgia to the ills of the present.[10] Foremost among the critics was Robert Hewison, who attacked what he termed the 'heritage industry' not simply because so many of its products are fantasies of a world that never was; not simply because at a deeper level it involves the preservation, indeed reassertion, of social values that the democratic progress of the twentieth century seemed to be doing away with, but because, far from ameliorating the climate of decline, it is actually worsening it.[11]

In the 'heritage wars' of the 1980s and 1990s, debates raged over whether the purpose of the heritage industry was to educate, or to focus on the economic benefits of entertainment. The transformation of industrial sites into heritage parks through regeneration projects faced particular criticism. While the authenticity of exhibitions was questioned, a more serious issue was the wider impact of the ownership of heritage for local people.[12]

At the turn of the twenty-first century, scholars of heritage increasingly criticized the hegemony of Western and white Anglocentric or Eurocentric narratives within heritage sites which excluded representations of minority groups. The distinction made by the cultural theorist Stuart Hall (1932–2014) between heritage and 'the Heritage' is very useful in this respect. While heritage covers all aspects of tangible and intangible inherited practices and artefacts, 'the Heritage' refers to those aspects perceived as 'the material embodiment of the spirit of the nation'.[13] Similarly, Laurajane Smith identifies an 'authorized heritage discourse' which is 'historically, institutionally and politically situated', based primarily on objects, emphasizes certain narratives of nationhood, and privileges professional and expert views.[14] The consequence of the 'authorized heritage discourse' is that without a sense of belonging being fostered through heritage, minority groups can feel marginalized in the present. Ultimately, 'the Heritage' can legitimize a continued imbalance of power relations.[15]

Who owns the past?

A consideration of who determines which objects are preserved and who owns those artefacts – in other words, who owns the past – demonstrates that power relations are evident at every stage of heritage creation, and that heritage overwhelmingly reflects the values of the most powerful groups in a society. The programmes of conservators reflect the policies and politics of large institutions and governments; rarely do we, the public, have a say in what is preserved. In the UK, as elsewhere, each individual museum has a collection policy, but funding plays a fundamental role in just what conservationists and curators choose to preserve and collect.[16] Artefacts of particular value are primarily owned by or in the trust of states and international organizations which closely monitor their protection and ensure their preservation for future generations.

In some extreme cases, the ownership and control of heritage can become part of an attempt by movements or groups to exercise and vie for power.

On 26 February 2001 Mullah Mohammed Omar, the spiritual leader of the Taliban, issued an edict to destroy all statues in Afghanistan. The destruction of Buddhist antiquities carried out by the terrorist Taliban-led regime included the annihilation of two fifth-century giant Buddha figures (38 and 58 m tall) carved into the hillside at Bamiyan. Figures 16.1 and 16.2 strikingly show the scale of the destruction. Widespread international outcry followed the attacks, thought to be a response to the UN-issued sanctions on Afghanistan.[17] In June 2015, Islamic State forces carried out the destruction of artefacts from the Assyrian and Akkadian empires at the Mosul Museum and at Nimrud in Iraq.[18] In both instances, the artefacts deemed worthy of World Heritage Status by UNESCO were argued to be idolatrous by Taliban and Islamic State terrorists. Destroying ancient artefacts, however, was about far more than religious beliefs. In the case of Islamic State in Iraq, this was a powerful and very public attempt to destroy the heritage of the region, and with it artefacts judged of archaeological value by the

FIGURE 16.1 *One of the fifth-century statues of Buddha which stood in the hillside at Bamiyan, Afghanistan.* © *Charles and Josette Lenars/Corbis (Image CJ004946).*

FIGURE 16.2 *The niche of the giant Buddha lies empty following its destruction by Taliban forces in March 2001. © David Bathgate/Corbis (Image DWF 15–1041295).*

West. Habib Afram, the President of the Syriac League in Lebanon, claimed Islamic State 'are not [only] destroying our present life, or only taking the villages, churches, and homes, or erasing our future – they want to erase our culture, past and civilisation'.[19]

The actions of the Taliban and Islamic State are extreme because they involve terrorist organizations and the actual premeditated destruction of heritage. Most debates about the preservation of heritage are instead focused on just what is deemed worthy of preservation. UNESCO, while carrying out incredibly important and valuable work in preserving and protecting heritage, has been criticized for appearing to privilege the material culture of Europe in contrast to the intangible cultural traditions which are a key part of the heritage of developing countries. Inclusion on the World Heritage List has become politicized because it brings prestige and economic benefits through tourism, and because the List is supposed to reflect the 'common heritage of mankind'.[20] The imbalance towards examples from developed, industrialized and Christian countries stems not only from the values of those who determine what is on the List, but the administrative and financial resources within certain countries which enable them to apply for inclusion on the List in the first place.[21]

The power of certain Western countries as revealed by the imbalance of the World Heritage List is also evident in other respects. During the expansion of European empires, it was common for victors to return with spoils from colonized countries. In the twentieth century, the ownership of items of national heritage by other states became an issue of much controversy and since the 1970s the repatriation of items of cultural patrimony has taken place.[22] Unlike other examples of the repatriation of artefacts, for example the return to rightful ownership of artworks seized by the Nazis during the Second World War, the return of long-held artefacts has not been straightforward because of the cultural, legal and financial implications for museums. The case of the Greek Parthenon marbles (popularly known as the Elgin marbles) at the British Museum highlights the complexities of this issue. In 1804 the British diplomat Lord Elgin (1766–1841) brought the marbles to Britain from Athens, which was then under Turkish rule, after he had struck a deal (*firman*) with the sultan of the Ottoman court. In a period when the display of artefacts from antiquity in museums was an important measure of national prestige, the Parthenon marbles (see Figure 16.3) became a prized exhibit in the British Museum, and a British national icon. To some extent, they have remained so.[23] Conversely, within Greece the continued absence of the marbles has been presented as a 'collective cultural trauma' because they are an important part of Greek nationhood. The call for the repatriation of the marbles is still ongoing, and the opening of the Acropolis Museum (Athens) in 2009 to house all Parthenon marbles has only heightened Greek demands.[24] If the British Museum were to return the marbles this would set a precedent, and has cultural, legal and financial implications for much of its collection and those of other European museums.[25]

FIGURE 16.3 *These sculptures form part of the controversial Parthenon marbles collection housed at the British Museum, London, since 1817.* © *Matt Mawson/ Corbis (Image 42–71839049).*

Repatriation is highly political because it involves acknowledgement of wrongful actions, and helps the descendants of those affected take ownership of their heritage. Nowhere is this more apparent than in the repatriation of human remains denied either a proper form of burial or lasting internment at a chosen sacred site.[26] In gaining the rightful ownership of ancestral remains, Indigenous peoples are both making an important connection with their heritage and challenging hegemonic national narratives which have marginalized that heritage and history. As we will see, the case of the National Museum Australia (NMA) is very telling of the power of artefacts and narratives of heritage within contemporary society.

Narratives, nation and power

The work of museums in Australia in the 1990s and early twenty-first century took place within a wider context of increased rights for Indigenous peoples and a conservative media and government keen to dispute what it disparagingly called 'politically correct' history. The incredibly acrimonious 'history wars' between professional historians and conservative politicians and media was sparked by the election of the Prime Minister John Howard and lasted for the duration of his premiership (1996–2007). Historians, largely on the left, concluded that the British settlement was an invasion and used oral testimonies, in the absence of written documentation, to reveal atrocities against Aboriginal Australians. They were attacked by Howard's supporters and the right-wing press who questioned the authenticity of a 'black-armband' view of Australian history.[27] Conservatives felt that Australians were being made to feel guilty for the actions of their forebears and ashamed of their history. Tellingly, these debates took place in the same period as the 1992 Mabo ruling (which recognized that land was stolen from Aboriginal Australians) and the 1997 'Bringing them Home' report into the Stolen Generations.[28]

The opening of the long-awaited NMA in 2001 only served to further tensions over national narratives. The NMA attempted to offer an alternative vision of the Australian past through a thematic approach which emphasized the stories of all Australian people. While the majority of visitors responded positively to the displays, the media and conservative Howard Government were angered by the decision not to have a clear chronology and the amount of attention given to the treatment of Indigenous people.[29] Faced with such scrutiny and criticism, the exhibitions were changed and the museum's director was sacked. Darryl McIntyre has raised the important point that we should not necessarily see this as a failure. The purpose of museums is to tackle difficult subjects in a balanced way, and in doing so 'controversial exhibitions mark the sometimes painful steps towards proper public discussion'.[30]

The heritage of Aboriginal people has only been included within Australian museums since the early 1980s. Recognition of Aboriginal heritage is not, however, just about inclusion in national narratives. The empowerment that the ownership of heritage can bring has been most evident in the repatriation from the 1980s of Aboriginal and Torres Strait Islander ancestral remains and secret/sacred objects to Indigenous communities. The NMA has been at the forefront in this work through a dedicated Repatriation Program Unit. The human remains found primarily in museums are overwhelmingly without means of identification, and the NMA team works to ascertain provenance and return the remains to the communities or places of origin. A sacred ceremony usually accompanies the return of remains and secret/sacred objects, and the NMA liaises directly with Indigenous communities.[31]

Although the remit of the Repatriation Program Unit is to return remains promptly, and not to carry out research, uncovering the provenance of remains has revealed further hidden histories of atrocities against Indigenous people by European settlers. For example, the Department of Anatomy at the University of Edinburgh has repatriated the remains of Aboriginal men and women killed at a massacre near Appin (south of Sydney) in 1816 and the remains of asylum and hospital patients from Adelaide stolen during the early twentieth century.[32] The head of the Aboriginal and Torres Strait Islander Program at the NMA, Michael Pickering, has shown that many of the Aboriginal people whose remains were eventually housed in museums were killed through atrocities either committed directly by agents of the state or implicitly condoned by those agents. The evidence of ritual killings counters suggestions by the right that frontier violence can be disputed because oral histories cannot be trusted. Pickering concludes:

> The repatriation experience provides cautionary tales. Over time, stories disappear. The horror and pain are lost to us. We do not hear the screams, or smell the odors, of the asylum; we do not hear the gunshots, the cries of families. The people are transformed into objects. Even the history becomes a commodity to be used by governments and commentators to suit political agendas. However, the impacts of these events persist. For the descendants of the victims, the scars remain. At numerous repatriation funerals I have attended, the desire to know what happened is strong, the tears and emotions, real. The events of the past resonate to the present. We have a responsibility to document these stories, in all of their manifestations, oral and written, tangible and intangible, objective and subjective, before the experiences are lost.[33]

The intervention of the Australian government and sections of the media at the opening of the NMA show quite clearly how politics and power play a pivotal role in shaping heritage, especially when it is felt the primacy of a particular narrative is threatened. The 'Destruction of the Country House' exhibition staged by the Victoria and Albert Museum (V&A), London, in 1974 is often cited as an example of the power relations of heritage in Britain. It sparked so much historical debate because it showcased the established view of national heritage as white, Anglocentric and elitist. Organized by the V&A director Roy Strong, the exhibition made a bold case for saving England's country houses. It was held primarily in response to the Labour Government's proposal to introduce an annual tax on properties over £100,000 and assets including works of art and collections of books, a measure some perceived as threatening the already uncertain future of estates.[34] The exhibition was undoubtedly polemical and clearly aimed to encourage sympathy for the plight of the country house and its aristocratic owners.

Roy Strong later recalled visitors crying after viewing the 'Hall of Lost Houses' part of the exhibition. This featured crumbling columns displaying the images of the estimated 1,000 homes which had been destroyed, and a soundtrack of the names of the lost houses being read over the noise of burning and collapsing buildings.[35] Visitors were warned that 'to have destroyed so much of beauty over such a length of time is a stain on our national history'.[36] Other intellectual and social elites also portrayed the privately-owned crumbling mansions of aristocrats as the property and heritage of the nation. Conservative MP Patrick Cormack argued that 'these houses are a special public possession for it is in them and in our churches that we perhaps come closest to the soul and spirit of England'.[37] This message garnered widespread attention following the V&A's exhibition. Over one million people signed a petition to save country houses and the press largely supported the measures.[38] The Labour Government eventually retreated on its plans for a wealth tax.

For Robert Hewison, the V&A exhibition went to the very heart of his fear that the British heritage industry sought to reinforce past power relations in the present. He argued that country houses

> do not merely preserve certain values of the past: hierarchy, a sturdy individualism on the part of their owners, privilege tempered by social duty, a deference and respect for social order on the past of those who service and support them. They reinforce these values in the present.[39]

The aristocracy (and the elite who supported its position) sought not only to protect its homes, but also its position within society. Hewison questioned the extent to which country houses were threatened at all and pointed out that under agreement with the National Trust, owners could continue to live in their estates and enjoy favourable tax breaks as a consequence.[40] Ultimately, the portrayal of country houses as national symbols helped to further privilege an Anglocentric and elitist version of heritage. Although in the 1970s and 1980s heritage was increasingly 'democratized' to include the narratives of women and the working class, the hegemony of elitist voices within national discourses of heritage persisted.[41] Moreover, even when the democratization of heritage is taken into account, heritage remained overwhelmingly exclusionary of other marginalized voices.

Heritage and belonging

Heritage sites cannot, of course, include all stories and just what visitors take away from an exhibition is highly subjective. How visitors 'fashion various imagined pasts' is shaped by factors including their 'forms of cultural capital' (e.g., non-economic assets such as education which help individuals to gain social prestige), knowledge gained (or not) from reading prior to the visit, whether the visit is for a specific purpose or just a trip out, age, and class, sexual, ethnic and gender identity.[42] Even when the role of the visitor in shaping meaning is taken into account, we must consider how potent particular narratives can be. For example, we could imagine how differently the future of country houses would have been presented had the V&A displayed the same objects under the title 'The Destruction of the Oppressive Old Order'. The accompanying wording could have celebrated the decline of the aristocracy, while a soundtrack played the names of working-class MPs over the happy laughter of people enjoying free access to healthcare and education.

If heritage sites help to create a sense of belonging then 'it follows that those who cannot see themselves reflected in its mirror cannot properly "belong"'.[43] In 1988 the American novelist Toni Morrison evocatively captured how alienating a lack of public heritage sites can be to those wishing to engage with their African-American heritage:

> There is no place you or I can go, to think about or not think about, to summon the presences of, or recollect the absences of slaves; nothing that reminds us of the ones who made the journey and of those who did not make it. There is no suitable memorial or plaque or wreath or wall or park or skyscraper lobby. There's no 300 foot tower. There's no small bench by the road. There is not even a tree scored, an initial that I can visit or you can visit in Charleston or Savannah or New York or Providence or, better still, on the banks of the Mississippi.[44]

The representation of ethnic minorities at heritage sites continues to be problematic. Jo Littler and Roshi Naidoo have identified three main problems with either the lack of inclusion of ethnic minorities, or the form inclusion has taken, within British heritage sites. First, there is 'an "uncritically imperialist" alignment' which continues to celebrate empire. For example, the Cadbury World historical exhibitions do not mention how slavery is part of the company's history.[45] Second, there are 'tokenistic approaches to "ethnic" heritage' that simply add the history of minorities on to a central white national narrative. Third, there is what they term the 'white heritage, multicultural present' paradigm where, all too often, the heritage of ethnic minorities is viewed as edgy and contemporary, usually post-1950s, in juxtaposition to a white and Anglocentric past.[46] The opening of Liverpool's International Slavery Museum in 2007 and the founding of permanent exhibitions, such as the 'The Atlantic: Slavery, Trade, Empire' gallery at the National Maritime Museum, Greenwich, are positive examples of attempts to explore the pre-twentieth-century heritage of ethnic minorities.[47] Other exhibitions and heritage sites which have considered ethnic minorities have tended to be temporary and fleeting, as the 2007 bicentenary celebrations of the abolition of the slave trade demonstrated.[48] However, as Littler and Naidoo pointed out, it is not simply the inclusion of ethnic minorities which is needed, it is more of a question of 'how "other" Britons are included'.[49]

The gallery trail 'Portraits, People and Abolition' at the National Portrait Gallery in London, curated by the historical geographer Caroline Bressey as part of the bicentenary celebrations, nicely highlighted the need to reconsider well-established 'uncritically imperialist' narratives and how this could be achieved. The trail led visitors around the gallery and offered alternative explanations to the artwork to highlight the racism of celebrated individuals and their involvement in the slave trade. For example, the historian and essayist Thomas Carlyle (1795–1881) is praised by the National Portrait Gallery for analysing 'brilliantly the sufferings of the common people'. Bressey pointed out in her trail that it must be recognized that he also wrote the deeply racist 'Occasional Discourse on the Nigger Question' (1853).[50] Given the scope and scale of the British empire, the tentacles of power and money gained through slavery must stretch into many corners of the heritage industry and this, like the uncomfortable origins of some artefacts, needs to be addressed. Furthermore, there is the need to consider the heritage of generations of ethnic minorities in Britain after slavery ended, and of those immigrants who settled in later years and not just in the immediately post–Second World War period.

The history of LGBT groups has also been, and continues to be, marginalized in heritage sites. The presentation of LGBT history has been disputed and difficult, not least because 'there are problems concerning the anachronism of "lesbian" or "gay" as identities in the past'.[51] In this case, the hegemonic narratives of heterosexual relationships and nuclear families have left the experience of those with alternative sexualities and life stories hidden.[52] Where LGBT histories have been explored, there has been a tendency to focus on narratives of 'homophobia, outing and community formation', and the experiences of bisexual and trans people have been woefully underrepresented.[53] Since 2005, in the UK a dedicated LGBT History Month in February has done much to encourage heritage sites to reconsider their existing collections and to orchestrate dedicated exhibitions. Like Bressey's approach to the history of ethnic minorities, some museums have included alternative LGBT trails, and therefore narratives, of their collections.[54] While important work is being carried out in presenting lesbian and gay history, there is a tendency within heritage sites to focus on modern artefacts and narratives. Similarly to the idea of a 'white heritage, multicultural present', there is a framework of 'heterosexual past, sexually diverse present' which dominates narratives at many heritage sites.

In 'uncovering' the heritage of black Britons in the 1970s and 1980s community groups often took a leading role. Alan Rice has advocated that forms of 'guerrilla memorialization' should continue to lead the way.[55] The role of community groups in uncovering histories and influencing museum displays is important, not least in ensuring ownership of heritage, but collecting artefacts and putting pressure on museums to transform established narratives should not only lie with minority groups. As Angela Vanegas notes, it is not right that within the heritage sector it is often seen as the responsibility of lesbian and gay curators or activists to collect relevant artefacts and organize exhibitions of LGBT history.[56] For minority groups to be better represented within heritage sites, to broaden the scope of exhibitions beyond living memory, and to offer alternative inclusive narratives, greater collaboration with historians can offer one potential route for change.

Historians and heritage

The responsibility for further challenging the dominance of Anglocentric, white and heterosexual narratives should not rest with curators. The influence of the work of historians within the heritage industry has helped to transform collections and narratives to include the history of the working class, women, ethnic minorities and LGBT people. However, historians have not always readily worked with curators. Indeed, Laurajane Smith has accused historians of contributing to the 'authorized heritage discourse' by favouring the primacy of written documents and their own authoritative view.[57] Smith focused on historians who had criticized the commercialization of industrial heritage sites and resulting mass tourism. Her views echo those of historian Raphael Samuel (1934–96) who provided the clearest, and still influential, condemnation of ideas of the public as passive consumers of history. Writing in 1994, Samuel felt that 'heritage-baiting has become a favourite sport of the metropolitan intelligentsia', who were guilty of snobbery for failing to see the value of visual materials. Engaging with history at heritage sites is very different from reading monographs and articles, Samuel argued, 'but not necessarily less taxing on historical reflection and thought'.[58]

Samuel's view that historians are simply one group amongst many creating histories has more recently been taken up by public historians. In their volume on public history and heritage, Paul Ashton and Hilda Kean give equal weight, and call for others to do the same, to the views of 'professional historians, community historians, archivists, museum curators and educators, re-enactors, teachers, artists and family and local historians'.[59] Public history is currently witnessing an expansion, driven both by the ethos outlined by Ashton and Kean, and the way in which the dissemination of research findings is embedded into funding criteria and the Research Excellence Framework (REF) which assesses the research quality of universities.[60]

The work of public historians offers an alternative collaborative model for professional historians and curators. Rather than professional historians simply telling 'the public' what their research findings are, historians can work together with curators to share knowledge and create exhibitions, as the next chapter shows. This proactive approach is advocated by Robert Mills to influence collection policies and displays of LGBT heritage.[61] A collaborative model can also work in the creation of heritage in communities. As discussed further in David Wyatt's chapter in this section, at Cardiff University the CAER heritage project has won numerous awards for its collaboration with community groups based in the Caerau and Ely districts of Cardiff, which face significant social and economic challenges. In this case, historians and other academics work with community groups to help facilitate research: local people take the lead in the creation, recognition and ownership of their own heritage.[62]

Conclusion

The critique of the heritage industry put forward here is not intended to discredit the vital work it completes. The heritage industry quenches a popular thirst for history, offers a window on to the past and provides a historical education. The heritage industry can also perform important work in unearthing marginalized histories and recognizing how the ownership of heritage is an empowering right. You need only consider the work of the NMA in returning ancestral remains to their rightful place of rest to see just how important museums are. It is because heritage sites are so important, not least as spaces where we can negotiate identity through engagement with our heritage, that as historians we must question the images and narratives presented to us. The tools of critique, analysis and the constant questioning of materials fostered by your history degree must equally be applied to museums. You must always consider what remains hidden and why. As this chapter has shown, both heritage sites and the ways in which people consume history transformed remarkably during the second half of the twentieth century. As the battle for ownership of the past through its objects continues, as national narratives are further contested and as minority groups remain active in attempting to find a voice, historians should move from the periphery and ensure that the most recent scholarship is reflected in museums, galleries and other heritage sites.

Acknowledgements

My thanks to Jane Henderson for an invaluable discussion on modern conservation practices.

STUDY QUESTIONS

- In what ways does heritage create a sense of belonging?
- How does the work of historians differ from that of museum curators?
- Does historical accuracy and authenticity matter at heritage sites?
- Why do you think visits to heritage sites are so popular?

Notes

1   K. El Beyrouty and A. Tessler (2013) *The Economic Impact of the UK Heritage Tourism Economy*, pp. 19–21: http://www.oxfordeconomics.com/my-oxford/projects/236505. Accessed 16 January 2016.

2   D. Lowenthal (1998) *The Heritage Crusade and the Spoils of History* (Cambridge: Cambridge University Press), p. 3.

3   R. Hewison (1987) *The Heritage Industry: Britain in a Climate of Decline* (London: Methuen London Ltd), p. 57; National Trust homepage: http://www.nationaltrust.org.uk/. Accessed 16 January 2016.

4   Lowenthal, *The Heritage Crusade*, p. 3.

5   L. Smith (2006) *Uses of Heritage* (London: Routledge), pp. 3, 11.

6   B. Graham and P. Howard (2008) 'Introduction: Heritage and Identity', in B. Graham and P. Howard (eds), *The Ashgate Research Companion to Heritage and Identity* (Aldershot: Ashgate), pp. 2–3.

7   A. Swenson (2013) *The Rise of Heritage: Preserving the Past in France, Germany and England, 1789–1914* (Cambridge: Cambridge University Press), p. 2.

8   UNESCO, the intellectual wing of the United Nations, was created in 1945 on the premise that 'peace must be established on the basis of humanity's moral and intellectual authority'. Following the 1972 World Heritage Convention UNESCO has had the power to intervene to protect cultural and natural heritage through inclusion on its World Heritage List. See UNESCO homepage: http://en.unesco.org/. Accessed 16 January 2016.

9   El Beyrouty and Tessler, *The Economic Impact of the UK Heritage Tourism Economy*, pp. 19–21.

10 P. Wright (1985) *On Living in an Old Country* (London: Verso); Lowenthal, *The Heritage Crusade*.

11 Hewison, *The Heritage Industry*, p. 10.

12 B. Dicks (2000) *Heritage, Place and Community* (Cardiff: University of Wales Press).

13 S. Hall (1999) 'Whose Heritage? Un-settling "The Heritage", Re-imagining the Post-Nation', *Third Text*, 49, pp. 3–4.

14 Smith, *Uses of Heritage*, pp. 4, 42.

15 J. Littler and R. Naidoo (2004) 'White Past, Multicultural Present: Heritage and National Stories', in H. Brocklehurst and R. Phillips (eds), *History, Nationhood and the Question of Britain* (London: Palgrave MacMillan), p. 333.

16 See, for example, the collection policy of the National Museum of Wales. National Museum Wales/Amgueddfa Cymru: Collection Management Policies: https://www.museumwales.ac.uk/68/. Accessed 16 January 2016.

17 L. Harding, 'Taliban Blow Apart 2,000 Years of Buddhist History', *Guardian*, 3 March 2001: http://www.theguardian.com/world/2001/mar/03/afghanistan. lukeharding; F. Bobin, 'Disputes Damage Hopes of Rebuilding Afghanistan's Bamiyan Buddhas', *Guardian*, 10 January 2015: http://www.theguardian. com/world/2015/jan/10/rebuild-bamiyan-buddhas-taliban-afghanistan. Both accessed 16 January 2016.

18 K. Shaheen, 'Isis Fighters Destroy Ancient Artefacts at Mosul Museum', *Guardian*, 26 February 2015: http://www.theguardian.com/world/2015/ feb/26/isis-fighters-destroy-ancient-artefacts-mosul-museum-iraq; K. Shaheen, 'Outcry over Isis Destruction of Ancient Assyrian Site of Nimrud', *Guardian*, 6 March 2015: http://www.theguardian.com/world/2015/mar/06/isis-destroys- ancient-assyrian-site-of-nimrud. Both accessed 16 January 2016.

19 Shaheen, 'Outcry over Isis Destruction'.

20 L. Steiner and B. S. Frey (2012) 'Creating the Imbalance of the World Heritage List: Did the UNESCO Strategy Work?', *Journal of International Organizations Study*, 3:1, p. 26.

21 UNESCO has recognized the need for greater diversity and is taking steps to include further examples of natural sites, intangible forms of heritage and those from developing countries. Steiner and Frey, 'Creating the Imbalance of the World Heritage List', pp. 25–8.

22 For an overview of this issue, see F. Kuitenbrouwer (2005) 'The Darker Side of Museum Art: Acquisition and Restitution of Cultural Objects with a Dubious Provenance', *European Review*, 13:4.

23 F. Rose-Greenland (2013) 'The Parthenon Marbles as Icons of Nationalism in Nineteenth-Century Britain', *Nations and Nationalism*, 19:4, pp. 658–9, 668.

24 Rose-Greenland, 'The Parthenon Marbles', pp. 654–5.

25 Kuitenbrouwer, 'The Darker Side of Museum Art', pp. 597–9.

26 Smith, *Uses of Heritage*, pp. 288–9.

27 M. McKenna (2013) 'The History Anxiety', in A. Bashford and S. Macintyre (eds), *The Cambridge History of Australia* (Cambridge: Cambridge University Press), pp. 571–8.

28 The Stolen Generations refers to mixed-race children who were forcibly removed from Aboriginal and Torres Strait Islander families up until the

1970s. McKenna, 'The History Anxiety', pp. 576–8; J. E. Stanton (2011) 'Ethnographic Museums and Collections: From the Past into the Future', in D. Griffin and L. Paroissien (eds), *Understanding Museums: Australian Museums and Museology* (National Museum of Australia): http://www.nma.gov.au/research/understanding-museums/_lib/pdf/Understanding_Museums_whole_2011.pdf. Accessed 16 January 2016.

29   P. Ashton and P. Hamilton (2012) 'Connecting with History: Australians and Their Pasts', in P. Ashton and H. Kean (eds), *Public History and Heritage Today: People and Their Pasts* (Basingstoke and New York: Palgrave Macmillan), p. 25.

30   D. McIntyre (2012) 'Creating New Pasts in Museums: Planning the Museum of London's Modern London Galleries', in Ashton and Kean (eds), *Public History and Heritage Today*, pp. 139–40.

31   M. Pickering and P. Gordan (2011) 'Repatriation: The End of the Beginning', in Griffin and Paroissien, *Understanding Museums*.

32   M. Pickering (2010) 'Where Are the Stories?', *The Public Historian*, 32:1.

33   Pickering, 'Where Are the Stories?', pp. 94–5.

34   Hewison, *The Heritage Industry*, p. 66.

35   R. Adams (2013) 'The V&A, The Destruction of the Country House and the Creation of "English Heritage"', *Museum and Society*, 11:1, p. 7.

36   Adams, 'The V&A', p. 8.

37   Quoted in J. Inglis (2009) 'The Changing Fortunes of Britain's "Heritage" of Historic Buildings since 1945', *History Compass*, 7:6, pp. 1513–15.

38   Hewison, *The Heritage Industry*, p. 67.

39   Hewison, *The Heritage Industry*, p. 53.

40   Hewison, *The Heritage Industry*, pp. 53–71.

41   J. Littler (2008) 'Heritage and Race', in Graham and Howard (eds), *Ashgate Research Companion to Heritage and Identity*, p. 91.

42   Adapted from the excellent explanation of visitor experiences in A. Oram (2012) 'Sexuality in Heterotopia: Time, Space and Love between Women in the Historic House', *Women's History Review*, 21:4, p. 538.

43   Hall, 'Whose Heritage?', p. 4.

44   Quoted in G. Quilley et al. (2012) 'Roundtable: Alan Rice's *Creating Memorials, Building Identities: The Politics of Memory in the Black Atlantic*', *Journal of American Studies*, 46:1, pp. 225–6.

45   The 'African Adventure Playground' is particularly distasteful. Cadbury World homepage: http://www.cadburyworld.co.uk/. Accessed 16 January 2016; Littler, 'Heritage and Race', p. 93.

46   Littler and Naidoo, 'White Past, Multicultural Present', pp. 334–6.

47   The International Slavery Museum developed out of a pioneering exhibition on transatlantic slavery at the Liverpool Maritime Museum.

48   For criticism of the 2007 exhibitions, see Quilley, 'Roundtable: Alan Rice's *Creating Memorials, Building Identities*', p. 224.

49   Littler and Naidoo, 'White Past, Multicultural Present', p. 337.

50   C. Bressey (2009) 'The Legacies of 2007: Remapping the Black Presence in Britain', *Geography Compass*, 3:3, pp. 908–9.

51   Oram, 'Sexuality in Heterotopia', p. 537.

52   Oram, 'Sexuality in Heterotopia', pp. 537–48.

53   R. Mills (2006) 'Queer Is Here? Lesbian, Gay, Bisexual and Transgender Histories and Public Culture', *History Workshop Journal*, 62, p. 256.

54   See, for example, the LGBTQ trail at Brighton Museum. R. White and K. Boddington (2013) LGBTQ Museum Trail: http://brightonmuseums.org.uk/brighton/what-to-see/lgbtq-museum-trail/. Accessed 16 January 2016.

55   Bressey, 'The Legacies of 2007', p. 907; Quilley, 'Roundtable: Alan Rice's *Creating Memorials, Building Identities*', p. 220.

56   A. Vanegas (2002) 'Representing Lesbians and Gay Men in British Social History Museums', in R. Sandell (ed.) (2012) *Museums, Society and Inequality* (London and New York: Routledge), p. 99.

57   Smith, *Uses of Heritage*, p. 33.

58   R. Samuel (1994) *Theatres of Memory. Volume 1: Past and Present in Contemporary Culture* (London and New York: Verso), pp. 259–71.

59   P. Ashton and H. Kean (2012) 'Introduction: People and Their Pasts and Public History Today', in Ashton and Kean, *Public History and Heritage Today*, pp. 1–2.

60   See the chapters by Matthew Grant, Jane Hamlett and David Wyatt in this volume for further discussion of the growth of public history, especially in relation to the REF.

61   Mills (2006) 'Queer Is Here?', pp. 259–62.

62   I was part of a team along with a sociologist, archaeologist, artists and community groups which created a heritage trail. CAER Heritage Project homepage: http://caerheritageproject.com/. Accessed 16 January 2016.

Further Reading

P. Ashton and H. Kean (eds) (2012) *Public History and Heritage Today: People and Their Pasts* (Basingstoke and New York: Palgrave Macmillan).

C. Bressey (2009) 'The Legacies of 2007: Remapping the Black Presence in Britain', *Geography Compass*, 3:3, pp. 903–17.

B. Graham and P. Howard (eds) (2008) *The Ashgate Research Companion to Heritage and Identity* (Aldershot: Ashgate).

S. Hall (1999) 'Whose Heritage? Un-settling "The Heritage", Re-imagining the Post-Nation', *Third Text*, 49, pp. 3–13.

R. Hewison (1987) *The Heritage Industry: Britain in a Climate of Decline* (London: Methuen London Ltd).

J. Inglis (2009) 'The Changing Fortunes of Britain's "Heritage" of Historic Buildings since 1945', *History Compass*, 7:6, pp. 1509–25.

J. Littler and R. Naidoo (2004) 'White Past, Multicultural Present: Heritage and National Stories', in H. Brocklehurst and R. Phillips (eds), *History, Nationhood and the Question of Britain* (London: Palgrave MacMillan), pp. 330–41.

D. Lowenthal (1998) *The Heritage Crusade and the Spoils of History* (Cambridge: Cambridge University Press).

R. Mills (2006) 'Queer Is Here? Lesbian, Gay, Bisexual and Transgender Histories and Public Culture', *History Workshop Journal*, 62, pp. 253–63.

A. Oram (2012) 'Sexuality in Heterotopia: Time, Space and Love between Women in the Historic House', *Women's History Review*, 21:4, pp. 533–51.

M. Pickering (2010) 'Where Are the Stories?', *The Public Historian*, 32:1, pp. 79–95.

F. Rose-Greenland (2013) 'The Parthenon Marbles as Icons of Nationalism in Nineteenth-Century Britain', *Nations and Nationalism*, 19:4, pp. 654–73.

R. Samuel (1994) *Theatres of Memory. Volume 1: Past and Present in Contemporary Culture* (London and New York: Verso).

L. Smith (2006) *Uses of Heritage* (London: Routledge).

17

Exhibiting History

Jane Hamlett

In the early 2000s, I worked on a PhD on gender and the domestic interior in nineteenth- and early twentieth-century Britain, looking at the way middle-class men and women used their homes. A few years after I had finished the project, in 2007, I had the opportunity to use some of this research in an exhibition called 'Choosing the Chintz: Men, Women and Furnishing the Home, 1850 to the Present', staged at the Geffrye Museum of the Home in Hoxton, East London. This essay is about my engagement with the world of museums as an academic historian, how I developed some of my own research for use in the exhibition and how visitors' responses to it made me think about this in new ways.

Museums, publics and historical imagination

There are many reasons why historians can and indeed should want to be involved with museums. Historical research is sometimes directly useful to curators when they make choices about how to display objects; a curator working on the recreation of past domestic interiors, for example, might refer to recent scholarship in this area when deciding what to put into an exhibition. But there is also scope for historians to play a more active role. Part of the attraction for historians is their sheer diversity; in the UK, as well as big, well-known institutions like the British Museum and the National Museum of Scotland, there are smaller establishments that cover a remarkable variety of subjects, from Cumberland's Pencil Museum to Boscastle's Museum of Witchcraft. All social levels are documented, from folk museums that display the material culture of working-class everyday life, to the elite palaces of the super-rich, preserved by the National Trust and English Heritage. Museums cover different kinds of institutions and activities as well as all sorts of working lives. Potentially, the range of history shown in museums is very broad and this offers a great deal of scope for historians. But again, perhaps the most important reason why historians (and certainly those who brand themselves as public historians) should want to work with museums is not just that they offer an arena for showing new aspects of the past to the public, but that they facilitate the engagement of the public with the past, and allow them to become active agents in its creation.

Museums are an important means by which public audiences engage with history. Curators create powerful narratives that explain and demonstrate the past in new ways. A museum with a particular purpose can influence the way in which important events figure in popular memory. A good example of the role of museums in creating national identity is the recent debate over the National Museum of Australia, which was opened in 2001 and took a controversial approach to the representation of the Australian national past, choosing to show this through the lives of everyday people rather than the already-known heroes of Australian foundation myth. As further discussed in Stephanie Ward's chapter in this volume, the museum sparked considerable criticism from government members and the press, and was eventually subjected to a substantial review in 2003, which although offering some praise for the museum was also critical of its failure to present visitors with clear and strong narratives.[1] Yet museums are not concerned simply with showing things from the past, or transferring knowledge, but in promoting and creating new ways in which visitors can interact with them. This can be seen in the increasing emphasis on interactivity in display, in the use of pull-out drawers, push buttons, iPads and screens and dressing-up costumes.[2] Museums do not simply relay facts; instead they present the past through works of art, objects or stories that are designed to provoke a response and to offer a new way of seeing the past. As Museum of London curator Darryl McIntyre puts it, museums draw on scholarly research but they also 'make possible a crucial interplay between intellectual and emotional knowledge. Museums want visitors to say: "I knew this happened, but I didn't know what it was actually like". Emotional connection founded on scholarship is what museums do best'.[3] For some time, curators have tried to bring new audiences within their walls, moving beyond the stereotype of the museum as an austere space, filled with glass cases, intelligible only to an educated elite.[4] Education departments in museums are also hugely important in introducing children to this world, often at very young ages. Most museums include educational activities as part of their aims in their mission statements, and activities are coordinated across the sector by the Group for Education in Museums (GEM).[5] In short, museums can transfer scholarly history to the public, but what is perhaps more important is their stake in how history is created in the public imagination.

This makes museums particularly important to historians who style themselves as 'public historians' or who want to engage with public history. The term 'public history' is a relatively recent one, at least in the UK. What does it mean?[6] Hilda Kean offers an expansive definition, arguing that public history can be seen as the process of 'looking at the value of the past in people's everyday lives', that is, any kind of history that continues to have significance to individuals or communities who are alive today.[7] Academic historians who engage with the public, be it through media, museums or research that has direct applicability to politics or social policies, as discussed in Matthew Grant's chapter in this book, are now sometimes described as public historians. The public significance of history is also an increasingly important part of how it is taught. The long-standing MA in public history at Ruskin College, Oxford, has recently been joined by courses at York and Royal Holloway, University of London. It is also a key component of a growing number of undergraduate courses. But as Kean points out, the point of public history in a larger sense is that it sees history as a shared activity that is not necessarily dictated by academic expertise. Public history can challenge the notion that history is created by scholars in universities and then simply transferred to a passive public.[8] Instead, there is an increasing focus, within public history, on how meaning and history itself are created through public engagement; that is, how the public themselves are actively involved in producing history and meaning, through family history research, the exploration of local archives or volunteering at National Trust houses, to name but a few activities. Museums have an important part to play in this, because, as curators have long recognized, the meaning they produce for visitors is created not just by the narrative and objects that are presented to them, but by the ideas and experiences that they bring in when they walk through the museum's doors. Museums do not offer historians the chance to present their research to the public, exactly, but rather to participate in a collaborative process in which the meaning of their research is transformed. Ideally, both sides can learn something from each other. This was certainly my experience when working with the Geffrye on 'Choosing the Chintz', as the rest of this essay will explore.

The research

Between 2001 and 2005, I was a PhD student at Royal Holloway, University of London, working on a thesis on gender and the domestic interior in middle-class English homes. I had come to this topic as I was very interested in the history of women, and in the way in which ideas of gender were both represented in society and played out in everyday life. One of the things that intrigued me was the question of how constricting ideals and expectations about gendered behaviour actually were in people's everyday lives, and how

far women in particular were really bound by them. Studying the material
world, that is the spaces and things that surrounded people in the past,
seemed like a good way of getting at this. It allowed me to look at both
the ideas that were attached to everyday objects, and how these reflected
society's conventions, as well as what ordinary men and women actually did
with goods on a day-to-day basis, which showed how gendered conventions
and rules could sometimes be broken.

So I became interested in the question of how space in Victorian middle-
class homes was divided up between men and women, and how the home
itself could work to create gendered ideals and identities. Historians had
often supposed that there were clear divisions in the Victorian middle-class
home, with dining rooms, studies, libraries, smoking rooms and billiard
rooms seen as male spaces, whereas drawing rooms, morning rooms and
boudoirs were thought to be the preserve of women. This separation was
usually associated with an unequal power divide between men and women.[9]
Male spaces were supposed to be decorated in dark colours, with heavy
furniture, and tokens of the hunt, while ideal female rooms were lighter and
more likely to be filled with ornaments. What I wanted to know was how
strongly these gendered meanings were articulated in nineteenth-century
culture, and why it was generally thought important to decorate the home
in a masculine or feminine way. But I was also interested in what people
actually did in their homes, and whether they felt obliged, or were able,
to follow these conventions.[10] To answer these questions, I turned to the
archives. By looking at how these rooms were presented in different sets of
sources, I hoped to access different levels of meaning.

To try and find out how these rooms were understood in nineteenth-
century culture, I began by looking at literature advising the middle
classes on how to decorate their homes. The gendered identities I had
been looking for were very strongly present in recommendations for
decoration and furnishing. These illustrations from an advice manual by
H.R. Jennings show a typical feminized piece of drawing room furniture,
from 'The Woman's Realm', as well as an image of an ideal dining room,
a masculine space, decorated in dark colours and furnished with heavy
oak furniture (Figure 17.1). Yet there was more to it than this. Not all the
advice books I looked at took the same line, and when I examined them
closely it became clear that the division of male and female space in the
home was actually the subject of heated debate. This centred on the use of
the third sitting room (a reception room other than the drawing room and
dining room). While male writers such as Jennings urged that this should
be used as a smoking room, female advisors such as Jane Ellen Panton
and Dorothy Constance Peel were determined that it should be a morning
room, a secluded spot devoted to women's work, household accounts or
even professional writing. So far from reinforcing women's inferior status,
some writers were arguing that gendered space could be seen as a direct
means of female empowerment.

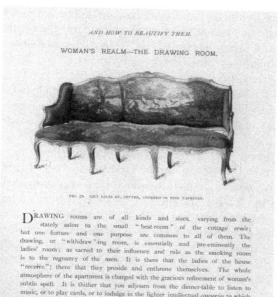

FIGURE 17.1 *Two pages from H.R. Jennings,* Our Homes and How to Beautify Them *(London: Harrison & Sons, 1902), showing the idealized feminine furniture for the drawing room, and the more masculine décor thought suitable for the drawing room.* © *Private Collection.*

Advice manuals, though, could only take me so far. What of how ordinary middle-class men and women used these spaces, and the identities that they created? It is often much harder to get at everyday practices than cultural expectations. Nonetheless, a wide range of sources are available to historians who want to find out about the everyday lives of the Victorian middle classes. I used around 200 inventories and sale catalogues (which listed some of things that people actually had in their homes) and photographs (these were sparser as it was difficult to take photos indoors in this period), to work out what the Victorians actually had in their homes. The inventories and sale catalogues usually offered lists of furniture on a room-by-room basis. They told a quite different story to the advice manuals. First, they showed that homes with extensive gendered spaces were really quite rare – only the very well-off could afford to have a library, billiard room or smoking room and morning rooms were even thinner on the ground. Instead, the main gender division in most middle-class homes lay between the masculine terrain of the dining room and the feminine drawing room. What was interesting though, was that in smaller homes the range of goods in these rooms suggested that far from being restricted to particular activities associated with either sex, these rooms were multifunctional. Despite the rigid gendered divides in advice literature, these spaces appeared to be used in a far less prescriptive and more fluid way.

To find out more about how these rooms were used, I surveyed around 200 contemporary autobiographies and 30 sets of family papers (manuscript sources that included personal writings such as diaries and letters). Autobiographies too bear testimony to the many uses of these places at different times of day. So the needs and demands of everyday life seem to have overcome strict gendered segregation. The individual testimonies presented in autobiographies and memoirs showed that the way in which Victorian families used space was often very complex, and varied between households. While studies and libraries were supposed to be the sacred territory of stern, patriarchal fathers, it was only in some homes that they were used for reprimanding the children, while in others they were frequently invaded by riotous offspring with scant respect for their father's sanctums.[11] Overall, from my research I concluded that although the material world of the home played an important part in the creation of gendered identities, this was much less restrictive and a great deal more fluid than previously thought. While these conclusions broke new historical ground, they were quite complex, and made sense primarily in terms of a response to what other historians had previously argued about gender and domestic interiors in nineteenth-century Britain. Nonetheless, the research material that I had amassed and the conclusions drawn were to come in very useful when I began working on 'Choosing the Chintz'.

From PhD to exhibition

So how did I come to be involved with the exhibition? The Geffrye Museum is relatively small. Opened in 1914, the museum started out primarily as a furniture collection but its remit has expanded considerably over the years and it now deals with all aspects of home life.[12] Its central display space is a series of period rooms, constructed in converted almshouses, which focus on the major transitions in urban living rooms from the late medieval period to the present day. As the museum focuses on the London middle-class home, it was naturally of interest to me as a PhD student. During the final year of my dissertation project I had a part-time job at the Geffrye, carrying out research to inform the refurbishment of their seventeenth- and eighteenth-century galleries, which gave me a chance to learn more about what the museum did first-hand. In 2006, the Geffrye approached me about working on what was to become 'Choosing the Chintz'. They were working with an exhibition proposal formulated by Deborah Cohen on male and female decorative choice. This was based on research from her ground-breaking book *Household Gods: The British and Their Possessions* (2006) which offered an exciting new vision of the meaning of domestic goods in the Victorian home, and argued that Victorian men had a much larger stake in domestic decoration than historians had previously thought.[13] But by the time the museum came to work on the proposal, Deborah had returned to the States and could not directly contribute. So the museum asked Lesley Hoskins, another historian of the nineteenth-century domestic interior, and me if we would be able to co-curate. I was delighted to have this opportunity, as at the same time I had applied for a year's ESRC postdoctoral fellowship to develop my thesis into a book, and the exhibition gave me a chance to get some of my research out to a public audience as well as an academic one. Our role as historians was to supply the material for the exhibition – images, testimony and objects – and to work closely with the curators on the development of the narrative for the exhibition. So in the months that followed we collected material and had a series of regular meetings with curators Eleanor John and Alex Goddard. We worked closely with the museum team over about six months, during which time we gathered and considered material, and slowly built a narrative.

So, beginning in the mid-nineteenth century, the exhibition told a story about who was responsible for choosing goods for the home, and how this shifted away from men towards women in the early twentieth century. One of the key points was that women did not always dominate homemaking. Here, we drew on the argument from Deborah's *Household Gods*, which showed that men played a far greater role in this than widely assumed. When putting together an exhibition, it is crucial to have something to show: points are made and hearts are won primarily through the display of objects and works of art, rather than the narrative. To demonstrate the prominence of men at home we chose three striking pieces of art: Colonel Harold Esdaile Malet's 'Interior at Cox Hoe' (1867–68), a painting in which the Colonel had used photomontage to insert an image of himself and his dog; George Smith's 'Evenings at Home' (1852), which showed Henry Cole and his family at their home in Kensington, West London; and George Townsend Cole's portrait of Henry Lambert (1858). Each of these was accompanied by a different illustrated diary and memoir, which I found during my research, displayed open in a glass box. One, 'Gleanings of the Pumphrey Family, 1835–1908', by Thomas Pumphrey, from Tyne and Wear Archive Service, was an autobiographical album compiled by a Newcastle-based grocer and leather-seller on his golden wedding anniversary. The album was open at 'In Our Cosy Chairs', a particularly striking photograph of Pumphrey and his wife seated in their parlour or drawing room, in companionable armchairs, reading (Figure 17.2). The second piece for display was the joint diaries of

IN OUR COSY CHAIRS. 1908. THOMAS

FIGURE 17.2 *Photograph showing Mr and Mrs Pumphrey 'In Our Cosy Chairs', from Pumphrey Family Golden Wedding Album, 1905. Tyne and Wear Archives, 1441/8. Reproduced by permission of Tyne and Wear Archives.*

Andrew and Aggie Donaldson (1879 and 1884) from London Metropolitan Archives, illustrated by artist Andrew. The diaries we displayed showed pictures of the family at the table at Christmas, and Aggie and the children with the family home above.

The next section of the exhibition, which explored gendered decoration and spaces in the nineteenth-century home, was directly informed by my research. The narrative showed how there were separate terrains for men and women, and that the main distinction was between the heavy, masculine dining room and the more feminine, ornamental drawing room. Here, we prioritized a quote from Jennings in the display: 'The drawing or "withdraw"-ing room, is essentially and pre-eminently the ladies' room; as sacred to their influence as the smoking room is to the regnancy of the men'.[14] Paintings and graphics from advice manuals and magazines were used to show dining rooms and drawing rooms, and we displayed a typical dining room chair alongside one from a drawing room, showing the contrast between the heavy, darker style thought suitable for the former, and the lighter, more ornamental for the latter. Two particularly fascinating objects, identified by Lesley, were also used to try and get the point across in a different way. The first, a doll's house (1860–65) from the V&A Museum of Childhood that had belonged to a Mrs Bryant, featured a drawing room and study in miniature, furnished in the feminine and masculine gendered conventions of the day (Figure 17.3). The second item was a highly unusual wallpaper order book, also from the V&A, from the firm of Cowtan and Son (1859–61). The book displayed samples of wallpaper chosen for drawing rooms and dining rooms, demonstrating that real-life consumers followed these gendered conventions in practice. We combined these things with several contemporary accounts on listening posts, including the autobiography of art critic and advice writer Charles Eastlake, who complained greatly over his wife's choice of ornaments in the drawing room.[15]

Our exhibition then turned to look in more detail at male spaces within the home, something with which we felt that our audience would probably be unfamiliar. This again drew on my research, which flagged up the prominence of rooms for men in some middle-class houses. Here we used two portraits to show men occupying specifically male spaces. And we brought together a group of objects to recreate the special, oriental style of decoration that was often found in the smoking room. Our display consisted of a full-blown Moorish decorative scheme for such a room (although emphasizing at the same time that this would have been quite rare), as well as an ubiquitous Moorish occasional table (c. 1890) from the Geffrye's own collections. We were also able to display some items of smoking paraphernalia including a Hookah or tobacco pipe (1880–90), borrowed from the Horniman Museum, and a tasselled smoking cap from the same period, from the Geffrye's collection. The showpiece of our display was a collector's cabinet (c. 1858) that had belonged to civil engineer and keen amateur geologist John Clark Hawkshaw, borrowed from Haslemere

FIGURE 17.3 *Doll's house known as 'Mrs Bryant's Pleasure', 1860–65.* © *Victoria and Albert Museum, London.*

Education Museum. This fascinating piece offered a material demonstration of the presence of male collecting practices in the home. However, with our narrative we tried to do justice to the nuances of some of this by explaining that while libraries and studies were designated as no-go areas they were frequently invaded by other family members. To do this we again deployed autobiographical extracts on listening posts, this time using Horace Collin's account of the frequent invasions of his father's library in Maida Vale in the 1890s, and his subsequent retreat to his bedroom.[16]

There were of course, some aspects of the research that could not be shown. The sources that we had surveyed for our various projects were too vast to be incorporated into a single exhibition, and it would not have been appropriate to do so. Our role as curators was to cherry-pick from what we had, selecting the most evocative and telling images, objects and stories to include. Here we relied on our interpretative skills as historians, sifting and selecting the evidence. There are obviously huge differences between exhibition texts and history books. The former are far, far shorter and must convey general points very precisely in a brief space. The academic language in which historians sometimes express their findings is inappropriate in this context and can be rather off-putting. Some of the quantitative analysis undertaken in my research could not be conveyed in a museum environment, yet the broad overall conclusions were used to underpin the direction of the narrative. Overall, we were pleased that our research was used in this way, but it was obviously very different to the way in which it was presented in an academic context.

It should be clear by now that 'Choosing the Chintz' was very much about teamwork. No one person's research material or conclusions dominated, and the resulting exhibition was a combination of ideas and material from Deborah, Lesley and me, brought together in a single narrative by the curators Eleanor and Alex. Nor should we overstate the contribution of historical research to an exhibition like this one. Our conclusions supplied the central historical story, and, for the most part, the materials displayed were drawn from sources we had found. Here our research experience was vital as we were able to draw on a vast body of contemporary sources that evoked the voices, words and lives of the past. Yet to make sense of these sources and to work out how the public might perceive them, we needed the help of the museum professionals on the curatorial team. The exhibition was mainly based on borrowed material rather than the museum's own collections. So that meant a protracted process of negotiating loans with various institutions, as well as negotiating the difficulties involved in offering the right conditions for storage and display. And the design of an exhibition – crucial in determining its final format – is also dealt with by professional designers. Andy Feast, Sharon Beard and Sally McIntosh were the exhibition and graphic designers for 'Choosing the Chintz'. Their role included designing the layout and use of space in the exhibition, working out how the images and narrative should be shown, and how the objects were displayed. In the last months of preparation, Lesley and I played a relatively small role; we just had to sit back and wait for the opening view (Figure 17.4).

Public engagement and response

Not only does the Geffrye Museum collect, document, preserve and display domestic furnishings and other household items, but one of the museum's strengths is its strong community role. It has a well-developed education department, which was established in the 1930s when the museum came to be funded by the London County Council's Education Committee.[17] The museum developed a reputation for its education programmes, and right from its early days, school parties have been taught in the period rooms, and allowed to touch and use special objects from the handling collection. Annually, the Education Department at the museum meets around 28,000 visitors face-to-face and 15,000 of these are school groups. About 60 per

FIGURE 17.4 *Installation view of exhibition 'Choosing the Chintz: Men, Women and Furnishing the Home, 1850 to the Present', 14 October 2008–22 February 2009. © Jayne Lloyd, Geffrye Museum Picture Library, archex_chintz_016. Reproduced by permission of The Geffrye, Museum of the Home.*

cent of school visitors are from the museum's local boroughs of Hackney and Tower Hamlets, and most school groups come from Greater London. Most visiting pupils are from primary schools, although since 2006 the secondary programme has brought around 800 secondary schoolchildren through the museum's doors each year. The museum offers a core programme for primary, secondary and special needs. Unusually for an institution of its size, it also plays a leading role in academic research. It has set up several research networks and runs a research centre for the study of the home with Queen Mary, University of London.[18] The museum's connections with academic research, as well as its wide-ranging educational activities, make it particularly attractive to historians seeking to work with wider audiences.

The 'Choosing the Chintz' exhibition was designed to reach out directly to visitors. To do this, we used displays that encouraged different kinds of engagement including listening posts and a video featuring contemporary couples discussing who 'chose the chintz' in their own homes. There was also an interactive game for visitors that involved looking at a series of interiors from London homes in the early 2000s and trying to guess which sex they belonged to. Some of these were surprisingly ambiguous, but there were a few 'giveaway' items in each one (Figure 17.5). 'Choosing the Chintz' was also used as part of the Geffrye's education programme,

FIGURE 17.5 *Interactive panels encouraging visitors to guess the sex of the occupants of twenty-first-century living spaces.* © *Jayne Lloyd, archex_chintz_015, Geffrye Museum Picture Library. Reproduced by permission of The Geffrye, Museum of the Home.*

hosting half-term activities for 253 children and a workshop for 102 children. Emma Dunn, Education Officer for Schools and Formal Learning at the Geffrye, introduced schoolchildren to the exhibition. She commented that explaining gender divides in the Victorian home to young children could be difficult, but this was made easier by one of the exhibition's focal points, a large nineteenth-century doll's house, which was 'compelling and understandable for younger pupils'. Young visitors were also introduced to the past through handling objects: 'Something that always works really well is the use of handling artefacts. We have a large collection of original Victorian household items – life size versions of those within the doll's house, which we use regularly at the Geffrye'. Some of the exhibits struck a chord with present-day home lives: 'Many of the Asian children told me that their homes are subdivided into masculine and feminine spaces, so they were able to relate to the subject'. This was a very interesting point, and not something that had occurred to us when we set the exhibition up. Here, the Geffrye's intervention in the wider community, and their active role in bringing diverse audiences into the museum, helped us see our research in new and different light. This is a good example of the value of exhibiting history, not just to the members of the public who visit museums, but also to the historians who carry out the research. Contact with wider audiences beyond the academy can help historians refine their ideas or see the purpose of their research in a new way. The meaning of history can be transformed if seen through the eyes of different ages, races or genders, as this book explored earlier in the chapter 'Identities'.

So how effective were our strategies for public engagement? Looking at what happened during the museum's education sessions is one way of working this out. Another thing we can measure is how many people actually turned out to see the exhibition. The museum recorded quite high numbers of visitors – 18,379 in total – and Eleanor John, Head Curator, stated that it was 'one of our most successful exhibitions'. The museum kept a book of comments and invited visitors to contribute their own stories about who chose what in their own households. We were also able to track the response to the exhibition by looking at how it was covered in the press – in fact, the idea of the home as the site for gendered decision making between men and women captured the imagination of quite a few features editors, and pieces appeared on Chintz in the *Sunday Times*, the *Guardian* and *Time Out*. These features tended to be light-hearted in tone, picking up on the comedy inherent in 'the struggle for the home' and 'the battle between the sexes'. This didn't exactly come as a surprise to us – we had, after all, hoped that the exhibition would be amusing and engaging and had deliberately picked material and the title with this in mind. But at the same time, after many months, and even years, of labouring over these questions in the archives this was perhaps a salutary reminder of the role of gender history in the popular imagination. Women, the home and private life are generally considered of less importance than more 'weighty' subjects, involving states, battles and great men. Yet despite this perception, home life is often viewed with a great deal of curiosity and pleasure by female viewers, readers and visitors in particular.

The meaning of an exhibition, and the history it conveys, is produced as much by the viewer who walks around it as the historians, curators and designers who have set it up. Here, the significance of the exhibition was created by visitors bringing their own experiences of home and gendered decision-making to bear on what they saw in front of them. The visitor numbers for the exhibition speak for themselves; entertainment and pleasure are of course major drivers of popular engagement with the past.

Conclusion

History as practised by academics and as created and used outside universities remain different things, but when the two work together the results can be beneficial for both groups. What, then, do historians get out of engaging with the public through exhibiting history? And what did I take away from the public engagement with our exhibition? By showing history in this way, professional historians are able to convey their research to much wider audiences. Academic work can be quite specific, and designed to answer questions raised by previous research or to move a field forward. Often, it complicates matters, rather than providing straightforward answers. Yet most historians also use their evidence to form broad interpretations about the past societies they study. The new ideas they offer can, with the help of curators and exhibition designers, be used to create stories or shows that 'speak' to the public and present the past in a new light. The role of the researcher in unearthing new evidence, or coming up with a novel interpretation, can also be essential to exhibitions which are premised on the idea that they show unknown material or that they have something new to say about it. However, this is not a one-way process. Presenting research to varied audiences can also help historians see its meaning and value in different ways. Looking at how people responded to 'Choosing the Chintz' was an interesting experience and it certainly made me think about my research in a new light. Seeing how the educational team were able to use the exhibition to introduce the Victorians to schoolchildren was fascinating, and made me feel proud of what we had been able to put together. As we saw in the chapter 'Evidence and Interpretation' earlier in this book, historians' perspectives are often shaped to some extent by their political ideas. As a feminist historian, I believe that our depictions of the past are always connected to the present. By studying past gender relations, we can take a more relational, informed view on how men and women interact now and (this may sound rather optimistic) move towards building a better, or at least more critical society. So by looking at the past and seeing how men and women divided up household tasks then and now, we can perhaps reflect on changes in the nature of those divisions in society. I do think that the exhibition genuinely challenged some public perceptions of male and female roles in the Victorian period – especially with regard to the home being a supposedly female sphere and the rigidity with which the Victorians are supposed to have adhered to gendered rules and conventions. But importantly, the exhibition also taught me something about why historical research can be valuable. Not just because it 'teaches lessons about the past', helps make current political decisions, or informs policy, but because of the role it plays in contributing to the formation of a broader historical culture in which entertainment, pleasure and enjoyment are as important as didacticism. I can't say how far the exhibition changed people's ideas about the Victorians, or about the operation of gender in society, then or now. But the fact that so many people came does at least reveal popular enthusiasm for the subject, that this was something that visitors wanted to look at and be part of. Public history is not important because it tells people things, but because people participate in making it. Helping curate this exhibition helped me see my research as something that figured in and connected to a broader public imagination, rather than something that I, the historian, set out to tell them.

Acknowledgements

I am very grateful to Lesley Hoskins, Eleanor John, Tracey Loughran, Laura MacCulloch and David Wilson who read a draft of this and provided some very useful comments.

STUDY QUESTIONS

- What is the value of historical research in a museum context?
- How can historians benefit from exhibiting history?
- What role do museums play in creating 'public history', and what part do museum visitors play in creating understandings of the past?
- Think of a museum you have visited and consider the following questions:
  - How has the museum chosen to display its objects? What strategies have been used?
  - What do you think the museum hopes to achieve from this?
  - How has the museum put these objects into historical context?
  - How successful do you think this is?
  - Does this museum seek to change established ideas about the past?

Notes

1   K. Message and C. Healey (2004) 'A Symptomatic Museum: The New, the NMA and the Culture Wars', *Borderlands E-Journal*, 3:3: http://www. borderlands.net.au/vol3no3_2004/messagehealy_symptom.htm. Accessed 16 January 2016.

2   For a discussion of changing display practices at the Museum of London, see D. McIntyre (2012) 'Creating New Pasts in Museums: Planning the Museum of London's Modern Galleries', in P. Ashton and H. Kean (eds), *Public History and Heritage Today: People and Their Pasts* (Basingstoke: Palgrave Macmillan), p. 131.

3   McIntyre, 'Creating New Pasts in Museums', p. 142.

4   N. Merriman (1991) *Beyond the Glass Case: The Past, the Heritage and the Public in Britain* (Leicester: Leicester University Press), especially the introduction.

5   GEM: The Voice for Heritage Learning: http://www.gem.org.uk/. Accessed 16 January 2016.

6 While at one time public history was defined as history that took place in institutions outside universities, increasingly it has come to include the activities of academic historians who communicate with public audiences. The word is used in different ways in different places. For a full discussion of this shift, and different definitions, see G. Smith (2011) 'Toward a Public Oral History', in D. A. Ritchie (ed.), *The Oxford Handbook of Oral History* (Oxford: Oxford University Press), pp. 429, 432.

7 H. Kean (2013) 'Introduction', in H. Kean and P. Martin (eds), *The Public History Reader* (London: Routledge), p. xiv.

8 Kean, 'Introduction', p. xv.

9 J. Kinchin (1996) 'Interior: Nineteenth-Century Essays on the "Masculine" and the "Feminine" Room', in P. Kirkham (ed.), *The Gendered Object* (Manchester: Manchester University Press), pp. 18–20.

10 For a full discussion of my findings, see J. Hamlett (2009) '"The Dining Room Should Be the Man's Paradise, as the Drawing Room Is the Woman's": Gender and Middle-Class Domestic Space in England, 1850–1910', *Gender & History*, 21:3.

11 J. Hamlett (2010) *Material Relations: Middle-Class Families and Domestic Interiors in England, 1850–1910* (Manchester: Manchester University Press), pp. 115–16.

12 See D. Dewing (2008) *The Geffrye Museum of the Home: A Guide to the Museum* (The Geffrye Museum: London).

13 D. Cohen (2006) *Household Gods: The British and Their Possessions* (London: Yale University Press).

14 H. R. Jennings (1902) *Our Homes and How to Beautify Them* (London: Harrison & Sons).

15 Hamlett, *Material Relations*, p. 95.

16 Hamlett, *Material Relations*, p. 116.

17 Dewing, *The Geffrye Museum of the Home*, pp. 48–9.

18 Queen Mary, University of London and The Geffrye, Centre for Studies of Home: http://www.studiesofhome.qmul.ac.uk/. Accessed 16 January 2016.

Further Reading

E. Barker (ed.) (1999) *Contemporary Cultures of Display* (London: Yale University Press).

C. Duncan (1995) *Civilising Rituals: Inside Public Art Museums* (London and New York: Routledge) (especially chapter 1, 'The Art Museum as Ritual').

J. B. Gardner (2004) 'Contested Terrains: History, Museums and the Public', *The Public Historian*, 26:4, pp. 11–21.

L. Jordanova (1989) 'Objects of Knowledge: A Historical Perspective on Museums', in P. Vergo (ed.), *The New Museology* (London: Reaktion Books), pp. 22–40.

H. Kean (2013) 'Introduction', in H. Kean and P. Martin (eds), *The Public History Reader* (London: Routledge), pp. xiii–xxxiii.

D. McIntyre (2012) 'Creating New Pasts in Museums: Planning the Museum of London's Modern Galleries', in P. Ashton and H. Kean (eds), *Public History and Heritage Today: People and Their Pasts* (Basingstoke: Palgrave Macmillan), pp. 131–45.

N. Merriman (1989) 'Museum Visiting as a Cultural Phenomenon', in P. Vergo (ed.), *The New Museology* (London: Reaktion Books), pp. 149–71.

N. Merriman (1991) *Beyond the Glass Case: The Past, the Heritage and the Public in Britain* (Leicester: Leicester University Press).

K. Message and C. Healey (2004) 'A Symptomatic Museum: The New, the NMA and the Culture Wars', *Borderlands E-Journal*, 3:3: http://www.borderlands.net.au/vol3no3_2004/messagehealy_symptom.htm.

D. A. Reid (2002) 'Making Gender Matter: Interpreting Male and Female Roles in Historic House Museums', in J. Foy Donnelly (ed.), *Interpreting Historic House Museums* (Oxford and New York: Altamira Press), pp. 81–110.

G. Smith (2011) 'Toward a Public Oral History', in D. A. Ritchie (ed.), *The Oxford Handbook of Oral History* (Oxford: Oxford University Press), pp. 429–48.

A. Woodhouse (2004) 'Museum Curators', in J. B. Gardner and P. S. LaPaglia (eds), *Public History: Essays from the Field* (Malabar, FL: Krieger Publishing Company), pp. 187–202.

18

Taking History into the World

David Wyatt

'What's the point of doing a history degree?' This is a familiar question for those of us who choose to become students of history. It can seemingly emanate from anywhere: relatives, close friends, work colleagues or casual acquaintances. Although it normally arises within a light-hearted jokey context, the question is still often tinged with an element of serious concern, and reveals some underlying assumptions and stereotypes about the nature of the subject: for example, that the study of history has no relevance to the 'real world'; that a history degree is, at best, an expensive educational side-street, and at worst an overindulgent intellectual hobby; and that studying history at university will provide you with few relevant life skills or avenues for career development, other than primary or secondary school teaching, that is. I am guessing that as you are reading this book, you've already decided that you don't agree with these assumptions, although you may well have been on the receiving end of them!

These enduring stereotypes about the value of studying history and its relevance to the 'real world' are actually underpinned by significant social, cultural and political perceptions and debates. These debates contest the nature, value and use of history within a twenty-first-century context of globalization, academic accountability, economic challenges and a highly competitive employment market. Many historians have felt the need to defend and justify their subject in the face of a perceived obligation to 'show their value-added nature to the taxpaying public and government customers'.[1] Yet the apparent need for a strenuous defence of the subject is also surprising given that that history is actually a booming 'industry', both in terms of public interest and in universities where tens of thousands of students choose to study it each year.[2]

Previous chapters have dealt critically and in some theoretical depth with such popular forms of history. What I do in this chapter is a little different and perhaps more practical. I will consider why and how academic historians interact with the public through engagement and outreach activities. I then relate this work to opportunities for students to similarly get involved in 'taking history into the world' during their time at university. In doing so, I hope to address some of the traditional stereotypes about the value of history and reveal how studying history provides a significant range of skills which prepare students for life after university.

Why take history into the world?

Before taking history into the world, we need to understand why we are doing it, and to what end. To disseminate knowledge of the past? To improve research? To develop employability skills? To challenge myths? To help communities? To be better, more fully rounded citizens? These are all potentially noble reasons, of course, but good historians always begin by exploring their own motivations before they approach a particular topic. So, in this section we will consider the reasons why academic historians are increasingly getting involved in public engagement, and examine their motivations for doing so.

To do this, we first need to consider the key strategic missions that drive universities and the academic historians employed within them. These missions will inevitably shape the nature of your experience as a student. This is because they directly impact on university research, teaching and learning by influencing the historical topics on offer for study and the ways in which courses are taught and assessed. They also help to shape extracurricular activities and public engagement opportunities, so it is quite useful to have a handle on them as you commence your life at university. These missions are: to advance knowledge through research; to impart knowledge to students through education; and to be of service to the wider world. This third mission concerns the social responsibility of universities: specifically, that knowledge and teaching expertise generated within these institutions may serve and strengthen communities, both locally and internationally. It should be immediately clear why these three missions have relevance to this chapter. Research generates historical knowledge and also directly informs teaching because academic historians are expected to teach courses based on their research (a process referred to as research-led teaching). Both research and teaching are underpinned by a wider social mission to share knowledge for the benefit of the wider world and also to produce responsible, enquiring and engaged citizens through the education of undergraduates.

This conception of a tripartite mission for universities is not new. These three goals have persisted as common threads throughout the history of the

Western university.[3] In theory, these three missions of research, teaching and social responsibility are closely interlinked and complement one another. However, ever since the professionalization of academic institutions in the nineteenth century, these three interdependent missions have often been compartmentalized or given differing priorities. More often than not, research has been regarded as by far the most important. This privileging of research has contributed towards the long-held perception that the academic world of research is separate from the 'real world'. Concerns regarding this perceived separation of academia from society are clearly evident in current debates surrounding the value and significance of history. They have led to increasing calls from within the academic discipline for historians to become more engaged in taking history into the world.[4] These concerns are exemplified by Justin Champion in his recent soul-searching article 'What Are Historians For?'. Champion cites 'anxieties' about the maintenance of historical objectivity as the specific reason for a perceived academic retreat into a closed, sheltered, discursive world of exclusive journals and expensive book publications. His concerns about the need for historians to expend more energy on reaching out to the world are underpinned by the emergence of two very powerful agendas over the last decade. These are the 'impact agenda' and the 'employability agenda'. It is therefore important that we briefly examine each of these in turn.

As seen in Matthew Grant's chapter in this volume, the impact agenda has arisen out of the publicly funded nature of research in the UK, and the mechanisms by which the quality of that research is assessed and made accountable to the public purse. It is true that the introduction of impact has been greeted by a fair degree of scepticism, suspicion and controversy by some academic historians. Yet in spite of these misgivings, the impact agenda has undoubtedly had positive effects too. Not least, it increasingly provides historians with significant economic and career-focused incentives to take history into the world. Debates around impact and the social role of universities are shaped by the wider context of global economic challenges and significant changes to the ways in which universities are funded. Universities are becoming increasingly marketized as a result of tuition fee rises and the resulting competition for student recruitment. They are also driven by clear government, business and student demands to equip undergraduates with the necessary employability skills for the highly competitive labour market of the twenty-first century.[5] Most undergraduate students regard higher university education as much more than a career development opportunity. But understandably, they also expect a return on their investment in terms of acquiring skills and abilities that will help them gain employment in a desired career.[6]

Historians have rightly highlighted that the 'transferable skills' inculcated by a history degree directly correlate to those skill sets most in demand from employers.[7] These include, among others, adaptability, initiative, oral and written communication, problem solving, analysis, creativity, team work and IT skills.[8] Such transferable skills have been firmly embedded into programmes of higher education teaching through the benchmark statements of the Quality Assurance Agency for Higher Education (QAA), an independent body that monitors and advises on standards and quality in UK higher education.[9] Detailed studies reveal the success of history graduates, armed with such skills, in securing good employment in diverse career pathways.[10]

Universities also place emphasis on providing support for extracurricular development and student volunteering. A recent survey of over 8,000 UK students and graduates entitled 'Bursting the Bubble' revealed that 63 per cent of those interviewed had taken part in formal volunteering since starting university. The majority of these had been involved in organizations or projects of benefit to people in communities outside of the university.[11] The survey noted the significant value of such volunteering for developing good employability skills. 51 per cent of the recent graduates surveyed stated that experience of volunteering had directly helped them in gaining employment.[12] Despite these obvious benefits in terms of personal development, the primary motivation for most of these student volunteers was actually far more altruistic. 95 per cent of those surveyed stated they got involved because of their desire 'to improve things or help people'.[13] The findings of the 'Bursting the Bubble' survey highlight a powerful student thirst for outreach and engagement, and especially work which is of benefit to those outside the academy. Of course, this culture of volunteering also has its downside. Unpaid work is just that – unpaid. Volunteer internships or placements have the potential to be exploitative, or even coercive, in a highly competitive employment environment where young people are desperate for a toehold within a specific profession.[14] Nevertheless, many students involved in ethically run volunteering programmes have highlighted the advantages of engagement for personal development, as well as the significant contribution students can make to the universities' 'third mission' of social responsibility to the wider world.

This brings us back to the subject of studying history – a pursuit long regarded as having much greater aspirational objectives than simply fostering core skills which help students to get jobs. In 1973, the historian J.H. Plumb (1911–2001) argued that the study of history improved individual self-awareness and provided a deeper understanding of society that might positively 'mould human attitudes and human actions'.[15] More recently, Beverley Southgate has reinforced this contention, arguing that the study of history helps to provide a more nuanced understanding of the complexities of human action, which can ultimately result in greater social tolerance.[16] Champion, too, highlights the role of history as a subject which inculcates students with an improved understanding of self and others, and instils a dynamic sense of citizenship. He passionately argues that it is the historian's *obligation* to take history into the world and 'to make every effort to connect the past to the public'.[17]

From the perspective of Plumb, Southgate and Champion, then, studying history develops students into more self-reflexive, tolerant and communicative citizens, and thereby improves society. I do not disagree with this premise, but it is interesting that historians who profess this view are often less specific on the exact form that engagement should take or who historians' proposed 'audiences' should be.[18] The term 'audience' is itself problematic in this context, as it assumes that academic historians stand on a notional stage magnanimously bestowing knowledge and empowering others. In my view, such terminology is counterproductive because it re-emphasizes the separation of the academy's 'ivory tower' from the wider world, and implies the exclusive nature of the academic historian's role. Instead, I argue that when we take history into the world it is very important to reflect on our methods and intentions, and to have a clear idea about who we hope to reach. So let us now turn to these more practical questions of how and who.

Taking history into the world – ideas and case studies

Agendas encouraging universities to become more engaged with the world are hardly unique to the UK. The global context includes UNESCO's World Declaration on Higher Education for the Twenty-First Century, which states that the opportunity for university education should be open to far more people across the globe. The declaration calls for significant reforms in university methods and practices so that they are 'based on new types of links and partnerships with the community and with the broadest sections of society'.[19] International drives for greater university engagement frequently focus on two key objectives: widening access to university, and assisting communities, especially in poor areas, through collaboration and the co-production of research knowledge ('co-production' here refers to the joint elaboration of knowledge by academic and non-academic partners).[20] These are not new ideas in the UK: the University Extension movement of the late nineteenth century was fired by similar imperatives to take the benefits of higher education into the world.[21] Indeed, it is probably no coincidence that historians were often at the forefront of these early endeavours.[22] Similarly, as Martin Wright discusses elsewhere in this volume, between the 1960s and 1980s left-leaning academic historians were heavily involved in adult education outreach and early co-production research collaborations such as the History Workshop.[23] These examples reveal that, far from being an exclusive and elitist pursuit, history can play a significant role in tackling serious social challenges, and in opening up new opportunities to those from more disadvantaged communities. Such objectives provide a clear focus for the empathetic, dynamic citizenship which Champion and others have persuasively argued is hardwired into the study of history. Schemes of this kind also provide a significant outlet for the altruistic motivations of many undergraduate student volunteers.

One important UK response to the challenges set out by UNESCO has been the creation of the National Coordinating Centre for Public Engagement (NCCPE). Established with public funds in 2008, the NCCPE's mission is to inspire and support universities, academics and students to engage more effectively with the public.[24] Indeed, in spite of the concerns regarding government influence discussed in the chapter 'History and Policy' in this volume, many academics have embraced the NCCPE's work, and the impact agenda more broadly. They recognize that they research and teach within a competitive, career-driven environment that has been moulded and shaped to predominantly benefit a powerful higher education establishment – an establishment which often reinforces rather than challenges elite power–knowledge relationships. Encouraging universities to think holistically about their missions of research, education and social responsibility is therefore regarded by many as no bad thing. Indeed, the NCCPE does not define public engagement in terms of a top-down dissemination of knowledge but rather as an interactive two-way process which is beneficial to all partners, both inside and outside of the academy.[25]

What does this all mean for studying history at university? Over the past decade, the combined factors of impact, employability, social mission and the establishment of the NCCPE have significantly improved student opportunities to get involved in public engagement work. Impact directives and related funding initiatives have acted as a catalyst encouraging more academics to undertake community-based history research projects. The continuing rise of the employability agenda means that universities are now more focused on skills delivery and embedding engagement into the curriculum. The ongoing social mission of universities has opened up opportunities for community work and widening access outreach in schools. What is more, substantial resources, including both funding opportunities and practical expertise, are now in place to facilitate engagement activities. The NCCPE has produced a series of accessible guides to these resources, and has also compiled a vast number of case studies of public engagement activities. All this material is of great value to both academics and students who want to get involved in public engagement.[26] These resources help to provide the historian with a clear focus and methods for taking history into the world.

In order to illustrate the potential of these new opportunities I conclude this chapter with two brief case studies from my own institution, the School of History, Archaeology and Religion (SHARE) at Cardiff University. Since 2009, the School has attempted to implement a holistic approach to the tripartite mission of the university. Our aim is to create a shift in culture, so that engagement is regarded as an integral element of research and teaching. Admittedly, we are still some way off achieving this stated goal. Nevertheless, as outlined below, this underpinning objective has generated some extremely exciting and beneficial projects. Similar projects are springing up in history and archaeology departments across the UK. These case studies offer a taste of the kinds of ways in which history undergraduates might get involved in public engagement over the course of their degrees.

Case Study 1 – the CAER Heritage Project

The Caerau And Ely Rediscovering Heritage Project (CAER) is a community co-produced research initiative funded by the AHRC Connected Communities Programme.[27] In 2011, historians and archaeologists from Cardiff University teamed up with community organization ACE (Action in Caerau and Ely), local residents and schools to explore the area's past and put local people at the heart of cutting-edge research. Nestled deep in a west Cardiff suburb, surrounded by houses, is one of the most important, yet little understood, monuments in the region – Caerau hillfort (see Figure 18.1). Surrounded on three sides by social housing estates, the huge earthwork defences of this Iron Age hillfort are hidden beneath woodland, a fact that means many people are unaware of its existence. The estates that surround the hillfort are home to more than 25,000 people. Despite strong community ties, many local residents are burdened by significant social and economic deprivation, particularly high unemployment. From the outset the CAER project's key objectives were therefore to employ history and archaeology to develop educational opportunities and to challenge stigmas and marginalization associated with these communities.

FIGURE 18.1 *An aerial view of Caerau hillfort during the 2015 community excavations which involved over 200 local volunteers. © Adam Stanford Aerial-Cam Ltd.*

The CAER project has had numerous and varied benefits to both academic and community partners, ranging from heightening awareness of heritage, to challenging negative stereotypes, developing skills and raising aspirations to go to university. Indeed, one local resident and long-term CAER project participant, Tom, recently observed that 'as an area we're pushed to the back a lot and have been for years, so all of us we're at the forefront for something you know which is pretty amazing really'.[28] The process of co-producing research with communities, and the new friendships and social and professional connections it has created between local residents, academics and students, is almost as interesting as the heritage that is being uncovered. At every stage, the project has involved undergraduate and postgraduate students who have worked side by side with community participants in a variety of co-produced research initiatives. These have included geophysical surveys, heritage-themed art installations, local history projects, museum exhibitions, adult learners' courses, the creation of heritage trails and large scale community archaeological excavations.

Case Study 2 – SHARE with Schools

Established in January 2011, SHARE with Schools (SwS) is a student-led volunteer schools outreach project (see Figure 18.2).[29] It seeks to break down barriers to aspirations for university education in targeted secondary schools, most of which are situated in poorer communities where uptake to higher education is currently low. The project is coordinated by a committed and capable team of hourly paid postgraduate students, who train and support an enthusiastic and dedicated body of undergraduate volunteers. Together they deliver an annual programme of interactive workshops in schools, based around the research and teaching conducted across SHARE. The workshops are designed to be engaging, hands-on, and relevant to pupils, who interact with historical sources and handle artefacts from their local area. Each workshop is delivered to a secondary school class (usually a history class) by a team of six to eight student volunteers and postgraduate coordinators. Each volunteer has to deliver a short presentational element and coordinate group work on sources and artefacts within a one-hour lesson time-slot. Workshops utilize a variety of 'toolkits' including presentations, worksheets, quizzes, artefacts and replicas, many of which are loaned from local museums. Topics covered include 'The Romans in Wales' and 'Life in the South Wales Valleys in the Nineteenth Century'.

Over the last three academic years, nearly 150 undergraduate volunteers have delivered 120 workshops in eight target schools to over 2,700 pupils and sixth-formers. Both pupil and teacher responses have been extremely positive. One history teacher commented that SwS 'has certainly impacted on pupil confidence and attitudes towards the prospect of higher education'. That the project is helping to erode educational barriers is exemplified by

FIGURE 18.2 *A pupil works on a poster about the CAER Heritage Project, as part of the SHARE with Schools scheme.* © *Paul Evans (2014).*

the experience of Jodie, who first encountered SwS in 2012 as a pupil at secondary school in Aberdare. This experience helped inspire her to progress onto a history degree at Cardiff University and, two years on, she became an SwS volunteer delivering workshops and acting as a role model to pupils in her old school. Indeed, student volunteers and postgraduate coordinators have also indicated that involvement in SwS has helped them to gain confidence and develop their expertise in communication, organization, project development and leadership. Student volunteer Kelsey recently commented that:

> SHARE with Schools has provided me with a plethora of transferable skills which I can use in the future. The whole SHARE with Schools experience has reassured me that I definitely want to apply for a Secondary Education PGCE and that it is well worth pursuing a career in teaching. SHARE with Schools has definitely been one of the highlights of my second year!

Conclusion

In this chapter, I have highlighted how the study of history at university inculcates a range of skills, both obvious and less immediately tangible. These skills directly address the demands of both employers and policy-makers for universities to produce intelligent, critically thinking, creative and communicative graduates. Academic history has always been instrumental in developing such talented and well-grounded individuals, but in recent years the impact and employability agendas have provided an important boost to universities' attempts to foster these skills.[30] I have also attempted to reveal how 'taking history into the world' through community and public engagement activities can significantly enhance skills and enrich the life experience and opportunities of students while at university. Now more than ever, then, there is opportunity for history students to develop their love of the subject, their research abilities, their communication skills and their empathetic connections with past peoples and cultures – not simply to improve their employability prospects, but to enliven and enrich their perspectives on life. Taking history into the world enables students to flex the muscles of skills acquired in the classroom before fully entering the world of work. In the process, they can achieve remarkable and positive outcomes for the local communities in which they live.

STUDY QUESTIONS

- Are stereotypical conceptions of universities as 'ivory towers' still warranted?
- Why might it be important to 'take history into the world'?
- Should historians be concerned about the impact agenda?
- What transferable skills do you think a history degree will give you?

Notes

1   R. Overy, 'The Historical Present', *Times Higher Education*, 29 April 2010, p. 30. See also J. Champion (2008) 'What Are Historians For?', *Historical Research*, 81:211, pp. 167–88; B. Southgate (2005) *What Is History For?* (Abingdon, Oxon and New York: Routledge) and M. MacMillan (2009) *The Uses and Abuses of History* (London: Profile Books).

2   Overy, 'Historical Present', pp. 30–1. See L. Jordanova (2000) *History in Practice*, 2nd edn (London: Hodder Arnold), pp. 140–7 and P. Ashton (2010) 'Introduction: Going Public', *Public History Review*, 17, p. 11.

3   T. Bourner (2008) 'The Fully Functioning University', *Higher Education Review*, 40:2, p. 26.

4   See Champion, 'What Are Historians For?', pp. 168–9; Southgate, *What Is History For?*, pp. 57–8; Jordanova, *History in Practice*, p. 171; Ashton 'Going

Public', pp. 3–4; and J. Tosh (2008) *Why History Matters* (Basingstoke and New York: Palgrave MacMillan), pp. 99–100, 119.

5   See K. Mason O'Connor et al. (2011) *Literature Review: Embedding Community Engagement in the Curriculum: An Example of University Public Engagement* (NCCPE and Higher Education Academy), pp. 10–11: http://www.publicengagement.ac.uk/sites/default/files/publication/cbl_literature_review.pdf. Accessed 16 January 2016.

6   D. Nicholls (2005) *The Employability of History Students: A Report to the Higher Education Academy Subject Centre for History, Classics and Archaeology* (Higher Education Academy), p. 9: https://www.heacademy.ac.uk/resource/employability-history-students. Accessed 16 January 2016.

7   Southgate, *What Is History For?*, p. 32.

8   Nicholls, *The Employability of History Students*, p. 4.

9   For the latest QAA Subject Benchmark Statement for History, see: http://www.qaa.ac.uk/en/Publications/Documents/SBS-history-14.pdf. Accessed 16 January 2016.

10 Nicholls, *The Employability of History Students*, pp. 1–2.

11 G. Brewis et al. (2010) *Bursting the Bubble: Students, Volunteering and Community Research Summary* (Institute for Volunteering Research and NCCPE), p. 2: http://www.publicengagement.ac.uk/sites/default/files/publication/bursting_the_bubble_summary_report.pdf. Accessed 16 January 2016.

12 Brewis, *Bursting the Bubble*, p. 2.

13 Brewis, *Bursting the Bubble*, p. 2.

14 C. Gerada (2013) *Interns in the Voluntary Sector: Time to End Exploitation* (Unite the Union): http://www.unitetheunion.org/uploaded/documents/UniteInternAware11-10685.pdf. Accessed 16 January 2016.

15 J. H. Plumb (1969) *The Death of the Past* (London: MacMillan), p. 106.

16 Southgate, *What Is History For?*, pp. 57–8.

17 Champion, 'What Are Historians For?', pp. 168–9.

18 Jordanova defines the public in public history very broadly in *History in Practice*, pp. 141–71. Tosh is similarly unspecific, focusing predominantly on an intelligent lay audience: Tosh, *Why History Matters*, pp. 99–119. Champion too advocates engagement in vague terms with 'the widest possible audiences', Champion, 'What Are Historians For?', p. 188.

19 *UNESCO World Declaration on Higher Education for the Twenty-First Century: Vision and Action* (1998), Article 9, Clause (a): http://www.unesco.org/education/educprog/wche/declaration_eng.htm. Accessed 16 January 2016.

20 *UNESCO World Declaration*, Article 9, Clause (a).

21 M. Williams (2008) *A History of Lifelong Learning at Cardiff University* (Cardiff: A. McLay), pp. 12–29.

22 Williams, *Lifelong Learning*, pp. 16, 22.

23 Tosh, *Why History Matters*, pp. 100, 105.

24 The NCCPE is funded by the UK's Higher Education Councils and Research Councils and the Wellcome Trust. See NCCPE (2012) *The History of the National Coordinating Centre for Public Engagement*, pp. 1–4: http://www.publicengagement.ac.uk/sites/default/files/publication/history_of_the_nccpe.pdf. Accessed 16 January 2016.

25 Mason O'Connor et al., *Embedding Community Engagement*, p. 2.

26 See NCCPE website: http://www.publicengagement.ac.uk/. Accessed 16 January 2016.

27 See CAER Heritage Project website: http://caerheritageproject.com/. Accessed 16 January 2016.

28 D. Wyatt, O. Davis and C. Ancarno (2015) 'Forging Communities: the CAER Heritage Project and the Dynamics of Co-production', in D. O'Brien and P. Matthews (eds), *After Urban Regeneration* (Bristol: Policy Press).

29 See SHARE with Schools website: http://sharewithschools.wordpress.com/. Accessed 16 January 2016.

30 Nicholls, *The Employability of History Students*, pp. 1–10.

Research Resources

I will leave you with just a few ideas on how you might begin to get involved in 'taking history into the world'. Don't be afraid to be proactive in this respect. If the academic department in which you are studying does not undertake a great deal of public engagement, then contact the NCCPE, become an ambassador for change and make it happen!

The NCCPE has a range of great resources and encourages students to become ambassadors for change: http://www.publicengagement.ac.uk/.

The heritage sector, archives and other institutions run numerous volunteer-based projects. Search the 'do-it' volunteer database for opportunities: http://www.do-it.org.uk/.

Students' Unions across the UK run history societies and provide diverse volunteering opportunities: http://www.nus.org.uk/en/students-unions/.

Learn more about AHRC-funded community-based history and archaeology research projects in the UK: http://www.archaeologists.net/sites/default/files/AHRC_Research_for_Community_Heritage.pdf.

INDEX

Note: The letters 'f' and 'n' following locators refer to figures and notes.